Curriculum for the Modern Elementary School

Curriculum for the Modern Elementary School

Walter T. Petty, **Editor**
State University of New York at Buffalo

Rand McNally College Publishing Company/Chicago

76 77 78   10 9 8 7 6 5 4 3 2 1

Preface

In this age of specialization it is difficult to find in a single textbook an authentic description of the elementary school—how it is organized and operates; the subject matter, skills, and attitudes taught; and the teaching and learning activities and procedures that should be used. The principal reason for this, of course, is that a single author usually does not have the depth of knowledge needed to write authoritatively about all of these aspects of elementary school education. This is the premise on which this book is based. It is the product, not of one author (or even two or three), but of twelve specialists. Each author is experienced in the elementary school and has studied and written extensively about his or her specialty. Thus, this book gives the reader specific insights into each curriculum area and provides a thoroughness of treatment limited only by the size of the book itself. Added to these assets is the concern that the authors have shown for writing a handbook that is a ready and useful reference for both preservice and in-service teachers.

This book is unique in many other ways. The central focus is on communication, which indicates the authors' recognition that most of what goes on in schools is language-based human interaction and that effectiveness in speaking, reading, listening, and writing is crucial to learning and development. This recognition led to the inclusion of five chapters about language, providing a core of information that is truly unusual. In addition, considerable attention is given to the open, or informal, classroom; to the importance of a motivating learning atmosphere; to the fostering of creativity; to the interrelatedness of subject matter; and to the role of evaluation and assessment in teaching and learning activities.

Perhaps it is not necessary to stress that the authors believe in schools and in teaching, but we want the reader to know this. We believe in teachers and we think they can do their jobs. But to do so they must be competent in all areas of the curriculum, and this competence is built on sound and innovative thinking and the attainment of knowledge that has its roots in research and effective practices. The strength of these beliefs is reflected in each chapter.

Many of the authors' colleagues and students have been helpful in preparing this book. These we most heartily thank. The editor also wants to thank each author; the cooperative spirit was appreciated during the months of preparation. In addition, Dick Drdek and Dick Salzer were especially helpful with the editing and in providing general advice. Appreciation is also due Professors John Cooper, Theodore Manolakes, and G. Wesley Sowards, who criticized and commented on the manuscript, and editor Charles H. Heinle for his patience and advice. Finally, my thanks are again expressed to my wife, Clem, for her understanding and professional aid and to Mrs. Julie Schneider, who uncomplainingly typed and retyped pages of manuscript.

W.T.P.

Contents

Chapter 2
The Child: Development and School Tasks 23
Richard E. Drdek

Chapter 3
Organizing for Learning   43
Richard T. Salzer and Richard E. Drdek

Chapter 4
The Curriculum Focus: Communication in the Classroom

Walter T. Petty

Chapter 5
Creative Dramatics for Learning and Teaching   89
Marion C. Cross

Chapter 6
Reading Instruction: A Total Curriculum Focus

Ramon Royal Ross

Chapter 7
Children's Literature Throughout the School Day

Paul C. Burns

Chapter 8
Children's Writing in Modern Classrooms

Walter T. Petty

Chapter 9
Social Studies and the Social World of the Child   217

Peter H. Martorella

Chapter 10
Mathematics for Today's World   245
Klaas Kramer

Chapter 11
Science in the Elementary School Classroom

Betsy Davidson Siegel

Chapter 12
Creative Expression Through Art

Juanita G. Russell

Chapter 13
Musical Environments for Every Child

T. Temple Tuttle

Chapter 14
Children's Health and Physical Education   359
Jerrold S. Greenberg

Chapter 15
A Look Ahead: The Elementary
School Beyond the 1970s   387

Richard T. Salzer and Walter T. Petty

Curriculum for the Modern Elementary School

This chapter effectively serves the dual purpose of introducing the reader to early- and middle-childhood education in the American elementary school and to the institution itself. The author presents a brief overview of the development and operation of the elementary school, the roles of school-associated individuals, and the issues and persistent problems within the system. The material is presented in a concise manner, which will appeal to the novice and the experienced professional alike. Beginning educators will want to investigate further many of the ideas presented here, and experienced teachers will find their interests and concerns renewed.

Anyone studying the curriculum of the elementary school must be aware of its determining forces. Content and learning activities do not appear out of the air. They are the product of history and tradition, political and social events and pressures, enactments of law, and the people involved—the children, teachers, and parents. The author of this chapter puts these forces into perspective and gives the reader a frame of reference for reading the remainder of this book and for studying the ideas and information presented.

W.T.P.

The American Elementary School
Development and Operation

Richard T. Salzer

1

THE ELEMENTARY SCHOOL DEFINED

Foreign visitors, as well as many of our own citizens, often express confusion over such terms as *elementary, grammar, parish, neighborhood, district, village,* or *grade* used in reference to American schools. Anyone who has grown up with the language understands that although these words have something in common, each one does have a shade of meaning all its own. Various terms are associated with particular historical periods, regions of the country, or views of what education for children should be like.

Some observers may attempt to reduce or end the confusion by pointing out that terminology is not important; the elementary school should be defined as that institution which provides instruction in the basic skills and otherwise introduces children to the culture. On examination, however, it appears that such a generalization helps little, since all schools—elementary, secondary, college, and university—teach basic skills and all enculturate. Nor is it satisfactory to say that the institution we are concerned with restricts its attention to the beginning stages of literacy and content fields, for pupils there may be found studying Far Eastern philosophy, analytic geometry, or the poems of Wordsworth.

Since the elementary school cannot be defined in any of these terms, other distinctions are necessary. These differences have to do with such matters as the age group enrolled, the legal status of the institution, and the relative rights of the government, the community, and the parents with respect to its operation. It will be noted in the following discussion that the factors affecting the definition are subject to change. Situations differ from what they were even a few years ago, and there are pressures that will likely lead to further alteration.

Age Group of Pupils

One important aspect of the definition simply acknowledges the elementary school as the agency that serves a particular age group—four to twelve years old, or six to fourteen, or five to thirteen, or any of several other alternatives, depending on locality or period in history. At the present time, most elementary schools enroll children of ages five to twelve, grades kindergarten through sixth. It should be noted, however, that other patterns exist and additional modifications are being examined.

Elementary school children, then, are old enough to take care of themselves in many situations but clearly too young to go into the world alone. During these years children grow slowly but steadily in physical stature, experience rather rapid development in muscle control, acquire academic skills and knowledge, and move through several developmental periods regarding establishment of relationships with others. All of these factors have important implications for the operation of schools. For example, children who have good diets and get regular rest but grow slowly need an outlet for their abundant energy. When such children run down the school corridor, they demonstrate not their defiance of rules so much as very real physical requirements. Six-year-olds may put more stock in what the teacher says than in the pronouncements of their own parents. But within three or four years the teacher's status will have slipped rather drastically in contrast with what the children's friends say and do.

The Compulsory Nature of Elementary Education

Because a modern nation-state cannot operate without a minimally educated citizenry, the elementary school has been established and parents are compelled to enroll their children or make some other arrangements acceptable to the authorities. While most elementary-age children appear to enjoy at least some aspects of the school program—and many of them eagerly attend—no pupil is there voluntarily.

It should be pointed out, of course, that nearly everyone accepts the necessity of school participation by the preadolescent child. Even among those who severely criticize the schools, there exists no substantial body of opinion that children of age eight or nine would be better off on the streets or at work. To agree that children must attend elementary school, or at least that they should be educated, marks only the beginning point of some debates, however. Disputes continually arise as to the acceptability of alternatives to the state system of education and as to the extent to which pupils may be required to participate in certain activities. Parents may be willing, even pleased, to have their children attend school, but most of them will want to have a say in which school that is and what transpires when their children get there.

"Free" Elementary Schooling

Society compels parents to have their children educated and provides institutions to serve this function. The taxpayers, just as they support police and fire protection, road maintenance, sewage disposal, and many other services, pay for school buildings, teachers' salaries, and school supplies and equipment. (In many localities the total expenditure for education now equals the budget for all other services combined.)

But with all these expenditures, parents find they must spend even more while their children attend school. Depending on the state or even the local school district, parents buy or rent books, purchase some supplies, take out school insurance, and day by day send money for photographs, field trips, entertainments, milk and lunches, and donation campaigns. No doubt these expenditures represent an important factor in family budgets; but considering what is required in the way of public spending to educate one child for a year (well over one thousand dollars in many areas), the amount paid by the parents appears relatively small. Certainly elementary schools are not without cost to those who use their services, but compared with subsequent levels of the educational system, there is enough validity in the term *free* to make the concept useful.

The Elementary School and the Community

Even though modern school-construction plans have meant that for most children the nearest building will no longer be found around the corner or just up the road, it remains true that the elementary school continues to be thought of as an institution that is in close communication with the home and related in many ways to the life of the immediate area. The average citizen remembers childhood experiences that include walking back and forth to school with friends, inviting a favorite teacher home for lunch, and participating in holiday events along with other residents of the community.

In many situations, however, because of social and political changes, the idealized picture of school-home-community cooperation no longer exists. Attendance areas may be so large and diverse that no "community" is discernible. The population of the immediate area has sometimes changed so suddenly and drastically that the administrators and teachers neither understand the children's families nor want to have much to do with them. And many educators do not consider their responsibilities to include extensive involvement with parents or other elements of a community in which they do not reside.

Another challenge to the traditional notion of the "neighborhood school" has come from the civil rights movement and associated concerns with racial isolation as found in communities and the schools that serve them. Plans for integrating the school system usually establish attendance patterns that mean at least some pupils will not be enrolled at the building located closest to their homes.

Parents and other citizens almost always strongly resist changes that would result in the disappearance or substantial alteration of what they consider to be "their" school. Whatever the causes of such feelings, justification of the position taken usually involves generalizations about the necessity of good relationships among home, school, and community. This belief about elementary schools sets them apart from other educational institutions.

THE HISTORY OF AMERICAN ELEMENTARY EDUCATION

The history of education in America may be viewed essentially as the account of the development of our elementary schools. Each major movement in education—establishment of tax-supported schools, preparation of students for citizenship, attempts to raise the quality of life through improvement of curriculums and instruction—had its inception at the elementary school level and gradually spread through the system.

In reviewing the sequence of trends in the story of our schools, it should be kept in mind that some of the greatest thinkers of each historical period have had something to say about education. If there exist any absolute truths in this field of human endeavor, they doubtlessly would have been discovered by now. What we do find is that because of events outside the school system, certain notions about education seem more attractive at a given time and place than others. In this section an attempt will be made simply to note the ideas that seem to have been dominant during various stages of American elementary education and that have left a residue of theory or practice.

The Colonies and the New Nation

Almost two hundred years elapsed between the time when schools first appeared in colonial settlements and the development of a distinctively American form of childhood education. During this long and complex period, all manner of instructional variation—everything from private tutors to boarding schools to charity classes for the poor—could be found. In terms of lasting influence, however, the system devised by the colonists of New England was the most important. In founding schools supported by the entire community, in specifying the instructional program, and in requiring attendance, the early New Englanders set the basic pattern for school governance in America. They furnished the educational ideals that moved westward with the settlers.

With the establishment of the new country there arose in the minds of many Americans the necessity to develop an educational program that would teach basic skills and instill a sense of nationhood in the diverse groups making up the population. Before long, young Americans were studying not only their own history and geography but also the country's distinctive literature, music, and language forms.

The Development of a System

By 1870 the American system of public elementary schooling somewhat resembled its present form. In order to provide an educated citizenry and work force, several states were requiring school attendance for the younger children, even though universal education was still many years away. The system known as "grading" had appeared, and schools in populated areas were organized in seven or eight separate and successive year-long classes.

Even in the one-room schools attended by children of various ages, the classes were designated by grade levels and the pupils were instructed in five- and ten-minute lessons so that all the subjects would be covered. And the subjects taught were many, including oral reading, penmanship, composition, grammar, spelling, arithmetic, history, geography, music, drawing, and sometimes physiology, nature study, elocution, calisthenics, and handwork. In most of these fields, series of graded textbooks began to appear, and the trend grew rapidly.

This situation—children placed in grades according to achievement and series of textbooks provided for them to study—characterized American common-school education for the latter part of the nineteenth century and many years thereafter. The prevailing instructional approach was recitation, the "re-citing" of what was in the books. Memorization was looked on as a method of instruction and a mind-strengthening value in its own right.

Attempts To Modify the System

In the decades immediately preceding and following the turn of the century, profound changes took place in American life. Of overriding importance was the process of rapid industrialization, which meant that the country was quickly becoming urban rather than rural and based on manufacturing instead of agriculture. This rather dramatic change from a farming society to an industrial one had important implications for the operation of the educational system.

The problems associated with the growth of the cities—including those of health, housing, working conditions, and child care and education—were difficult for everyone but especially so for the hundreds of thousands of immigrants arriving each year. Awareness of these conditions brought forth a substantial response from an increasingly alarmed citizenry.

While the inappropriateness of the rigid and limited traditional school seemed self-evident in the case of immigrant children, some observers maintained that in violating principles revealed by new knowledge about human behavior, the existing educational program demonstrated its inadequacy for all pupils. The "Progressives," as the reformers came to be called, sought to establish schools that looked outward on the real world, took account of the nature and interests of children, and included activities of much greater variety and potential significance than those that centered around textbooks, chalkboards, and other paraphernalia of conventional classrooms. They advocated learning environments made up of workshops, gardens, animal pens, and open space. And they hoped to find warm and responsive teachers who would be eager to introduce children to the worlds of nature and the arts.

Wars and Depression

Although in many ways the schools of the early twentieth century seemed poised for major change, the energies required to accomplish educational reform were diverted to more immediate national concerns. Within a period of thirty years the country participated in two major wars and suffered through a crippling economic depression. Faced with events of this magnitude, the American people understandably gave little attention to those who told them that the educational system of which they were generally quite proud required extensive alteration.

Important developments—even though their impact was not as yet very great—were taking place in a number of fields. Out of the work being done on the measurement of intelligence came an extensive series of group tests of mental ability and academic achievement, and the resulting knowledge increased awareness of variation among individuals. The systematic study of human development was leading to better understanding of childhood as a period of life with distinct characteristics. Certainly much that was being discovered in these areas was consistent with such Progressive principles as an emphasis on flexibility of instructional content and activity-oriented learning experiences. When the time came for practical implementation, however, it was clear that these ideas represented too drastic a departure from traditional schooling to be acceptable as anything more than a set of slogans and clichés.

For whatever reasons, the schools did change, but slowly and only slightly. Textbooks were produced in more attractive forms and provided material at least somewhat oriented to the life experiences of children. Several districts constructed the first large, one-floor buildings, some of which contained specialized facilities and equipment to support programs much in advance of any generally available. In addition, reformers continued to discuss ideas concerning what school ought to be like for children, although increasingly their audience became limited to teachers and other educators.

As is usually the case, the attitudes of the general public toward schools were conditioned more by events of the time than by the thoughts of educators. Living through a war causes some people to wonder if the schools were overly nationalistic and whether or not more attention should be given to international understanding and concern with world government, while others raised questions regarding the steps being taken in the schools to encourage patriotism and a willingness to sacrifice for the good of the country. The Great Depression led some individuals to question the viability of the capitalist system and to insist that the schools introduce or even indoctrinate a different set of beliefs; others became increasingly suspicious of plans to permit discussion of economics in schools.

A Conservative Challenge

After World War II most citizens hoped that "normal" living would resume, but instead the nation confronted a number of critical social and political problems, ranging from an increase in juvenile delinquency to concerns about internal subversion of the government. The causes of these problems were sought in many quarters, and the school system received at least its share of attention.

Although the process of education differed little from what it had been forty years earlier and certainly had not come under the domination of Progressives, it became more and more reasonable to a growing number of people that schools which no longer taught letter sounds, conducted spelling contests, spanked naughty children, gave numerical marks, and required the memorization of state capitals were responsible in large part for apparent threats to the welfare of the family and the security of the nation. Critics encouraged attacks on the schools, teachers, administrators, and college and university education departments.

Since teachers and administrators generally value academic achievement very highly, many of them were pleased to hear of a renewed emphasis on the traditional forms of education. And parents, especially the powerful middle-class group, came out of the depression and the war more convinced than ever before that their children needed higher education and whatever sort of rigid educational effort that was required to prepare them for it.

These attitudes had a significant impact on education in many localities. There was an upsurge of "ability grouping," arrangements whereby bright, average, and slow children were placed in separate classrooms. Committees examined report cards in order to assure what they saw as proper attention to the measurement of academic progress. In some districts, four or five times as many children were being required to repeat a grade level as was the case under previous conditions. Reading programs were subjected to the closest examination, and a book condemning the traditional basal reading series became a best seller. Corporal punishment was specifically instituted in some school systems and prohibition against it removed in others.

The New Curriculum Movement

In the midst of the conservative activity a rather different trend began to develop. Some whose attention had been directed toward the schools decided that an outmoded curriculum was the basis of many of the faults being found with schools. In particular, partly because of competition with other nations in space exploration and defense matters, attention was given to the fields of mathematics, science, and foreign language. By the early 1960s many school systems were trying out innovative programs in one or more subjects and the "new curriculum" movement was under way.

Largely because of the international political situation, substantial appropriations of federal funds became available for this curriculum revision work. With such a high level of support, the projects were able to secure the services of individuals from many varied backgrounds. Scholars in academic disciplines were especially prominent in identifying the most significant content to be taught, an idea that was fundamental to the new programs. In each field, academicians determined what was considered "basic"—mathematics as an interrelated system of concepts, science as a set of processes for knowing, and linguistics as a means of analyzing language, for some prominent examples. While emphasizing content and academic disciplines and thus appealing to educational conservatives, the advocates of the new programs were mainly progressive with respect to teaching methodology. They promoted such principles as active involvement of the learners, contact with concrete materials, and investigation and discovery rather than memorization.

Questioning Assumptions

Of course, large numbers of schools, almost untouched by the trends discussed in the preceding section, continue to operate much as they would have fifty or sixty years ago. And even the changes that have taken place represent to some observers only slight modifications of traditional ways, with teaching machines now presenting material once included in workbooks, for example. Social critics stress that the school needs to do more than make insignificant adjustments in content, methods, and organization. Fundamental changes are called for to help children meet the life demands of the present and the future.

One group attacks traditional education on the grounds that the school system appears to base its procedures on the assumption that pupils are being prepared for industrial work. These analysts insist that through its provision of minimal education in a few areas, the school produces citizens suited only for occupations involving routine tasks. Additionally, it has been argued that such factory-oriented thinking has influenced the conduct of education, placing emphasis on time schedules and essentially meaningless activities carried out under the close supervision of someone who is more concerned with conformity and measurable results than with what happens to the people involved.

Criticism of the schools for adopting the factory model is particularly interesting in view of the trend in industry to provide working conditions that make for a much more satisfying situation for employees. In other sectors of society, concern for the quality of life is also being demonstrated. As an institution that touches the lives of nearly every citizen, the educational system has been urged to determine where improvements might be made in such areas as interpersonal relationships and expressive communication.

It should be noted that the schools as presently operated have not even succeeded in teaching all pupils the minimum competencies needed in an industrial society. Large numbers of children, most of them from poverty backgrounds, have sat year after year in classrooms and gained little from the experience. Attempts to deal with the problem of school failure by disadvantaged children have represented for the most part only minor alterations of existing efforts— starting school a year earlier, using different books, or learning lessons in smaller classes. Ultimately, devising an educational system that successfully meets such serious challenges may require fundamental alteration of what is now known as "elementary education."

THE ELEMENTARY SCHOOL TODAY

While most of the chapters that follow provide information in considerable detail about what elementary schools are like today—along with an occasional prophecy about the future—their focus is on curriculum content and activities rather than on buildings, staff, and overall program considerations. In this section these latter elements of the elementary school are discussed within the framework of present-day conditions.

Buildings

At one time it was customary for the local elementary school to serve as a community center—a gathering place for social events, for quasi-legal assemblages of citizens, and, of course, for ceremonial activities centering on the school itself, events such as Christmas programs and the "class day" at the end of the year. Although some of these activities continue and there have been concerted attempts in a few communities to recapture such an atmosphere, for the most part local elementary schools now serve an educative function only and that during the day.

The average citizen considers the school building and related structures as important factors in any assessment of school-system quality. Indeed, some boosters who claim "good schools" for their community usually are equating superior physical facilities with outstanding instructional programs. Some teachers, too, appear highly conscious of the building in which they serve.

Because the physical makeup of a school building does somewhat affect the learning atmosphere, districts that value education highly tend to spend sizable portions of their budgets on maintaining existing schools and replacing older ones. It should not be concluded, however, that buildings control the type of education offered there. New construction designs, technological innovations, and modern furnishings do not in themselves produce quality learning experiences for children. On the other hand, a classroom crowded with bulky furniture and lacking running water, electrical outlets, work surfaces, and storage space severely handicaps the teacher who is interested in designing effective programs. No one doubts that good buildings are to be preferred over poor ones.

Types of Buildings

There still exist a few "schoolhouses" of simple frame or concrete-block construction that are attended by a few dozen children from the immediate vicinity, but this type of building is the exception. More likely, a school has been built of some combination of stone, brick, steel, glass, or aluminum and houses five hundred to two thousand pupils, some of whom travel long distances to get there. These structures often cost as much as one million dollars and may include swimming pools, television studios, and electronic computers.

There are many varieties of school buildings, some of which are "composites" resulting from additions made in successive decades. But most fall into one of several categories, even though some concession to local architectural style may be in evidence.

One-Floor Plan with Long Corridors   Prototypes for the "spread-out" elementary school appeared as early as the late 1920s, but the big expansion in their number occurred in the housing boom following World War II. School districts in rural and suburban areas have used this plan almost exclusively in recent years, and it is now very likely the most common type of elementary school building.

Typically, the design provides for two major wings, one for the kindergarten/primary level and one for the intermediate grades. Classrooms may open off one or both sides of the corridors. Service centers, such as the administrative headquarters, the nurse's office, the library, and a large multipurpose area, are usually located at the junction of the two wings.

New Multistory Buildings   In cities and other congested areas, building sites have not been large enough to accommodate the one-floor plan. In these situations even the newest buildings have two stories, with the intermediate grades upstairs. But generally the layout of these buildings resembles that of the single-story design. Large areas, such as auditoriums, will be located on the ground floor, but the library, the nurse's rooms, and other facilities may well be found upstairs.

Old Multistory Buildings   The nineteenth-century schools still in use typically consist of four floors, although the top one has often been abandoned as a fire hazard. Such a building usually has the lavatories in the basement, along with the furnace and maintenance area, and perhaps, a lunchroom. The principal's office, the auditorium, the gymnasium, and other service rooms, along with the kindergarten and a few classrooms, are located on the ground floor, with advanced grades on successively higher levels. Customarily there is a single wide corridor on each floor and rooms open off both sides.

The early decades of the twentieth century saw the construction of exceptionally large "grade schools," many of which remain in use. Since in many cases these buildings were planned for kindergarten through grade eight attendance, they included such facilities as home economics and workshop complexes, art and music rooms, and science laboratories. Swimming pools and large libraries were also often provided. The structure was usually a three- or four-story hollow square, with classrooms opening off one side of each corridor and service rooms located inside the courtyard.

Changing Building Concepts

Social factors, instructional and curriculum decisions, and developments in the fields of architecture and the construction industry all lead to changes in the design of school buildings. Principles and practices now evolving have caused several communities to select building plans quite different from the ones that have been most favored in recent years.

Community Facilities In the construction of totally "new" towns and in the rebuilding of urban areas, careful attention has usually been given to the placement and design of elementary schools. An important consideration has been the desirability of arranging such facilities as gymnasiums, swimming pools, and art rooms so that the community has easy access to them in after-school hours. Community planners have also proposed in some situations that classrooms for the younger children be integrated with the housing complexes in which the families reside.

Open-Plan Buildings A large number of the elementary school buildings now being planned and constructed have been designed to provide rather extensive areas of open, uninterrupted floor space. Such provision is a response to criticism of even relatively new buildings in which thousands of square feet of space are taken up by corridors and permanent walls divide almost all of the learning area into conventional classrooms.

Many educators and architects agree that assigning nearly all of the floor space to ordinary classrooms greatly limits the flexibility of the instructional program. One of the alternative plans provides for almost total openness under one roof, an entire school with very few permanent walls. A less-drastic design is one in which permanent "pods" the size of four or five conventional classrooms are constructed. In these open buildings, decisions concerning the use of space are purposely left to the people who will develop the educational program.

While these buildings provide flexibility in terms of wall placement and furniture arrangement, they are sometimes criticized for their uniform carpeting, sound characteristics, and lack of appropriate work areas. A varied school program requires differentiated space—areas for noisy and messy activities as well as places for quiet study and reading. Buildings providing such varied environments are "open" in the sense of interconnectedness and ready access for children and teachers.

Staff

The school staff includes the professional employees—teachers, principal, psychologists, librarians, and so on—and non-professionals—clerks, custodians, lunchroom workers, bus drivers, and teachers' aides. The members of the staff who are directly charged with educating the children are identified below and their roles briefly discussed.

Classroom Teachers

Elementary school teachers make up a large and fairly complex occupational group. Most of them are women, but only a few resemble the stereotype of the prim old maid. Teachers usually marry and have the same kinds of family lives as other citizens. On the whole, teachers are now rather well compensated for their services, although when a teacher's income is the only one in a family, the standard of living will not be lavish.

In terms of background, teachers have tended to come from the lower sector of the middle class, from families in which the father is a skilled worker, an owner of a small business, or a lower-echelon manager. For many in the teaching profession, their vocation represents a step or two up the social-class hierarchy. Their out-of-school activities vary widely but ordinarily resemble those chosen by the great majority of Americans rather than those of an intellectual elite.

Most elementary school teachers received their higher educations in more or less single-purpose teachers' colleges, institutions now claiming to be multipurpose by virtue of having dropped any portion of their previous name that implied an exclusive concern with teacher education. While there have been many hardworking and sincere individuals on the staffs of these institutions, and not a few distinguished scholars, the level of academic work generally has not been outstanding. Elementary school teachers have complained about the quality of their professional education and the inferior general education offered them.

Historically, the American teaching force has not been a mobile group. Teachers have usually grown up in a particular region, attended college there or not far away, and taken jobs in the same community. Since World War II, however, the greater mobility of the population has particularly affected the suburban areas of metropolitan centers and other rapidly growing regions of the country. In such areas the teaching staff will represent a diversity of backgrounds not usually found elsewhere.

Taking into account the social-class origins of elementary school teachers, the similarity of their educations, and their relative geographic stability, it becomes easier to understand what some observers see as the pervasive conservatism of the group. And although teachers are no longer dismissed for smoking cigarettes or forbidden to enter cocktail lounges or required to teach Sunday school, they still represent for many citizens the repository of traditional values. Teachers have been told, implicitly and explicitly, to instill certain principles in their pupils and are often judged on the basis of how well such training appears to have been accomplished.

But the situation of elementary school teachers is changing. More men have entered the field, and in a masculine-oriented society this means that the role commands greater respect. Elementary school teaching is increasingly less likely to be seen as a "nice job" for unmarried women or simply an opportunity for mothers to augment the family income. Then, too, a predominantly female occupational group, such as elementary school teachers, benefits from the improving status of women in this culture. Female teachers are insisting on equal opportunities to secure advanced administrative positions in school systems. Others are using teaching as a springboard to commercial and governmental positions, just as men have done in the past.

Teachers are also acquiring some degree of control over their own profession, an important element in determining status. Teachers' organizations in several states now work closely with colleges and state governments to approve patterns of professional preparation and determine who will be admitted to teaching. Collective bargaining, which permits teachers to exercise significant influence over the terms and conditions of their employment, is now either mandated or permitted in some localities. Other aspects of the changing role of the classroom teacher are discussed in Chapter 3.

Principals

The role of the elementary school administrator began as that of the chief, or principal, teacher in the building, and for a very small proportion of those in the position such description is still valid. But as schools have grown larger and the operation of educational systems has become increasingly complex, the building principal has had to devote more and more attention to administering—scheduling the use of facilities and services, implementing policies emanating from the district's central office, engaging in public relations activities, gathering information for agencies and officials, relating to colleges and other institutions that have continuing contact with the school, and in many ways attempting to facilitate the work of the rest of the staff.

In carrying out these many responsibilities, the principal may be aided by one or even two assistant principals, depending on the size of the building and local school-district policies. There are also very likely to be office clerks, building custodians, and a group of food-service employees. In view of the large size of the professional and supporting staff assigned to a school, an elementary school principal has a major personnel management responsibility.

It would appear, then, that the principal who deals with all of these administrative matters will not be able to devote much time to such areas as the instructional program. And many principals do state that they find it impossible to become deeply involved in making decisions concerning curriculum planning or teaching methods. On the other hand, others in equally demanding situations do seem to find the time to provide instructional leadership in their buildings.

Other Professional Staff Members

Although there are elementary school staffs that consist only of a principal and classroom teachers, it is much more likely that the complement of professional personnel includes a number of other individuals, some of whom will work at one school exclusively. It has become common, of course, for specialists to teach art, music, and physical education, at least to the children in the upper grades. And although not at all usual, teachers of foreign language may also be employed. Depending on such factors as the affluence of the district and the size of the particular school, these specialists devote their attention to one building or two or even several.

Elementary school libraries or more comprehensive resource centers have become relatively widespread and require at least part-time staffing by trained personnel. Some school systems have also experimented with the concept of media specialists, teachers who are responsible for helping their colleagues use audiovisual devices effectively.

A number of children have learning problems that require attention but do not necessitate their assignment to special classes. The difficulty that some pupils experience in reading is often recognized by the inclusion of a special reading teacher, who oversees the total program and meets regularly with certain children. Therapists usually come to an elementary school on a regular basis to help pupils with speech difficulties.

School psychologists or counselors are sometimes available to work on education-related problems with individuals or groups of children. Such professionals may also supervise the program of standardized testing and concern themselves with other pupil-personnel matters. Health considerations often receive systematic attention from a school-system or public-health nurse, who visits the school regularly. Increasingly, school social workers and attendance officers provide services to elementary schools.

Program

The term *broad-fields curriculum* best characterizes the elementary school instructional program now in widest use. The academic fields referred to are those of language arts, social studies, mathematics, and science, with physical education, music, and art being treated as separate areas. Customarily, classroom teachers accept responsibility for academic fields and specialists teach the other subjects.

Mathematics, social studies, and science are preceived as subjects that encompass various content areas. Elementary mathematics, for example, includes work in geometry; the science program is composed of materials from biological and physical areas; and several social sciences make up social studies. The language arts field, on the other hand, is usually divided into instructional programs in reading, spelling, English, and writing.

While most teachers make some attempt to relate school subjects to one another and at least occasionally deal with topics that involve several fields of knowledge, the conventional practice is to divide the day into periods and have all the members of the class work on a single subject at the same time. This style of teaching derives in large part from the widespread assumption that a teacher's chief responsiblity is that of guiding students through given amounts of pre-selected and organized subject matter. Obviously, a regular schedule of work in compartmentalized areas facilitates such an approach. Additionally, state laws or local policies typically mandate the amount of time to be devoted to each field of study, and adherence to a time schedule readily demonstrates that a particular program meets requirements.

The great majority of classroom teachers spend most of their six-hour school day in a single room with thirty children of about the same age. Increasingly, as school systems are agreeing to employ aides in a variety of roles, teachers are being relieved of the responsibility of supervising lunchrooms and playgrounds. Districts in which the rights of staff members have been vigorously asserted often guarantee teachers "free" periods during the week, usually when a specialist teacher takes the class.

Although much teaching centers around textbooks, most elementary school teachers employ a reasonably large variety of instructional practices. Teachers of the first three grades tend to form small reading-instruction groups that meet regularly, and they may use a similar approach in other skill subjects. Generally, however, in the fields other than reading, primary-grade teachers make presentations to the entire class and then provide follow-up activities. And at this level it is not uncommon for teachers to be responsible for their own class in music, physical education, and art. In grade four and up, teaching customarily takes the form of class presentations, except in reading, for which some types of grouping or individual activities are provided. Pupils often undertake small-group work or independent-study projects within the framework of a class topic.

Large numbers of school districts now offer kindergarten programs as an integral part of the instructional sequence. Children in kindergarten usually attend school for one-half of the day, during which they have experiences that assist them in learning about school, other people, and the world outside the home.

In Chapter 3 and subsequent sections of this book, emphasis will be placed on alternatives to the conventional program just described. The reader should note that the field of elementary education is quite diverse, with many possible types of organization, curricular patterns, and teaching strategies in use. It should be kept in mind, however, that many schools, perhaps a majority, have not been substantially influenced by the developments discussed throughout this chapter.

IMPORTANT INFLUENCES IN THE ELEMENTARY SCHOOL

The elementary school is a unique institution in that nearly every citizen has had a significant amount of contact with it. This does not necessarily mean that everyone considers himself or herself an expert on how the schools should be run, but it does imply that each person has a background of experience from which to make judgments about a particular school or elementary education in general. And since, in our open society, the citizen may find many opportunities to attempt to influence public affairs, it is to be expected that the elementary school will always receive much attention.

Tradition

One important source of influence is, of course, the force of tradition, which clearly affects the attitudes of the average citizen. If schools have typically operated in certain ways, the adoption of a different practice will automatically be viewed as suspect by some observers. Schools have been conducted in approximately the same manner for several hundred years, so no one should be surprised that there exist rather well established notions of what teachers should do and how pupils should react. In addition to these widely accepted understandings, each locality has its own set of practices that have become well established by the passage of time. And any attempts to tamper with these practices are made only at the risk of some reaction. Superintendents have been challenged for altering the time at which school begins each day as well as for proposing a twelve-month operational year for the system.

Legal Constraints

Another influence on schools has to do with legal matters. It is widely accepted that in the United States, education is a function of the individual states, which in turn delegate much of their authority to local school districts. As has already been noted, states may require that school programs provide particular kinds and amounts of instruction. And anyone who has been involved in school administration can verify the fact that state laws and regulations touch the school in numerous important ways. States specify who may teach, what services will be offered to children, and how the school district should conduct its business.

In recent years the federal government has become more and more involved in school affairs. Court decisions and department regulations have affected such matters as the assignment of pupils to buildings. And the schools have discovered that funds from the national level are accompanied by regulations concerning how the money may be spent and how the programs sponsored are to be operated and evaluated.

Local Formal Control

The delegation of the state's authority over education to local districts has resulted in most decisions concerning elementary schools being made at the local level. The board of education—a group of private citizens charged with the responsibility of guiding the educational process—possesses ultimate authority but delegates power to their chief administrative officer, the superintendent of schools, and his or her staff. The school board sets policies regarding how a staff is to be assigned duties, how much employees should be paid, what the instructional program ought to be, what size classes should be organized, which schools children in the district are to attend, and many other matters that would be under the control of professional educators in most countries. It should be pointed out that in recent years, concerns such as class size and teachers' salaries have become subject to negotiation with teachers' organizations. Also, items such as selection of books to be read and assignment of pupils to school buildings have in many areas become focal points for pressure groups in the community.

Theoretically, the central administrative staff of a school system carries out the policies made by the board of education. Depending on such factors as the size and affluence of a school district and the philosophy of the board and the superintendent, a particular elementary school may or may not have extensive direct contact with the central office. As general guidelines and specific directives are implemented, however, there will be communication between the school and certain individuals.

In most central offices there will be a person charged with the responsibility of supervising the elementary schools in a general sort of way. On that official's staff, or in some other office in the district, there will be experts in the various instructional fields—supervisors of mathematics, coordinators of reading programs, and so on. There will be other people who oversee the district's offerings in physical education or who look after the libraries or who assume responsibility for audiovisual equipment and educational television. Although these supervisory and administrative personnel may come to an individual elementary school only rarely, they still have some influence on the overall program. Other central-office staff members concern themselves with pupil records, provisions for children with special problems, and other matters having to do with individual children rather than more general considerations.

Local Informal Control

In every community there exist extralegal forces that significantly affect the schools. Various groups and private citizens exert subtle pressure or make outright political appeals in order to bring about the acceptance of a favored policy or practice. Of course, the influence of existing political, corporate, religious, or labor groups may be so pervasive in some communities that the school program will almost always be affected in important ways. In these cases, disputes arise only when someone in a distinct minority or with a strong sense of mission is disturbed enough to object. But most influences are not thought of as objectionable by the majority of citizens. A conservation group wants the children to plant a tree on Arbor Day; a veterans' organization desires to present ceremoniously a flag that has flown over the nation's Capitol; or the local historical society offers to organize a school assembly program on the founding of the town.

Increasingly in recent years, however, the pressures on elementary schools have been of the type that most observers view as controversial. A group of parents wants a pupil-exchange program between schools that enroll children from different racial backgrounds; at a time of national debate on a crucial issue, an organization offers the school a set of posters that some citizens find offensive; a teacher or a book in the library is found to be exposing children to a religious point of view not acceptable in the local community. Discussion and resolution of such controversies affects the operation of elementary schools.

PERSISTENT PROBLEMS IN ELEMENTARY EDUCATION

Because of the inherent complexity of such an institution as the American elementary school and of the social forces that affect education, a number of topics consistently appear on any list of school-related problems. These difficulties have been with us so long that they appear almost unsolvable unless the basic nature of schooling is changed. Consideration of these problematic areas will serve, it is hoped, to prepare the reader to some extent for the discussions presented in this book.

Providing for Individual Differences

The operation of the typical elementary school often appears to be based on the assumption that children are nearly identical, varying significantly only in age and sex. Curriculums, teachers' expectations, testing programs, and tradition all act to reinforce the notion that children closely resemble one another. There are some pupils who do receive special treatment, those who are handicapped in some obvious way, for example, or, less often, those who are especially able academically. Variations of this type are frankly acknowledged, with classes for such children designated as "special," or "exceptional."

The fact is, of course, that all children differ from one another in most important respects—physical size and coordination, growth rate, visual and auditory acuity, personality, emotional stability, social graces, talent, knowledge, and interests. The material in Chapter 2 well documents the significance of differences among children.

Some observers conclude that the range of individual differences in a school are reduced significantly when a building serves families who are highly similar in terms of socioeconomic status. But political and social developments may lead, as they already have in several localities, to the planning of enrollments so that pupils from varied backgrounds attend the same school. And even if children do come from similar home situations, teachers still find substantial variation in their personalities, talents, and academic aptitudes.

Traditionally, schools have all but ignored differences among children. Teachers have provided the same program for all pupils and have evaluated the work according to a fixed standard, utilizing procedures whereby only particular sorts of abilities have been rewarded. Some educators, recognizing the inefficiency of such a system, attempt to meet differences by grouping pupils according to mental ability, performance level in a subject, or other similar criteria. Approaches of this sort have been criticized for not meeting differences adequately and for causing negative feelings among pupils.

Chapter 3 includes discussions of plans for dealing with variations among pupils. The chapters devoted to the instructional programs in school subjects also contain material related to the problem of meeting individual differences.

Evaluating and Reporting Pupil Progress

Almost all teachers insist that "giving grades" and "making out report cards" are the least-liked aspects of their role. Many observers of the educational system believe that the usual methods of evaluating and reporting actually impede the work of teachers by seriously affecting their relationships with pupils. Disputes over evaluation raise questions that concern the very nature of teaching and learning. The traditional view is that the teacher has a responsibility to teach basic skills and impart knowledge, to make judgments concerning how well the pupils are learning, and to summarize these conclusions for various interested parties. The summaries often take the form of numerals, percentages, or letter grades.

Critics of these essentially judgmental practices argue that the system fails in two important ways—by not improving learning and by communicating important information inadequately. In support of the first contention these observers point to evidence showing that consistently negative evaluations of performances often lead the learners to abandon their efforts rather than to increase or redirect them. An additional source of difficulty is that bright children who hardly work at all may be praised and rewarded while their less-able but more-diligent classmates receive mainly discouraging feedback. On the matter of inadequate information giving, some critics make the point by asking if anyone would be satisfied with a medical examination in which the physician awarded him or her a "B−" in "lungs" and a "68" in "heart."

When attempts are made to evaluate and report in ways that take into account the child's ability or the evidence of his or her application to tasks, the possibility exists for an able pupil to be rated relatively lower than the child performing at a mediocre level. While proponents of the approach contend that such a likelihood constitutes an advantage, the reporting of this type of information to parents and the school system sometimes results in much confusion. In addition, there are always questions having to do with the standard of comparison being utilized. Is the pupil being compared with other members of the class? With other children of the same age in the school or district? With the results of a national standardized test? With some absolute idea of what the child's status should be? Answers to such questions would make a difference in what gets "reported."

Good teachers constantly "evaluate," of course, as they go about the business of organizing class work, assisting individual pupils, and examining their own techniques and procedures. Many teachers utilize checklists for recording progress in skill development, notes on children's concept development, samples of pupils' work, or even the results of fairly extensive interviews with children. It seems likely that the sort of information most useful to the classroom teacher would also be of great interest to parents and other teachers. But many people, both within and outside the school system, would need an explanation of the advantages of such an approach before they could appreciate its strengths in comparison with conventional evaluating and reporting.

In considering the material in the chapters devoted to the subject fields, the reader should bear in mind that schools with the most forward-looking instructional programs may still require teachers to summarize pupil progress with a letter grade. Also, it may prove enlightening to decide what type of information would be required in order to make valid judgments as to whether or not objectives described by the authors are being attained.

Managing and Controlling Pupils

Teachers with twenty years of experience as well as beginners typically rate discipline as one of their chief problems, if not the main source of difficulty. The pervasiveness of this concern with children's conduct in school indicates that much more than an occupational hazard for teachers is involved. It may be that what appears to be a problem requiring solution is, rather, a perpetual condition with a natural explanation.

The explanation lies, of course, in the fact that, historically, schools have worked at cross-purposes with children. Casual observation and systematic study both confirm that children are naturally active and social, but conventional school regulations require silence and quiescence. As has already been mentioned, the range of individual differences among pupils causes difficulty for the teacher, especially since the dominant instructional technique, the group lesson, is almost always irrelevant for a large proportion of any class. No one should be surprised that discipline problems arise when one adult attempts to keep thirty active, friendly children in their seats, quiet, and paying attention to lessons that may be appropriate to only a few of them.

It has become common practice for supervisors to tell student teachers and those just beginning in the profession that discipline problems can be overcome only by good teaching—the careful planning of interesting lessons and the provision of activities to accommodate varied abilities, aptitudes, and interests. Certainly the teachers able to create these sorts of conditions are well on their way toward solution of management and control problems in their classrooms.

Other sources of the discipline problem may be found outside the classroom and the school. These factors relate to social and economic difficulties that impinge directly on the lives of children and affect their behavior in important ways but are not under the control of teachers. Children who suffer most from poverty, inadequate public services, and disorganized family life tend to be concentrated in schools serving particular neighborhoods and communities. In reacting to the behavior difficulties of these pupils, professional school personnel often simply redouble their efforts to keep the children seated and quiet, with these procedures sometimes becoming objectives in themselves.

While studying the remainder of this volume, the reader may find it interesting to recall from time to time that many teachers would be examining every proposal of the authors in terms of the likelihood of discipline problems being intensified should the practice be adopted. Such an exercise would lead to a greater appreciation of the magnitude of the task confronting those who seek to change the schools.

EXERCISES FOR THOUGHT AND ACTION

1. Interview senior citizens and ask them to recall their childhood and school. How do they remember their teachers? The school program? Their classmates?
2. Visit your local historical society and inquire as to the availability of pictures and other materials related to the schools of a particular period. What can you find out about class size, room furnishings, and teacher qualifications and salary?
3. Interview a building principal or curriculum director. Find out what they consider the important problems confronting them in their work. Compare the results with discussions in this chapter.
4. Skim through professional books or official pamphlets for a checklist by which an elementary school may be evaluated. Then apply the criteria to a specific school.
5. Interview a pupil and ask about his or her school. Find out what the child does and how he or she reacts to what occurs in the classroom.
6. Examine a particular newspaper for a few weeks, noting the school-related news stories and letters to the editor. What are the predominant concerns?

SELECTED READINGS

Cremin, Lawrence A. *The Transformation of the School.* New York: Alfred A. Knopf, 1961. This is a treatment of the Progressive movement, including the period from the turn of the century to the late 1950s. The volume presents good background material for an understanding of the development of modern elementary education. The account of the controversies occurring after World War II is especially illuminating.

Goodlad, John I., and Shane, Harold G., eds. *The Elementary School in the United States.* Seventy-second Yearbook of the National Society for the Study of Education, part 2. Chicago: University of Chicago Press, 1973. Four sections of this useful volume are "The Elementary School in Perspective," "Forces and Ideas Shaping the Elementary School," "Challenges and Options for Today," and "Change: Today and Tomorrow." The chapter on "Views of the Child" brings out some important issues.

Reisner, Edward H. *The Evolution of the Common School.* New York: Macmillan, 1930. The author provides a full description of the development of elementary education from the Middle Ages to the Progressive era. Most attention is devoted to American schools, but their development is related to events and thinking occurring elsewhere.

Silberman, Charles E. *Crisis in the Classroom.* New York: Random House, 1970. This is a general attack on traditional "joyless" schools and "mindless" educators. The author reviews many types of innovative school programs designed to improve instruction and points out their deficiencies.

This chapter is about the child, but it is also about what the school climate should be to maximize learning, to foster personal development, and to help children live in the reality of the world.

The author assumes that the reader has a good deal of basic knowledge of child development as it relates to the specifics of the elementary school curriculum as well as the ability to pursue in greater depth the ideas presented here. He has avoided the use of educational and psychological jargon and the tendency to dwell on differences in various theorists' points of view and beliefs about human learning. Instead, the author uses down-to-earth terms and chooses to discuss only those elements of various theories that appear to have the widest acceptance and that are most related to the concerns of this book.

This chapter sets the stage for much that is said in other chapters. The cognitive tasks for children identified here are placed in descriptive frameworks that may be used for reference in the discussions on curriculums and methods in other chapters.

W.T.P.

The Child
Development and School Tasks

Richard E. Drdek

2

Each child comes into the world as a unique individual and with an inheritance dating back to the beginning of life itself. The phenomenon of humankind is the uniqueness of the individual in spite of a common biological heritage and grossly similar environments. Throughout recorded history and deep into legendary records, there appear individuals whose traits and deeds were so distinguishable as to merit remembering. Extraordinary heroes, artists, philosophers, teachers, and villains mark humankind's passage through time and give evidence of the range of individual differences.

Although the diversities in human nature have been a part of that nature since some far-removed era, curiosity about the uniqueness of individuals is relatively recent. The earliest recorded explanations for human disparities attributed them to divine bequests or, in cases of evil, to the overpowering influences of malevolent spirits. It wasn't until this century that nonspiritual causes for human differences were diligently pursued. Human behavior became a science in the twentieth century.

This chapter is neither a review of human growth and development nor an extensive treatment of children's learning. The assumption is made that the reader has some background in these areas but would be helped by an overview of the nature of human differences that must be dealt with in a viable elementary school curriculum. The chapters that discuss particular disciplines refer to stages in children's development and maturation in terms of the appropriateness of subject-matter content and learning activities.

This chapter does explore some of the theories that attempt to account for human differences, presents a list of tasks that children are required to master in spite of individual differences, and suggests factors that are important to everyone who wants to help children learn.

HEREDITY AND ENVIRONMENT

As recently as the 1890s genius and insanity were coupled as being equal parts of the same gift. So universally accepted was that notion, it is now suspected that many individuals who were considered—or wished to be considered— geniuses demonstrated irrational behavior because it was expected of them or because they had an exonerating excuse for not adhering to the norms of the times. When it was no longer stylish for gifted persons to behave flamboyantly, the image presented by them became more subdued. Theories on the influences of heredity, which delineated and separated inheritable characteristics, may have affected courses of behavior as well as explained them.

What the Child Inherits

Chance is the primary determiner of the characteristics that an individual inherits. Each of a child's parents contributes twenty-three chromosomes to the forty-six that determine everything the child inherits. Chance selects which twenty-three chromosomes each parent transfers. Mathematically, there are more than sixteen million possible combinations. Furthermore, it is possible for each pair of father-mother chromosomes to separate and exchange genes. The result is a chromosome with some of the mother's and some of the father's genes. Because of the probability of gene crossovers, the sixteen million possibilities are raised mathematically by the number of genes in the forty-six chromosomes. Considering the fact that each gene carries one specific characteristic from a fantastically large pool of possibilities, it can be said that each child born is a genetically unique individual, unless the child is one of a pair of identical twins. The child may not display any of the characteristics of either parent. He may more nearly resemble an aunt or an uncle, a grandparent, or some distant relative. Some parents have a child so unlike them in temperament that they sometimes wonder if the child is really theirs.

What the child inherits from his parents, then, is a set of chromosomes containing a set of unique genes. The genes establish the nervous system and physical structure of the child. And although particular behaviors are not inherited, a predisposition toward certain patterns can be. A child may be born with a nervous system highly subject to outside stimuli and, as a result, exhibits tendencies toward distractability and hyperactivity. Another child may inherit a far-less-excitable nervous system and appear to be a calm and placid child.

Chance determines yet another important variable: the immediate environment into which a child is born and in which the child spends the early, formative years of life. The influence of the environment can be illustrated by the case of the calm child who lives in a nervous and erratic household. The calm infant becomes bewildered, anxious, and sometimes frightened. On the other hand, if the baby with hyperactive tendencies lives in a flexible, permissible, and understanding home, she may learn to direct her energies toward positive goals. However, when such a child finds herself in a superbly ordered, highly structured, and strictly regulated environment, it is likely that the parents and the child may virtually become antagonists.

Much of the research that led to the coining of the term *culturally disadvantaged* called attention to the contrary effects of certain home environments on inherited, culturally valued characteristics. It was found that the home environment can enhance or subvert those valued variables estimated by the Stanford-Binet scale and similar measures.

"Intelligence" as some kind of mystical, fixed quantity is not inherited. The genes transmit certain physiological structures that may influence the individual's chance for interacting successfully with certain variables in the environment. The physiological structures are genetically determined, but beyond that point they are subject to the vagaries of the cultural environment. For many years, those variables tested for on the Stanford-Binet scale and its many descendants were regarded as particles of intelligence, when in fact they are no more than indicators of behavior related to success in school and to selected occupations.

Because our culture values the advancement of commerce and industry, those individuals whose inherited physiological structures enhance their possibilities for success in those fields have an advantage over others. Also, certain physical characteristics hold cultural preferences and therefore help determine the course of one's life. Our culture values tallness in males and petiteness in females. Certain facial features are epitomized while others are scorned. And the pigment of a person's skin has a remarkable influence on the course of his life, regardless of all other inherited traits.

Inherited characteristics, then, must be viewed according to the predominant values of the culture in which the individual lives. A person's behavior is the product of the interaction between individual uniqueness and the environment.

Error also influences the genetic uniqueness of the individual. Sometimes one parent will transmit twenty-four or twenty-two chromosomes, and the child will have forty-seven or forty-five instead of forty-six. Too many or too few chromosomes are associated with mental retardation, sex aberrations, personality disorders, and physical anomalies.

Chance enters during the prenatal period as well as the conceptual one. After the fertilized cell begins to develop, the multiplying cells may group themselves in such a way that twins will result. Should two or more female sex cells each be fertilized by a male cell, another form of multiple pregnancy will take place. (Just how uterine crowding affects the characteristics of children born of multiple births is still under investigation.)

Both chance and error, then, play major roles in determining the psychological and physiological characteristics with which the child enters the world and which make him unique. Some ancestor a thousand generations ago may have had some strength or weakness in eye or hand or mind or heart that is randomly passed on to descendants. An unknown or forgotten predecessor may bequeath a supersensitive ear, good muscular coordination, or a brain that is highly sensitive to stimuli. The detailed makeup of an individual's physical structures has its beginnings in the past and is exposed to alterations caused by chance and error.

Thus, the child enters the world with a set of predetermined characteristics. The color of hair, eyes, and skin; the general body build; and the quantity and arrangement of cells in the central nervous system have been established randomly from a pool of extraordinary possibilities.

Health of the Mother

Individuals are influenced by and react to their environment nine months before birth. The uterus, while being a highly specialized environment, is far from being the safe and secure nest that poets declaim. The mother's dietary habits affect the growing cells. In extreme cases of malnutrition, the fetus may not survive the mother's disease. A deficiency in the mother's protein intake can retard the development of the fetus's brain cells as well as the cellular structure of the whole body.

The nutritional-intake level of the mother is generally determined by the economic conditions of the family. Protein-rich foods are more expensive than high-starch foods. Consequently, mothers in low-income families tend to give birth to infants who are in poorer physical condition than the children born to middle-or high-income families. Furthermore, evidence shows that such children seldom catch up. And this means that when the economically deprived female child matures, her chances of producing a child who is physically comparable to a middle-class child are slight. To break the chain, a nurtritionally balanced diet needs to be fed to the mother before and during pregnancy and then to the child during the growing years.

Besides nutrition, other aspects of the mother's health are important to the child in the prenatal environment. Infectious viruses and bacteria carried by the mother can seriously afflict the unborn child. Rubella, or German measles, is one example. Studies show that mothers infected with rubella during the first two or three months of pregnancy bear children with one or more abnormalities. Some common rubella-related defects are cardiac lesions, blindness, deaf-muteness, and microcephaly.

Mothers addicted to herion bear children who enter the world craving the drug and displaying withdrawal symptoms. Some of the babies have to be given the narcotic or a substitute to preserve their lives. LSD is suspected of causing chromosome damage to the user, so that in the chromosome exchange at fertilization, children not only stand a good chance to bear defects, but their genes will be damaged and *their* children may be deformed. (At present this is an unproved theory that warrants further study.) Controversy also continues as to whether a mother's intake of alcohol and her smoking habits have any relationship to the health and physical condition of the baby. The point is that whatever the mother takes into her body finds its way into her bloodstream and that of the fetus. Thus the condition of the mother's body may drastically alter the inherited characteristics of her child.

ADAPTABILITY AND COMPENSATION

While human beings have the widest range of differences of all living crea-
tures, they have the remarkable ability to adapt their inherited traits to their needs
and to compensate for whatever deficiencies they may possess. Although each
child is different from any other in genetic inheritance—physical size, muscular
coordination, visual acuity, quantity and arrangement of cells in the central nervous system, formation of the body—the human ability to learn reduces the effects
of the differences. The two percent or so of a population's children who are
considered "uneducable" are not excluded from the process of adaptability.
Uneducable is a legal term; children who are labeled as such do adjust to their
environments. Genetic inheritance has only an indirect regulatory influence on
all aspects of learning and influences only the degree to which a child can master
the complexity of learning. There are, however, some genetic combinations that
contribute to insanity or produce organic brain deterioration that inhibits adaptability.

Human Adaptability

The ability to adapt to the demands of different environments is due to the
transactional nature of human beings. A child does not choose an environment
that is most suitable to him. He is forced by circumstances beyond his control to
adjust to environments that not only vary from time to time but may be entirely
different. He lives in a climate, a home, a school, and a neighborhood. One or all
of these social and physical environments may suddenly change when the family
moves from one part of the community to another or from one region of the
country to another. But the human individual is not a passive passenger on some
environmental voyage. He is continually interacting with those environments.
While the factors in an environment are acting on him, he is reacting to them. He
may be able to do no more than put on a heavy coat and wear gloves to go to
school on a cold day, but his response shows that he is transacting with the
weather. In the same way, the child is far from being molded or formed by his
parents, teachers, and adult relatives as if he were some kind of plastic clay.
While they are putting pressures on him, he is exerting an influence on them.

The Transacting Child

As far back as nine months before birth, the child may influence the lives of
the parents. The child's existence as an unborn member of the family may make
the parents decide to move to a new residence, a larger apartment, or a home in
the suburbs. The father may look for a new job. Perhaps the parents will contemplate a change in environment in consideration of the general well-being and
future education of the child.

When the child is born, her presence influences the routines of the household. Her voice, which at first is only a cry, is heard and given some degree of
consideration. As her language skills develop, the ability to transact with her
environment increases. She discovers that through language she can have her

needs satisfied. At the same time, the adults and her older siblings are using language in an attempt to control her behavior. The child also interacts through physical actions. She acts out her wants and displeasures, and sometimes the dislikes of her parents are acted out on her. From these experiences she acquires knowledge, and the cognitive insights acquired and how they are acquired become her adaptations. Thus, very early in life, the child begins to modify her inherited characteristics and her personality is being formed.

Circumstances in the environment play a major role in determining the extent to which the child's inherited potentials will be realized. Very early in life the child realizes that her welfare, if not her very existence, rests on her ability to cope with her environment, no matter how erratic it may be. She discovers through her transactions that many forces in her environment are stronger than she is. Her parents are physically stronger; they control her intake of food; they can give or withdraw affection. The child has very few weapons for retaliation. Even her screams may go unheeded.

As the child strives to fit into the environment, her struggles influence that environment, causing it to respond to her efforts. The result is that the child accommodates herself to certain tasks of the environment, and the environment in turn makes some accommodations to the child. Even if the cries of the child go unanswered by the other humans within hearing range, a response is being made. The hearers may have decided that the cries are to be ignored, and so they have responded. Ignoring the cries is an accommodation. The child is then forced to change her strategy. She may yell louder, bang her head against the side of the crib, toss out the playthings, or simply give up. Any choice or combination of choices is a response, furthering the transaction.

The environment is neither so inflexible that the child has no influence on it nor so malleable as to be controllable by the child. What is important in the child's transactions with the home, the school, and the neighborhood is the relative flexibility-inflexibility of each. No environment is static; each is subject to all the social, economic, and natural forces that are parts of the environment. The individual's ability to adapt her inherited characteristics to environmental needs and to make accommodations when they are demanded will have an important influence on the course of her life. Both the cockroach and the dinosaur evolved at about the same time in history, but one lacked the flexibility to adapt to an ever-changing environment.

Environmental Effects on Transactions

A child's development, as stated previously, is greatly influenced through his transactions with his environment. The child enters an environment with certain inherited physiological characteristics, but conditions within the environment may modify those traits considerably. One means of modification is through the child's attempts to adapt to the tasks of the environment, the most demanding of which are cognitive tasks (discussed in the following section). The quality of the accommodative transactions are products of the individual's cognitive processes. Transactions, consequently, are limited to the extent that the cognitive processes are limited.

There are other conditions of the environment that are substantially beyond influence by the child's transactions, yet which modify inherited characteristics. An example can be seen in considering what intelligence tests measure—that is, a combination of inherited characteristics and the effects of the environment on them. Environment in this sense is cumulative; thus, it includes all the variables in contact with the child from conception onward. Already shown are the influences of the mother's health on the inherited characteristics of the child. The damaging intake of drugs by the child's mother during pregnancy is outside the child's ability to influence. After birth, the child, depending on the extent of the damage, may make some ameliorating adaptations. Those children whose central thought processes have been severely damaged may survive after delivery, but only with the outside assistance of medical technology.

Other environmental conditions that bear on the child's ability to transact are related to the opportunities for richness in his interactions. The conditions of these surroundings pertain both to the existence of stimuli and to the child's opportunities for transacting with them. Included in the stimuli of any environment are the human resources present. The humans more or less provide affection, help build the child's image of himself, act as models for behavior, stimulate his curiosity-creative impulses, and supply him with language labels for feelings and things within his experience.

The child who spends his preschool years in a narrow environment can be expected to demonstrate behaviors somewhat below his inherited capabilities. The child reared with the fewest adult contacts has the least amount of usable data to draw on. He may come to know an object for its use but be unable to call it by name. He may know that an apple is good to eat and may desire one but not be able to ask for it when it's out of sight. Without the words that denote quantity and quality, the child cannot adequately describe a thing or a feeling. Without such labels at his command, the child can be expected to demonstrate an inability to adequately transact with his environment.

The human mind is much like a computer—constantly running, always ready to take in data. The adults in the child's life, as well as the adolescents, contribute the most quantitative and qualitative data for storage. These data are chiefly in the form of labels for the things the child sees, hears, tastes, smells, touches, and feels inside himself. The child's ability to solve problems depends greatly on the experiences and labels in his memory bank. Creative thought is feedback from previously stored data.

Besides experiences with people, the child needs contacts with things. From his manipulation of objects he acquires knowledge. Let the reader imagine a child exploring a toy dump truck for the first time. What discoveries can the child make about the construction and operation of the truck? When he actuates the mechanism of the toy, what can he, the operator, make the truck do? If the same procedures were followed using a doll or a teddy bear, what knowledge can be gained? What knowledge is given when the doll is made to talk, to walk, to dance, and to be disobedient? The child eventually acquires the ability to conduct operations in his mind, as the reader may have done with the toy truck and the doll mentioned here. In the barest of environments, the child has few challenges for the mind, few opportunities to expand his knowledge. The child whose world is filled with many interesting articles within the home and who is provided with guided opportunities to explore the countless natural and artificial wonders outside the home has much more data to store and recall.

Language contacts with adults make another contribution to the child's ability to transact. They are those contacts that fill the child's imagination with wonders, real and fanciful, beyond the child's senses. A star is a diamond in the sky or one of heaven's windows or a distant sun. A cat can wear boots or a stovepipe hat and do wondrous things. A group of different animals can live together in harmony and enjoy fantastic adventures. Language as literature opens up for the child the treasure chests of metaphor and make-believe, stuffs that daydreams are built on. When children act out their daydreams, they exhibit creative behavior. Playing "let's pretend" draws on the child's stored fantasies and fairy tales, both old and new, that were created by adults. Creative input feeds creative output. Those enterprises that are called literary arts, dramatic arts, and fine arts are disciplined daydreams, usually presenting the world not as it is but as it might or could be. A relationship exists between the adult's creative work and his imaginative intake as a very young child.

School readiness can be modified by the extent of the child's transactions; that is, the normal child who has had a dearth of experiential transactions may not be able to meet the tasks required in the first grade, whereas the child who has had a wealth of experiences may be able to do first grade tasks while still in kindergarten.

The trend today is not to wait for the child to become ready to learn. It is advocated that children who are not ready be provided with specialized experiences to modify the rate of development. As previously mentioned, it can be anticipated that some children born into deprived socioeconomic environments will not be as ready for learning as children born into more favorable environments. To offset the disadvantages, special preschool programs are provided the the children in the first group (even though the provision of these experiences is not at the optimum time to be of maximum help to the child).

As a transacting being, the individual is never complete. An individual's uniqueness is continually evolving as he continues to transact with his environment. When the individual is a child, his transactions are controlled to a large extent by the adults in his life. Eventually and hopefully the individual will take over and control his own transactions. The school has the obligation of helping him accomplish this, and the task may be begun in the earliest years of the elementary grades.

The following section is a discussion of transactions as they pertain to some major tasks that are imposed by society. These are cognitive tasks—knowledge and skills that children must acquire to function efficiently in the culture. The handling of cognitive tasks requires adaptations in the sense that the individual child approaches the tasks with a unique background of inherited and environmentally modified characteristics.

COGNITIVE TASKS OF CHILDREN

Cognition has to do with the things individuals know, how they use what they know, and how they came to know. Handling cognitive tasks demands adaptations. To be confronted with tasks establishes instabilities or disequilibrium in the individual. Because the organic system of the individual cannot tolerate the instabilities, the person seeks to restore equilibrium.

To handle the tasks, the child must transact with the environment. These transactions are different from those influenced by the environment over which the child has no control, such as the economic level of the family and the quality and quantity of food brought into the home. The child also has no control over the unplanned contacts he has with the adults in the vicinity of the home. The people in the neighborhood, regardless of their idiosyncrasies, are unavoidably there and play a part in the child's transactions, as do the various neighborhood stores, playgrounds, and other local features.

Cognitive tasks compel the child to seek specific transactions; the instabilities direct the transactions. In school, specific experiences are organized and controlled to facilitate some of the child's transactions, and they become central factors in the curriculum.

The focus in this section is on cognitive tasks rather than on any behavioral outcomes, which are dealt with in the chapters that discuss curriculum and instruction in specific disciplines. The knowledge and skills the child needs to acquire and use are grouped arbitrarily simply to facilitate the discussion. Although enumerated, these tasks should not be regarded as separate entities. They are merely facets of a total cognitive adaptation, and the list is not meant to be exhaustive.

1. *Finding labels for perceptual experiences.* Perceptual experiences include all the things the child discovers or comes in contact with through the use of the senses. The term includes everything that happens to the child, the happenings she envisions, and the space in which the perception occurs. It also includes varied representations of realia, illustrations, dramatizations, and symbolizations. Children need to attach labels to their experiences in order to communicate with others about them and to facilitate their recalling of specific experiences in reaction to a stimulus from some other experience.

Much of the child's first twelve years of life are spent in acquiring labels. At first, very young children learn the labels for those people around them, followed by labels for the things they can grasp. Then their horizons expand to such an extent that by the time they leave the elementary grades, they have built repertoires of highly specialized labels that are pertinent to the social studies, the sciences, math, literature, and art.

2. *Discovering patterns.* Whether patterns have a prior existence or whether patterning is a peculiar human drive, the child's world is filled with them. Recognizing patterns makes predicting possible. When the young child learns the family's routines for a twenty-four-hour period, he is able to anticipate daily events. Life embodies many, many patterns that the child needs to learn if he is to function properly.

Spatial patterns surround children. Homes are made up of rooms that are designed or used for specific activities. Doors, windows, halls, outdoor walkways, streets, city blocks, shopping centers, schools, and churches—each as an entity and their relationships to each other in space are patterns. Before children leave the elementary grades, they will need to comprehend highly complex patterns in which both time and space are involved.

Children must learn that our number system has a basic pattern of ten. And numbers themselves, used in seriations, are employed to identify other patterns.

Geometry uses patterns on which rules for organizing and predicting spatial relationships are established. The face of a clock shows patterns of five and twelve. A yardstick holds a pattern of twelves and fractional parts of one. Those sequences of practices necessary for working toward the solutions of mathematical problems are patterns. They tell children where to begin, which algorisms to use in what sequence, and how to test the answers.

Patterns include the use of colors in series. Kindergarten children meet them in replicating the arrangement of color sequences in a string of beads. They meet more complex color patterns when they interpret diagrams, maps, and other illustrations. Children apply their knowledge of patterns in the things they create. Included in their creative endeavors are their literary projects. Poetry involves highly sophisticated patterns of words that are organized in rhythm and rhyme. Prose follows somewhat standardized organizational patterns.

Related to the ability to recognize and use patterns is children's awareness of likenesses and differences and their skills in reconciling the two. A pear and an apple are quite different in shape, taste, and coloration, and yet they share many other characteristics in common. A Cortland is quite different from a Delicious, yet they are both recognized as apples. Children learn to discriminate between apples and pears and between kinds of apples by patterns of shape, color, and taste. Then children reconcile the differences when they discover a common pattern that they may call "treats" or "dessert."

3. *Classifying and categorizing.* To reconcile differences is to generalize, a step toward classifying. Children start to generalize early in life when they put all persons having grossly similar characteristics into groups of "mommies" or "daddies." The classes formed early in life tend to be very broad. As children experience more things and do more classifying, they begin to refine their classes according to the difference they realize. For instance, young children may include in their classification of *bowwows* all dogs, cats, raccoon, and other medium-sized, four-legged furry mammals. When children begin to separate the different members they have so classified and form more refined classes, they are categorizing. Their class of bowwows is then limited to only those mammals they perceive as being doglike. Their class of *cats* is restricted to lions and tigers and all mammals bearing characteristics similar to the house cat they are familiar with. As children grow older, their classifications and categories must become more precise and at the same time admit an ever-increasing membership. Much of the schoolwork deals with forming classes and categories and with breaking down classes into categories and classes into members. The ability of children to generalize and specify in these ways helps them to understand and describe their universe.

Children are also required to maintain a degree of flexibility in their classifying and categorizing. They find that they must be able to generalize on several contingencies. Any given thing can be a member of several groups, depending on its place or use. A tree can be a weed if it's growing where it's not wanted, like a seedling that sprouts in a garden or in the gutters of a house. An automobile can be a vehicle or junk or a priceless antique.

4. *Conceptualizing.* Concepts are the usable products of perceptions. Details of a stimulus are perceived and are organized into some kind of scheme. The scheme holds all of the perceived details, including all the emotional reactions prompted by the stimulus. Concepts are highly personal; they exist in the mind

and are brought out by some internal or external stimulus. The output of a concept may be in the form of a generalization, a class, or a category. And it is only through this output, such as a statement, an illustration, or an observable action, that we know someone else's concept. An observer does not know a child's concept of *mother, horse, house, apple,* or anything else until or unless the child demonstrates it in some way. The observer knows that conceptualizing is occurring when she observes conceptual behavior. Yet when concepts are demonstrated through behaviors, it does not always mean that communication is taking place. No matter by what means an individual articulates a concept, the receiver must interpret and restructure it. In that sense, concepts cannot be transmitted exactly or exchanged. They are built or rebuilt in the mind of the perceiver and are subject to all the nuances of prejudices and preferences that affect all perceptions. The visual images that the child has while listening or reading are influenced by the same preconditions. Most adults try to transmit concepts through verbal images, and this process is often unreliable. Consider an adult who is attempting to describe an elephant to a child who has never seen one. The adult relies on principles of likenesses and differences that he has observed, and when put into language, those principles are expressed as metaphors. Example: "An elephant is like a horse, only much, much bigger. Huge! Big as a house. And it has a nose that looks like a hose and touches the ground." The only way that a child can truly build a valid concept of *elephant* is by examining the real thing, although the use of a model or an illustration may substitute to a limited extent.

Yet without a doubt, language-related concepts are the most useful ones because they are the only ones that can explain themselves. A painting or a dance may communicate a concept, but neither of those two media can discuss itself; only language concepts serve as discussion media.

A book on astronomy can contribute to the child's concept of a star, and a book on some distant place can create impressions that the child might never be able to experience. Many valuable notions about places and things beyond the child's reach are stimulated through verbal communications with her peers as well as with adults. When a classmate describes a trip she has taken or a happening she has experienced, she may be conveying the nuclei on which the receivers build concepts. Many useful concepts have their origins in vague impressions.

Labeling is one of the primary functions of language. Labels are symbols mutually agreed on by a societal group to represent things, places, positions, feelings, actions, quantities, and qualities. Labels give a permanence to experiences. By stating the name of an article, the communicator continues the existence of the concept of that article. However, saying or writing the label is not necessary for keeping a concept alive; the individual need only think the label. Through the manipulation of language-based thoughts, the individual can test ideas before she follows through on them. Thus, through a process of mental trial and error, the individual may solve problems without much expenditure of physical energy. And thinking in words supplies the individual with cues for chaining concepts.

Another contribution of language is that it enables individuals to construct classes and categories, which simplify their thinking and communicating. Labeling as related to categories and classifications enables the individual to manipulate them both mentally and vocally.

The child's ability to conceptualize is demanded by the entire school program. The qualities of her conceptualizations will depend, in part, on the qualities of the models she experiences. Included in quality are the consistencies of the models. When the models vary from day to day, the child is confused and her conceptualizations are vague. Because education is so completely involved in concept building and conceptual behavior, the nature of concepts and how they are developed are extremely important to curriculum specialists.

5. *Identifying self.* It is difficult for the child to discover and know himself, to know his capabilities, and to know where and how he stands in his environment. The task is made more difficult because the maturation process is constantly producing physical and mental changes in him.

Much of the information a child has for building his self-image is based on the reflections communicated by the adults and peers in the environment. Every human contact becomes a mirror and reflects an image of the child as the contact sees the child. The image is made known by how the reflector looks at the child, speaks to the child, and treats the child. If the contact views the child as being hopelessly incompetent, the child will receive that reflection. The difficulty lies not only in how an influential adult sees a child but also in how the child *thinks* the adult sees him.

The child needs to learn to recognize his uniqueness and to evaluate the reflections of himself that he sees in others. To do so is a difficult task because there is no other individual, no model, like him. Teachers—because of their professional training and because they are in contact with the widest range of individual differences—are in the best position to present the child with strong and sympathetic reflections. It is also in the power of the teacher to reflect ego-destroying images.

Personal goals and values evolve from one's self-image. To establish healthy and worthwhile goals, the child must learn to evaluate himself and his progress toward his goals. He must learn to examine the reflections of others and discern whether the images they show him are really in his interests. This is especially relevant for the images his peers present. Peer groups are inclined toward reflecting what is to their advantage. Some adults with whom the child is in close contact tend to transfer to the child their interests and aspirations. Rather than asking "Who am I?" the child should be concerned with "Who am I becoming?" Knowing himself is probably one of the most difficult cognitive tasks the child faces.

Of importance for the development of a healthy self-image is the child's concept of himself as a sexual human being. This does not imply that the child must understand all the biological facts of reproduction. It means that the child must recognize all of the aspects of the sex he or she is. These include the masculine-feminine responsibilities to each member of the family.

It is in the early years that the child builds or fails to build the necessary foundations for effective functioning as a sexual human being. To help the child understand himself or herself, the girls need to have some knowledge of the social roles of the male, and the boys need to appreciate those of the female. Stereotyped images, such as women have babies and men work, need to be avoided; sexual roles should be placed in their proper context. It is important that the child understands that both females and males can function in a variety of roles without losing their sexual identities as long as individuals maintain their sexual self-images.

6. *Solving problems.* The child is confronted with problems very early in life. If the adults around the child are anxious to solve all her problems, the child's confidence in herself as a self-functioning human being may fail to develop. The child's independency relates directly to her ability to solve problems. The types of problems the child meets can be grouped as goal-oriented, dilemmas, quandaries, and academic.

Goal-oriented problems pertain to both immediate and long-range goals. An example of an immediate goal for a young child is that of desiring a cookie out of her reach. The child may attain the goal by dragging a chair up to the table and using it as a ladder or by sitting on the floor and yelling.

Long-range goals are those that are not immediately attainable. Reaching the goal depends on persistence in the problem-solving technique as well as on the technique itself. The child is required to develop a scheme compatible with her abilities and to recognize the importance of persistence. It frequently happens that the child chooses goal-achievement methods that are too large or too complex for her abilities. She needs to learn from her failures as well as from her successes.

Dilemmas are of a personal nature; they pertain to conflicts between the individual and other people. The resolution of a dilemma demands a choice between two or more equally unpleasant alternatives. Example: A ten-year-old is invited by a playmate to participate in a highly enjoyable activity, while her parent invites her to an afternoon outing. If the child chooses her playmate, she offends the parent; if she rejects the playmate, she may fear that she will lose position or face with him. Some of the dilemmas children face are so threatening that they seriously trouble them. In the interest of mental health, children need the help of adults in establishing guidelines for resolving dilemmas. In the end, the alternative chosen is a value decision and is related to the child's self-image. The worst choice a child could make is to postpone a decision, hoping that one or both alternatives will be withdrawn.

Quandaries are situations in which the child must choose between two equally rewarding alternatives. A classic example is the child with a coin to spend. Should she spend it on ice cream or on a toy? She has to decide in advance which alternative will be more satisfying. The situation that was used to illustrate a dilemma would be a quandary if the child were to weigh in balance the rewards of each conflicting alternative. It depends on whether she views the problem according to what she may lose or what she may gain. Some dilemmas are easily resolved by turning them into quandaries. Again values play an important role in the decision making. There are, however, some children who are so fearful of making a decision that they make no choice at all.

The child must also be able to solve problems related to academics. Generally speaking, academic problems are those found in workbooks, assignments, or in classroom dialogues. The resolution of these problems involve the application of skills and knowledge introduced in the classroom. For the most part, the purpose of this kind of problem solving is an evaluative one. To function effectively in this area, children need to know the required methods and procedures for attacking the problems. In arithmetic, the algorism is usually specified in the textbook. In written composition, the textbook presents outlines and guidelines. In other situations, it may be that the child's ability to memorize facts and/or procedures is being evaluated. In fairness to the child, she should be made aware of what is being measured and what the performance criteria are. The teacher should also view the work of the children as a reflection on the teaching procedures used in the classroom.

Academic problems frequently become dilemmas when the emphasis is placed on the product rather than the process. When the adult stresses the "correct" answer, conceptual behavior is directed toward avoiding the punishment of incorrectness. In the so-called discussions that usually follow reading or social studies lessons, the child is chiefly concerned with giving answers that do not displease the teacher. In some situations the students spend more time studying the teacher than the lesson. Instead of reasoning sessions, discussions often tend to deteriorate into a game of twenty questions. The rejected answers serve as clues to finding the acceptable one. Very little learning takes place in such sessions, for the child cannot learn when she is in a threatening atmosphere and when she and her classmates are being cross-examined. But by emphasizing reason, the teacher demonstrates logical procedures for arriving at conclusions and making decisions. And that's what problem solving and resolving dilemmas and quandaries are all about—predicting and examining all the possible consequences and weighing them against each other.

7. *Disciplining self.* Responding to inner controls relates to the individual's knowledge of himself and his ability to solve problems. The child can achieve self-discipline if he views himself as a competent individual who can meet contingencies, anticipate consequences, and make decisions. The child who is pictured by adults as being incompetent and unable to seek solutions to problems can be expected to rely on those adults for control of himself. The extent of a child's self-discipline is related to the degree of his dependence or independence. A paradox is seen in some parents' and teachers' attempts to maintain a high degree of dependence in the child while decrying his lack of self-discipline. Many adults subconsciously treat children as inferior human beings rather than as individuals who are progressing toward self-fulfillment. Some teachers present a similar attitude in teaching a lesson. Such a teacher assumes the pose that she is all-knowing, all-wise, never wrong—an omnipotent master of all knowledge. The child is never permitted to enjoy the satisfaction that comes from accomplishing a task. Nothing can please the master because the child always has so much further to go. In this type of atmosphere, the child can never get to know himself because the self is unable to emerge.

Encouraging independence does not mean, however, that support is withdrawn. The child must feel confident that the teacher is there to help when problems seem unsolvable. The child who has mastered self-discipline not only feels secure with himself but also has faith in his teacher as a reliable, nonaccusing, nondemeaning source in problem solving.

A child needs self-discipline not only for his personal well-being but for living in society as well. There are a number of social rules that are established for the common benefit. Some rules are absolute do's and don'ts; others are codes of behavior, which are set up to induce pleasant human associations. The child needs to know both types by the verbal images transmitted by the teacher and other models. In the first case, the teacher verbally states the rules as do's and don'ts and then enforces them. When the teacher takes action against an unwanted behavior, the enforcement is a model. It is precise. The children experience an example of what is not permitted. The social niceties are also demonstrated through models. The children observe which behaviors are rewarded and which are frowned on. Models of good behavior abound in literature, but perhaps the best model is the teacher herself when she is displaying the desired behaviors in her relationships with the pupils. And her consistency in behaviors is of primary importance.

In coping with various situations, including school problems, the child builds his self-esteem, the basis for self-discipline. Educational programs should not only provide the child with opportunities to solve problems but should have built-in plateaus at which the child can rest on his laurels and savor his successes. The child needs time to look at himself and to examine past occurrences to see how far he has come.

8. *Using symbols.* Humankind has demonstrated a canny penchant for filling the world with symbolic representations. It is only through the use of symbols that people can share experiences and transmit the lore of the culture. Among all the classes of symbols the child must know, the most important are those related to the language arts and mathematics. A knowledge of these symbols is required to interpret all other symbols, such as maps, charts, diagrams, illustrations, and models. While each of the fine arts has its own communication symbols, those symbols can only be explained through the symbols of language. In that sense, the language symbols and/or math symbols are intimately involved in all other classes of symbols.

As may be expected, the child learns the meaning of symbols according to the opportunities she has to experience them. She gains insights chiefly through her contacts with the adults in her immediate environment. Because she has limited opportunities in her home environment to acquire skills in the uses of symbols, she is sent to school and put into the hands of professionals. The child uses almost all of the possible combinations of the verbal symbols by the time she is seven years old. On completing her elementary school years, she is expected to have progressed in her verbal-symbol usage so that she can compose clear, concise, and orderly presentations within standard syntax, perceive verbal symbols and build them into concepts, and recognize as many as twenty thousand written symbols and interpret their meanings. In addition, she is expected to compose and express concepts in written form according to various precepts. And all of these tasks include an enormous inventory of symbols in the language arts, mathematics, science, social studies, music, art, dramatics, and physical education.

Symbols that are frequently overlooked in teaching procedures are models. They fall into three groups: three-dimensional, two-dimensional, and verbal. All models are abstractions of the real, with the three-dimensional being closest to the real. What is frequently overlooked is that the children need help in attacking them just as they need assistance in attacking printed language symbols. They need to know how to extract information from them. Until the child has a scheme for doing so, her conclusions may reflect the ambiguity of the models.

9. *Memorizing.* The child needs to memorize certain data not only to make progress in school but to fulfill his personal needs as well. The accomplishment of this task requires more than recollecting. Specific information must be so ingrained that it is recalled automatically. On entering school, the child must have memorized his name, his parents' names, his address, and perhaps his telephone

number. For his safety and well-being, he must memorize a list of do's and don'ts enumerated by the teacher. The child soon discovers that there are a number of tasks that he can do more efficiently if he memorizes the routines.

The very young child finds that he has to memorize rhymes, jingles, and songs and then some basics of arithmetic and spelling. As the child progresses through the grades, he is called on to demonstrate his ability to memorize the sequencing of events he has experienced either personally or from what he has read or heard. Sequencing of events in historical order pertains not only to social studies but to fiction, biography, and the sciences as well.

There are so many stimuli being poured into the child's mind at one time that it is remarkable how much the child does retain. A number of systems that are designed to aid memory have been used in schools. However, the teacher can be of greatest assistance to the child through her sympathetic understanding. Since anxiety-imposed thoughts are the greatest blocks to developing a good memory, the teacher must strive to provide a nonthreatening atmosphere. The child who does not have to fear the consequences if he forgets a particular fact is more apt to develop a good memory than one who feels threatened.

10. *Creating.* Creative behavior is present when the child produces some thought that is entirely new to herself. The thought need not be expressed immediately, nor may it ever be expressed. It may be stored in her memory bank and then used at some future time in response to some stimuli or in combination with other creative thoughts.

A considerable amount of creative activity is demanded by the school programs. Not only are there creative tasks in written and oral composition and in arts and crafts, but much of the science, math, and social studies programs require children to gain insights and reach conclusions that are new to them. Because teachers have already made those discoveries, they may fail to regard the child's thoughts as creative output. Having this kind of attitude deprives a child of a true understanding of creativity.

Creativity is related to reasoning power, which, incidentally, cannot necessarily be measured by intelligence tests. There undoubtedly is a degree of intelligence below which creative outputs diminish in quality, but it cannot be assumed that the power to create ascends along with scores on intelligence tests. Some intellectual geniuses may be highly creative, but many creative geniuses score in the high-average or above-average bracket. Many factors other than intelligence are involved, one of which is adult expectancy. If the teacher is willing to accept the proposition that every child in the classroom is capable of producing something creative, there will be much creative output.

Creativity has its roots in perceptions. No matter what the media of expression is, the child has to draw on her perceptual experiences. The quality of the finished product depends on the quality of the material the child has stored. The teacher makes his greatest contribution by teaching the children what to perceive, how to do it, and how to interpret the perceptions. If a walk in the woods is to precede the writing of a composition about autumn (which it should, if possible), the teacher may need to call attention to the colors of the fallen leaves, their textures, their odor, and the sounds they make underfoot. The sky, the weather, and the atmosphere need to be discussed along with the subjective feelings the total scene arouses.

Fantasizing, or daydreaming, is a creative act. Young children act out their fantasies when they play "let's pretend." Kindergarten children are encouraged to respond to their creative impulses and play out roles spontaneously. For some reason, children are no longer encouraged in these activities from grade five and up. And as soon as they burst out the door at the end of the day, they become a variety of make-believe characters. Pretending is a form of creative behavior and belongs in the classroom—not to amuse an audience but to give the children another means of expressing creative thought.

Self-confidence is required for creative behavior. To help a child feel confident, the teacher needs to give well-timed encouragement, not lavish praise; children are clever enough to detect undeserved applause. Also needed is constructive criticism—and the teacher does not need to be an accomplished artist, novelist, or poet to give it. The teacher can use his own works, not necessarily as models for the children to imitate, but as examples of technique. Nothing does a better job of teaching the child how to appraise creative work than does self-criticism by the teacher of his own attempts. When a teacher assigns creative tasks, he can gain beneficial insights into what is being required by performing the tasks himself. Teacher dependence on guides and answer keys can deprive the teacher of opportunities to share experiences with the children.

Persistence plays a big role in the quality of creative work. The individual who can cling to a thought, refine it, and re-refine it demonstrates persistence. She is the one least likely to turn in her first effort. In some cases, she would rather not turn in anything than submit an attempt she is not satisfied with. Unfortunately, the desirable attribute of persistence may sometimes be driven out of the child in deference to the daily schedule. Giving a child twenty or thirty minutes to create a written composition or to produce a painting results in her learning that completing the task is more likely to gain teacher approval than striving for quality.

Time also works against the persistent individual in oral lessons. Some teachers seem to abhor periods of silence, those spaces between the asking of a question and the responses. The child who gives an answer off the top of her head is generally rewarded more for breaking the silence than for the quality of the answer. Many times the persistent thinker does not get the opportunity to make a contribution. By the time she has resolved the question to her own satisfaction, the teacher has moved on to the next question.

Adults who associate successfully with groups of children, successful parents, foster parents, teachers, and others have learned to practice the science of perceiving and advancing individual differences. The ability to do so is not a gift; it is a cognitive process that needs to be developed. Many adults fail to do so because they have been and continue to be compared to some imaginary norm by those who direct their activities and by their colleagues.

An attempt has been made to describe ten major classes of cognitive tasks facing each elementary school child. They were purposely presented from a child-centered view to emphasize the enormity and complexity of what lies ahead for the new-born child. The list also points out the enormity and complexity of the teachers' responsibilities in facilitating the transactions that are necessary for each young unique individual to adapt herself for meeting the tasks successfully.

LANGUAGE DEVELOPMENT

As is seen in the tasks just described, language is the most valuable tool the child has in attaining the goals established for him and by him. Practically every task depends on the ability to use language and to build and manipulate concepts. Consequently, the teacher's greatest concern needs to be language development. All applications of language—speaking and writing and listening and reading——are parts of an overall skill. All four applications of language use closely related symbols and deal with concepts. The child who is adept in oral composition can be expected to read, write, and listen better than his counterpart who is not. The child who reads more skillfully usually speaks, listens, and writes better.

Not all children develop language ability with equal ease. The disparity in the language performances among children who are completing study in elementary schools is great and has precipitated much study. The differences appear to be related to hereditary and environmental and emotional factors.

There are strong arguments to suggest that language learning abilities have their base in what is inherited. For example, it seems an impossibility for a child to develop language skills so completely and so rapidly from environmental contacts in the short span of time that it ordinarily takes. While it is true that every child acquires much of his oral language skills by imitating those in his environment who speak, he cannot have heard all of the many sentences he uses during his first five or six years. To do so would mean that he would have heard as many as several billion different forms. The child appears to learn, at a very young age, to form implicit rules about the structure of language, rules that indicate a high-level mental activity.

Theories about hereditary influences do not cancel out the influences of the environment by any means. No person learns to talk without experiencing contacts with other people. Neither do all children speak the same language nor even the same dialect. And it is from the environment that meanings become attached to words. Children learn to use language if they are exposed to it, but more than exposure is needed to gain the verbal control necessary for many learning tasks.

EXERCISES FOR THOUGHT AND ACTION

1. Observe two children of the same sex and chronological age and note differences in their physical growth, motor skills, emotional development, and social skills. If possible, investigate the home environments of these children. Do you find conditions that may account for some of their differences?

2. Investigate L.S. Vygotsky's research and theory concerning speech and thought. What is the relevance of this theory to school learning?

3. Why is the child's self-concept important in the learning process? What does a child need to learn about himself?

4. Would you make a grouping (and labeling) of problems the child meets other than the one presented in this chapter? Why?

5. Report to the class on environmental factors that are important in the development of creativity. Critique each of those factors in terms of your observations of children and your examinations of educational literature on creativity.

6. What are the effects of malnutrition of the mother on her unborn child? Can these effects ever be altered if the child is subjected to several preschool years of improper nutrition?

7. Based on your study of this chapter, describe what a classroom should be like in order to maximize the child's success in learning.

SELECTED READINGS

Almy, M.C., et al. *Young Children's Thinking.* New York: Teachers College Press, 1966.

Bloom, B.S. *Stability and Change in Human Characteristics.* New York: John Wiley, 1964.

Brown, R.W., and Bellugi, U. "Three Processes in the Child's Acquisition of Syntax." *Harvard Educational Review* 34 (1964): 133-51.

Bruner, J.S., et al. *Studies in Cognitive Growth.* New York: John Wiley, 1967.

Carroll, J.B., ed. *Language, Thought, and Reality.* New York: John Wiley, 1965.

Foss, B.M., ed. *Determinants of Infant Behavior.* New York: John Wiley, 1961.

Frost, J.L., ed. *Early Childhood Education Rediscovered.* New York: Holt, 1968.

Gibson, E.J. *Principles of Perceptual Learning and Development.* New York: Appleton-Century-Crofts, 1969.

Hertzler, J.O. *A Sociology of Language.* New York: Random House, 1965.

Hunt, E.B. *Concept Learning.* New York: John Wiley, 1962.

Hunt, J. McV. *Intelligence and Experience.* New York: Ronald Press, 1961.

Landreth, C. *Early Childhood; Behavior and Learning.* New York: Alfred A. Knopf, 1967.

Lenneberg E. *Biological Foundations of Language.* New York: John Wiley, 1967.

Lewis, M.M. *Language, Thought and Personality in Infancy and Childhood.* New York: Basic Books, 1963.

Lorenz, K. *Evolution and Modification of Behavior.* Chicago: University of Chicago Press, 1965.

Piaget, J. *The Science of Education and the Psychology of the Child.* New York: Viking Press, 1970.

Rebelsky, F., and Dorman, L., eds. *Child Development and Behavior.* New York: Alfred A. Knopf, 1970.

Spencer, T.D., and Kass, N. *Perspectives in Child Development.* New York: McGraw-Hill, 1970.

Torrance, E.P. *Guiding Creative Talent.* Englewood Cliffs, N.J.: Prentice-Hall, 1962.

Vygotsky, L.S. *Thought and Language.* Cambridge: MIT Press, 1962.

Winich, M. "Malnutrition and Brain Development." *Journal of Pediatrics* 74 (1969): 667.

Wright, J., and Kagan, J. "Basic Cognitive Processes in Children." Monographs of the Society for Research in Child Development, 2nd ser., 28, no. 86 (1963).

Much of what happens in an elementary school classroom depends on factors that are a part of, or are related to, how the classroom is organized. In this chapter the authors discuss the organization of schools as well as individual classrooms. They show that many aspects of school, district, and state policies affect the organization for learning in individual classrooms.

The authors strongly advocate the open informal classroom—a position that developed from their extensive experiences in teaching in elementary schools, supervising beginning teachers, teaching preservice and in-service curriculum and methods courses, and observing in British primary schools.

A reader may possibly be disturbed by the authors' descriptions of many—if not a substantial majority—of present-day classrooms. However, striving to disturb complacency is a goal of this chapter as well as of the entire book. What is done in many classrooms is less than desirable; improvement is needed. Too many children receive too little education in our schools. Critics of schools are numerous but not many of them offer more than fault-finding. The authors of this chapter do not fall into that category; they are specific in suggesting how a classroom should be organized and operated.

W.T.P.

Organizing for Learning

Richard T. Salzer and
Richard E. Drdek

3

Elementary schools in the United States enroll thirty million children and utilize the services of over one million teachers, principals, aides, clerks, custodians, food-service personnel, and other employees. Operation of such a large institution requires a substantial amount of organizational planning and administrative control. Although there are numerous federal and state agencies concerned with education in our society, most administrative efforts have been concentrated at the school-district level.

A wide range of types of educational decisions must be made regarding the operation of schools—what supplies to purchase, how to organize the instructional program, what system to use for scheduling the day and utilizing the facilities, and so forth. At the local level the school board and professional staff share authority for setting the policies and adopting procedures that significantly affect what takes place in the buildings and classrooms.

IMPORTANT FACTORS IN SCHOOL ORGANIZATION

The degree of control a building principal and staff have over their own activities depends on the amount of decision-making power retained in the central office of the school system. In many districts the regulations of the school board or superintendent's office exert substantial control over the day-by-day operation of schools. For example, grouping students by academic ability may be required in some systems, forbidden in others, and left to the discretion of the principal and staff elsewhere. Even at the building level there will be variation in the extent to which the administrator shares decision-making authority with teachers and others involved in operating the school.

Regardless of the formal organizational structure of the school system, there are a number of factors that influence the manner in which all educational decisions are made and schools actually operated.

Large School Enrollments

Modern education has been marked by a dramatic increase in the size of individual schools. As mentioned in Chapter 1, the era of the small school attended by a few local children has all but ended. Such buildings were replaced because their enrollments were not sufficiently large to justify expenditures for the facilities, equipment, supplies, and services that are considered essential to good education.

The argument for the larger school is that concentration of funds will mean the availability of swimming pools, audiovisual equipment, remedial reading teachers, and much else that seems necessary. While most authorities accept the "efficiency" point of view, it is clear that large schools have proved to be a mixed blessing. Some of the problems associated with them stem from the sheer size of the building. It is understandable that children and even teachers may suffer a loss of identity in a building of two thousand pupils and a one-hundred-member staff. This lack of a feeling of belonging, a source of serious personal difficulty in its own right, is also related to such social problems as vandalism, alienation, interpersonal antagonism, and even violence. While these difficulties have been most commonly associated with secondary schools, it seems likely that large elementary buildings contribute to the general problem. Big schools may themselves be a source of fear for small children and even adults, and this may be a reason why parents in some communities stay away.

In rural and suburban districts, large enrollments are possible only when the attendance district for a particular building is extensive—encompassing in many cases an area of one hundred square miles or more. Such an arrangement may cause feelings of alienation, since the school will not be an integral part of the lives of more than a few families. Contact with all but the most interested or aggressive parents is inhibited under these conditions.

Anyone who has been involved with rural or suburban schools knows that extensive attendance districts require much attention to transportation of pupils. The school bus has become a significant factor in the lives of many families and nearly every school-system administration. Dependence on buses usually means that children can neither go to school early nor stay late for extra attention or special opportunities. The bus schedule may even dictate that the school day be so concentrated as to permit pupils only a few minutes for breaks from classroom routines and a very short lunch period. The appearance of the school bus has meant substantial change in the daily programs of elementary schools.

The development of large schools has been accompanied by the creation of an extensive system of internal management: the appointment of assistant principals who are given particular administrative assignments and the designation of some members of the staff as lead, or master, teachers or as grade-level coordinators who supervise a portion of the building or an aspect of the program. While these arrangements appear essential in many schools and occasionally work reasonably well, in other situations what results is a cumbersome administrative hierarchy within the building, with consequent loss of a sense of community and mutual confidence.

Relation of School to Community

As implied in the preceding section, the location of a school, especially if in suburban or rural areas, may substantially affect its internal organization. And as discussed in Chapter 1, there have been some recent attempts to recapture the spirit of close school-community cooperation that once characterized much of elementary education in this society. In many residential areas, of course, the local elementary school continues to be the only institution with extensive direct contact with the majority of homes.

When a school is located in a densely populated community, with most of the local children in attendance, it is often described as a "neighborhood school." This term once implied only that the building was of moderate size and well placed to serve the children living near it. Supporters of the neighborhood school claim for it the advantage of a close relationship between classroom and home, significant independence for children as they walk to and from the building with friends and siblings, the greater possibility of using neighborhood resources for learning, and better financial and moral support from the community. In opposition are those who advocate plans that would, if adopted, abolish the neighborhood school. These critics maintain that the supposed virtues of the neighborhood school no longer exist in anything like their idealized form. They point out that a high proportion of mothers are employed and thus unavailable for contacts during the day, and that, for reasons of safety and convenience, parents often transport their children to school, even when the family lives close by. And, it is often added, few teachers either know much about the locality in which they teach or use it for instructional purposes.

Instead of neighborhood schools, some citizens and educators support the establishment of very large attendance centers, such as campuses for grades kindergarten though senior high or schools organized so that children of different grade levels are transported out of their home areas. For the most part, the intent of such proposals is the creation of a more diverse school population than that usually found in a single neighborhood.

As indicated in Chapter 2, it has become increasingly apparent that environment largely determines the course of a child's development. Educators recognize the validity of this finding, and many are seeking ways to have more contact with the early environment, particularly the home. Federally funded projects for poverty-level children uniformly require parental involvement and usually strongly suggest that teachers' aides and similar personnel be hired from the community in which the school is located. School systems are not only employing ordinary citizens to help with the operation of schools but also are encouraging parents and other adults to come into the school on a voluntary basis to assist in various ways. Specific activities as well as the general trend toward involvement of the community have implications for school organization.

Nature of the Individual School

The atmosphere, tradition, and staff of a particular school partially determine how it is organized. For example, a school is likely to be resistant to change if it is long established, located in a residential area with a low rate of transience and consistent parental expectations, and staffed by teachers with many years of experience in that building. It is usually true that in this type of school, there exist relatively fixed and conventional ideas concerning the grouping of children for instruction, the roles of classroom and special teachers, the pattern of library use, and most other organizational matters.

In newly established schools, however, the important decisions are often made by the incoming staff, or sometimes a group of teachers has been specially selected to reflect a particular orientation. In these cases, plans for the organization of a school may derive from the implementation of a specific set of principles regarding the nature of education, rather than the personal beliefs or habits of a few individuals.

New developments in school organization are stimulated to some extent by the availability of architectural innovations that provide wide latitude for decision making with respect to the use of space. School designs and renovation plans often evolve from concerted attempts to develop structures that support particular concepts in educational programming. And sometimes a building plan that is drastically different from the existing architecture is adopted by a district in order to compel change in school organization and program offerings.

Even if the architecture of a building remains the same, new forms of operation and management can appear. Theories of education come and go, of course, which alters the ways of doing things. The appointment of a new principal or a major turnover of teachers affects the balance of power and the decision-making process in a building. The nature of the neighborhood population changes, perhaps with implications for the organization of the school.

Complexity of the Educational Program

Decisions concerning school organization necessarily are complex undertakings, even if considered only from the standpoints of the number of people involved and the varied nature of the relationships among personnel, facilities, and programs. The size of the staff of a modern elementary school is large, and the administrative superstructure governing it is diverse and complicated. All of these factors must be considered in planning and implementing the instructional program if sound administrative practices are to be followed.

Certainly logistical problems arise in school operation, and various forms of organization require different types of equipment. Books, chalk, and paper are required for conventional programs, of course. Technologically oriented approaches require audio tapes, bulbs, batteries, cords, television receivers, and projectors. Lumber, hamster food, and clay are some of the necessities in activity-oriented programs.

Curriculum decisions also affect school organization arrangements. For example, when mathematics offerings became more complex at the elementary school level (see Chapter 10), observers noted a substantial increase of teacher interest in departmentalization plans that permitted one or two members of the staff to teach mathematics. Proposals for improving the reading program of a school also sometimes require reorganization of the entire building or a major section of it.

Proposals to change the age range of the children served have implications for school organization. If pupils move to a "middle school" at age ten or if four-year-olds are admitted to elementary schools, there are important questions to be answered regarding school administration.

PROGRAMS AND SCHOOL ORGANIZATION

Decisions about school organization are often important enough that the adoption of one or another approach may result in a school being characterized as being of a particular type. In certain communities a particular school is identified as "the place where they do all of the grouping," "the school where they have the team teaching," or "the one that has levels instead of grades." While it often appears to some observers that organizational plans are selected for the wrong reasons or no reasons at all, most educators, in following a particular plan, are usually attempting to deal with a specific set of circumstances. The questions to be dealt with are very simple and quite important: Who will attend which school? How will pupils be organized when they get there? How will their learning be supervised?

Age Groups of Pupils

For the purposes of this discussion the elementary school is defined as including the age group five through twelve, grades kindergarten through sixth. Although this pattern has been dominant for some time, it is by no means universal. Earlier forms of age grouping have been retained in some areas. For one important matter, several states still do not include kindergarten in the public school system. In many instances, especially in private schools, the seventh and eighth grades have been retained in the "grade-school" buildings.

Organizational patterns such as the "primary school" for grades kindergarten through three and the "intermediate building" for older students have received some attention. But the really significant changes adopted or proposed have to do with a reassessment of the age groups assigned to the elementary school level.

Including Young Children

Chapter 2 presents evidence concerning the growing recognition of the importance of the early years of life. In acknowledgment of these findings, it has been proposed in some states that classes for four-year-olds be included in the public school system. Large numbers of three- and four-year-old children have already participated in programs funded by the federal government but operated by school systems and other agencies. Early-childhood classes are now an accepted part of the elementary school in many localities. But since parents and other citizens as well as educators are not all convinced of the value of young children attending school on a regular basis, enrollment in such programs in always voluntary on the part of the family.

Development of Middle Schools

In some communities school reorganization has meant that sixth graders, or sometimes fifth and sixth graders, attend middle, or intermediate, schools, usually with seventh and eighth graders. The rationale for this change is based on the earlier physical and social maturation of children and the complexity of the school program at the upper elementary level. In a few situations a genuinely different type of school has been evolving, one that retains some of the aspects of the conventional elementary classroom while providing a good variety of exploratory opportunities for pupils. But for the most part, unfortunately, the middle school represents little more than a name change from "junior high."

Grouping of Pupils

While children of widely varying ages sat in colonial, frontier, and rural schools, the separation of pupils into age groups has been the general practice in recent times. When grade levels were first introduced, educators often rigorously enforced the system. Children were frequently required to spend two or more years in a grade before being passed to the next, whereas academically talented pupils were often allowed to "skip" a grade.

The strict enforcement of promotion standards finds favor from time to time in different communities but is not generally supported by educators. Not only does the practice not lead to substantial narrowing of the range of achievement in classes but also seems to produce harmful effects in terms of children's attitudes toward themselves and school.

Since children of the same age do vary widely in their academic abilities, educators are continually seeking ways to improve the present grade-level system that means frustration for some children and boredom for others.

Achievement Grouping

The practice of grouping by achievement levels is based on recognition of the fact that children vary in their knowledge and skill in different school subjects. Achievement grouping within the normal, self-contained classroom means that several pupils of approximately the same level of performance are brought together for instruction. Such groups may be temporary, designed to accomplish a specific teaching objective, or more or less permanent, meeting regularly for the entire school year. The latter type of grouping is almost universal for primary-grades instruction in reading and may sometimes be used in other skill areas such as mathematics and spelling.

Achievement grouping, especially with older children, is often combined with departmentalization. In this arrangement several classrooms schedule the same subject at the same time, and each pupil is assigned to a particular class on the basis of his or her performance in that field of study.

Although achievement grouping as a concept is popular with many teachers and administrators, there is no stubstantial body of evidence to indicate that the benefits of actual programs outweigh the possible negative effects of labeling children as mediocre or poor performers.

Ability Grouping

In ability grouping an attempt is made to place in a given classroom children who are of similar general academic aptitude. The criteria for this type of practice normally include such factors as intelligence, reading level, competency in study skills, and teacher judgment of individual pupils. The assignment of a child to a particular classroom group is usually done for a year at a time. Such placement has significance for the individual's entire academic career, however, since the classes often progress at different rates through a similar instructional program. Children assigned to a "slow first grade" ordinarily can be found in a "slow sixth grade" five years later.

Ability grouping rises and falls in popularity as do the other organizational practices. In many schools the approach has been tried but then abandoned when it was found that since not many children do equally well or poorly in all school subjects, the complexity of the teacher's task was not reduced very much. Furthermore, some educators express concern about the negative effects produced when a large proportion of the school population is publicly labeled "inferior."

Proposed Grouping Plans

While organization plans based on achievement and ability are the most frequently adopted alternatives to the heterogeneous age-group class, many other types of programs have been considered—including grouping pupils according to sex, friendship preferences, and personality match with the teacher. In view of the generalization that grouping pupils by age is a relatively recent practice which "outdated" the placement of children of different ages in the same classroom, it is interesting to note that one alternative practice now proposed involves the deliberate placement of children of different ages in the same room.

Providing for Pupils with Special Needs

The area of special, or exceptional, education is a large and complex field and cannot be sufficiently dealt with in a general curriculum and methods textbook. In terms of the overall elementary school program, however, it is important to point out that a number of authorities are taking the position that while children with outstanding academic aptitude or those with handicaps should be identified early in their school years and provided with assistance, this additional attention need not take the form of isolation in special classes. More and more children with special needs are appearing in regular classrooms, in which they spend all or most of their time.

The placement of handicapped children in normal classes may be viewed as helpful to all concerned—the pupils with difficulties have the opportunity to learn how to function in a realistic situation, and the other children are helped to realize that classmates with special problems are more like them than they are different. For some of the same reasons it may be argued that the extremely bright and able pupil is also better off in a class of normal children, especially if the classroom program is flexibly organized so that individualized work is possible.

When children who are seriously handicapped in areas of vision, hearing, speech, mental ability, or mobility are placed in regular classrooms, the demands made on the teacher undoubtedly increase. But with the help of resource people who know how to meet the difficulties that arise, the situation can be handled in ways which benefit all the pupils. Another desirable outcome is that the teacher, in working to meet the special needs of one or two pupils, may become more sensitive to the individuality of all children.

Monitoring Pupil Progress

An important consideration in school organization has to do with the responsibility for seeing that children make regular academic progress. In the most traditional forms of schooling, the teacher takes the class through an externally imposed program of studies, makes judgments concerning each child's learning of skills and acquiring of knowledge, and keeps records having to do with such evaluations.

In some situations the difficulties presented by the conventional evaluation process are confronted by grouping the pupils in various ways. Such procedures are intended to reduce the magnitude of the testing and recording tasks facing the teacher. The other general approach to solving some of the evaluation problems involves organization of the program of study.

Nongraded Schools

The nongraded system may be thought of as more a general point of view than a set of specific administrative procedures. In one sense the term refers to much of current elementary education, in that pupils are usually automatically promoted to the next grade, with only a few instances of enforcement of performance standards. There are a few buildings and systems in which *nongraded* refers to a school program that is organized without reference to the placement of content at particular levels or the attainment of specific objectives by all pupils. In such schools curricular emphasis tends toward concrete and creative experiences and attention to the development of the individual child.

The nongraded primary form of organization, limited as the name indicates to the first years of schooling, has been in use for a number of years in some districts. This practice, also known as the "primary unit," grows out of a concern on the part of many educators that because of the unevenness of the developmental pattern of young children, no decision to require a child to repeat a grade should be made until after three or four years of school. Such a method of operation permits many slow starters to avoid the difficulties often associated with having had a "failure" experience.

Continuous Progress Plans

Sometimes combined with nongraded programs are plans that rather carefully specify the content and sequence of what pupils should learn but do not associate material with particular years in school. *Levels program* and *continuous progress plan* are the terms most often used in referring to such an approach.

The basic idea in continuous progress planning is the division of the curriculum into relatively small, consecutive units for each subject area. Rather large numbers of these units, modules, or levels are identified and described for the elementary school years. As a child or, more likely, a group of children completes one of these units, the achievement is recorded and the learner moves on to the next level. The pupil, accompanied by his or her records, goes on to a different classroom each year. It is assumed that subsequent teachers will find it possible to take up instruction at the point it has been left off. Thus, the progress of the child should be continuous since the material studied is appropriate to his or her level of performance.

Levels programs have been criticized for the amount of record keeping involved and an almost inevitable tendency to combine these types of plans with some form of achievement grouping.

Individualization Approaches

The term *individualization* may refer to practices as varied as the routine completion of hundreds of work sheets in serial order to programs involving independent research projects specifically designed for particular children. These activities have in common the assumption that learners should work on their own rather than as members of a class or instructional group.

Trends toward individualization have been stimulated by the development of commercial packets of materials and electronic equipment designed for individual use. These aids may be offered as either programs complete in themselves or as components of a larger instructional system. In some cases advocates of certain kinds of individualization have gone so far as to claim that they can "diagnose" the child and then "prescribe" what is needed for his or her academic development. Then, too, some programs utilize such terms as *individual guidance* and *personal needs* but actually base their operation on some form of achievement grouping.

Although individualization of instruction seems to be one of those ideas that precludes disagreement, the means of achieving such a goal are not always above criticism. The mechanistic approaches are considered by some educators to be unattractive to most children and the independent-learning systems are thought to often exclude pupils from important social-interaction experiences.

Staff Utilization

Most elementary school teachers work only with their own group of children in conventional classroom situations. Quite a large group of other teachers are included in administrative arrangements that cause them to interact with several other adults and a large number of pupils during the day. These different plans for utilizing a staff are often combined with one or another of the grouping or organizational schemes.

Departmentalization

Some elementary schools have adopted the secondary-level style of subject departmentalization. Occasionally such an arrangement may be used at the primary level, but ordinarily it is implemented in the upper grades, largely as a response to the growing complexity of the curriculum for older children. Many sixth-grade teachers contend that hardly any one person possesses the competence needed to teach the most advanced programs in all subject fields. They advocate that one teacher work with all the sixth graders in mathematics, another in science, and so on.

Departmentalization does offer teachers an opportunity to specialize, but it also introduces into the elementary school all the difficulties associated with secondary school teaching—a rigid schedule, lack of opportunity to get to know pupils, and the likelihood of an emphasis on the covering of material rather than on learning experiences suited to the children.

Differentiated Staffing

The term *staff differentiation* refers to organizational plans that involve hierarchical assignments for the adults working with pupils. Team teaching is placed in this category when fully qualified teachers only are involved.

The most extreme form of differentiated staffing is usually associated with open-space buildings in which one hundred or more children and several adults are often placed in what amounts to the same room. Under this arrangement, one teacher, called a "team leader," or "coordinator," assumes administrative responsibility for several adults, including regular classroom teachers, instructional and clerical aides, student teachers, and volunteers. In planning the educational program, all of these individuals may be consulted, along with any specialists who have been provided by the school district.

Differentiated staffing offers many possible benefits, but these must be weighed against the drawbacks inherent in any activity that requires several persons to work together closely and continually. It should also be emphasized that some people view teaching as a very personal matter, something special between one teacher and a group of pupils, and this relationship cannot be interfered with without destroying it.

The Pupil's Day

Any organizational plan adopted affects the daily activities of the pupils, of course. But there are a few types that relate principally to the scheduling of the child's time.

Discretionary Time

The allotment of unscheduled time for pupils as a regular feature of the instructional program has been implemented most frequently at the upper levels of the school system. But some elementary schools have also provided a period during which children may select from a variety of club and creative activities or a list of minicourses. In terms of strictly academic work, a free-time approach may be utilized in a building in which the library has expanded into a resource center, furnished with filmstrips and film loops, audio and video tapes, and independent-study materials of all kinds. Here, the students may receive assistance with investigations they have undertaken for personal reasons or in connection with classroom work.

Dual Arrangements

Some organizational plans combine heterogeneous grouping with a type of selection by ability or achievement. In the most widely adopted of these dual arrangements, for one-half of the day children of the same age but varying abilities work with one teacher in programs that emphasize language arts and social studies. For the other half of the day pupils are grouped by achievement level for the remaining subjects, each of which is taught by a different teacher.

CLASSROOM ORGANIZATION

The preceding sections have dealt with organizational plans and issues affecting entire schools. While such arrangements as the grouping of pupils affect the operation of classrooms, it is in the individual room and in the interaction of teacher and children that education takes place.

Standard Classroom Program

Although the modern classroom, with its bright lights, functional and attractive furnishings, and extensive equipment does not physically resemble its counterpart of one hundred years ago, the "modern" pattern of instructional activities usually does approximate rather closely the nineteenth-century approach to teaching. Even allowing for the modifications described in the preceding section, educative arrangements have remained largely unchanged; the roles of teachers and pupils have not altered, and the basic nature of the program persists in nineteenth-century form.

Teacher Centeredness

It has become axiomatic in education that the teacher is the really crucial element in the learning situation and that the quality of the program in any school depends on the qualities of the staff members. To a large extent, these generalizations refer to the teacher as a person—his or her friendliness, likableness, sense of humor, and sympathetic attitude toward pupils. The principle has even wider applicability to the instructional program offered the class, however, for in the conventional classroom very nearly all pupil activities come under the direct control of the teacher.

While persons other than those on the elementary school staff largely determine the school curriculum, the teacher ordinarily enjoys substantial latitude in selecting the procedures by which the program is implemented. The many differences often observed among the work of classes that cover the same material in a single school system or building demonstrates how much teachers may influence what takes place.

A visitor to a conventional classroom readily notes that nearly everything revolves around the teacher—the making of explanations, the asking of questions, the offering of demonstrations, the conduct of discussions, and so on. The teacher makes almost all the decisions and follows through on their implementation. Even under organizational arrangements that involve differentiated staffing, the adults retain all decision-making authority. They define the procedures, designate the activities, establish the schedule, and select the materials.

In playing such a central role the classroom teacher may be likened to an entertainer whose reputation depends on the audience's enjoyment of the performance. Thus, it is no mystery why people who are judged good at teaching tend to be outgoing individuals who have strong personalities and a flair for the dramatic.

Sequential Programming

As presented to children the conventional school program represents a body of experiences the content and sequence of which have been well established by tradition and authority. The assumptions underlying this general orientation have to do with conceptions of how knowledge ought to be organized and made available to learners.

Those in charge of the upper levels of the educational system have divided skills and information into subjects, areas of knowledge that supposedly possess a focus and internal consistency. Within each subject field, components have been arranged in hierarchies of complexity. Using these systems in school programs becomes a matter of devising activities that begin at the simplest levels for the youngest children and proceed through predetermined stages of academic learning as the children grow older.

The systematic programs are usually presented in series of textbooks. Additionally, sequential programming necessitates a set of procedures for monitoring the progress of pupils and reporting the findings to parents and other interested parties. Particular attention is given to such matters as the development of marking systems that attempt to indicate how well or rapidly work is completed, the finding of means for speeding up the progress of pupils with good aptitudes, and the establishment of special groups or classes for children who are not progressing adequately.

Innovations in this type of programming have centered on how the school work and the classes should be organized and what means might be used to record pupil growth. These kinds of alterations, however, raise no fundamental questions concerning the nature of educational arrangements. Too frequently, their proponents seem to seek to do a better job of instruction merely by employing machines or prescribing which of a set number of activities a child ought to undertake at a given point.

Pupil's Role

The operation of the conventional school classroom appears to demand that children adopt basically passive and receptive roles. Such assumptions are obvious when desks are provided at which children are to sit while receiving instruction or studying the books that have been provided.

Group instruction, the dominant mode of classroom procedure, requires that the child be able to "pay attention," "sit still," and "keep quiet." To pay attention means to attend to those experiences that are being directed by the teacher and to ignore distracting elements in the environment. The pupils' attention is directed to the salient points of a lesson, and they are expected to recall these because they will soon be set to work on their own at tasks requiring the application, practice, and testing of the information and skills presented. The extent to which the individual pupil can remember instructions and apply what has been presented will determine his or her success in school. Remaining still and quiet have traditionally been deemed necessary for individual concentration and so that the attention of others will not be diverted.

For the most part the pupil must learn meanings for the words and other symbols presented by the teacher or textbook. The child is then expected to manipulate these symbols in ways that conform to certain standards—guidelines emphasizing precision in following directions, neatness, and speed. These procedures are usually carried out in a general context that emphasizes competition with other children in the class.

In recent years a somewhat wider range of pupil behavior has been accepted in many classrooms. Some teachers have at least a portion of their program devoted to small-group and individual activities that permit children to intereact freely with one another. New approaches to the teaching of such subjects as science require much direct pupil involvement with laboratory equipment and similar materials. For the most part, however, it is still assumed by educators and private citizens alike that children attend school to sit quietly and follow directions in order to complete routine tasks.

Major Criticisms of the Conventional Classroom

As discussed previously, many proposals have been made for improving the schools by revising the ways in which children are grouped and their progress charted, the staff utilized, and the day organized. For the most part, however, these programs and projects have not led to fundamental alteration of educative practices—teachers and other adults remain the central figures; activities are not being related to the individual child; and the pupil continues to be a relatively passive reactor.

Insufficient Personalization

Even when a classroom program is organized so that teacher and pupils remain together for much of the day, it often happens that they do not get to know one another very well. When the dominant mode of operation is group instruction and the activities center around textbooks and duplicated work sheets, there is often little opportunity for the kind of interchange that furthers mutual understanding of a personal nature.

Under conventional arrangements the child is not met as a distinct human being with unique background, needs, and pattern of strengths and weaknesses. Rather, children are exposed to the same course of study, and each individual is judged against either a set standard or the performance of others who have different abilities. When only a limited range of talents receives recognition, a child stands little chance of being accepted as a unique and valued human being.

Attempts to individualize instruction generally have accomplished little more than the provision of means by which all pupils progress through identical or highly similar material at a somewhat different rate. Only the most sophisticated electronically based programs of the prepackaged and preplanned approaches can take into account pupil characteristics and performance and actually provide different experiences for different pupils. And working with a television screen has limited acceptance as a personalized experience.

Even though the traditional classroom revolves around the teacher, the situation often prevents him or her from behaving in ways that are personally most satisfying. Neither the regular program nor the currently available innovations permit the full force of the teacher's personality to come through.

Inadequacies of Traditional Instruction

The most fundamental problem with the systematic program is that the concepts and skills to be learned have ordinarily been selected and organized from an adult viewpoint, with little attention to the ways in which the child's mind functions. Another fault, which of course is not inherent in the material or its organization, is that usually only a narrow range of types of learning activities is presented or suggested in the programs utilized.

Traditional instruction that emphasizes the direct transferral of information from the teacher or textbooks to the child has been attacked from a number of quarters for many decades. This form of teaching persists in large part simply because it is traditional, most teachers having experienced no other approach as students. As a procedure it is readily understood, and the straightforward presentation of the material is rather easy to do. Recent developments in several curriculum areas have brought about a few reforms; some science and mathematics materials, for example, are now based on how a child's thought processes function and grow. But generally speaking, many of the innovative programs are packaged in such a way that their presentation does not require teachers to alter their style of working with a class. Other attempts to improve instruction involve the use of special audiovisual equipment in place of the teacher, with everything else remaining unchanged.

Several experimental curriculum projects in science and social studies have eliminated textbooks and encouraged teachers to have the pupils spend most of their time working with concrete materials and direct experiences. While these programs have been enthusiastically received in a few schools, most teachers find them too different to consider.

Lack of Pupil Involvement

The child in the traditional classroom engages in a limited variety of activities under direct supervision. Given such conditions, there will be little opportunity for the individual pupil to have much influence over what happens to him or her; all the important decisions have been made by others. The conventionally operated classroom is not conducive to providing those experiences through which members of a group form a sense of purpose by shared planning.

Pupils need to participate in genuine problem-solving activities and have continuing contact with the real materials of the world. A classroom limited to textbooks and the other conventional paraphernalia of education does not sufficiently engage the interest and attention of most children. After four or five years of the same kinds of activities, many youngsters lose interest and voice negative opinions about school.

Children need to be productively involved with one another on a regular basis in order to have an effective educational experience. Both their academic and personal lives become richer as a result of cooperative effort in the context of significant work. In the regular classroom, however, purposeful group activity has been rare, and children are generally discouraged from talking with one another. In recent years, there have been some innovative programs that stress such learning activities as discovery and problem solving, but most of them primarily advocate individual exercises to be performed according to a prescribed format.

Limited Effectiveness

The standard school offering, with its emphasis on verbal facility and physical quiescence, has been successfully pursued by only a proportion of the school-age population. Generally, the children who succeed in such an atmosphere come from a home background in which books and learning are important, there is much use of the same kind of language that is taught in school, and values such as deferment of gratification, control of impulses, orderliness, time consciousness, and competition are taught. Most children from this type of home readily adapt to the regimen of the conventional classroom. And they possess the general knowledge, experiences, and behaviors on which the school program has been predicated.

Large numbers of children, of course, are not from backgrounds of the type described. They may get along well in their own cultural group and then find that the school demands different behavior—a child helps a friend and is called a "cheater"; a lack of concern with time is termed "laziness"; the label of "disrupter" is pinned on anyone who talks to a neighbor. And perhaps most importantly, the traditional program demands careful use of a language that may be quite different from that found in the home.

A great deal of money and effort has been expended in special efforts to assist all children to succeed in school. In general, however, the approaches adopted have represented only minor modifications of the conventional classroom. Class size is reduced, but the activities are still teacher-centered. Additional adults are brought in and used to maintain more rigid control over the pupils. "Poor" textbooks are replaced by "good" ones. All of the basic assumptions about education are retained, and some are even emphasized.

The Open Informal Classroom

While the classroom organization familiar to most readers may have been modified in a number of ways in some elementary schools, it is only in recent years that there has come into existence a type of classroom regarded by many as fundamentally different from the one that fits the conventional description. This "open," or "open informal," style of operation appears to have achieved enough acceptance among teachers to warrant considering it as a genuine alternative to the traditional way of teaching.

The threads of open education are found throughout the history of schools, but widespread interest has only occurred as a result of the efforts undertaken in Britain over the last few decades. The example provided by the informal British primary schools has been followed by numerous teachers and a few school systems in various parts of the world.

There has been a good deal of variation in what has been said and written about this new movement. Naturally, then, teachers do not all follow the same pattern, but there are several factors that do characterize all open classroom approaches, as distinguished from conventional means of organizing elementary education.

Provision for Choices

The most significant differences between open, or informal, approaches and standard forms of schooling have to do with the matter of choice on the part of pupils. In the traditional school nearly all decisions have been made by the teacher or the teacher's superiors, while in informally organized classes children have a substantial degree of control over learning activities and the conditions governing their work.

In the open classroom pupils do not have absolute freedom, of course, for the teacher represents society's interest in seeing that the basic skills are learned, knowledge gained, and positive attitudes developed. But the informal-classroom teacher recognizes that children learn in many ways and that learning may proceed better if the pupils have some control over their time schedules and the physical space and facilities of the room.

When children have the opportunity to choose among alternatives and receive guidance in making the choices most appropriate to their developmental levels, they grow in that ability. In the open classroom, pupils are typically given some control over the disposition of time, with occasional interventions by the teacher. The child's daily or weekly schedule may include regular commitments, with other segments planned cooperatively by pupil and teacher. For a significant portion of the hours spent in school, however, the pupil has the responsibility of deciding how to use the available time to meet the teacher's expectations and his or her goals.

The child in the open situation also exercises some choice in the use of learning materials, since the classroom structure ordinarily provides alternative ways of meeting instructional objectives. For example, all pupils are expected to learn the multiplication facts, and in the open classroom there will be, perhaps, six or seven general approaches available. The teacher is there to assure that the tables are learned and may suggest the two or three modes that seem particularly appropriate for a given child, but the pupil is also involved in the choice.

Use of the learning environment is to some degree under the control of the individual child. Depending on the room arrangement and the ancillary space available, the pupil may choose where he or she desires to work. And because of the emphasis on cooperative effort among children, a pupil has some latitude for choosing the classmates with whom he or she prefers to associate for a given activity.

Classroom Arrangements

Although informal programs have been developed in open-space buildings, most of the better examples are to be found in self-contained classrooms occupied by one teacher and one class of pupils. Here, the physical arrangement and general appearance will differ significantly from typical schoolrooms. Most often, separate areas corresponding to the usual subject fields will have been created and supplied with the materials of instruction related to those subjects.

The open classroom is often furnished differently from the conventional room, with pupils' desks replaced by a variety of types of seating, from tables and chairs to stools, sofas, and pillows. Bookshelves, screens, pegboards, and display racks separate one section of floor space from other areas. One or two areas, especially library or reading corners, are usually covered with carpeting or rugs.

Each learning space is supplied with a variety of materials, supplies, and equipment. The mathematics corner, for example, provides firsthand materials such as stones and nuts and bolts for counting and weighing and commercial blocks and geometric-form boards for concept development. The collection may also include various measuring devices, puzzles, games, books for practice and enrichment, and work cards that provide practice on skills and facts in the basic processes. Other areas of the room are similarly equipped for science, reading, creative writing, social studies, arts and crafts, and other fields. Some teachers also stress particular activities such as raising plants and animals, cooking, pottery, carpentry, and needlework. The room will likely also contain the usual complement of instructional equipment, from chalkboards to electronic gadgetry, all of which is available for direct use by the pupils.

Daily Program

In the open classroom the school day is much less rigidly scheduled than under conventional arrangements. Some teachers have gone so far as to have no demarcations of the day at all; pupils simply work on individual and group projects and confer with the teacher. Most open-classroom pupils continue to meet with specialist teachers for physical education, music, and art, but in a few instances these fields have been integrated into the total program. There are also schools in which music and art are offered on an open basis, with these instructors and their specialized facilities available to children at various times during the day.

The open-classroom school day characteristically begins with a group planning session, during which routines are dealt with and agreements are reached concerning the use of facilities. At this time the teacher makes requests of the class and arranges meetings with individual children. The day sometimes concludes with another group meeting devoted to evaluation and a review of the activities that have taken place.

The teacher usually attempts to develop a classroom program that provides a balance among total-group sessions, small-group work, and individual activity. The class meets as a total group, for example, to plan, interview guests, and provide an audience for a classmate who has written a story. Pupils group together in threes and fours to work with a teacher on a skill, prepare a presentation for the class, and share interesting activities. Individuals work on the full range of educational experiences, from writing poetry to drilling on number facts.

In planning a program the open-classroom teacher usually intends to provide for total-class study topics, learning centers involving varied experiences, and developmental sequences for the basic skills. The general topics or units taken up by the class may come from either the curriculum set by the school district or interests that occur in the classroom. Whatever the source, such a topic as "trees" furnishes opportunities for work in all curricular fields—from mathematics to literature to interpretative dancing. This type of approach provides children with many creative opportunities, gives them a realistic setting for using their developing skills, and guards against an exclusive emphasis on separate subjects by emphasizing the unity of knowledge.

Along with the work on the overall class topics, pupils in an open classroom find opportunities to utilize the learning centers in the room. Individual and small-group interests may range from model-boat building and care of baby hamsters to flower transplanting, cake baking, and weaving. The classroom program must also be organized to insure that substantial attention will be given to systematic development of basic skills. Application and growth will come out of topic study and other experiences to some extent. But it is also necessary for the teacher, whether through the material placed in learning centers or by means of instructional groups, to provide structured activities that are designed to develop specific understandings and skills.

Pupil's Role

Children in the informal classroom exercise a greater degree of control over their lives than do pupils in the conventional school situation. Because they are required to plan many of their activities, the children have opportunities for developing abilities related to decision making, self-discipline, and acceptance of responsibility.

A significant number of children's learning experiences in the open classroom centers on aspects of topics or other experiences of particular concern to the individual pupil. This situation, if properly capitalized on by the teacher, provides children with exceptionally rich learnings in the communications skills as they discuss what concerns them, read and gather information, and formulate their own ideas for written and oral presentation.

Pupils in the open classroom have substantial freedom to move about and talk with the teacher and their classmates. Under such regulations, the standards of conduct differ significantly from those existing in the conventional situation. Also, the conditions that give rise to misbehavior in the traditional classroom are relieved to some extent in the less-formal setting in which children use up energy in natural ways, moving about and working with tools and other manipulative devices.

Teacher's Role

The open-classroom teacher works in a variety of ways to insure an effective learning environment. Much attention must be given to the organization of the room, the provision of learning materials, and the structuring of experiences. In many cases the teacher has personally developed much of the learning material, since specific activities not available in commercial programs will have developed from the projects undertaken by the class. In dealing with children mostly as individuals and as members of small groups, the teacher has an excellent opportunity to become well acquainted with pupils from both personal and professional viewpoints. Such knowledge can then be used to make the school program more responsive and relevant to each child.

Although the record-keeping task appears formidable, the teacher who has been deeply involved with getting to know the pupils and in developing meaningful experiences for them has a good basis for devising an effective system. Some records, in the form of plan books or journals, are kept by the pupils. Check-off sheets and similar devices may be an integral part of the organization of the learning centers in the room. And the teacher will often engage in diagnostic teaching in the skill areas, an approach that requires record keeping as an integral part of the instructional sequence.

Teachers who have taught in traditional ways and then reorganized their rooms report that they enjoy teaching much more after having made the change.

Not only do they derive satisfaction from becoming well acquainted with the children, but also they stress that the teacher is much more of a person in the open classroom, participating fully in many of the activities and finding additional outlets for expression of his or her own individuality.

Conventional and Open Classrooms

The open-classroom approach appears to meet the objections raised against the traditional form of organization. Children have a greater likelihood of being treated as individuals. They receive personal attention from the teacher, and they make significant decisions that affect their own education. In the open classroom sequential programming is an aspect of the overall educational effort rather than the dominant feature, as is the case in most conventional situations. The range of potential learning activities is much wider in the open environment than in the traditional program, which could result in a greater proportion of children making adequate academic progress.

The authors of the chapters that follow are not in total agreement as to the extent to which they recommend the adoption of the open informal type of classroom organization. But they do stress such principles as the need to consider the individual child when making educational decisions. In examining the chapters on such diverse topics as science, dramatics, and health education, the reader will note the emphasis on attention to the individual and on the need for flexibility in teaching-learning situations. While an author may not formally mention the open classroom, the reader should appreciate that much of what is advocated in terms of procedures and content can be best accomplished within the framework of such an environment.

EXERCISES FOR THOUGHT AND ACTION

1. Visit an elementary school, find out about its operation, and draw an organizational chart that shows the relationships among the positions held by adults.

2. List the advantages and disadvantages of subject-matter departmentalized teaching at the elementary school level.

3. Visit a classroom that you consider traditionally organized andpick out an individual child for observation. To what extent does the pupil fit the requirements to "stay seated and quiet" and to "pay attention"?

4. Interview an elementary school teacher. Find out something about the range of intellectual abilities and academic aptitudes of the children in this teacher's classroom and the means he or she uses for coping with the differences.

5. Locate a recent magazine or book devoted to school architecture. Note any attempts to relate the building structures to the educational program.

SELECTED READINGS

Anderson, Robert H. "Organizing and Staffing the School." In *The Elementary School in the United States*. Seventy-second Yearbook of the National Society for the Study of Education, part 2, edited by John I. Goodlad and Harold G. Shane, pp. 221-42. Chicago: University of Chicago Press, 1973. The author briefly but comprehensively touches on most of the varieties of organization of interest to educators. He makes a balanced presentation and provides a helpful context.

Leeper, Sarah Hammond, et al. *Good Schools for Young Children*. New York: Macmillan Co., 1974. This volume focuses mainly on the nursery school years, but the basic point of view has application to the development of programs through the primary grades.

Sergiovanni, Thomas J., and Elliott, David L. *Educational and Organizational Leadership in Elementary Schools*. Englewood Cliffs, N.J.: Prentice-Hall, 1975. The authors discuss the general question of the nature of instructional leadership in elementary schools. Many types of innovative programs and projects are described.

Silberman, Charles E., ed. *The Open Classroom Reader*. New York: Vintage, 1973. The editor has collected many resources pertinent to the open classroom movement. The selections deal with both British and North American schools and cover theoretical as well as practical topics.

Toffler, Alvin. *Future Shock*. New York: Random House, 1970. This is a general treatment of major changes likely to occur in our culture. The author gives specific attention to the disparity between the assumptions underlying the present school program and conditions that seem to be challenging those beliefs.

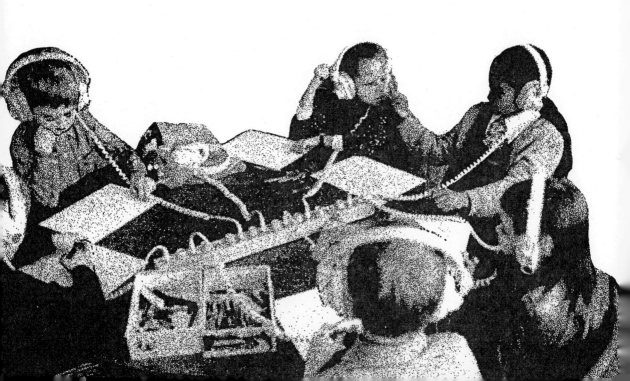

This chapter, like the preceding three, continues to stress the importance of the individual child. Particular attention is given to the child's growth in the use of language and to the role of communication in his or her development. Since communication is a part of every area of the curriculum, emphasis is on the significance of attention being given at each level of schooling to teaching the skills essential to effective communication.

Much of the content of this chapter is about listening and speaking because the child comes to school with some ability in both of these areas and because of their importance in the classroom. Other aspects of the language arts—reading and writing—are discussed in later chapters.

Consideration of listening and speaking in this chapter does not mean that they are ignored in other chapters. To the contrary: The following three chapters also give attention to these areas, and because of the importance of language, every chapter is concerned with communication in the classroom.

W.T.P.

The Curriculum Focus
Communication in the Classroom

Walter T. Petty

4

Teaching and learning in the elementary school is a process of communication. Some of the communication is accomplished through seeing—watching a demonstration, observing on a field trip, or noting a facial expression. However, most communication makes use of language. The role of language in communication is shown as a child reads a story or finds information in a textbook, listens to the teacher's directions, views and listens to a film, talks to other children and responds to them, and writes about ideas. Communication is the focus of all these activities, as it is when the teacher speaks, listens, reads, and writes—to the children, and about and for them in planning, instructing, evaluating, and reporting. Communication is the lifeblood of the school curriculum.

Teachers are the major facilitators of the communication. They give instruction in the skills that permit communication and plan for and guide curricula which focus on communication. Other communicators in the classroom are those who have written the books, produced the films, and developed the materials. Furthermore, those theorists and researchers whose ideas and collected information are in the materials as well as in the minds of both teacher and pupils are significant communicators. Most importantly, in classrooms with the most effective programs, the children themselves are truly notable communicators.

COMMUNICATION AND THE LANGUAGE ARTS

Long before children enter school they discover that language is a powerful resource, an absolute necessity in many situations, and something over which they have a great deal of control. The importance of language and of children's development in the use of it was discussed in Chapter 2. As pointed out in that chapter, using language is an important activity to preschool children. While they may communicate in nonverbal ways, they generally use speaking and listening to make their wants known and as the basis for their responses to others.

The very extent and diversity of knowledge, which inevitably are reflected in the planned and the unplanned activities in the classroom, generate a wide use of and diversity in language. To develop children's abilities in using language with maximum proficiency, much of the school program should be, and ordinarily is, designed to teach and to further develop language skills, to foster attitudes important to the most effective use of these skills, and to build appreciation of the role of language in increasing an individual's resources as a human being.

The Place of the Language Arts

Because language is needed to exchange information, to share ideas, and to record knowledge, it is basic to all living and learning. Thus, the program in developing skill in the use of language is the foundation of the school curriculum. This has been true since colonial days—and precolonial days—when schools were established for the purpose of teaching reading and writing. This curriculum emphasis has continued with the subsequent increases in school populations and the extension of the program to include the teaching of speaking and listening. It continues regardless of technological changes, the expansion of knowledge, and the increasingly pluralistic nature of society.

Communication is crucial to everyone's social, economic, and political well-being. Yet the personal and vocational environments each person lives in are becoming more and more specialized, with the result that unique language and ways of communicating develop, which, in turn, lead to class and status barriers that limit the communicative give-and-take essential to human relationships. Developing the full capabilities of all children for communication is recognized in effective elementary school curriculums as necessary for lowering these barriers by maximizing cooperation among people and by developing their respect for the rights and privileges of every human being.

In the language arts, as in all curriculum areas, there must be diversity in the curriculum to do the most for each child. Yet the language arts activities in classrooms may often have a common focus because of the similarity of children's needs. An effective language arts curriculum provides for both the differences and similarities among children.

Defining the Language Arts

The language arts includes the *receptive* language activities of listening and reading and the *expressive* language activities of speaking and writing. Sometimes reference is made to "thinking" as a language art, but there seems to be a degree of artificiality to this classification, since all expression and reception requires thinking. Another common element in each of the language arts is language itself; thus, to a great extent the language arts may be considered a unified field and perhaps as a curriculum area should simply be called "language." However, most curriculum guides, textbooks, courses of study, and program schedules separate the activities that involve language. For example, literature, which is an aspect of reading, is often considered a subject in itself. Writing is often viewed as a separate subject, with even spelling and handwriting taught apart from it.

Some schools favor the use of the term *English* for this curriculum area, largely because of a belief that this designation properly narrows the content of the instruction to writing, grammar, and literature and prevents what is construed as a fragmentation and weakening of the area as a discipline through the use of the broader term. In programs that use the label *English,* reading is treated as a separate subject and there often is little or no attention given to listening.

Sometimes only the term *language* is used, but often, regardless of the unifying nature of the term, reading as well as spelling and handwriting are taught separately. However, increasingly there are designations given to this curriculum area that seek to suggest the common elements and unity—*Communication Arts* and *English Language Arts,* for example.

What a curriculum area is called is important because there is evidence that the name tends to determine what is included in it. The terms used often become the basis for planning, determining objectives, selecting materials, and choosing many instructional procedures and learning activities. Thus, using the term *language arts* to describe this curriculum area, and defining it as including speaking, listening, writing, and reading, is important to establishing a program that develops abilities and attitudes necessary for effective communication.

Interrelationships Among the Language Arts

Even a superficial consideration of elementary school programs leads to the conclusion that any subject matter area is difficult if not impossible to separate from most others. Of course, some curriculum areas of the typical elementary school program, and even some aspects of the language arts, may be separated from others for purposes of particular instructional emphasis. However, the language arts surely must be taught all day long, since rarely does any single language skill or ability function independently of many others.

While there has been considerable research concerned with the interrelationships among the language arts, the obviousness of many of the relationships requires no investigation. For example, speaking (expression) and listening (reception) are opposing processes of a single communicative act. The speaker is affected by the listeners and must consider their abilities and the circumstances of their listening. Likewise, a listener's reception is highly dependent on the speaker's tone, organization of ideas, and manner of expression. One person transmits a message and the other receives it, but both the transmittal and the reception are affected by the interaction of the two processes. Although this kind of relationship is apparent, it is sometimes given too little attention in the curriculum. The other expressive-receptive processes, writing and reading, are also often separated so that children may not really realize that what they read was written by someone writing in the same way they write.

The interrelationships are further shown by the fact that an individual's first contact with language is through listening and that it is from the listening that the person learns the words, the speech patterns, the dialect that he or she later speaks. A child's speech greatly affects his or her reading and writing, since achievement in either area is especially related to the words the child knows and uses in speaking.

Writing is particularly related to the ability to use language orally, with the effectiveness of both speaking and writing dependent on compositional skill—the putting together of ideas and information in a coherent and appealing manner. The compositional elements are also important in receiving information by reading or listening. Likewise, those skills that are especially a part of writing—spelling, punctuation, and capitalization—are of major importance to gaining meaning by reading.

Reading and listening both require the perception and identification of words, the securing of meaning from clues present in the context, and the organization of the message heard or read.

As discussed here and in Chapter 2, the child does not use language skills in a compartmentalized manner. Thus, it is imperative that the interrelatedness and essential unity of the language arts be acknowledged and often stressed in curriculum activities.

The Language Arts and Other Curriculum Areas

Since there is no communication without content, much of the language arts program must focus on expressing and receiving ideas and knowledge related to social studies, science, music, health, mathematics, and other subject areas. Most of the chapters in this book show how language arts activities are related to the subject matter areas.

It is unrealistic, however, to expect all of the important attitudes, skills, and abilities necessary for optimum effectiveness in speaking, listening, writing, and reading to be learned in association with other subjects, for which the emphasis is rightly placed on the content of those subjects. For example, while the difficulties encountered by pioneers moving westward may be the focus of a discussion, attention to teaching listening and speaking skills during the discussion may prevent the children from gaining sufficient knowledge of the topic. Too, there are many occasions for communication that have no direct relationship to specific subject areas. For example, an occurrence on the playground may cause so much enthusiasm that the ensuing discussion is a more genuine occasion for teaching such discussion skills as "sticking to the point," organizing thoughts, and speaking clearly and calmly. Furthermore, there needs to be planned specific instruction in some language skills in order to avoid their never being taught. As suggested later in this chapter, planning the language arts program to use genuine communicative situations capitalizes on the content in subject areas when it is advantageous to do so.

Determining What Should Be Taught

The premises and principles operating in a program are of utmost concern if the instructional effort of a teacher is to accomplish anything worthwhile. In the language arts, as in all curriculum areas, the content of curriculum guides and textbooks, the findings of research, and the policies and standards of the school all provide bases for determining what should be taught. However, these are all guides; fundamentally, the curriculum is decided by the teacher. Programs in which teachers adequately recognize this role are guided by principles:

1. The curriculum should be based on the communication needs of the children in the classroom. Factors that must be considered include children's backgrounds and levels of development, the knowledge and skills they do and do not have and will need to have mastered before progressing further in school, and the ongoing activities that develop from day to day in the classroom.

2. The instructional emphasis should be on how skills and knowledge are used rather than on rules, definitions, and abstractions. The curriculum needs to reflect the conditions and the situations fundamental to communication rather than ones that are hypothetical and artificial.

Supplementing these principles are the following questions, the answers to which provide guidance in deciding what skills, information, and attitudes to teach:

1. How frequently is this skill or information needed and used in the lives of children and adults? For example, colons are used much less frequently than commas and telling a story is done more often than choral speaking.
2. How crucial is this skill, ability, or attitude when the need for it arises? Many people, for instance, do not write business letters frequently, but when the need arises, it is usually important that the letter be written well.
3. How universal is the need for this skill or ability? That is, while giving a book report may be an important school activity, writing letters is almost universally done.
4. Does this skill, ability, or attitude give evidence of meeting a permanent need? For example, some of the first words a child learns to spell are the same words adults use most frequently in their writing.
5. Is the child ready to learn this skill, ability, or attitude? In other words, does the child need to use the skill at this point in his or her development? Does the child have the background for learning it? Is he or she motivated to learn it?

LANGUAGE AND THE COMMUNICATION SKILLS

While the fundamental role of language in listening, reading, speaking, and writing may be understood by practically everyone, just what this role means in terms of learning and instruction is not so clear and is often misunderstood. There has been a long-established effort to determine the place of studying about language in the teaching of its use for more effective communication. The extent of this effort is probably most readily noted by examining the amount of research that has been done on this issue. For example, one report cites more than one hundred studies concerned with determining the effects of studying about language on the quality of pupils' writing.[1] The intent of most of these studies was to find out if the study of grammar affected writing efforts, the assumption being that pupils must be able to verbalize about how language operates in order to use it with skill. As this report states, the findings of the many studies are very heavily weighted in the direction of little or no positive effects on writing from the kinds of language study engaged in by the pupils in the studies.

A major factor related to the findings of these studies is the fact that children know much about their language before entering school. They can put words together into sentences, which is sure evidence of the knowledge they have. The value of raising this knowledge to the conscious level is the real issue, with the major concern being the amount of variability shown in the language used by the children in most classrooms and what to do about it. The question of studying about language is discussed further in the following sections, along with a consideration of factors influencing language development.

Factors that Influence Language Development

Although it appears that children have an inborn faculty for learning a language, the actual learning is not natural or instinctive. The factors that affect language learning are important to the elementary school curriculum, since the school's function is helping children learn. These elements include characteristics of both the child and his or her environment. The child's physical and mental conditions and capabilities, the environment in which he or she has lived and is living, and the kinds of stimulation he or she receives for using language all bear on the development of the child's language ability. Any handicap to sight or hearing or to the ability to perform neuromuscular acts necessary to producing speech sounds is likely to interfere with a child's language development.

The fact that measures of intelligence correlate highly with those of language ability should be an important consideration in the curriculum. While much of the development of both intelligence and language ability takes place in the preschool years, the existence of the relationship needs to be respected in the school environment.

The environment that a child lives in plays the most important part in determining his or her language development. For instance, an only child, through close association with adults, usually develops a larger vocabulary and greater facility in expression than a child who has brothers and sisters. Similarly, the child whose parents talk with him or her a great deal develops language facility earlier

---

1. J. Stephen Sherwin, *Four Problems in Teaching English: A Critique of Research* (Scranton, Pa.: International Textbook Co., 1969), chap. 3.

than the child who lives in an environment in which there is little language exchange with adults. The child who plays alone or only with other children at home has a limited number of opportunities to gain new ideas and concepts. Television does not contribute to a child's language development as much as is often thought since the element of exchange is missing. Of course, seeing pictures of things and hearing words in association with them undoubtedly provides stimuli for the child who lives in a limiting environment.

An Environment for Language Growth

Children's use of language after entering school continues to be influenced by the experiences they had prior to school entrance. Their home and neighborhood environments continue to add to these experiences. However, the environment of the school does begin to have an influence on language development. The daily learning climate, the activities of the classroom, the content of the curriculum, and the attitudes of teachers and other school personnel become major factors in each child's language growth.

The attitudes of the teacher toward children and toward how communication effectiveness is learned are recognized as being of utmost importance in quality language arts programs. Evidence of possession of these desirable attitudes is shown by a teacher who:

1. Shows each child that he or she is an accepted and important member of the classroom group.
2. Encourages attitudes of friendliness and mutual respect among the children, including respect for differences as well as likenesses.
3. Talks with and listens to children individually and in groups, encouraging them to exchange ideas and experiences.
4. Receives ideas and information expressed by the children as evidence of their interests and capitalizes on the information in planning.
5. Shows appreciation of each child's efforts toward expression.
6. Shows enthusiasm—and allows children to do so—about the activities of the classroom.
7. Shows sensitivity to and awareness of the world, encouraging children to notice the way things look, sound, smell, feel, work, grow, and so forth.
8. Allows children to see that they enjoy language in the stories read and written, in discovering word origins, and in the images that words and phrases create.

The physical conditions of the classroom are also important to environment. Little stimulation of language growth comes from drabness. Wall and bulletin board decorations, displays, pictures, things to handle and talk about are all important. And of course, there must be language—signs, captions, records, tapes, tables and shelves of books, writing areas, conversation corners, and so on.

Finally, and most importantly, a classroom in which language growth takes place is one that exhibits evidence of the children themselves having taken part in planning, preparing, and arranging the environment and showing freedom and confidence as they move about in it.

Dialects and Standard English

The suggestions in the preceding section emphasize attitudes that show acceptance of the child, thus implying the importance of accepting the language the child uses. In general, this attitude is a departure from the historical one that has been ingrained in teachers by tradition and language purists to teach children "correct" English. The change in emphasis has come about largely from an increasingly widespread recognition that it is not only the people in the South or Brooklyn or Boston—or even blacks or immigrants from Europe—who speak dialects. The effect of this recognition is the realization that everyone speaks a dialect (some are able to speak more than one), that a dialect cannot be equated with either "correct" or "incorrect" language, and that all persons vary the language they use in ways appropriate to the situations in which they communicate.

The major difficulty in teaching children greater variability in their use of the language is that appropriate instructional procedures are not as well defined by either research or practice as is needed. On the other hand, many processes that are frequently used—learning definitions of parts of speech, completing usage exercises of the "choosing the correct word" variety, reading about usage in a textbook or being told by a teacher, and studying about how language works (grammar)—are known to be largely fruitless. Apparently though, there is a persistent hope that these practices will succeed, since many teachers and textbook writers continue to uphold their use.

What is overlooked by these advocates is the mound of evidence accumulated during the past sixty or so years indicating that such practices do not accomplish what is sought. They also fail to recognize that language habits are really that—habits—and that habits are not easily changed. Certainly they are never changed unless they are dealt with directly. And learning rules and doing exercises removed from actual communication is not dealing with the habits directly. For children to learn to speak and write in acceptable ways, they must practice speaking and writing in situations and on occasions that demand acceptable English and yet are important to them. This means that every possible procedure must be utilized for relating the activities of the classroom to the basic goals of each child. Children must feel that a specific usage item being taught is actually in widespread use in the situations and for the occasions advocated and that learning it will benefit them personally. They must be shown that their communication in such situations is more effective. For a teacher to do this generally means that many notions of acceptability and correctness will have to be looked at more realistically than they have been in the past.

Grammar Teaching: The Dilemma

As has been suggested earlier in this chapter, the value from teaching grammar is seriously open to question. Yet the content of many textbooks continues to include grammar rules, definitions, and exercises, emphasizing the role grammar has traditionally had in schools. The persistence of this tradition causes a curriculum problem that is not easily solved. The difficulty is further compounded by misunderstandings about the place of linguistics (discussed in the following section) in the program and the susceptibility of many teachers and curriculum authorities to accept new "solutions" to complex problems.

It is true that there are some persons—particularly some linguists—who believe that the study of language is valuable in and of itself; that is, although they do not hold that such study improves written composition or changes language usage, they do believe that the basis for its inclusion in a language arts curriculum is comparable to that for including history in the school program, since both areas are concerned with humanity. While the validity of this point of view may be accepted, at issue is what about language should be studied, and when. Opinions differ on this matter, but most often considerable study of grammar is thought to be necessary. Thus, the acceptance of this point of view means that a large portion of the program may be devoted to such study, with the amount of time given to the meaningful use of the communication skills being considerably reduced.

Anyone who observes children in classrooms for very long discovers that few children generate much enthusiasm for the activities of a program that is centered around a textbook which insists it is wrong to say "Don't go in the house" or that it is normal and proper to say "The team is we." No greater enthusiasm will be shown for exercises calling for identifying nouns, verbs, and adjectives; for underlining complete predicates; or for learning definitions for phoneme, high vowels, and noun phrases.

Programs that effectively combat tradition and pressure may teach some grammatical terminology, but in the context of children's speaking and writing. Their main focus is on communication. They do not allocate particular grammar items to specific grade levels. Instead they teach anything about grammar—and language in general—in natural communicative situations.

Linguistics and the Language Arts

As suggested previously, problems related to grammar teaching have been affected in recent years by the rising influence of linguistics—the scientific study of language. While linguistics as a field of study has a history of more than one hundred years, the attempt to relate it to school programs is a recent and continuing development.

Linguistics is defined in one curriculum guide as "the study of human speech; the units, nature, structure, and modifications of language, languages, or a language, including especially such factors as phonetics, phonology, morphology, accent, syntax, semantics, general or philosophical grammar, and the relation between writing and speech."[2] The condensed definition of "the scientific study of language" is expanded by one author who says: "Such study may concentrate on the sounds of language (phonology), the origin and changing meaning of words (etymology and semantics), or the arrangements of words in a meaningful context in different languages (syntax-structural or transformational grammar)."[3] More recently linguistics has been defined as including the study of language behavior and learning (psycholinguistics), society and language

---

2. Nebraska Curriculum Development Center, *A Curriculum for English: Language Explorations for the Elementary Grades* (Lincoln: University of Nebraska Press, 1966), p. 2.
3. Pose Lamb, *Linguistics in Proper Perspective* (Columbus, Ohio: Charles E. Merrill Publishing Co., 1967), p. 4.

(sociolinguistics), and the more inclusive relationships between language behavior and other modes of human behavior (metalinguistics).

Considering the broadness of these definitions, it is difficult to determine what aspects of the study of language might be appropriate for the elementary school. Certainly to say that linguistics should be a part of the language arts curriculum—as some educators and linguists have said—is an oversimplification. Likewise, the increasing use of such terms as *new English* and *linguistic method* are not particularly helpful. In fact, the propriety of their use has been questioned by an eminent linguist.[4] However, both terms—as well as simply *linguistics*—have affected the content of language arts curriculums, as indicated by the first definition of linguistics cited in the curriculum guide mentioned earlier. As that definition suggests, there has been an injection of new terminology and, generally, of a greater amount of study of language structure into those language arts curriculums that are based on the curriculum guide from which the definition was taken or on similar guides or textbooks.

At issue is whether the language study suggested is different from traditional grammar study in both content and purpose. As has been stated, no study of language structure has been shown to result in desired changes in pupils' speaking and writing habits. Of course, language study does not have to be only about structure, nor does it require the learning of technical terms. Such matters as the origins of words, changes in word meanings, the uniqueness of many words and phrases, patterns in orthography, dialect differences, restructuring and combining sentences, inflections in speech, and so on may all be properly considered as areas of language study. Pupils may learn about these various areas within the framework of the kind of communication that is necessary for keeping children involved and motivated.

THE ROLE OF LISTENING

Listening is a comparatively recent concern of elementary school teachers, and even now this teaching receives much less attention than it deserves. Language textbooks have included listening activities only since the early 1950s, and reading textbooks generally included nothing about listening until even later. Furthermore, a survey taken only a few years ago showed that less than one percent of the content of textbooks is devoted to listening lessons.[5]

While listening has always been regarded as important, it was not until the results of a pioneer study became known that it began to be taught. This study showed that pupils spend thirty percent of their language activities each day in speaking, nine percent in writing, sixteen percent in reading, and forty-five per-

---

4. Albert H. Markwardt, "A Glance at the Past: A Look Toward the Future," in *Linguistics in School Programs*, Sixty-ninth Yearbook of the National Society for the Study of Education, part 2, ed. A.H. Markwardt (Chicago: University of Chicago Press, 1970), p. 325.

5. Kenneth L. Brown, "Speech and Listening in Language Arts Textbooks," *Elementary English* 44 (April 1967): part 1, 336; (May 1967): part 2, 461–65.

cent in listening.[6] These findings led to other research, including that of showing the need for listening to be taught and, for best results, to be taught through relating it to the other language arts.[7]

The Nature of Listening

Listening is more than just hearing or paying attention. It is more than being quiet in a situation in which there is speech, music, or other sounds. The listener must be a participant for communication to occur. Listening requires active and conscious attention to sounds in order to gain meaning from them. The sounds may be those of a speaker, a fine orchestra, neighborhood children at play, or the traffic on an expressway. In all instances, if listening is taking place, there is reaction to what is heard.

The listening process may be thought of in terms of a series of steps: (1) hearing, (2) understanding, (3) evaluating, and (4) responding. That is, listeners first perceive a sound or pattern of sounds; next, they recognize or otherwise attach meaning to them; they then appraise the meaning in terms of their individual experience backgrounds; finally, they react to this understanding—audibly or by movement, further thought, facial expression, and so on. Thus, the process is a complex one that requires the listener to move through all of the steps for genuine communication to occur.

Some writers define listening as only a two-step process: the receiving of sound and the interpreting of sound.[8] This definition of course includes both gaining meaning as well as responding to it in the second step. The important curriculum consideration, regardless of the number of steps thought to be in the process, is full awareness that listening goes beyond hearing and that the mental activity necessary for communication to take place requires skill, effort, and thoughtful attention.

The importance of hearing to the process should not be minimized, however. To determine whether a hearing problem exists, such factors as auditory acuity, binaural hearing, auditory perception and discrimination, and the masking of communication by other sounds should be checked. Any problems in these areas or actual hearing losses may require medical and other specialized attention as well as adjustments within the classroom. On the other hand, it is important that inattention, boredom, indifference, and poor concentration not be confused with hearing losses to excuse poor listening. Even with less than total hearing loss, an individual can listen.

Listening effectiveness may be affected by lack of attention and concentration, by the means or ways an individual has for identifying and attaching meaning to sounds, and by the rate at which sounds flow. In addition, listening is influenced most importantly by the experience and background of the listener

---

6. Paul T. Rankin, "The Importance of Listening Ability," *English Journal,* college ed. 17 (October 1928): 623–30.

7. *Ends and Issues: 1965-1966; Points of Decision in the Development of the English Curriculum* (Urbana, Ill.: The National Council of Teachers of English, 1966), pp. 29–30.

8. Ralph G. Nichols and Thomas R. Lewis, *Speaking and Listening,* (Dubuque, Iowa: William C. Brown Co., 1965), p. 6.

and by his or her capacity to use language. Attention and concentration are affected by the tone, style, and manner of the speaker, the content of the message and its organization, and the listening environment—temperature, the presence or absence of distractions, acoustics, and so forth. Attention is not necessarily shown by quietness; in fact, in the program advocated in this book, the activity of the children precludes an atmosphere in which there always will be quiet as they need to listen. Certainly, too, concentration is not always reflected in facial expression or absence of any physical activity. On the other hand, distractions of noise and movement as well as the speakers themselves do affect attention and the concentration required for effective listening.

Types of Listening

Everyone listens in different ways at various times and in various situations. These ways or types of listening suggest that instruction not only take into account the nature of listening and the specific skills necessary for communication to take place in particular situations but also the types of listening that are commonly done. There have been various classifications of these types: appreciational, informational, and critical; or attentive, purposeful, critical, and responsive. The Commission on the English Curriculum has defined the types of listening as passive, or marginal; appreciative; attentive; and analytical.[9]

Another type of classification is that which identifies various levels of listening; that is, for the various types of listening a person does, he or she may be considered as performing at the following levels:

1. Hearing sounds or words but not reacting beyond bare recognition of them
2. Intermittent listening, with the mind wandering in between
3. Half-listening or listening only closely enough to know when it is his or her turn to do something
4. Listening passively with little or no response
5. Listening narrowly, missing significant parts but accepting that which is familiar or agreeable to him or her
6. Listening and forming associations with related items from his or her own experiences
7. Listening closely enough to get the organization of the material heard—to get the main ideas and supporting details
8. Listening critically, including asking for more data on statements made
9. Appreciative and creative listening with genuine mental and emotional response[10]

It might be argued that several of these are not really listening levels but are examples of activities in which listening is not taking place. However, this listing does describe situations or activities that do occur and need to be recognized in

---

9. Commission on the English Curriculum, The National Council of Teachers of English, *Language Arts for Today's Children* (New York: Appleton-Century-Crofts, 1954), p. 80.
10. Harry A. Greene and Walter T. Petty, *Developing Language Skills in the Elementary Schools*, 4th ed. (Boston: Allyn & Bacon, 1971), p. 162.

planning a program. The point of concern is that while listening varies, all forms of it require specific abilities and skills. It is obvious that individuals listen to particular sounds for particular purposes; they do not just listen.

The Listening Skills

The identification of skills that can be defended as being ones specifically associated with listening has been the concern of much educational research. Unfortunately, this research has not achieved results that permit complete assurance for stating what these skills are. Obviously, listening is something of a state of mind; it is a process that, after basic sound reception has been made, closely parallels or is identical with thinking. People do listen; they listened before listening was considered a language arts instructional area. Children without instruction in listening can listen well (or at least adequately) when they wish to do so. Most mothers and teachers will readily attest to the accuracy of this statement. Furthermore, children must have listened quite well or they would not have learned the many words that they know or have the understanding they have of many ideas and concepts.

Following this line of reasoning can lead the curriculum developer astray, however, because children can learn to listen more effectively when instructional efforts are made. Therefore, an effective program incorporates instructional procedures for developing two groups or types of skills or abilities that appear to be needed: (1) those concerned with accurate perception of sound symbols and (2) those concerned with interpretation of and reaction to what is received.

The first group includes:
1. Skill in perceiving individual sounds and in discriminating one from another
2. Skill in identifying a group of sounds—usually a word but possibly a longer speech element—to which meaning is attached
3. Skill in deducing the meanings of words and longer expressions from the context of what is heard

The second group includes:
1. Skill in comprehending or gaining meaning from that which has been identified through such means as noting details and fitting them together, determining main and subordinate ideas, and selecting information pertinent to a specific reason for listening
2. Skill in relating the comprehension to previous learning in order to develop new understandings

Both groups of skills are virtually identical with reading skills. Those in the first group are quite similar to those reading skills generally termed *word recognition, word identification,* or *word analysis.* The second group corresponds to the meaning or comprehension reading skills. The extent of this relationship is being increasingly recognized in the school curriculum. Most noticeable is the inclusion of listening lessons and activities as integral parts of commercial basal reader materials.

Other listings of skills are sometimes made, with these possibly implying that more skills are involved in listening than those suggested in the two groups. For example, each of these "skills" may suggest other skills or subskills:

1. Listening to answer questions or to gain specific information
2. Determining the speaker's purpose and means for accomplishing it
3. Selecting items or particular content for summary or for the drawing of conclusions
4. Separating fact from opinion
5. Recognizing emotional appeal in the content
6. Detecting bias, prejudice, or propaganda
7. Responding to mood or setting of what is heard
8. Understanding the use of asides, satire, and voice inflections
9. Creating visual images from verbal descriptions

Listening as a Curriculum Area

With the increasing recognition of the need to teach listening and the inclusion of listening activities in the curriculum, it is often difficult to determine the extent to which the skills are actually taught. Certainly few if any teachers list listening on their daily program schedules as a separate subject area. The teaching is often made a part of some more all-inclusive area or is done in relation to reading. This procedure is highly appropriate, since there is the constant need for meaningful integration of subject matter.

Nevertheless, if the teaching of listening is approached incidentally, the desired results may not be accomplished. Effective programs provide for specific instruction in the listening skills, just as they provide for specific instruction in other skill areas. But this does not mean that a listening lesson or activity may not be interrelated with the subject matter from another area of the curriculum. In fact, as with teaching any of the communication skills, the teaching of listening requires relation to subject matter in order to gain the content and purpose that interest children.

Guidelines for Teaching Listening

There are a number of principles to be observed in planning the listening curriculum. *First,* features of the climate of classrooms as recommended in Chapter 3 and earlier in this chapter are significant. The most effective teaching of listening needs a teacher with a relaxed, unhurried, nonthreatening voice, along with facial expressions that are responsive and supportive.

Second, purposes *for* listening need to be developed with the children rather than demanding that they listen *to* something. Listening should be done *for* information that can be gained, *for* appreciation of the language in a poem, *for* propaganda words and content that shows bias, *tor* directions about how something should be done, and so on. Establishing standards for the listening, providing for individual and class reactions, and discussing listening skills needed all help children discover the importance of listening and the skills they need to do it effectively.

The *third* principle is that listening activities need to be related to or made an integral part of the ongoing activities of the class. These activities should be within the interest and comprehension levels of the children and such that they become personally involved, thus avoiding "tuning out." Interest is also more likely to be maintained if intensive listening is not required for too long a time and if changes in activities are provided for—questions, discussion, drawing or writing something as a result of the listening.

A *fourth* principle is related to the need to provide as much variety as possible in the listening experiences that are used for teaching the skills; that is, films, individual and group reports, dramatic activities, demonstrations in science, game descriptions, explanations of activities, discussions, conversations, flannel board stories, and so on may all be used as the bases for listening lessons.

In addition, attention needs to be given to a number of other factors. For example, some variation in physical arrangements may assist the teaching. A close grouping of the children around the storyteller will be appropriate in one instance, while sitting in rows may be the best arrangement for watching a film. An effective program also provides for individual differences. Certainly, always placing those children with hearing problems as advantageously as possible is necessary. It is also important to help pupils ignore distractions, take notes, develop enough vocabulary knowledge to recognize word clues, and learn to make use of changes in the tone of voice or manner of the speaker.

Listening Lessons and Activities

While every oral communication situation is an opportunity for developing listening skills and fostering good listening habits, an organized program (planned for in some detail and evaluated with adequate attention to objectives) is a part of effective curriculums. A planned program includes specific lessons designed to teach the skills as well as activities that build interest in learning to listen well.

The listening lessons in such a program are often quite informal, and usually they should be. However, a good listening lesson does have several identifiable characteristics that are necessary for the learning of skills and the practice of good habits:

1. *Stated purpose.* The purpose of the listening experience (to follow directions, to get word meanings from context, and so on) may need to be clearly defined and stated so that the children understand and appreciate the purpose. This usually means that some discussion is necessary, with the children themselves stating the reason or reasons for listening.

2. *Learning new words.* Preliminary attention to unfamiliar vocabulary often is necessary; that is, words that are likely to be unknown may need to be written on the board and related to words children know and to experiences they have had. Naturally this preliminary vocabulary work can be overdone. For example, the meanings of all words need not be known to appreciate some stories and poems. Also, one listening skill that is very important is that of getting meaning from the context, so not all new words need to be discussed.

3. *Listening guides.* Guides similar to study outlines or guides used for directing reading are sometimes used in listening lessons. These should be prepared in advance and used by the children as they listen. Some listening activities (ap-

preciational, for instance) may be harmed by the degree of formality the guides may invoke; therefore, decisions as to using them depend on the purpose for the listening.

4. *Follow-up.* Some follow-up should be a part of all listening lessons; that is, the purposes need to be examined in light of what has been listened to in order for the listening act to be complete. The amount and type of this follow-up varies, depending on the effectiveness of the listening. However, if the purpose for the listening has not been accomplished, extended follow-up discussion will not help very much. Time is better spent in re-listening.

In teaching attentive, analytical, and critical listening, supplemental activities such as note-taking, outlining, writing summaries, and using reference sources to check on the reliability of the material heard may need to be taught first or in conjunction with the listening lessons. These will help children organize their thinking and remember what they have listened to.

Simply asking children to listen to something is not a listening lesson. Doing this does not identify for them the listening skills they will need, nor does it teach these skills or promote the habits that are vital for them to learn. Teachers should have no difficulty in constructing effective lessons (or in selecting commercially prepared ones)[11] if they give attention to types of listening, to the purposes for particular types, and to the skills needed for achieving each purpose.

SPEAKING SKILLS IN THE CURRICULUM

While practically all children come to school with reasonably adequate ability to voice their thoughts and feelings, this ability is only a foundation for the mastery of the skills necessary for effective oral communication throughout their school years and beyond. Planned and continuous instructional opportunities must be provided in order to reinforce this foundation and build on it.

The need for planned oral language programs in all classrooms—programs that recognize the development of each child—is supported by the fact observable in many meetings and other social settings that shows many individuals, even though they may have sound and constructive ideas and strong feelings, are unable to express their thoughts effectively. Many persons are actually afraid to appear before a group of their associates and read an announcement, make a report, or express an opinion. Many may even be uncomfortable making small talk or engaging in conversation. Those who are so lacking in speaking ability or skill—in this broad sense—are handicapped in societal effectiveness and thus may be unfulfilled as individuals.

Competence in oral expression is first taught and developed in elementary

---

11. In many basal reading materials; also in Stanford E. Taylor, *Teaching Listening* (Washington, D.C.: National Education Association, 1964); David H. and Elizabeth F. Russell, *Listening Aids Through the Grades* (New York: Bureau of Publications, Teachers College, Columbia University, 1959); and Guy Wagner, Max Hosier, and Mildred Blackman, *Listening Games* (Darien, Conn.: Teachers Publishing Corp., 1962).

schools through attention to (1) the speech skills—the production of sounds accurately and easily; the control of the voice in matters of audibility, flexibility, and quality; and the use of correct intonation, suitable tempo, and good phrasing; (2) the physical movements and mannerisms related to the act of expression; and (3) the situations in which there is the need to speak. The curriculum should include all three areas, though actual ability to use language orally largely comes from practice in the various situations in which individuals naturally find themselves speaking. Effective programs recognize this fact and utilize natural situations to give instructional attention to the speech skills, to behavioral attitudes and habits, and to the matter of what is said.

Instructional Objectives

While learning to speak is a process of maturation and enculturation, each child's development of this ability to the extent most beneficial to him or her personally, socially, and educationally requires an instructional focus that seeks to achieve realistic objectives. Several of these objectives are identical with ones that are often stated for the elementary school curriculum generally, and others obviously are closely related to or are segments of the larger objectives. Since communication is viewed here as the core of the curriculum, and oral expression is basic to all means and modes of expression and reception that make use of language as a tool and a process, the commonality and relatedness of objectives is to be expected. Certainly without considerable success in attaining the objectives of the oral language program, many of the objectives of the total elementary school program will not be achieved.

Objectives for instructional programs should be as specific as possible and directed at children individually. Thus, the following objectives for the oral language program need to be made more specific in order to take into account the differences among children.

1. *Fostering fluency and naturalness in speaking.* While children have an instinctive desire to express themselves, they often do not have the fluency needed to express their true feelings and the knowledge they possess. Many very common and crucial speaking situations are much less satisfactory than they might be if the speakers do not have this fluency or do not feel at ease about speaking.

2. *Developing the child as a social being.* This objective is closely related to the first one, but the focus is more on interaction. Speaking must be recognized in its social context; it is not an individual act. A child must be taught to listen to others, recognize that they may have something to say, or simply be courteous and considerate—all of which are necessary if the child's speaking is to result in communication.

3. *Developing skill in enunciating, pronouncing, and controlling the voice.* This objective is also related to the first one in that naturalness should be stressed in enunciating and pronouncing rather than placing emphasis on particular phonemes or syllables that result in any sort of affectation. The goal is the development of an easy, pleasant manner in speaking, good voice control both in

volume and tone, enunciation and articulation that does not restrict communication, and pronunciation that is acceptable in the dialect standard for the speaker's environment.

4. *Organizing the content of expression.* Organization that facilitates and clarifies thoughts and ideas is essential in speaking situations. In learning to speak, children gain satisfactory command of the grammar of the language, how it is put together and works. They often have difficulty, however, with the sequencing of sentences they speak in attempting to communicate with others. In addition to sequence, effective organization also may require that content not related to the communication be eliminated, that some aspects of the message should be repeated or restated, that more details need to be added, or that the content should be related to the experiences of others or to what they have said. This objective, of course, is really directed at developing thinking abilities. But since the effects of thinking are only shown in behavior—in this case, what is said—the objective can be given particular attention in the oral language program.

5. *Developing skill in social settings and situations.* Speaking is usually done for specific communication purposes and in identifiable situations and settings. Thus, there is a need for teaching children to speak in these situations. As shown later in this chapter, such occasions occur naturally in classrooms that provide for active learning programs. However, there is a need to plan to maximize these and to provide the practice that reinforces the learning.

Attention to Speech Skills

Aside from the content of what is said, which is always of primary importance, effective oral expression results from speech that is pleasing to the ear and is produced with ease and confidence. This speech occurs because it is rhythmic; free from many hesitations, repetitions, and interruptions; and produced at a suitable tempo and volume for the content and the audience, with all of the sounds clearly articulated and distinctly enunciated.

If children have heard and assimilated enough pleasing speech in their early years (and many children have), they are well on their way to a good development of speaking skills. But this does not mean that they cannot profit from speech instruction—all children can. And there are some children who definitely need instructional guidance to correct specific speech problems. For example, some children always seem to speak too loudly, and others can scarcely be heard even when they are near. Many children have not learned to adjust their voices to the size of the room or to the speaking situation. Some children speak in monotonous tones; others speak in shrill ones. The voices of some children are nasal, breathy, hoarse, or thin. Some children speak so rapidly that the meaning of the communication is lost; others speak so slowly the result is the same. Some of these problems can be resolved through the recording of voices and subsequent playbacks, class assessment of speech according to set standards and guidelines, and choral speaking. Other more serious problems require the services of speech specialists.

Children's emotional, social, and mental reactions are often manifested in their speech. Voice quality, tone, pitch, and tempo are often indicators of an emotional state. Children who are upset, tense, or worried usually show it in their voices. Self-reliant, alert children show their confidence by pleasing voices. Eager, happy children are friendly and talkative. Children who are emotionally and socially insecure are unable to express themselves in fluent, articulate speech. Youngsters who are overly aggressive, perhaps reflecting emotional insecurity, are apt to speak in loud voices, talk a great deal, and insist on monopolizing conversations. Children who have speech problems due to emotional makeup can sometimes be helped by the teacher's encouragement and understanding and the atmosphere of a nonthreatening classroom group, but others need specific programs to help them overcome insecurity and social inadequacy. Still others may need the corrective work prescribed and directed by a specialist.

Programs should also make children aware that oral communication often includes more than speech. It is virtually impossible for individuals to express themselves orally without using some body movements (which should be natural and in harmony with the speech activity and the content of the communication). Children need to be helped to avoid such annoying physical mannerisms as fidgeting, head jerking, hand twisting, exaggerated facial expressions, and other undue physical movements. Many of these problems can be overcome by the elimination of self-consciousness through the practice of speech in realistic, meaningful situations.

Instructional Settings and Situations

An active learning environment provides natural settings and situations for learning to speak effectively—the class discussing a problem, a small group working on a project, two or three children conversing, children reporting to classmates. These situations and activities are genuine and meaningful by being truly concerned with communication. Using realistic situations increases the children's acceptance of the teaching of speech skills, which in turn maximizes their possibilities for learning.

The situations suggested below can and should be settings for learning to use language effectively. Each one has specific characteristics related to its purpose; each also is nonspecific in that the subject matter of the speaking is virtually unlimited, thus facilitating the adaption of the situation to the curriculum, to children's interest in science, social studies, health, music, mathematics, and so on. Many of these situations are not discrete, or certainly are not so always; that is, a discussion may lead to several people reporting, storytelling may turn into a conversation (see Chapter 7), sharing and a discussion may be intertwined, or choral speaking may include drama characteristics (see Chapter 5).

1. *Conversations.* Occasions for conversations occur very frequently in the classroom, just as they do in our daily lives. There may be occasions to converse before school in the morning, during the day as children and teachers work with one another, as children plan in small groups, and the many other times that conversing is the natural thing to do. Due to their relative intimacy, conversational situations provide especially good settings for a teacher to help the shy child develop ease in speaking.

2. *Sharing.* The sharing of information is a part of the curriculum in the

primary grades in most schools. This sharing is frequently done during a specific time called "share and tell," or "telling time." The original idea for this activity —and one that needs reconsideration in most classrooms—was that children who are shy about speaking could *show* an object (a toy, new sweater, a drawing, or a similar item) and gain security in speaking from holding it. Thus, a better name for the sharing time is "show and tell." Showing something also guides the composition of what is said by the very nature of the act of telling about it, whereas simply relating something that happened too often does not show the minimal composition qualities discussed earlier.

3. *Discussions.* The naturalness of this activity is apparent since in any group the size of the typical classroom, discussion is bound to arise. Many of the issues that arise in the day-to-day activities of the classroom may be the subject of a discussion. A discussion differs from a conversation—in addition to the differences usually in the size of the group—in that there is a more specific focus on a topic, a more purposeful goal. Discussion also requires more "speaking up" so that all may hear. Characteristics such as "taking turns," avoiding unnecessary repetition, and listening to others are common to both conversation and discussion as well as to other oral activities.

4. *Storytelling.* Storytelling is closely related to the sharing of experiences, which takes place in many settings. However, the curriculum should provide for helping children develop traditional storytelling skills; that is, there should be the telling of stories from literature (written and oral) in which particular attention is given to getting attention through the beginning; holding it with details, dialogue, and sequence; and the building to and relating of a climax. Certainly there is no one way to tell stories, either those that are real or imaginary, or those read or heard or simply "made up." It is important, though, for children to have many opportunities to hear stories, to read stories, and to practice the skills necessary to hold an audience's attention.

5. *Reporting.* Good reporting requires skill in selecting appropriate information to report on, organizing this material, and giving the report accurately and interestingly. To attain these skills there must be provision for teaching children how to use the library, how to prepare notes and other reporting guides, and how to use visual and other aids to convey the information. As with discussion, the breadth of the elementary school curriculum makes the number of possible situations for reporting almost unlimited. Chapter 7 has numerous suggestions for reporting in relation to children's literature.

6. *Dramatic Activities.* Children love to play roles, to imagine being someone else, to be creative. The importance of the many dramatic activities—from rhythmic games to pantomime to dramatic play to formal drama to the elementary school generally as well as to the development of oral expression—is the reason there is an entire chapter (Chapter 5) in this book about it.

7. *Interviewing.* An interview is a good method for securing information and provides the interviewer with the opportunity to use speaking skills, organize his or her thinking, and develop listening ability. Children may have opportunities to be both interviewer and interviewee if the possibilities for the activity are capitalized on. Almost anyone with special information—parents, a returned traveler, a child with an interesting hobby, another teacher—may be interviewed

with profit to the class and with a special learning opportunity for the interviewer.

8. *Telephoning.* Many children now come to school experienced in talking by telephone. Many have not, however, learned how to identify themselves properly when answering or making a call, how to formulate and receive messages, and how to end telephone conversations. They also may not observe telephone courtesies in asking permission to use a phone, placing calls at convenient times, and not monopolizing a phone.

9. *Announcements and Directions.* Giving announcements has become a part of school life, with many schools having regular opening announcements through a speaker system. Some schools incorporate this activity into the curriculum by providing for children to make some of these announcements as well as some of their own. In addition, there are many opportunities in classrooms for announcing something. There are also many opportunities for giving directions—for a game, how to perform some task, traveling to a particular place, and so forth.

10. *Participating in Meetings.* Most elementary school children become interested in clubs of one sort or another. Outside of school they often are in scouting groups and neighborhood and church clubs. While interest in clubs does not automatically mean interest in learning how to conduct club business effectively and efficiently, children can become interested in basic parliamentary procedure if it is taught in the context of a club's actual business.

11. *Choral Speaking.* Choral speaking serves as a most enjoyable way to interpret literature orally (see Chapter 7). Experience with choral speaking helps children learn to sense mood development and understand the role of rhythm in speaking and the importance of volume, tone, and quality of the voice (see Chapter 5). Fluency, clarity of enunciation, and speaking with expression are improved through this activity. Choral speaking also helps children who are too shy to speak up, those who are too loud to tone down, and those who do not respect the rights of others to participate in a group activity.

12. *Amenities.* Children often do not learn out of school such amenities as making and responding to introductions, welcoming a newcomer, thanking people for kindnesses, and responding to invitations. These and similar activities are important to most people and need to be learned. To be learned well, the learning should begin in the elementary school.

Evaluating Oral Expression

While children's abilities in expressing themselves orally cannot be measured by paper-and-pencil tests, assessment of overall ability and the development of skills in specific speaking situations can be made. For instance, guidelines and statements of rules or standards of performance developed by teachers and pupils for all oral language situations should be used in all programs. Standards for conversing might simply state that only one person at a time should talk, that everyone should speak clearly and listen carefully, and that good language should be used. Of course, the standards are to reflect the children's maturity and their ways of looking at things, but they should also reflect the teacher's recognition of the performance levels possible. The standards or rules should also be evolving; that is, they should reflect growth from one period of time to another.

In addition to the use of standards of performance, the program should provide for using checklists in which behavior with respect to specific skills are systematically recorded—again to reflect development over periods of time. A speaking checklist might list such questions as "Is my voice pleasant to hear?" with provision for check marks to be placed when a particular question can be answered affirmatively. Checklists may also be developed by children themselves or by the teacher and children and may be used by both or by children individually.

Most importantly, evaluation of oral language expression and reception as well as evaluation of any aspect of children's behavior must be thought of in broader terms than simply something done in connection with giving grades to pupils. Evaluation is a process, an essential component of the larger process of instruction. It is directly related to the attainment of curriculum objectives. Evaluation is made to determine what has been learned and what has not been learned and thus needs more instructional attention. It is a process that includes all of the evaluative procedures used by the teacher, the children, and all others involved in the instructional program. As a procedure, evaluation includes these steps: formulating goals in terms of behavior that can be measured or appraised, securing evidence regarding the extent of achievement of these objectives, interpreting or analyzing this evidence in terms of the objectives and learning activities, and using the interpretation to extend learning. Thus, evaluation is a basic element of the curriculum.

EXERCISES FOR THOUGHT AND ACTION

1. Examine curriculum guides and elementary school language textbooks for references to language arts curriculum organization and how the various language arts areas may be taught in an integrated manner. Critique the references in terms of your own beliefs.
2. Devise checklists for evaluating skill development in listening and speaking that can be used by the pupils themselves. Identify the age/grade level of your checklists and tell how they should be used.
3. Record the speech of several children in natural communicative situations. Evaluate these recordings in terms of dialect differences, possible usage problems, and speech production faults.
4. How important is it to seek to have all children speak a standard dialect? What is the evidence for your answer?
5. What evidence can you present that environment affects language development? Is there evidence that all children's language is grammatical? What variations in language are caused by environmental differences? How do you know?
6. Examine the principles for curriculum determination given on page 69. Do you agree with these? Why or why not? Have you others to suggest?

Burling, Robbins. *English in Black and White*. New York: Holt, Rinehart & Winston, 1973. This small book presents many of the linguists' ideas about "black English" and what teachers should do about teaching children who speak nonstandard dialects.

Burns, Paul C., and Schell, Leon M., eds. *Elementary School Language Arts: Selected Readings*. Chicago: Rand McNally & Co., 1969. Part 3 includes articles about listening and speaking. Several of these deal with interrelationships between listening and speaking and other language arts areas.

De Stefano, Johanna S., and Fox, Sharon E., eds. *Language and the Language Arts*. Boston: Little, Brown & Co., 1974. A book of readings that has some useful sections. The articles in Chapter 1 give an introductory overview of the function of language.

Greene, Harry A., and Petty, Walter T. *Developing Language Skills in the Elementary Schools*. 5th ed. Boston: Allyn & Bacon, 1975. The first three chapters discuss in depth the planning of the language arts program and the roles of dialects and linguistics in the program. Other chapters present curriculum bases and instructional methodology in all areas of the language arts.

Petty, Walter T.; Petty, Dorothy C.; and Becking, Marjorie F. *Experiences in Language: Tools and Techniques for Language Arts Methods*. Boston: Allyn & Bacon, 1973. This text presents detailed teaching suggestions for each language arts area. Particularly helpful are the independent activities for children.

Phillips, Gerald M., et al. *The Development of Oral Communication in the Classroom*. Indianapolis: Bobbs-Merrill, 1970. This is a general presentation of the classroom as a verbal community as viewed by the speech specialist. Particularly helpful is the discussion on poverty and class differences and how they both affect the teaching of oral expression.

The reader may wonder about the placement of this chapter toward the beginning of the book since drama is often considered to be something that is done if there is time or if parents need to be entertained. But dramatics is a way of learning, one that is often overlooked in consideration of the receptive and expressive aspects of language or of the instructional methods and techniques that may be used. For this reason it needs to be discussed early in the study of areas of the curriculum.

The author of this chapter is especially enthusiastic about the importance of creative dramatics to learning. She also feels strongly about the interrelatedness of all aspects of the language arts and the ties among various areas of the curriculum—and how these relationships may be made the most of in the curriculum.

Many schools are instituting programs in aesthetics, which includes music, art, and movement, as well as drama. Of course, all of the language arts and many areas of social studies may be made a part of such programs. The reader should particularly relate the content of this chapter to the contents of Chapters 12 (art), 13 (music), and 14 (health and physical education).

The author of this chapter wishes to acknowledge the helpful suggestions provided by Mr. William Moore, Coordinator of English, Hamilton Board of Education, Hamilton, Ontario.

W.T.P.

Creative Dramatics for Learning and Teaching

Marion C. Cross

5

Drama is most often thought of in terms of scenery and scripts, costumes and curtains, audiences and rehearsals, and learning lines. Much less frequently does this word come to mind as someone observes children playing in yards and streets, sees a child pretending to feed a doll, or laughs as youngsters mimic someone who has annoyed them. Even less often is drama thought of as a way of learning, an instructional method.

The discussion of dramatics in the pages that follow is not about "how to put on a play." Neither is it about the value of theater to children, although learning about this dramatic form certainly is valuable. Rather, the concern in this chapter is with capitalizing on the natural activity of children in teaching and learning dramatics. After all, dramatics is about "being" and "doing." From infancy children find out about themselves and the world around them as they play at being the people and things encountered in the environment. Later children move further afield: They more deeply express feelings and interpret and reenact increasingly more complex situations.

By the time children come to school, they are experienced at being and doing, for much of what they know has been learned this way. As one writer put it: "Drama comes in the door of every school with the child."[1]

VALUES IN CREATIVE DRAMATICS

Creative dramatics is a way of learning, a means for expression, and an art form. It provides for an individual's involvement through both thought and action. With the increasing need for school environments that maximize each child's development, teachers need to be aware of what creative dramatics can do for a child—and do within the framework of the total curriculum. The following values are the objectives of a program—aims to be accomplished through realistic situations in a nonthreatening environment.

Developing Awareness and Sensitivity

From birth the child tastes, touches, listens, looks, and smells in an effort to find out about himself and his world. But as the child matures and becomes acquainted with the printed symbol as a source of information, there is a danger that his perceptions of much that is about him will diminish. To counteract this possibility, creative dramatics can be used to help sharpen the child's awareness and sensitivity. To playact an old person, the child must note many details that show the quality of oldness; to use the body to express the color red, he must observe color around him and become aware of how it influences him. Specific observation and discussion of the characteristics of objects in the environment should be an integral part of all elementary school programs. Visually the focus might be on the colors, sizes, shapes, and movements of the leaves on a tree; auditorily, it might be the rhythm, pitch, and volume of cars rushing by on the highway. Observation interpreted in dramatic form builds a conceptual base for expression in language, in music, and in the visual arts.

Fostering Imaginative and Independent Thinking

Through creative dramatic activities the child develops a potential for imaginative and independent thinking. While much has been written about creativity and creative expression, too often the emphasis has been on the product rather than the process. In dramatic activities the teacher has the opportunity to challenge the child to use her experiences in presenting an interpretation that is uniquely her own.

The child faced with this challenge must choose from among a number of

---

1. Winifred Ward, *Drama with and for Children*, U.S. Department of Health, Education, and Welfare, Bulletin no. 30 (Washington, D.C.), p. 1.

available alternatives, must use imaginative powers, and must think independently. This is the process that raises the creativity of spontaneous play of early childhood to the level of a challenging problem to be solved. In addition, the cyclic effect operates: The dramatic activity stimulates the child's imagination and encourages further creativity.

Increasing Expressional Skill

Through speech, body movements, and combinations of both these acts, the child exhibits increasing facility and confidence in self-expression. In playing a role that requires speech, the child practices control of volume, tempo, pitch, and diction; if movement is involved, then he tries to avoid awkwardness. While the child's progress is usually gradual and somewhat developmental, his participation in a variety of dramatic forms during the primary and intermediate years results in increasing sophistication in the ability to concentrate, to control voice and physical movement, and to express himself as he wishes.

Developing Interest in Other Art Forms

While participation in creative dramatic activities may not necessarily lead the child to an interest in formal drama, the active involvement in this expressive form helps the child to develop a sensitivity to the magic and make-believe of the theater. Through the process of representing her experiences and ideas dramatically, she begins to sense the underlying qualities that are shared by music, sculpture, painting, poetry, or any other of the creative art forms and to formulate some comparative guidelines to use in her appreciation of the arts. Creative dramatics particularly presents the opportunity to become acquainted with good literature.

Building Cooperative Skills and Social Awareness

Through creative dramatic activities the child develops a better understanding of himself and others. In dramatic play the child has the opportunity to act out his ideas and to test and evaluate them in an accepting environment. As he takes on the roles of other people, he is compelled to consider the factors that make them who they are and influence them in what they do. Even the youngest child who pretends to be someone else is showing insights into the behavior exhibited by his fellow human beings. This role playing helps the child to build a positive self-concept and to increase his tolerance of other people.

Releasing Emotions in a Healthy Manner

At some time or another everyone feels anger, fear, anxiety, jealousy, resentment, and negativism as well as joy, happiness, and love—yet there is an inner desire to control oneself. Through playing a part suppression is avoided, a fact that the child learns to appreciate; thus he recognizes that creative dramatics is an expressional mode that is satisfying and enjoyable.

AN ENVIRONMENT FOR CREATIVE DRAMATICS

The fact that creative dramatics may occur in many types of activities means that its initiation and success in a particular classroom may well depend on the capabilities and interests of the teacher. A beginning may be made in any one of three basic activities—speech, movement, or stories. Since all three areas are involved in·creative dramatics, they are all interrelated with one another.

Thus, a teacher who is interested in choral speaking may begin with this speech activity by introducing the class to verses, and then pantomime or other action may be added in keeping with the content of the poem. For other teachers, story sessions or body movements may be the most comfortable way of easing into the beginnings of creative dramatics.

In whatever form children are introduced to creative drama, their expression depends on other experiences they have had and the general atmosphere that pervades the classroom. This atmosphere or climate should be relaxed, safe, and flexible. But it needs to be more than that, as has been described in the preceding two chapters.

Every classroom should be an extension of the real world. A variety of concrete materials relating to topics currently being studied needs to be available for pupils to manipulate and explore. If there are opportunities to handle and talk about materials in the immediate environment, children will establish conceptual bases for their expressive endeavors. A child who has felt and discussed objects that are smooth, cold, and slippery, or soft, warm, and fluffy will bring this knowledge to a dramatic experience in which she is crawling up a cold, slippery, glasslike iceberg, or one in which she must wrap herself in a warm, woolly coat for protection from the cold.

The child should also have opportunities for moving beyond the walls of the classroom to further enrich the impressions she can weave into her dràmatic activities. Pictures, films, television and radio, books and newspapers, and adults with experiences to share—all add dimension to the child's real world. The teacher is himself an important resource and activator as he shares the experiences with his class, particularly as he questions to produce insight and reads to add dimension. It is the teacher who largely determines the attitudes that prevail in the classroom, by the way he structures tasks and by the manner in which he expresses his acceptance of the child's productive efforts. It is imperative that the teacher clearly establishes from the beginning that there are no right or wrong ways to express an idea. Through gestures and comments the teacher conveys this attitude to the class, and for the most part, children will reflect these feelings toward the efforts of their fellow classmates.

Materials and activities should suggest to the child *what* she may do in dramatic expression but allow her the freedom to make decisions as to *how* she will organize and produce her expression. This chapter contains many examples of such challenges and the ways in which they may be structured for maximum pupil growth.

BEGINNING SCHOOL EXPERIENCES IN CREATIVE DRAMATICS

Most children—whether from the inner city or suburbia—come to school with rich backgrounds in imitating people and things that they have met in their real worlds, including what they have seen on television. The kindergarten and primary classrooms, by using suitable materials and good organization, may stimulate the child to continue and expand this informal-play activity. Interest centers designed for individual and small-group activities (which often may be planned and instituted by the children themselves) as well as teacher-directed activities built around story-plays or choral verse contribute to the child's growth in creativity.

Interest Centers as Starting Points

For many years kindergarten classrooms have contained play and work areas. As teachers of primary and intermediate grades become familiar with the potential of activity areas, more and more classrooms in the elementary school are being organized in this manner.

Each interest center is supplied with materials related to a particular activity or activities. The areas are often separated from one another by dividers especially designed for the purpose or by furniture such as a bookcase or piano. These physical divisions give the children a sense of security and a degree of intimacy and at the same time keep their activities from disturbing children in other centers. Children are allowed reasonably large blocks of time to circulate from one center to another on their own initiative or in a manner structured by the teacher. Some centers that foster creative-dramatic expression are as follows:

1. *Family center.* This type of center, sometimes called the "doll center" or "Wendy center," contains a collection of toys such as dolls and doll clothes, dishes, furniture, telephones, and irons, all of which are arranged to suggest a home setting. In it children play the roles of the people in their homes and neighborhoods—a relative, a neighbor, a mail carrier, and so forth. A few articles of clothing—a man's hat, a lady's purse, a lunch pail, an apron, for example——further stimulate the children's imaginations. Only enough wearing apparel should be provided to suggest a character, since the child is expected to rely on words and actions to portray the character he is thinking about. A young boy was heard to say to his "wife" as he swung into the family center and thumped his lunch pail down on the table, "Boy! What a day! Is there any cold beer in the frig?"

The teacher, observing the direction of the play taking place in the center, may decide to extend the children's thinking by asking questions like the following: "Is your baby sick?" "How are you going to care for him?" "You are having company for dinner, are you?" "What are you going to cook for them to eat?" At other times the teacher may decide to join in the action and chat with the family. In this way the teacher is able to present patterns of behavior that the children may model in their play as well as in their daily lives.

Sometimes the class may wish to convert the family center into a play store filled with boxes, cans, and other items that the children have contributed; a doctor's office; a post office; or some other setting. Occasionally the center may take on a completely different design. A large paper wigwam with some complementary play items, such as a few sticks and stones for a campfire, transports the child's imagination to the excitement of family life in other cultures and other days.

2. *Puppetry center.* From the humorous puppets of the educational program "Sesame Street" to those depicting the Three Billy Goats Gruff or some other favorite fairy-tale characters, puppets and the skits that are built around them fascinate young children. Indeed, for most children puppetry is probably the first dramatic form that is geared to their level and in which they can fully enjoy the observer role. A puppetry center in the classroom capitalizes on this interest as it provides excellent opportunities for the children to develop a story-play. Within the security of the theater walls, the children are free to express their emotions and play out short sequences built around the puppet characters.

While the center could contain a commercial-type theater and puppets, children reap equal benefit from ones made by a teacher and pupils.[2] When the center is first introduced, the number of puppets should be limited; only a few characters such as a dog, a rabbit, and a cat can be used to capture the interest of young children. After the children have experimented with the puppets and have exercised their potential for expressing ideas, additional characters may be added. Audience is not important in the early stage of puppet play, but as children become increasingly interested they become anxious to share episodes with friends.

3. *Dress-up center.* A dress-up center is closely related to the family center, but the concentration of the former is on using clothing and other personal articles to stimulate make-believe about various personalities. The center usually consists of a large cardboard box or chest, which is used to store an assortment of items such as hats (a soldier's, a fire fighter's, a farmer's, a lady's); a sword; large chiffon scarves and lengths of bright-colored material that can be draped, folded, or tied for a variety of effects; an old wig; jewelry; and a small hand-mirror. Most of the items for such a box will be contributed by the children if the teacher gives them incentive and encouragement.

Using this kind of collection, children in the late primary and intermediate grades can plan story-plays to enrich the understandings of stories in reading

---

2. For aid in puppet making, see L. V. Wall et al., eds., *The Puppet Book: A Practical Guide to Puppetry in Schools, Training Colleges and Clubs,* 2nd ed. (London: Faber & Faber, 1965).

programs or to extend their interests in the people and times encountered in eocial studies.

Guiding Beginning Informal Dramatics

The teacher plays a crucial role as an observer of the activities in the centers. She must be sensitive to the developmental needs of the pupils in order to decide whether to intervene or to allow a dramatization to continue uninterrupted. This decision should be based in part on the following considerations of children's dramatic expression:

1. In each new encounter with informal dramatics, there will be a period of random manipulation of materials, during which time the children become familiar with the handling and the expressive potential of the objects.
2. Young children are naturally repetitive in their play. Children enjoy acting out some stories and skits a number of times, with each repetition giving additional pleasure and satisfaction to the children as they gain confidence in the expression.
3. Children's play will at times appear to be rather aggressive, since role playing often acts as a satisfying outlet for release of feelings that may have been restricted by a home or school environment.
4. The dramatic activities initiated by children will always reflect the amount of motivation potential of the materials in the center and the degree of stimulation in the classroom atmosphere.

Beginning Teacher-Directed Activities

For some beginning dramatic activities the teacher may take a more active role than that of guiding and observing as identified with the centers. By initiating some directed activities the teacher helps to nurture each child's dramatic expression. The following descriptions of teacher-directed activities suggest a variety of ways this may be accomplished in the classroom.

The Story-Play

The telling or reading of a story may lead directly to a dramatic activity. The teacher may start a dramatic activity by inviting the children to help bring the story to life by making some of the sounds that happen in the story. Or the teacher may begin by telling or reading a portion of the story, with the children pantomiming. Opportunity should be provided for total group participation, without the restrictions of an audience. Sometimes a musical instrument, such as a piano or a drum, may be used to accompany action. Variations such as this are subject to the interests of the teacher and the children and to the general tone of the story-play being developed.

Story-plays may be built around science or social studies interests and stories; fairy tales or nursery rhymes; or in general, any story made up. The total physical involvement demanded by the story-play satisfies the young child's need for active learning and gives the activity a quality closely akin to movement and dance, which are discussed in a later section. The following examples suggest different ways the teacher may approach this form of dramatic play:

1. *Family living.* In a unit on family life intended to emphasize good health habits, a story-play can be used to reinforce a discussion. While the teacher tells the story, the children mime it. To begin, the children are lying on the floor in random formation and pretending that they are asleep.

> Mother is calling, "Yoo-hoo, time to get up." Oh! It's so hard to wake up. You rub your eyes....You stretch your legs . . . wiggle your toes . . . Oh, oh. There's Mother calling again. You throw back the cover and jump out of bed. You had better get dressed first. Undo the buttons on your pajamas. . . . Pull out your arms. . . . now your legs. Carefully put on your clothes for school. Don't forget to hang up your pajamas.

The story-play continues with descriptions of washing, eating, and other family routines that the teacher wishes to emphasize.

2. *Leaves in the fall.* A science unit on the signs of fall may have a story development in which a musical instrument adds dimension to the action. Children may be given scarves from the dress-up box to flutter in their hands to simulate the floating of falling leaves. The use of scarves or crepe-paper streamers encourages children to forget about themselves and to direct their attention to the person or thing they are miming.

To begin this sequence, the children, holding their bright-colored scarves, are in scatter formation about the room.

> All through the summer the little leaves hung on tightly to the branch of the big tree. Sometimes a gentle breeze blew through the tree and rocked the leaves. *(The teacher may play a short selection on a piano, shake a tambourine gently, or lightly tap a drum.)* All too soon fall days came and the days grew cooler. A strong, cold wind began to blow and it shook the branches of the tree. At last the little leaves could hang on no longer. Away they went, whirling and twirling in the frosty fall air. *(Once again suitable musical accompaniment may be provided as the children move about the room.)*

The story continues as the leaves float down to a quiet rest on the ground. The scarves or streamers are set aside, and the children mime the raking of leaves into big piles. The children then mime the games they like to play in the leaves.

While these examples are indicative of the use and value of the story-play, they are very elementary. With some imagination, a teacher and/or pupils can create increasingly sophisticated story-plays—ones that integrate programs in literature and other subject areas.

Verse Speaking

Fortunately many children have shared Mother Goose rhymes with their parents by chanting the short, lyrical verses and moving their hands and bodies in time with the variety of rhythms and speeds. Once children are old enough to play outdoors, they are initiated to a multitude of skipping rhymes like the following one:

> Bubble gum, in a dish.
> How many bubble gums do you wish?
> One, two, three. . . .

Such rhymes, while somewhat unique to geographical areas and cultures, have similarities that are characteristic of the concerns of childhood. Preschoolers are exposed to sing-along commercials on television, and from radio they learn folk songs and ballads that they take delight in performing for a captive audience.

Teachers of kindergarten and the primary grades build on this beginning with colorful spectrums of poetry for children to share. Nursery rhymes may be chanted, sung, and acted out. If wisely chosen, poetry exposes children to many different rhythms, as suggested by the following list:

Marching: "The Grand Old Duke of York"
Skipping: "Hippity Hop to the Barber Shop"
Galloping: "Ride a Cock Horse to Banbury Cross"
Rocking: "Rock-a-Bye Baby in the Tree-Top"

Finger plays, a simple means for showing action, involve hands in representing the thought and are related to verse speaking. Often finger plays can be made into playlets, with some children taking the speaking parts and others acting out the scene as suggested by the lines of the poem. The finger play "Five Fat Squirrels" provides an example of this technique.

> Five fat squirrels sitting in a tree,
> The first one said, "What did I see?"
> The second one said, "I see a gun."
> The third one said, "Let's run, let's run."
> The fourth one said, "Let's hide in the shade."
> The fifth one said, "I'm not afraid!"
> Bang went the gun! See them all run.

Five children who are chosen to be the squirrels group themselves together on the floor. Each "squirrel" says a line in turn. All the children in the class share the last line, and the "squirrels" scatter to their places.

Fun with Word-Sounds

Just as children enjoy manipulating materials with their hands, they find pleasure in using their voices to create different kinds of sounds and impressions. Two examples of voice manipulation are described below. The first, a story, is fun for children and helps increase their awareness of sounds around them.

> I was walking to school today, when up the street came a big black dog. I knew he was angry because he was barking loudly. *(The children produce the sound of the dog.)* Running up the street behind the dog was a little old lady. She had a leash in her hand and was shouting at the dog. What do

you think she would say to the dog? *(The children make suggestions and then choose the one they wish to use.) (The story continues in this fashion.)*

Once the story has been completed, the children will probably enjoy going through it a number of times without interruption while using the sounds they have decided on.

The second activity gives the children the opportunity to make and compare sounds:

Can you tell me what a cat says? Make the sounds for me.
What does a kitten say? Make the sound for me.
How would a hungry kitten sound? *(The child makes the sound.)*
How would a kitten that has lost its mother sound?
What would an angry cat say?
Growl like a little cat.
Growl like a big lion.
Purr like a kitten.
Purr like a mother cat.
Purr like a big lion.

As the children do this exercise they will chat informally about the sounds they are making and about the ways in which the sounds are the same or different.

DEVELOPMENTAL PROGRAMS IN CREATIVE DRAMATICS

Following children's first experiences with creative dramatics, teachers of the later primary and intermediate grades have the opportunity to develop a program that encourages increasing sophistication in dramatics. More attention can be given to specific details in the three areas that were used as starting points— movement, speech, and stories—and to interrelating creative dramatics with other aspects of the total school program.

Dramatic Development Through Body Posture and Movement

Movement is natural and often pleasurable and it provides an acceptable means for relieving tensions. Since movement is more primitive in its beginnings than speech, it is often an easier mode of expression for children as well as for adults.

Creative dramatic expression through movement is initiated through gross physical activity that makes the child aware of all of the parts of his body. Through this awareness, the child is able to develop the muscle control needed in depicting characters and feelings. Expressive movement permits children a direct, immediate, and spontaneous expression of their thoughts and feelings. It enables them to derive pleasure easily and freely—satisfactions that are increased as skill in the control of the body is developed. Not to be overlooked is the fact that meaningful movement may add to overall communication ability.

Each movement has a quality of weight and time, and it is the interaction of these elements that makes movement expressive. Table 5.1, based in part on the movement theory of Rudolf Laban, identifies and describes the basic elements and suggests the potential for their development.[3]

Table 5.1. Movement: Elements and Development Activities

Basic Elements	Description
Body awareness	Any part of the body may begin a movement—head, shoulders, hands, feet, fingers. The different parts of the body move in relationship to one another.
Space	Movement may go in different directions—toward the walls, ceiling, floor—and be carried out on three levels—high, medium, or low. The body moves through space in open or closed positions. Open positions suggest happy, relaxed feelings while tight, cramped positions convey feelings of discomfort. Movement may be direct or twist through space.
Speed	A variety of locomotions—walking, running, leaping, jumping—carry the body through space in speeds ranging from fast to slow. Any flow of movement may be terminated with either a sudden or a gradual stop.
Weight	Movements range from strong, firm acts to light, gentle ones.

Source: Adapted from Vera Gray and Rachel Percival, *Music, Movement and Mime for Children* (Oxford: Oxford University Press, 1962), p. 14.

The activities presented in Chart 5.1 may be used to initiate and develop expression through movement:

Chart 5.1. Expression Through Movement Activities

Space

To begin: 1. *Space is all around you.* (Children tend to move into space in front of them, forgetting that they can also move backward or to the left or right.)
Slowly lift your arm in front of you. Slowly lift your arm behind you. Slowly lift your arm to your right, and then to your left. Move your arm forward, backward, sideways, and round and round.
Shake your leg in front of you. Shake your leg to your right, to your left, and behind you.
2. *Space is above you, all around you, and at your feet.*
Be a giant. Stretch as tall as you can.
Be a spot on the floor. Make yourself as small as you can.
Be a huge machine. Make yourself as large as you can.

3. Adapted from Vera Gray and Rachel Percival, *Music, Movement and Mime for Children* (Oxford: Oxford University Press, 1962).

3. *You may move through space in direct or twisted movements.*
Be a sunflower. Grow up to the sun as straight as you can.
Be a morning glory. Slowly twist your way up the fence.
4. *You may change your body shape from one position to another.*
Slowly become a round, fat balloon as someone fills you with air.
A little girl pricks you with a pin. Suddenly make yourself
limp and thin.

To develop: Pretend that you are a toy. Are you big or are you small? Are you
wide or are you thin? Can you move forward, backward,
sideways? Does someone have to wind you up? Move about
the room as a toy.
What do you like to ride in? Pretend that you are your favorite
vehicle. Move about the room. You may make sound effects
for your vehicle. On my signal, stop your vehicle.
Show me with your body:
I am a king.
I am very sick.
I have worked very hard today. I am very tired.

Time
    To begin: Run lightly to the front of the room.
Push your feet slowly about the room. Push forward, backward,
and sideways.

    To develop: You are riding on your bicycle. You are going up a hill and you
have to push very hard. Finally you reach the top and go
zooming down the other side.
With a partner, pretend that you are a moving part in a clock.
Your partner winds you up and you go very fast and then
slowly run down.

Force
    To begin: With your hands, punch up to the ceiling as quickly as you can.
Crouch down to the floor. Slowly and gently raise youself as high
as you can.
    To develop: Be a dandelion seed. Float and twirl through the air. Drop slowly
down to the ground.
You are in a crowded department store. Push your way through
the crowd to the front door. Get away from the store as
quickly as you can without running.

The Use of Pantomime

Pantomime (more commonly, mime) builds on the skills developed through
movement activities. It is a product of physical and mental coordination to interpret and express an experience without sound. Its effectiveness depends on the
development of the powers of observation, concentration, and the physical skills
of the performer. For example, if a pupil wishes to mime a rather stout person
boarding a bus, the pantomimist must first consider movement—the way the

person carries himself, facial expressions, the actions of hands and feet. Thus, it is necessary for the pantomimist to have observed the movements of one or more heavy persons in order to make the decisions these considerations require. Then he must try to express the actions by controlling his own gestures and body movements. This requires concentration and physical capability.

In its more sophisticated form, dramatic expression by mime is based on eight basic expressive movements—outgrowths of the elements of time, space, and weight as described above. These movements are identified by specific adjectives, which suggest their use to show characterizations and feelings.

Punching: quick, straight, and strong
Pressing: slow, straight, and strong
Wringing: slow, twisted, and strong
Slashing: quick, twisted, and strong
Flicking: quick, twisted, and light
Floating: slow, twisted, and light
Dabbing: quick, straight, and light
Gliding: slow, straight, and light[4]

As children build interest in mime, they may discuss these movements and begin to visualize the potential of each. They may be led to discussions by suggestions such as the following:

1. You are a strong, proud soldier. Which movement do you use to portray a soldier? *(Punching)* Why? Show us how a soldier moves.
2. You are the queen of the ball. Show how a queen moves. Which movement did you use? *(Floating)* Why?

In the beginning the teacher should generally challenge the children to mime a character in a short-story sequence in the simplicity of the story-plays discussed earlier. An experience to be mimed should be familiar to the child so that she may draw on memory for the expressive movements she will use. Here are some suggestions for mime:

1. You are very tired. Climb up a long flight of stairs to your bedroom.
2. Set the table for dinner. Remember where the dishes are kept, the knives and forks, the food.
3. You are a mail carrier with a heavy bag of Christmas mail. It snowed last night and the street is very slippery. Make your way down the street and deliver the mail.
4. You are picking berries and putting them in the cardboard box you are holding. Suddenly you hear a strange sound behind you, and you turn to see what it is. At the same time, you drop the box and the berries fall to the ground. You try to save as many as you can.
5. It is Christmas time and you are walking down the street. All at once you come to a shop window which has a toy train that runs around a Christmas tree. You are fascinated by the train as it goes round and round. You are sorry to leave the window.

---

4. Gray and Percival, *Music, Movement and Mime*, p. 38.

As the children become more proficient in their control of movement, a greater variety of experiences may be mimed, including those in stories and poems and ones made up by the children themselves. Besides solo miming, a group may plan and present a mimed sequence for the rest of the class.

The following examples further suggest situations and procedures for teaching mime and movement for creative dramatic expression. These exercises progress through the steps of presentation of a challenge by the teacher, a discussion of the challenge by the children, the mime activity based on the challenge, and an evaluation and/or presentation in response to the challenge.

1. *Dancing with a robot.* The situation or challenge: Under your Christmas tree, you discover a windup robot doll. Excitedly you wind up the toy and watch as it begins to dance. You are so happy that you begin to dance with the doll. It slowly winds down and stops, and you put it back under the tree.

The teacher may ask questions such as the following to start the children thinking about the challenge:

How would you feel if you saw a large windup robot under your tree?
What body movements show that feeling?
What kind of movements do you think a robot doll makes?
How would you feel if your doll began to run down? Why?

Following this discussion the class may break into working units to plan and informally perform the movements. The teacher should move from one group to another to answer questions or to stimulate the planning with questions and ideas. After the children have had enough time to plan, the teacher brings the class together again to discuss the different ways in which the challenge was approached and the variety of actions that could be mimed. Then the groups may be invited—but never forced—to make their presentations. And those mimes that are presented should be respected as creative endeavors. Comments by both children and teacher should be directed toward the positive qualities of the total impression and of the specific movements.

2. *Patrolling the beat.* The challenge: You are a police officer patrolling your beat at night. You hear a noise in a store, and you walk over to find out what it could be. Then you discover that the back door is open. You creep into the store and spot what appears to be a burglar. You try to capture the burglar.

The teacher asks the children to work in pairs and plan and mime a sequence that tells something of the police officer/burglar meeting. The interaction may begin without any suggestions from the class, or the teacher may use questions such as the following to direct the thinking:

How would the police officer approach the burglar?
What may happen if the police officer were to chase after the burglar?
What movements would you use to show the police officer?
What movements would you use as the burglar?
Is it necessary to tell the whole story in your presentation? What part would you like to use? Why?

Once the partners begin working to plan their mime, the teacher should move about the room and act as a resource person, providing guidance or stimulation as needed. At the end of the group activity, the class may come together again to evaluate their presentation experiences through discussion.

3. *Little Red Riding Hood.* The challenge for this mime is in the story of Little Red Riding Hood. After sharing the story, the teacher may start the discussion by asking the following questions:

> If we were to plan a mime sequence for this story, what characters would we need to have?
>
> What movements would you use for the little girl? The wolf? Grandmother?

The children should work in groups of four or five to plan a presentation for this fairy tale. The teaching sequence for this challenge is similar to those described previously.

4. *Children's own stories.* This example is different from the previous ones in that children must create their own stories, and after working in small groups to plan movement sequences for sets of characters, all the children get together to coordinate their efforts into one mime presentation. The challenge and subsequent questions to stimulate discussion are as follows:

> We have made mime sequences using stories or experiences that we have heard or seen. Today we are going to compose a story of our own, and let's use some unusual characters as a beginning. Suppose we had a story that told about an adventure involving witches, fairies, and children. What do you think may happen in a story like this? What kinds of movements would show the witches? The fairies? The children?

The suggestions of the children should be used to create a plot. After a story line has been agreed on, the children should be arranged in three groups according to which one of the three character types interests them. The teacher should ask the children to plan a movement that tells about what their characters do in the story. This mime should eventually become a complete story, involving children in different movement sequences as related to the characters whom they are depicting.

Creativity in Dance-Drama

Dance-drama is an extension of movement and mime; it involves the expression of a story in the language of movement and is structured by musical accompaniment. In the elementary school, accompaniment for dance-drama may be provided by records that have colorful contrasts in rhythm, melody, and volume and therefore suggest a variety of moods and scenes to the ears of young listeners. Sometimes children prefer to plan their own accompaniment by using musical instruments or homemade substitutes. Often tapping a pot lid with a stick or shaking a tin can filled with beans is every bit as effective as playing drums, tambourines, or cymbals.

Some records, such as Moussorgsky's "Night on Bald Mountain," have a definite story line, which may be shared with the children before they listen to the music. In this particular story, witches meet with the devil on Bald Mountain on All Saints' Eve. The music powerfully portrays their activities and struggles. Suddenly the clock strikes and the spirits flee. The music becomes very soft and the listener experiences a musical interpretation of the breaking of dawn. Having heard the music, children should be encouraged to talk about words that describe the movements of the witches and the kinds of body movements they would use to depict them. While playing the record to structure their physical movement, the children use their bodies to express the struggles of the spirits as described in the music.

Other records, such as "La Mer" by Debussy, are more open to interpretation and therefore should be experienced in a different manner. The children listen to the music first and then make suggestions for possible story lines. The group decides which suggestion to use and then plans movement patterns to support their choice.

Sometimes a story or poem that is either read by the teacher or created by the children may be used as a story line for dance-drama. And the music could be planned and played by the children. Themes based on subjects that have emotional overtones, such as a season of the year, a color, a feeling, particularly lend themselves to the imaginative expression of ideas and feelings through movement and sound.

Tableau as Drama

A tableau is a scene depicted without motion or sound. It is a valuable dramatic experience for children as it requires concentration on body posture and facial expressions to communicate action and feeling. To be truly interesting a tableau should depict a dramatic incident. Children working in small groups may plan a tableau around a moment in history or literature: a Pilgrim carves the turkey at the first Thanksgiving, or Cinderella discovers that the glass slipper fits her foot. The use of simple costumes and stage props may add dimension to a scene planned by the children.

Groups may plan a series of tableaus to depict the highlights of a story. Using a narrator or a tape recorder to tell the story, the tableaus may be presented in sequence and become what is known as a "tableau play."

Dramatic Development Through Choral Speaking

In the early days of Greek drama, a speaking chorus was used to provide the audience with the background of the play or to relate certain events as the drama developed. Within the classroom setting a speech choir may be the focal point for the creative dramatic activities that the teacher plans or may be used in combination with movement or story-play. After some experimentation, exciting dramatic effects may be achieved by using variations in choral arrangements, sound accompaniment, or visuals to complement the spoken lines. As discussed later in the chapter, choral speaking provides a pleasurable interaction with poetry; aids in voice control; and as a group activity, it involves everyone in the class, thereby giving some children more confidence.

Choosing Selections for Choral Speaking

Selections for choral speaking may be either poetry of prose. In choosing poetry it is important to select themes or topics that are interesting and relevant to the children. A few years ago the author had the opportunity to use Eugene Field's "A Seein' Things at Night" with a group of nine-year-olds. Each time the poem was recited, the class members delighted in sharing their fears and concerns about darkness and night. Needless to say, they thoroughly enjoyed the content of the poem and their recitation of it.

As children build a background in choral speaking, they begin to appreciate the effects from different arrangements and interpretations, which are made possible by changing tone, expression, speed, and rhythm. It is important, then, that the selections chosen for development have this kind of potential. Two good poetry anthologies for choral speaking are suggested at the end of this chapter.

Children may wish to prepare a narrative selection from a book or one which they have written to accompany a tableau play, a story-play, or a series of pictures that they have mounted for viewing. Sometimes these selections may be taped for ready use or for variety in presentation.

Choral Arrangements that May Be Used

A unison speaking—the entire group speaking as a unit—is generally the most successful arrangement, particularly for beginners. It is important that everyone speaks together and that the voices blend together as one voice. In another type of arrangement the class is divided into two groups, with one group presenting a question or an appeal and the other the response. Usually the two groups are divided into contrasting light and heavy voices.

Many poems lend themselves to recitation by a combination of voices: solo and choir, several solo parts and choir response, or a number of groups to create contrasts in sound. The manner in which the selection is "orchestrated" should contribute to the message it contains.

Preparing a Choral-Speaking Selection

Depending on the age and reading ability of the children, the teacher may introduce a selection by reading it aloud, distributing copies of it for the children to read, or using a combination of the two methods. If the teacher reads the selection first, the children are being subjected to an interpretation. Thus, this method is not always the best procedure to follow, although it may be usable for teaching beginners or with a selection that may be difficult for the children to read. With young children the teacher may use some kind of visuals, such as flannel board materials, to help them understand and learn the poem.

After children have been introduced to the selection, they may decide how it should be recited. Questions such as the following may help stimulate ideas for manner of presentation:

What words are important in each line?
Does this line suggest sadness, anger?

Should this line be said in a loud or soft voice, fast or slow?
Can this poem be recited in parts?

As decisions are being made about the way the poem is to be presented, the children should try out their ideas, sometimes evaluating as they say the lines and other times hearing parts of the selection on the tape recorder. During the evaluation the selection needs to be read, repeated, and heard so frequently that it may possibly be committed to memory. Decisions also need to be made concerning the use of visuals, such as movement or mime and any sound or lighting effects, to accompany the voices.

Not all choral speaking needs to be shared with an audience; children often simply enjoy the process of production. On some occasions, however, they may wish to present their selection to another class, teachers from within the school, or their parents in order to share their creative efforts.

Extending Choral Speaking

As children's creative sensitivities are developed, some pupils may wish to share their favorite poems with other members of the class in a poetry-reading session. A theme for one of these readings may be "Halloween," "feelings," "winter," or some other topic of general interest. For this activity the children may group themselves in a casual seating arrangement. Some, or all of the students, may individually read a poem or series of poems that they have chosen and prepared. Sometimes copies of the poems to be read may be distributed, with the children following the lines while a reading takes place. However, it should be understood that no one reads ahead or turns pages unnecessarily while a classmate is reading.

Pupils who can play a guitar, harmonica, or some other instrument may provide pleasant accompaniment for poetry selections. Children may even devise homemade instruments to use in making sound effects to blend with the reader's voice.

Choral speaking may be combined with both music and movement. For this activity the class should be divided into groups of about ten pupils each, with every group given copies of the same poem or different ones for their interpretations. Each group plans a choral presentation, with part of the group reciting the selection, another part providing suitable movement, and the remainder of the group creating accompaniment with musical instruments or homemade sound effects.

Dramatic Development Through Informal Dramatization

Children have daily contact with many people—parents, neighbors, teachers. From the days of early childhood, children have noted differentiating characteristics in the people they have met and have enjoyed and learned from imitating them. As stated previously, this imitating for fun is the beginning of informal dramatization. In a creative dramatics program, informal dramatization may be planned to raise the performance of the children from a surface mirroring of others to a "crawling under the skin" of the characters by using appropriate movements and speech.

Objectives in Informal Dramatization

There are a number of objectives for developing children's abilities in dramatization, and some of these are common to all forms of creative dramatics:

1. To deepen children's reactions to conflict as met in literature and social studies and as encountered in their own lives
2. To develop the children's control of their speech and actions in order that they may better depict the intended character
3. To provide the children with opportunities for role playing as a problem-solving technique
4. To stimulate children's imaginations, which then will be reflected in their storytelling and creative writing

Informal Dramatization Without an Audience

Because the reader may be so accustomed to dramatics in which there is an audience and a group of performers, it may be difficult to envision a classroom dramatization in which all the children are players. Yet with careful structuring and plannning, generally in the same way as previously suggested, this type of dramatization can be enacted and can be an enjoyable and energy-releasing experience for children. The following guidelines may be used to get the action under way:

1. Provide precise description of the action to take place.
2. Allow only a short time for the action—about three minutes in most instances.
3. Keep evaluation positive and begin refining the dramatic expression only after the children are comfortable and receptive to suggestions from others.

Dramatizing selections from realistic and imaginative passages in literature, as well as events in history, places children in situations in which they must consider different points of view, conflicts, compromises, and the strengths and frailties of humankind. Many selections may be dramatized—as well as ideas provoked by any number of selections—but consider these three settings that come naturally from the study of Christopher Columbus.

1. What kind of person do you think Columbus must have been? What leads you to this impression? Why did many people think he had a crazy idea when he talked of reaching China by sailing west? Working in groups of three, pretend that one of you is Columbus, and you are trying to convince two of your friends to invest money in a venture to reach China by sailing into the setting sun. Your friends are firmly convinced that the world is flat.
2. The trip has been a long and perilous one, and many members of the ship's crew want to give up on the venture and return home. Working in

groups of four, plan a scene that may have taken place aboard ship as two sailors try to persuade two others to stage a mutiny.

3. Land is finally reached, but many members of the crew think that the voyage has been in vain since they have not reached China. Instead, the crew has landed in a country inhabited by a strange people. In small groups, act out a scene that may have taken place among the sailors as they discuss the situation.

In order to dramatize these scenes, the children need to discuss generally the historical conditions of the time. Reference materials should also be used to provide information. After the children have general knowledge of the conditions that faced the characters, they then try to project themselves into the time and place of the scene. After a dramatization of the scene, which should be kept fairly short, the pupils discuss the experiences they had during the role playing. The children may also discuss the effects of Columbus's decisions on the world in his time as well as on the world of today, along with ideas of what might have happened had he resolved his problems in a different way.

Children may also dramatize situations based on their own direct experiences. In this kind of dramatization they have an opportunity to look at their own lives through the eyes of other people. For example, by acting out a common situation such as children riding on a school bus, the pupils see how a number of children on the bus aggravate the driver by teasing other children. In dramatizing a particular situation, the teacher may simply wish to present the situation, without making specific reference to the problem. A situation like the following may be presented:

Bill, a boy in grade five, likes to tease the other children on the bus. The bus driver is becoming rather disturbed about it and is thinking of putting Bill off the bus.

The children may be grouped in fours and fives to act out several bus scenes related to the situation and to the solution of the problem.

CREATIVE DRAMATICS AS A TEACHING METHOD

Throughout this chapter consideration has been given to the value of creative dramatic activities in the elementary school and to the development of the related expression skills in children. It is important to remember, however, that dramatic expression should be thought of in the context of the total school program, and particularly it should be recognized as only one facet of the language arts.

As discussed in previous chapters—particularly Chapter 4—the elementary school program is based on communication. And children will often choose the dramatic mode to communicate their ideas and feelings if they are given opportunities for dramatic expression and have achieved the skills needed to do it effectively. Dramatics is also a way to learn. Attempting to experience how another person feels is a very real learning experience, one that is much less abstract than those provided by verbal, visual, and auditory symbols alone. Thus, for both the receptive and expressive acts in learning, dramatics is an instructional method that every teacher should use.

EXERCISES FOR THOUGHT AND ACTION

1. Describe ways other than those suggested in this chapter for using creative dramatics in the several areas of the curriculum.
2. Make a collection of poems that are suitable for choral speaking at a grade level of your choice. Categorize these as to their suitability for unison speaking, two-part, solo and choir, and so forth.
3. Select one of the references in the "Selected Readings" and prepare a report on it for the class.
4. Make some suggestions for mime, using experiences that are familiar to children.
5. Collect materials that can be used in a family center.
6. Evaluate the section "Values in Creative Dramatics." Are there other values? Do you agree that all the values listed belong there?

SELECTED READINGS

I. Books

Barton, Robert, et al. *Nobody in the Cast.* Toronto: Longmans, 1969. Even though this is a student handbook for the junior high level, the elementary school teacher will find it to be a valuable source book since it presents a philosophy of creative dramatics through suggested activities and materials that may readily be adapted for younger children.

Bruford, Rose. *Teaching Mime.* London: Methuen, 1964. This is particularly useful in suggesting ways in which mime can be used as a method for stimulating interest in many areas of study.

Courtney, Richard. *Teaching Drama.* London: Cassell, 1965. A short but comprehensive outline of various dramatic activities for all ages.

Edwards, G. N., ed. *Let's Enjoy Poetry, Kindergarten to Grade 3.* Toronto: J. M. Dent & Sons, 1957. This book contains a collection of poems suitable for young children, with suggestions for orchestrating the poems for choral presentation.

Edwards, Rosalind. *Let's Enjoy Poetry, Grades 4 to 6.* Toronto: J. M. Dent & Sons, 1961. A book containing a collection of poems suitable for children in the intermediate grades, with suggestions for orchestrating the poems for choral presentation.

Gray, Vera, and Percival, Rachel. *Music, Movement and Mime for Children.* Oxford: Oxford University Press, 1962. This is a concise, little book describing the interrelationships among movement, music, and mime. It contains many practical suggestions for activities and materials for use with primary-age children.

Hodgson, John, and Richards, Ernest. *Improvisation: Discovery and Creativity in Drama.* London: Methuen, 1966. This book discusses the nature and purpose of improvisation and interprets the philosophy presented in many detailed exercises and related activities.

Slade, Peter. *An Introduction to Child Drama.* London: University of London Press, 1958. This is a condensed version of the author's theory of child drama as it relates to education and behavior, with some practical suggestions for the teacher.

Wall, L.V., et al., eds. *The Puppet Book: A Practical Guide to Puppetry in Schools, Training Colleges and Clubs.* 2nd ed. London: Faber & Faber, 1965. A complete, practical, and well-illustrated guide to making and using all kinds of puppets.

Way, Brian. *Development Through Drama.* London: Longmans, 1967. The author's many years of working in drama with young people are crystalized in this useful book on the theory and practice of creative drama.

II. Other Aids

Creative Drama. Stacey Publication, 1 Hawthorndene Rd., Hayes, Bromley, Kent, England. This publication is edited by people directly involved in creative drama.

Educational Theatre Journal. American Educational Theatre Association, John F. Kennedy Center, 726 Jackson Pl., N.W., Washington, D.C. 20566. This official publication of the American Educational Theatre Association contains reviews, research, and surveys of work being done at all levels of education. It is published quarterly and is available at reduced rates for association members.

Theatre News. American Educational Theatre Association, John F. Kennedy Center, 726 Jackson Pl., N.W., Washington, D.C. 20566. This monthly newsletter is available to members of the association.

Any consideration of elementary school curriculums and methods must give prominence to reading. Attempting to discuss in one chapter the many issues and problems seemingly inherent in reading instruction and to make suggestions about what should be taught and when and how is a herculean task. Yet Professor Ross, in a most appealing, personal way, has handled this challenge remarkably well.

In this chapter, the author stresses the relationship of reading to all other areas of the curriculum. Particular attention is given to such program aspects as storytelling, dramatics, and children's literature. The concern for individualizing instruction—a consideration in preceding chapters—is discussed here also.

Previous chapters discussed how language is learned, issues related to dialects and grammar, and how children's use of language is facilitated in such activities as drama, choral speech, reporting, and conversations. The importance of language facility to learning to read receives special treatment, including comments on the beneficial effects of acceptance of each child's language on the motivation to read.

W.T.P.

Reading Instruction
A Total Curriculum Focus

Ramon Royal Ross

6

Reading has been and continues to be the instructional concern receiving the greatest attention in school programs. Reading is a common topic of politicians, parents, business executives, physicians, and newspaper columnists. If children are taught to read, parents are pleased; school boards bask in reflected glory; teachers walk the streets of the community with pride; and pupils hug books to themselves with affection.

Much is known about reading, but much remains veiled. In this chapter a number of aspects of reading will be discussed, including issues in defining it, characteristics that help a child become a reader, the curriculum of reading, and techniques and approaches for developing competent readers.

WHAT IS READING?

"Reading is interpreting visual experiences." If one accepts this popular definition, perhaps ninety percent of the children in America can "read" before they enter kindergarten. Should you doubt this, borrow a four-year-old for an afternoon stroll through your community. Walk him past a Shell station, a McDonald's restaurant, and a Tastee Freeze. Stop at the traffic light and ask him to tell you when to walk. Visit a grocery store and let him point out which carton holds milk and which holds buttermilk. Ask him to show you Tootsie Rolls, Hershey bars, Cracker Jacks, Coca-Cola, Crest, or Fritos. Flick on the television and observe the number of commercials and program introductions that he recognizes.

Such reading is related to the "organic" words that Sylvia Ashton Warner describes in her book, *Teacher*.[1] Why the child knows these words is patent——they are significant in his domain. They are words that touch on aspects of his life—the family car, food and drink, pleasure and fulfillment, wishes he may be making for the days to come. Reading of this sort begins by making visual discriminations. Very early in life, children begin to make such distinctions between visually seen objects. The child can pick out his mother when she is with several other women her age and general size and shape. Children learn to "read" colors, clothing, familiar streets and houses, the family dog and cat. These discriminations become increasingly refined as children mature, until they learn that SHELL is somehow related to the fuel that makes the car move and that KENTUCKY FRIED CHICKEN goes with picnics and snacks.

"Reading is knowing all the words," Carla, a five-year-old kindergartner, said one morning when the class was talking about reading. Carla's view is shared by persons who think of the reading process as one of decoding printed symbols. According to this theory, the reader learns to begin at the left-hand side of a page of print and works his way through word after word by finding the voiced or unvoiced oral equivalent of the words and saying them to herself. This process is viewed as a precise and logical skill. Printed words stand for spoken words, and the reader's task is to unlock the code of the written symbols by letter identification, the general configuration of the word, and knowledge of sound-symbol patterns and of such structural elements as root words, prefixes, and suffixes.

Our culture assigns a high value to reading. Parents of beginning school children consistently rank reading as the top learning priority for their children. And young children—first and second graders—echo that concern. "I want to learn to read," children respond when asked what they want most out of school.[2]

Many creative persons have placed great significance on their first encounters with books and have written recollections of their keen desire to learn to read. Jean-Paul Sartre, in *The Words*, tells how he listened to his grandfather read and then he read the same book to himself, mastering the code, until those "little dried herbals," as he called the words, were his.[3] Model setting—adults the child admires are observed reading—exerts a powerful influence on the young child. If children see father, mother, a big brother or sister, or their teacher reading, then they begin to view reading as a desirable act.

---

1. Sylvia Ashton Warner, *Teacher* (New York: Simon & Schuster, 1963).
2. From interviews conducted by the author with parents and children at Greg Rogers School, Chula Vista, California, Fall 1971.
3. Jean-Paul Sartre, *The Words* (New York: Fawcett World, 1964), p. 28.

"Reading is a 'psycholinguistic guessing game.'"[4] According to Kenneth Goodman, reading—printed page reading—is far from being the precise and exacting skill envisioned by those who describe reading as the decoding of words. Rather, Goodman tends to think of reading as the interaction of thought and language. According to him, efficient reading is not the result of knowing (saying) every single word; it is the skill of selecting cues necessary to produce accurate guesses. Anticipating, testing out, trying to "make sense," using what has been read before, drawing on personal experiences to assist in the bringing of meaning to the page—these are the processes that a skillful reader goes through. Thus while readers may err in specific words read, as long as they gather in the gist of the author's intent, success is theirs.

Certainly it is true that the years of language buildup come to the aid of readers. They may not be able to articulate the difference between a noun and a verb, but they do sense, almost intuitively, when a sentence is complete and when it is garbled nonsense. Such sensing is not in fact intuitive; rather, it is the result of language learning that is so thorough as to require little conscious thought.

Lisa, aged six, reads for her teacher. "Little . . . pig . . . stas . . . her." She looks up. "That doesn't make sense," she comments. And, indeed, she's quite right. It doesn't.

"Try again," the teacher urges. "See if you can get it to make sense."

Lisa studies the words. "Little . . . pig . . . stays . . . here." "Now I get it," she says. "That sounds better."

Lisa exemplifies the spirit of the successful reader. She knows that books contain words and that the words link together to form ideas as expressed within the conventions of language. She approaches reading by looking for meaning and tests out what she reads by comparing it with what she believes the words ought to say. Had she read—or misread—"Little pig stops here," Lisa would no doubt have accepted her misreading, since the substitution is a sensible one and fits within the context of what had preceded that sentence.

While the exact process involved in reading is not certain, the steps may go something like this:

1. The child scans along a line of print, eyes moving from left to right, line by line, down the page.
2. In this movement, there are frequent fixations, with some print in focus and some only peripherally so.
3. In the focus field, the reader picks up graphic cues while being guided by constraints set up through prior choices, language knowledge, and word identification tactics that she has developed.
4. The reader forms a perceptual image by using the graphic cues and other cues she expects to find.
5. Now the reader tests the cues against her memory to see if they contain meaning for her. She may look again to test that meaning.

---

4. Kenneth S. Goodman, "Reading: A Psycholinguistic Guessing Game," in *Readings on Reading,* eds. Albert Harris and Edward Sipay (New York: David McKay Co., 1972), p. 54.

6. At this point the reader may make a tentative guess that is consistent with the cues she has received. Semantic analysis helps her decode at this point. ("Little pig stas her.")
7. If no guess is possible, she looks again to see if she can gather more cues.
8. If the reader is able to decode, she tests her guess for semantic and grammatical acceptability in the context developed by prior choices and decoding.
9. If the tentative choice is not acceptable semantically or syntactically ("Little pig stas her. . . . That doesn't make sense."), the reader regresses, scanning from left to right along the line, then back again, looking for a point at which she can get back on the track of meaning.
10. If she accepts the choice, then meaning is assimilated with prior meaning; and using the information now available, she continues to read, making guesses concerning input that lies ahead.
11. The cycle continues.[5]

As indicated previously, there is no certainty as to the exactness of this model. There does appear to be evidence from a variety of sources that substantiates the process, however. Consider the problems of meaning that occur with a single word—cactus, for example. A reader, encountering that word, may have had many different experiences with cactus, ranging from seeing it in the desert lands of Baja California to viewing it in travelogues on television to examining a tiny, potted cactus in a nursery to standing in the shade of a saguaro giant in Arizona. In reading the word cactus, then, the reader derives the meaning of the word from his own varied experiences with the object.

Furthermore, words are rarely used in isolation. Consider the following:
1. "Mother, may we buy this cactus plant? It only costs a dollar."
2. Old Cactus Pete swaggered out to the corral and mounted his bronco.
3. The organ-pipe cactus is capable of storing more than eight gallons of water in its thick-walled reservoir.

The reader, encountering the word cactus in each of these sentences, has context to deal with. Furthermore, in each sentence, the need to know the word cactus varies. In the first sentence, "May we buy this . . . plant?" makes sense, even without the word cactus. For in the first sentence, cactus simply helps illuminate the full meaning of the sentence. Nor does "Old . . . Pete swaggered. . . ." need the word cactus. Pete got on his horse. That's all the reader needs to know. Cactus adds little more than color to the sentence. But in the third sentence, not knowing the word cactus throws away the meaning of the rest of the sentence. Cactus is critical to meaning in that statement.

So, as the reader moves through sentences imbedded in large chunks of textual material, he picks cues, tests them out, and relates them to his experience. In the process, he misses some, gets close with others, makes guesses, accepts or rejects those guesses, and fits in the guesses with what comes next. He continues this perceptual, physiological process throughout the material.

---

5. Adapted from a model proposed by Kenneth Goodman, "Reading," p. 62.

What is reading? In the preceding discussion, reading has been examined in terms of its social, experiential, language, perceptual, and physiological components. It may be that no single definition for reading will suffice. What the young child thinks of as reading is pretty much a word-calling game—a process of decoding printed symbols. Once reading gets beyond that initial stage, the act becomes a meaning-getting, meaning-giving process, one which involves the whole child—her backbround of experiences, the memories banked in her mind, her perceptual apparatus, and her abilities to take bits of information and make guesses from them and to continually add data to her memory bank as she moves further and further into the text.

VP, AP, LofC; The will toR.
Prediction & K

READING READINESS

It may be that the beginning reader has as his most important single task the cracking of the code—the realization that printed words represent ideas and the ability to identify letters and words so that the process of reading can get under way. The preparation for that task has come to be known as "reading readiness." At least since the 1920s, when the measurement and testing movement first got under way, first grade teachers have tried to answer the question: "Is the child ready?" Some prerequisites for reading are common to all learning: good health, family support, security, emotional stability, mental alertness. There are, however, specific factors that are related more directly to success in reading.

Visual Perception

As suggested earlier, it is likely that probably ninety percent of the children in America know how to read. They know such words—in context—as *Shell*, *McDonald's*, *Texaco*, and *milk*. Most children, using the clues they receive from logos, specific settings, and color combinations, recognize these words in association with the service stations or the restaurant or a carton. But if these words——thought to be so familiar—are typed or printed on a card, chances are that most children will not recognize them.

Young readers may not be able to make the transition from one type of print to another. They know SHELL but may not know "shell" or *shell*. To talk about what a child does not know, however, is quibbling, in light of all that he does know. That he is able to distinguish between *Texaco* and *Shell* or between *Jack in the Box* and *McDonald's* indicates that his visual and perceptual apparatus is intact and that he has a basic sense of what symbols are, what they do in giving meaning to what he sees.

Many visual discriminations are challenging even for an adult. Paul McKee has illustrated this by presenting reading material using graphic forms that are different from ones we know.[6] Using these symbols the material begins with

6. Paul McKee, *A Primer for Parents* (Boston: Houghton Mifflin Co., 1971).

simple words and then progresses to an increasing number of words on the page. The adult who attempts to learn these symbols may sense the frustration of the beginning reader.

Consider the following, patterned after McKee's work:

a = ⟊
e = ⟋
i = ⊢
g = ⟊
p = ⟖
s = ∅

Now read these words:

∅ ⊢ ⟖

⟊ ⟊ ∅

∅ ⟊ ⟊

⟊ ⟊∅∅

Try this sentence:

⊢ ∅⟊⟊ ⟊ ⟖⊢⟊.

What procedures does one use to read this sentence? Most adults look for something distinctive in the shape of the symbol—the circle of the symbol representing s or the horizontal bar representing i. The difference between some shapes is, of course, confusing. ⟊ and ⟋ are pretty much alike, varying only in direction. The same is true with the letters b and d in the alphabet that our children learn. Some persons verbalize to remember a shape. "The p (⟖) looks like an anchor," they may say. And in reading the sample sentence, an adult enjoys several advantages over the beginning reader. The adult knows that reading goes from left to right, that the spaces separate words, and that the dot signifies the end of the sentence.

Undoubtedly, reading requires visual discrimination. Readiness tests assess that ability. Thomas C. Barrett analyzed the *Gates Reading Readiness Tests*, the *Harrison Stroud Reading Readiness Profile*, the *Lee-Clark Reading Readiness Test*, the *Metropolitan Readiness Test*, and the *Murphy-Durrell Diagnostic Reading Readiness Tests* and found that visual discrimination of words was measured in all but one of these tests.[7] Barrett also reported that the more the sections on visual

---

7. Thomas C. Barrett, "The Relationship Between Measures of Prereading Visual Discrimination and First Grade Reading Achievement: A Review of the Literature," *Reading Research Quarterly* 1 (Fall 1965): 51-76.

discrimination tasks in the tests resemble actual reading, the better they will be in predicting reading success.

However, the research investigating the effect of visual training as a prelude to reading points to the apparent futility of much of that training in enhancing reading achievement. Helen M. Robinson, in summarizing the research on visual perceptual training, concluded that while most of the programs appear to benefit specific perceptual performance, there is often too little carry-over into reading itself.[8] It does appear that the more directly visual training is related to reading, the more effective it is. Work with words and letters, for example, is more helpful to the young reader than equivalent amounts of time spent in learning to recognize, match, or reproduce assorted shapes or designs.[9]

Auditory Perception

Even before coming to school, children are skilled in perceiving and distinguishing among sounds. They are able to tell the difference between sounds that may seem quite similar: the ringing of the telephone and the ringing of the doorbell; the hum of the vacuum cleaner and the hum of the washing machine. And, too, they differentiate between words that are similar in sound formation: *big* and *pig*; *little* and *letter*. The child's ability to produce sounds may be not fully complete, so that he may say *free* for *three*, or *aminals* for *animals*, but this does not necessarily mean that he does not *hear* the differences between those words. Reading readiness programs often presume that children do not perceive the differences in sounds of similar sounding words and so will have difficulty distinguishing between printed symbols of such words. Research on the significance of auditory discrimination has been summarized by Robert Dykstra.[10] He reported that, in general, correlations between the measures of auditory discrimination and first-grade reading achievement scores are low to moderate.

Certainly if some children do have difficulty with auditory discrimination, the school day abounds with opportunities to sharpen their awareness of sounds. Children, young children, love words—words like *squishy*, *gooey*, *icky*, *scrumdubulous*, *mulligawumpers*, *Walla Walla Wash*—and refrains and rhymes:

> And the father pulled;
> And the mother pulled;
> And the daughter with the new blue shoes pulled. . . .

They like to sing "Comin' Round the Mountain," "Kum Bai Yah," "He's Got the Whole World in His Hand." They enjoy choral speaking, and one of the best opportunities to help them hear differences in pitch, intonation, and inflection is echo reading, in which the teacher says a line, with the children repeating it by matching the teacher's voice pattern.

---

8. Helen M. Robinson, "Perceptual Training—Does It Result in Reading Improvement?" in *Some Persistent Questions on Beginning Reading*, ed. Robert C. Aukerman (Newark, Del.: International Reading Association, 1972), pp. 135-50.

9. Margaret LaPray and Ramon Ross, "Visual Perception and Beginning Reading" (Paper delivered at California Education Research Association Meeting, Spring 1964).

10. Robert Dykstra, "Auditory Discrimination Abilities and Reading Achievement," *Reading Research Quarterly* 1 (Spring 1966): 5-34.

The classroom teacher may use a portable cassette tape recorder to collect sounds from the environment and play them back in the classroom so that children can become interested in listening for fine differences among sounds. One kindergarten teacher collected a series of taped bits from around her community—the sounds of the surf on the beach, a rainstorm, street traffic, and the like. She also recorded sounds from around the school—the cafeteria, the playground, the kitchen. She taped birds singing, dogs barking, and vacuum cleaners running. All these sounds were then spliced into a single tape, with intervals of silence separating them. Children listened to the tape and described what they heard. Their teacher encouraged them to compare sounds in terms of loud or soft, high or low. But she also directed them to develop their own descriptions. "It sounds kind of crackly, like when Mamma cooks meats," one child said of the rainstorm. Another said, "I think of paper crunching up." This same teacher engaged her class in a game in which one child would speak while the others closed their eyes and listened. They then tried to identify the speaker. Games were played, repeating phrases and sentences. Out of these and related experiences the children developed a new appreciation for the messages they could acquire through their auditory senses.

The Language of Children

It has been commonplace for early-childhood education specialists to act as if children possess little or few language skills when they come to school. But just the opposite is true. Five- and six-year-olds speak in beautiful and complex patterns. In a kindergarten, on a rainy morning after a police officer had visited the classroom, Bobby painted a picture and dictated the following story:

> Officer Smith is in his paddy wagon.
> He chases the bad guys.
> His siren is blowing, wooooooooooooooo.

And that's stilted compared to the language Bobby showed in regular classroom activities and on the playground.

This language fluency is not limited to white, middle-class children. William Labov explored the notion that children from the lower class or from minority groups use inferior speech or have language deficiencies.[11] In his judgment, based on analyses of interviews with such children, the apparent "differences" in their language are related to the interviewer (or teacher); that is, problems may arise if the interviewer is from another culture, speaks a dialect different from that used by these children, or represents an authority figure. But who among us has not experienced difficulty in understanding others? For example, when humanists and scientists talk, when we are in another culture, or even when we sit next to a pompous stranger at a stilted dinner party, understanding may be impossible.[12]

11.   William Labov, "Academic Ignorance and Black Intelligence," *Atlantic*, June 1972.
12.   Much the same point regarding language is made by Yetta Goodman in her description of language patterns among black children in Detroit. On November 2, 1972, Goodman, addressing the California Reading Association Meeting, Anaheim, California, stated that we tend to value certain forms of American English (a Bostonian accent, for example) much more than others. Thus we would never consider correcting the Bostonian's "peculiar" accent. And yet we don't think twice about pointing out other, equally established, dialectically different speech patterns.

Rather than acting as if the child were a linguistically deficient individual, the teacher would do better to accept the child's speech and learn to appreciate its richness and variety. The teacher may also learn the child's language and find reading matter that comes close to the child's awareness and experiences. One way in which this may be done is by using language experience reading and writing activities. Illustrations of this technique will be given later.

The Will To Read

An aspect of reading readiness seldom discussed is the entire issue of wanting to learn. Learning to read requires that the child be able to attend to instruction. Sean, as bright a six-year-old as one could imagine, spends as much of each day as possible wrestling with classmates. For Sean, reading at this time holds no promise. He remains much more interested in large muscle, physical activities. Why do Sean and many other children demonstrate excessive activity? There appear to be many reasons. One physical cause may be "minimal brain dysfunctioning," a label physicians often apply to the child who is "explosive," labile, distractable, impulsive, and relatively unresponsive to the usual teacher tactics of reward and punishment. A nonphysical cause of excessive activity may lie in the child's home environment. A child, growning up with low parental expectations, then faced suddenly with the demands of the classroom—conformity, sitting still, attending to a task demanding fine focus of attention—has a long way to go before he may be expected to enter into something as intellectually demanding as reading.

But for some children, the home environment favorably influences the young reader's will to read by the modeling behavior it provides. The child who sees her family engaged in reading comes to school wanting to read. That keen desire goes far in making reading possible for her.

Home is the place where the beginning reader may get his first taste of the specifics of reading. Jeanne Chall reviewed the studies relating knowledge of letters and beginning reading, and she concluded that the child's ability to identify letters by name in kindergarten or the beginning of the first grade was an important predictor of success—a higher indicator, for that matter, than mental ability or other tests of language ability and verbal ability.[13]

Where does the child learn letters? In many instances, he learns from caring family members—father, mother, and older brother or sister. So the home environment, and the concern demonstrated by the child's family, influences not only the attitudes the child brings to school, but specific information, as well.

Predicting Reading Readiness

Albert J. Harris, discussing reading readiness measures, concluded that current reading readiness tests generally include three or more of the following types of measures and activities:

---

13. Jeanne Chall, *Learning To Read: The Great Debate* (New York: McGraw-Hill, 1967), pp. 141-49.

1. Visual perception, including the matching of pictures, geometrical forms, letters, and words
2. Verbal comprehension of words and concepts, sentence comprehension, and the ability to follow directions
3. Auditory perception, including recognizing whether words are the same or different, recognizing rhyming sounds, and finding words with similar initial consonant sounds
4. Identification of letters of the alphabet and digits
5. Sample lessons, in which a small number of words are taught in a specified length of time, followed by checking the ability to recognize the same words
6. Rating scales for use by teachers in evaluating the children on characteristics that are not tested in the objective subtests
7. Drawing or copying an illustration[14]

Each of these items has been found to have some relevance to the total picture of reading readiness. Published tests, such as the *Lee Clark Reading Readiness Test* and the *Metropolitan Readiness Tests* assess such abilities as found in this list. However, it is scarcely fair to conclude that the child needs all these abilities if he is to read.

For too long we have been asking the question: Is the child ready? Such a question focuses on the child and implies that the curriculum is an inflexible and unbending Procrustean bed into which he must fit.

Another way of looking at readiness is to ask: how can the teacher plan instruction so that more children will be ready? Whether or not a child is successful in learning to read appears to depend to a large extent on the kind and quality of instruction that is offered. The child who is not ready for one kind of instruction may be ready for another. Delores Durkin points out that there are some reading materials and methods that a child with a mental age of five can master with reasonable ease, and there are others which would give a child with a mental age of seven difficulty.[15] Much this same point was made by Lillian Orme, who investigated the effects of adjusting beginning instruction to the needs of children entering first grade.[16] She developed methods and materials for an experimental group of first-graders. The project included reading readiness books; preparatory books; and supplementary materials, such as picture cards and phonics cards. Interest centers in the experimental room were arranged to give the children experience in free reading, painting, dramatic play, and working with science and mathematics materials. Teachers of children in two control groups proceeded with their reading instruction in as conventional manner as possible.

At the end of the first year, all the children were tested, and the scores showed that the experimental group was two months ahead of the first control

---

14. Albert J. Harris, "Evaluating Reading Readiness Tests," in *Problem Areas in Reading—Some Observations and Recommendations,* ed. Coleman Morrison (New York: Oxford University Press, 1965), p. 11.

15. Delores Durkin, "What Does Research Say About the Time To Begin Reading Instruction?" *Journal of Educational Research,* October 1970, pp. 52-56.

16. Lillian Orme, "Building Readiness for Reading in First Grade Children Through Special Instruction," *National Elementary Principal* 35 (September 1955): 43-46.

group and three months ahead of the second control group. By the end of the second year, although no further experimental work had been done, children in the experimental group maintained superiority in all areas of the tests, while those children identified in readiness testing as being "poor risks" but who had received no adjusted program of instruction continued to do badly in reading. Orme concluded that rather than retain the child with low readiness scores or push him ahead in spite of lack of success, the teacher would do better to adjust methods and materials to meet individual needs.

THE READING CURRICULUM

Thus far the nature of reading and what goes into getting ready for reading have been discussed. Now, before examining teaching/learning procedures, a look at what constitutes the reading curriculum is necessary. If one thinks of a curriculum as the content within textbooks, then there is no such thing as a generalized reading curriculum. True, basal reading series tend to have much in common; they have preprimers and readiness books, first and second grade readers, and books for older children. They have workbooks and exercises to accompany the basal books and teachers' manuals to help the teacher use the materials more effectively. They may, in part, even be similar in content: family situations, animal stories, some informational articles and accounts, a balance of poetry and fiction, and both serious and light literature. But not all schools use basal readers and even within basal readers, one does not study a particular subject at a particular time. In a fifth grade social studies class in California, children may be studying Mexico, Canada, and Central America. In a fifth grade reading class, however, it is difficult, if not impossible, to predict what the children will be studying. They may be reading—or at least some of them may be reading—from a fifth grade reader, and hopefully, the reader will serve as a springboard into new insights about themselves and their world. But what they are learning—what the teacher is concerned with teaching—are reading skills, and it is these skills that come closest to being the reading curriculum.

What are the skills of reading? A scope and sequence chart of reading skills generally accompanies a basal reader series. While these charts may vary from series to series, they tend to include the following: visual and auditory perception skills, word language structure knowledge, study skills, and critical and appreciative skills. In the beginning grades, major emphasis is on auditory and visual structures; in the later grades, more time is spend on comprehension, study skills, and critical and appreciative reading.

To illustrate, Chart 6.1 lists statements that may be encountered in a first grade reading curriculum.

Chart 6.1. Reading Curriculum Statements (First Grade)

Language structure
  1. Listen to and complete sentences.
  2. Dictate stories to teacher.

    3. Arrange known words into sentences.
    4. Listen to recordings of stories.

Word structure
    1. Work with identification of letter shapes and names by matching, saying, and reproducing.
    2. Develop awareness of consistent letter clusters, such as *-it, -un, -at, -er.*
    3. Develop basic service vocabulary.

Visual perception
    1. Trace letters, gradually eliminating parts so that the child can use minimal clues, such as dots, to write letters.
    2. Identify relationships between capital and small letters.
    3. Match letters and words that are the same, except for size.

Auditory perception
    1. Supply rhyming words.
    2. Recognize words that begin with the same sound.
    3. Differentiate between singular and plural forms.

Note: These statements were formulated by the author in developing a basal reader series.

In the intermediate grades, curricular statements are directed more toward the use of reading as a tool for learning, as evidenced in Chart 6.2.

Chart 6.2. Reading Curriculum Statements (Intermediate Grades)

Language structure
    1. Explore formal and informal language patterns, noting the style used by an author.
    2. Explore changes in meaning when word shift occurs.

Study skills
    1. Use the encyclopedia and other reference tools to compare information.
    2. Work with map and graph reading skills.
    3. Analyze editorials and compare them with news reports.
    4. Develop scanning and surveying skills.

Critical and appreciative skills
    1. Develop awareness of cliché and stereotype.
    2. Analyze various sentence styles and note author's particular use of sentences to develop writing style.

Note: These statements were formulated by the author in developing a basal reader series.

Though these curricular statements were selected at random, two major aspects of the reading process run through them. First, there is the aspect of reading instruction that consists essentially of decoding. Letter and word identification, the acquiring of a sight vocabulary, the application of phonemic and structural knowledge in correctly unlocking an unknown word—all of these fit under the decoding category.

Paralleling the decoding strand of reading is comprehension. The word *comprehension* refers, broadly, to one's ability to understand, to grasp meanings, to relate to. When an individual comprehends written material, the person draws literal, interpretative, and critical meanings from it. As a result of reading, the child who comprehends demonstrates behaviors like the ones listed below:

1. Answers factual questions relating to information
2. Supplies detail when questioned
3. Relates without assistance the account read
4. Differentiates between main ideas and supportive detail
5. Follows directions
6. Relates illustrative materials to the point they illustrate
7. Relates ideas expressed by different authors
8. Differentiates between connotative and denotative use of words
9. Describes the mood or tone of the writing
10. Interprets the author's purpose
11. Identifies figurative language, symbolism, and other artistic use of language and relates them to the author's purpose

Comprehension development needs to proceed apace with decoding. This notion has been generally accepted by persons developing materials for beginning readers, and it accounts for the concern for questioning that precedes and follows reading in most classrooms. In the list of behaviors just identified, clearly some comprehension activities are easier than others. In the first grade, Karen reads her story, and the teacher asks questions, such as: "What did Father do when he saw the ball rolling out of the yard?" Karen answers the question, and the teacher may move on to another question or search for detail, asking Karen to explain what certain phrases mean.

In Kenneth's sixth grade class, the discussion may center around the use of particular words Scott O'Dell has used in *Island of the Blue Dolphins* to convey the mood of a primitive, unschooled girl telling her life story.[17] An intellectual and informational span exists between those two activities, since for Kenneth to discuss with any sensitivity word choice and author style, he needs first of all to be able to do automatically what Karen is learning—that is, the specific, factual reporting of what has been read.

Later in this chapter, sections concerning strategies for the teaching of reading will give specific examples of teaching both decoding and comprehension.

MATERIALS FOR READING INSTRUCTION

From the days when the hornbook constituted the sole device for reading instruction in a classroom, our society has moved to a point at which there exists an overwhelming choice of books, filmstrips, programmed materials, and kits to

---

17. Scott O'Dell, *Island of the Blue Dolphins* (Boston: Houghton Mifflin Co., 1960).

use in teaching reading. The teacher, examining those materials and trying to decide which will best serve the instructional needs of the children, faces complicated decisions. Should he use a basal reader, with its sequential development, wide and varied choice of reading selections, and teacher's guide? Or should he choose the programmed texts, with their high level of pupil involvement and their attractive gadgetry? What about individualized instruction, with its reliance on the pupil's self-selection of trade books. Or should he use experiential reading, involving the printed word in all its faces as it is encountered in the newspaper and on television, street signs, and billboards?

No single program works for all children. There are, however, aspects to different programs that may make them appealing to certain teachers and their pupils. In the next few pages the major types of reading programs presently employed are described, along with examples of their use.

Basal Reader Services

While it is true that no single approach to reading is effective for use with all children nor satisfactory to all teachers, it has been well demonstrated that a reading program utilizing a well-organized, systematic skills program is generally more effective in helping children learn to read than a casual and unsystematic program.[18] This is a major reason for many schools using a basal reading program and making the series of children's books and teacher materials the core of the reading program.

Most basal reader programs contain some form of readiness materials. These generally are directed at helping the child learn left to right sequencing, letter recognition, initial sound identification, sequence in a story, concepts such as singular and plural, and a few basic words that will be used in the preprimers of the series. Children have an opportunity to follow directions and complete tasks related to reading. They gain experience in writing and forming words. One activity that can be used for this type of learning is found in many of the newer readiness materials. They involve the child in completing partially written letters and then writing the letters in the spaces provided. Increasingly, readiness books are moving away from such activities as the matching of pictures of objects and are concerned with the real stuff of reading—words, letter sounds, and language. Children are no longer being asked to find the ball that looks like another ball on the far left of the page or to spot the house with no chimney among houses with chimneys. Such activities help children learn to locate detail in pictures, but they are not particularly related to reading.[19]

By the time a child completes the readiness book, she probably knows most of the letters of the alphabet and can write her name. She knows a few words that have been taught to her as sight words: *Mom, school, I, can, go*. She has had experience with stories told by herself and others and has retold stories and

---

18. Guy L. Bond and Robert Dykstra, *The Cooperative Research Program in First Grade Instruction*. (Washington, D.C.: U.S. Department of Health, Education, and Welfare, February, 1967).

19.   Barrett, "The Relationship Between Measures."

arranged pictures in sequence. She knows that words—written words—are discrete units and must be separated from one another and that writing moves from left to right across the page. She has begun to be aware of the sounds of words. Listening to stories as the teacher reads, she knows that books contain ideas, recipes, laughter.

She is ready for a book of her own. For many children, that first book is the soft-bound preprimer of a basal reader series. It contains perhaps twenty-five to thirty different words, which are utilized in a number of sentences. The child gets an opportunity to read a word again and again in a variety of contexts. There are instructions for the teacher so that he may provide help in word learning and reading.

Beyond the primary books, basal readers are usually anthologies, with selections drawn from a wide variety of sources in various literary forms. Often these materials are based on themes or generalizations. They may contain stories, plays, poems, and essays dealing with space exploration, for example. Another theme used may be interpersonal relationships.

As to amounts of material, a basal series will generally consist of a readiness book, three soft-bound primers, and a hardback book at the first grade level; two hardback books at each of the second and third grade levels; and a single hardback book at each level from the fourth grade through the eighth. In each successive book, a limited number of new words are introduced. While the books make use of the work of many well-known children's authors, there may be some editing so that there is a progression of difficulty in the stories as the books advance in grade level. The literary quality of many basal readers is high; a glance through the table of contents of a typical fourth-grade-reader may reveal the names of such outstanding writers as Eve Merriam, Scott O'Dell, Elizabeth Yates, Astrid Lindgren, Carl Sandburg, John Ciardi, and Marguerite Henry.[20]

Accompanying the children's books are the teacher's manuals, with their suggestions for teaching decoding, language skills, and comprehension. The manuals give numerous suggestions for enrichment, including the use of recordings, filmstrips, films, and related books and articles as well as suggestions for projects as based on the stories. Many basal reader series also provide test materials, which the classroom teacher may use to help determine strengths and deficiencies in the reading skills of the pupils.

Critics of basal readers have faulted them for the insipid quality of their writing, the limited and repetitious vocabulary, the hidden lessons regarding values, and the prescriptiveness of suggestions for the teacher. There has been truth in some of these criticisms, and this has resulted in better programs in newer series. However, a limited number of words in the first reading experiences, for example, can be very encouraging to the young child, as he finds that he can read rather easily. But these words should be used imaginatively, so that the child remains interested and challenged. Theodor Geisel, in such simple Dr. Seuss books as *Hop on Pop*, shows how creatively a few words may be arranged and

---

20. Leo Fay and Paul S. Anderson, *Young America Basic Reading Program*, Level 12 (Chicago: Lyons & Carnahan, 1972).

rearranged.[21] Bill Martin's *Instant Readers* provide the young child with delightful sentences that he can learn by listening to someone else read and can then read for himself.[22]

Characters in primary basal readers have tended to be stereotyped. The father who arrives home from a hard day's work but is never too tired to play with the children; the mother whose apparent mission in life is to cook and bake in her spic-and-span kitchen, to sew, and to entertain children; the beautiful grandparents who are snug on their farm, with its cows and chickens and pigs and growing crops—these are the materials of a 1930s movie but are not closely related to what children of today know or understand. On the other hand, with the diversity of culture in America, there is no way in which an author can write stories that all children can identify with.

Fortunately, there are some human truths that transcend class and culture. The making and maintaining of friendships, the excitement of holidays, the wonder of animals and the world and moving things, love of someone for you—these are common to all children. Writers of books for young children—good writers—are able within the confines of a limited vocabulary to deal with these learnings.

People read to sense the joy and exuberance of the world. Not all that a child reads about should be within her own experience. Reading is a way for even the youngest child to learn about the experiences of others. In one basal reader series, the first episodes center around a boy, his mother and father, a pig, a balding middle-aged bachelor, a kangaroo, a cowboy, and a wonderfully strong-willed girl. Each of these characters assumes genuine proportions as a person, though the vocabulary is limited.

Finally, critics attack basal readers for the teacher's manuals. These can be tedious and pedantic if they are not used with discretion. The best manuals suggest, rather than mandate. They view the teacher as a busy person who needs as much help as he can get in planning activities to help the children learn to read. If a teacher's manual is looked on as a resource book of ideas arranged in sequence, then it can be an invaluable tool for the teacher.

Programmed Instruction

During the last few years, programmed materials have been utilized to teach reading. While these materials come in many forms, they tend to have some common features:

1. Information is presented in small bits—much smaller, for instance, than in basal readers. For example, in a basal reader the child may read a five-page story and then answer a series of questions relating to that story, while in programmed instruction he may read no more than a sentence before he is expected to respond in some fashion.
2. Pupil participation is active; an overt response is required. Using either

---

21. Theodor Seuss Geisel, *Hop on Pop* (New York: Beginner Books, 1963).
22. Bill Martin, *Instant Readers* (New York: Holt, Rinehart & Winston, 1970).

answer sheets, the reading booklet itself, or a machine, the pupil marks a response, writes in a word, speaks into a microphone, or selects and punches a button.

3. Feedback regarding the response is immediate; the child knows whether he chose the correct response and can either reread and correct his error or advance.

4. Good record keeping is possible with those systems requiring the pupil to write a response or punch a button that records answers on tape. The teacher, using these response sheets, can discover a pupil's strengths and deficiencies and can select new programs based on needs.

5. Individualization is possible, as the teacher utilizes appropriate programs to fit the individual pupil's needs in terms of skill building, work habits, and interests.

As teachers and parents become increasingly concerned with the overemphasis on competition in the school setting, programmed instruction offers attractive alternatives. Invidious comparisons ("You're in the slow group") may become less common when each child is pursuing a program that accommodates his own needs for reading skills. Competition, when it does exist, may be within the individual. A child who takes five minutes to complete his rate builder, with three items missed, works to cut his time to four minutes, with the same number of errors or fewer.

Programmed instruction is not without its limitations. A steady diet of programmed bits of reading data may soon tire the young reader, who prefers to get involved with a story in which persons and plot are developed and a more realistic reading situation prevails. Difficult as the vocabulary may be, the child will persist in reading Ezra Jack Keats's *The Snowy Day*[23] or Roald Dahl's *James and the Magic Peach*,[24] for he finds the content fascinating. This reaction is quite different from the one that may follow the young reader's encounter with sentence after sentence, after which he answers "yes" or "no."

For this reason, programmed instruction tends to focus primarily on skills development. For example, in the Sullivan Associates Programs, instruction begins with activities designed to teach the relationship between printed symbols and speech sounds.[25] By the time the child completes the prereading course, he will have learned the names of the letters and how to print them. He will have been taught—by working with the letters *a, f, m, n, t, th*, and *i*—that letters represent sounds. The child will also learn that reading goes from left to right across the page, that words are groups of letters, and how to recognize the words *yes* and *no*.

Even in beginning materials, the Sullivan program stresses comprehension. For example, the child answers "yes" or "no" as he reads each of the following sentences:

---

23. Ezra Jack Keats, *The Snowy Day* (New York: Viking Press, 1962).
24. Roald Dahl, *James and the Magic Peach* (New York: Alfred A. Knopf, 1961).
25. M. W. Sullivan et al., *Programmed Reading* (Manchester, Mo.: McGraw-Hill, Webster Division, 1968).

I am a man.
I am an ant.
I am a mat.
I am a pin.
I am tan.

The Sullivan materials stress a careful control of sound-letter correspondence. In the example just given, one may note that the "short" sounds represented by *a* and *i* are used. Certain words that do not conform to those generalizations are taught, but these are held to a minimum and are ones deemed essential for meaning.

The Sullivan program consists of core books, word cards, filmstrips, supplementary storybooks, and ditto masters. There are twenty-one levels to the Sullivan program, with one book at each level. The levels are divided into three sequences, with seven books in each sequence. But not every child who uses the program begins with the first book. A test is given, and the child is placed according to the results of that test. After placement, a child moves through each succeeding book, step by step. At the end of each book, he must pass a test before moving on to the next one. Furthermore, at the end of each sequence, he must pass a special test before being allowed to advance to the next sequence.

Programs like the one just described rely primarily on the printed page. Other programs are moving more to the use of hardware—tape recordings, records, and filmstrips. Hoffman Information Systems (HIS), with programs for reading readiness, primary reading, and intermediate reading, makes use of a Mark IV projector, slides, and synchronized recordings.[26] Materials are attractively arranged in albums and are organized so that a young child can insert the strip and the record. Accompanying the lessons are work sheets and small booklets for reading. For the intermediate grades, the Hoffman system provides audiovisual instruction designed for individual and small-group instruction. In actual practice, the child listens to a recording and watches a filmstrip at the same time. For example, the topic for one of these sessions is entitled "The Deadly Piranha." After listening to the recording and watching the filmstrip, the pupil will then use the record and filmstrip "Flashback on Facts," which assists the child with recall and comprehension, stresses study skills, and gives vocabulary reinforcement. This is followed by "Mirror on Meanings," an audiovisual presentation designed to help the pupil gain multiple meanings of words and further comprehension. A final presentation, "Spotlight on Sounds," gives help with word analysis, phonetic and structural analysis, word attack strategies, and word origins.

Accompanying the audiovisual presentation is a word book. The pupil writes in her book, pushes a button on the projector, checks her response, and moves on to the next question after verifying the answer. The presentation is followed up with the *Encore Readers,* which are small books that contain practice exercises for the reading skills taught.

---

26. Hoffman Information Systems, Inc., Hoffman Electronics Corporation, El Monte, California 91730.

Individualized Reading Programs

When the concept of individualized instruction was first developed, teachers were urged to use library books and adapt word study, comprehension development, and enrichment activity programs to the content of these books. For many a harried teacher, the task proved too demanding, and the goal—instructing children in reading skills by using books they had personally selected—was not attained. The reading program became little more than a time for library book reading, with the teacher trying her best to listen to each child read from a book for five minutes each week.

Responding to a need for some structuring of individualized reading, several companies have developed "classroom libraries." One example is Individualized Reading, a program that includes 185 paperback books ranging in reading difficulty from first through fourth grade.[27] The first eighty-five books are considered the Primary I unit *(Reaching Out)* and have a three-grade readability span. The remaining one hundred books are the Primary II unit *(Reaching Up)* and have a four-year readability span. The quality of these paperback books is high; they are reprints of books children have shown a fondness for. They include such titles as *Curious George* by Hans Augusto Rey;[28] *Goodnight Moon* by Margaret Wise Brown and illustrated by Clement Hurd;[29] *Clifford, the Big Red Dog* by Norman Bridwell;[30] and *Nobody Listens to Andrew* by Elizabeth Guilfoile and illustrated by Mary Stevens.[31]

Accompanying the books are several different kinds of materials. There is an informal reading inventory, which the teacher uses to help the child make an appropriate selection.

Conference cards give a short summary of a book listed on the reading inventory and questions for the teacher to use in bringing out the child's understanding of the book and in helping him relate the content to his own experience.

For preselected books, there are discussion cards, which summarize the books and offer questions that can be used for group work. These cards are aimed at helping the teacher and children enjoy the sharing of a book that has been read by several members of the class.

Activity cards suggest things to do after the book has been read. For instance, the card for *Curious George* recommends the following:

1. Draw George on a big piece of paper. Make a big yellow hat for him. Or make a clay model of George.
2. Make up a title for a new *Curious George* book. Draw a book jacket to go with the title.
3. Make a collage of George in his new home in the zoo. Use colored paper for the balloons and add strings to them.

27. Priscilla Lynch, *Individualized Reading from Scholastic* (New York: Scholastic Magazines, 1972).
28. Hans Augusto Rey, *Curious George* (Boston: Houghton Mifflin Co., 1941).
29. Margaret Wise Brown, *Goodnight Moon* (New York: Harper, 1947).
30. Norman Bridwell, *Clifford, the Big Red Dog* (New York: Scholastic Magazines, 1963).
31. Elizabeth Guilfoile, *Nobody Listens to Andrew* (Chicago: Follett Publishing Co., 1957).

Recordings have been made for many of the books, so that the child, using a listening post, may listen to the record along with reading the book.

Accompanying all of these materials are skill activity games, a diagnostic master work-sheet book, a flannel board with cutouts for the *Reaching Up* series, a teacher's guide, and a reading log in which the child lists new words learned and writes in summaries of stories.

The teacher's guide gives practical help for initiating an individualized program. It suggests that the teacher may wish to begin with one pupil, or two, and gradually expand to include a larger number of his pupils as the year progresses. Recommendations are also made for parental involvement in a basal program.

One particularly useful aspect of this individualized reading program is the conference notebook, which gives examples of the techniques a teacher might use in maintaining records of pupil progress.

Even when programs like the one just described are not available, it is still possible to individualize a reading program. Basal reader programs provide books that may be used selectively, according to the progress of the individual child. As the pupil demonstrates his capabilities, he may push ahead on his own. The advantages of using basal readers for such individualized instruction are twofold: They have an accumulating and controlled vocabulary, and the stories and articles within a single book are generally of the same level of difficulty. Before the child is allowed to move on to a succeeding book, the teacher should glance at the vocabulary at the back of the book being used and then ask the child to read a few random pages to verify that he knows the words listed and is able to read them in context.

Basal readers also provide help for individualized instruction through their accompanying teacher's manuals and workbook materials. The manuals contain suggestions the teacher may employ to help teach skills, as problems in word attack and comprehension are noted during conference periods with children. Used with discretion—not assigned as busy work—workbook pages can be selected to give practice in these same areas.

TEACHING THE CHILD TO READ

Thus far, the nature of reading, the reader, characteristics of the reading curriculum, and materials for reading instruction have been discussed. This section suggests classroom practices that aid in the development of the desire to learn to read and the skills necessary for achieving that desire.

Sustained Silent Reading

All readers—even beginners in the kindergarten and first-grade age group—need to learn what it feels like to be readers. This is an opportunity that can be presented in every classroom. Even before children actually read, they can be put in that quiet, tranquil, and intellectually stimulating environment that is a part of reading. Sustained Silent Reading (SSR) is a quiet time when children—

and even teachers—can read without fear of being interrupted or questioned on what has been read or asked to read aloud. SSR is a time when children and books can get together.

Here is how one teacher used SSR in his classroom. Before the reading period he placed piles of books—books that have proved to be of interest to children—on the rug, on tables, and wherever children sit to read. Since he was working with primary children, he chose books that consist entirely of pictures and ones that are fairly difficult in nature. Eventually, most children brought books that they had chosen on their own. But during those first few days of SSR, the teacher's selection aided the children who were having difficulty in choosing books themselves.

The first time SSR is held, brief rules are explained:

1. We continue reading until a bell tells us it's time to stop.
2. We read without talking, since even if reading aloud is done very softly, it will disturb others, and we don't want to do that.
3. This is a special time for reading. We have a time for talking and a time for playing ball. This is a time for reading.

During the first periods there were opportunities for browsing among the piles of books. Then it was announced, after two or three minutes, that SSR was about to begin. The children found the places where they wished to sit, and a kitchen timer was set. At first, the time for reading was very short—no more than three or four minutes. But during that time each person could count on not being disturbed. If someone interrupted the SSR time, then the period was over; there would be another opportunity on the following day.

During SSR everyone read: teacher, classroom visitors, and children. The timer was used to establish the parameters of the reading period; once set, it could be trusted to remind the group when the period was concluded. The time given to SSR during the first few periods was slowly extended to ten minutes, then fifteen, and eventually to twenty minutes a day.

For SSR to be successful, it is important that the teacher read—and read what interests her: adult books or children's books too good to miss. The teacher whose program was described above read—during a month's time—A.S. Neill's *Summerhill*,[32] Duncan Emrich's *Folklore on the American Land*,[33] and Richard Goldstein's *The Poetry of Rock*.[34] He also read these children's books: Scott O'Dell's *Sing Down the Moon*[35] and Richard Chase's *Grandfather Tales: American-English Folk Tales*.[36] He read these two because he enjoys children's books and not because he felt that he should be reading books on a level with those being read by the children.

In this teacher's classroom the children began to prize their time with books. They would set new goals for themselves: "Let's see if we can go for fifteen

---

32. A.S. Neill, *Summerhill* (New York: Hart Publishing Co., 1960).

33. Duncan Emrich, *Folklore on the American Land* (Boston: Little, Brown & Co., 1972).

34. Richard Goldstein, *The Poetry of Rock* (New York: Bantam Books, 1969).

35. Scott O'Dell, *Sing Down the Moon* (Boston: Houghton Mifflin Co., 1970).

36. Richard Chase, *Grandfather Tales: American-English Folk Tales* (Boston: Houghton Mifflin Co., 1948).

minutes today." To a great extent it was in SSR that they came to know the feeling of getting caught up in a book and of knowing what it was like to sit with others who were equally captivated. They were able to see their teacher in a different light; that is, the teacher was regarded not as someone who checks their progress but as a person who wanted to read certain books and valued the time spent in doing so.

Why did the children value this time set aside for reading? Perhaps they felt mature and proud to know that they were able to engage in the intellectual achievement that reading is. True, the younger ones in the class may not have known any words, or only a few words, but they could choose books in which there were pictures to provide clues, and furthermore, they were in an environment in which not knowing a word meant no disgrace. So they were free to try without fear of embarrassment should they fail. And the younger children, although not reading in the strict sense, were enjoying the intellectual achievement in their own way.

What happened each day after SSR? Did the children discuss what they had read? Did the teacher ask questions or talk about the books with children? Occasionally, but those sessions tended to be informal, low-key discussions. Perhaps one of the children had read something that he was bursting to share. That may have been told. Questions may have been asked of that child because of the class interest he generated. But, as often as not, children moved on to other work and nothing was shared. SSR would happen again, tomorrow.

Language Experiences and Reading

A child's experiences are a vital source of material for early reading. While it is true that there is fascination for young children in the little preprimers and primers with their array of mythological characters, it is also true that there is equal—and perhaps even greater—fascination in the world that buzzes and roars and clicks around them. That world can be the basis for language experiences, including telling and writing and reading.

As Dorris M. Lee and R.V. Allen express it:

1. What a child thinks about he can talk about.
2. What he can talk about can be expressed in painting, writing, or some other form.
3. Anything he writes can be read.
4. He can read what he writes and what other people write.
5. As he represents his speech sounds with symbols, he uses the same symbols (letters) over and over.
6. Each letter in the alphabet stands for one or more sounds that he makes when he talks.
7. Every word begins with a sound that he can write down.
8. Most words have an ending sound.
9. Many words have something in between.
10. Some words are used over and over in our language and some words are not used very often.

11. What he has to say and write is as important to him as what other people have written for him to read.
12. Most of the words he uses are the same ones which are used by other people who write for him to read.[37]

Many teachers of young children have seen this theory put into practice. One teacher, at Christmastime, walked with her children to a nearby farm where Christmas trees were grown. There they sniffed the fragrance and admired the green foliage as they ambled up and down the rows. On returning to the classroom, they worked as a group to develop a story about the walk:

> Today we went for a walk to look at Christmas trees.
> Lucy fell down and skinned her knee.
> John found a snake skin, but it was empty.
> The Christmas trees smelled good, but they cost a lot of money.
> Mrs. Moran [the tree farmer] gave us each a lollipop to eat.

Using a felt pen, the story was written on a large chart. Then the teacher copied the story on paper and distributed ditto sheets of it to the children. With scissors and paste and colored paper, each child constructed her own book by cutting the sentences apart and pasting them, one sentence per page, in a Christmas tree book of her own design. Each child illustrated her own book by drawing or using a collage to illuminate the meaning of each sentence.

Another teacher found that flannel board stories were a successful beginning point for children in developing their own stories.[38] Working with older children who were having reading problems, he first told a flannel board story and then asked if one of the children would like to tell a story—either the one that had just been told or another—using the felt characters and the board. Taking out a piece of paper and a thin-line felt pen, he explained that he was going to write the story as the child told it. Spatial limits were set. In this case, the story could not exceed one sheet of paper. Then the telling began.

Why specify the length of the story? Why not let the child tell his account naturally, without limits? In part, limits were set because the teacher wished the child to have a workable piece of prose from which reading instruction might begin. Furthermore, limits help the child to develop a sense of the elements of a story: a beginning, a middle, and an ending. A limited amount of space encourages the child to concentrate on these elements in order to give unity to his story. At first, it was hard for some children not to run on and on. Using the flannel board and the felt figures, they began to tell the story but then would ramble from one event to another and would end up with a story that made little sense. The teacher talked about that story, explained the limits, and the child tried again.

As the child told the story, the teacher wrote down exactly what he said. Then the teacher asked the child to read back what had been written and to

37. Dorris M. Lee and R.V. Allen, *Learning To Read Through Experience*, 2nd ed. (New York: Appleton-Century-Crofts, 1963), pp. 4-8.

38. The flannel board technique is treated at greater length in Ramon R. Ross, "Frank and Frannie and the Flannel Board," *The Reading Teacher*, October 1973, pp. 43-47.

underline those words he knew. Teacher and child then read the story together—the child reading underlined words and the teacher reading all other words. As the story progressed, the child often would find that he knew more words than he had underlined. Sometimes a child would know nearly all the words in a story. The emphasis in this activity was placed on what the child knew—two words or three or fifteen—and instruction began at that point.

Here is an example of a story using this technique. The original tale told by the teacher was "The Tiger, the Brahman, and the Jackal." The following is Frannie's telling, after she had heard the story:[39]

> Once upon a time there lived a lion.
> He lived in a cage.
> The butcher came in and took him out of the cage.
> "I want to eat you for dinner," the lion said.
> "I will bring my puppy in the house and eat you for supper," said the man.
> The puppy was fat. "Do not eat me, Puppy," said the tiger.
> So the man took the tiger out and the tiger lived alone after that.
> The end.

Frannie was a third grader who was going to a reading clinic because she had severe problems with reading first grade materials. Yet she knew most of the words in *her* story. After Frannie and her teacher read her story together as a team, she visited another clinician and read the entire story by herself. Incidentally, notice how Frannie immediately changed the tiger in the original story to a lion and then switched back to tiger. Note, too, the subtle humor in the threat, "I'll eat you for supper!"

Once a story has been written and read by teacher and child together, there are many other activities that can make use of the material. For instance, the teacher can cut the sentences apart and ask the child to arrange them so that the story is in the same order as originally told. Or the child may be asked to arrange the sentences so that the final unit makes "good sense." Sometimes, in rearranging parts of a story, a better order is found than that of the original writing.

Learning sight words is possible with the content of a flannel board story. For example, the story written by Frannie includes these words, which are among the 220 most frequently used words as enumerated in the Kucera-Francis list.[40]

once	in	out	said	not
upon	the	of	will	me
a	came	I	my	so
time	and	want	house	after
there	took	you	man	that
he	him	for	do	

39. The underlined words are those Frannie knew.
40. H. Kucera and W.N. Francis, *Computational Analysis of Present Day English* (Providence, R.I.: Brown University Press, 1967).

Twenty-nine of the words Frannie chose, then, are among the most commonly used ones in our language. The others are these twelve:

lived	eat	dinner
lion	bring	fat
cage	puppy	tiger
butcher	supper	alone

This illustrates the tendency of English-speaking people to rely on a relatively small number of words for much of their communication. No matter which story Frannie chooses to tell, there is a good possibility that approximately three out of every four words will be on a common-words list. These common words also are characteristically used in basal readers and other carefully structured instructional materials.

What can a teacher do with the words a child uses in her story? Frannie's teacher wrote them on cards to be used for isolated-word drill. Since these were Frannie's words, she had no difficulty learning them out of context. Using those words, games such as the following are possible:

1. Make a duplicate set of word cards. Place one pile face down on a table. Deal the duplicate set to players, who then try to match their cards with those drawn from the pile.

2. Locate words that have elements in common. For example, *a* and *I* are both single-letter words; *he, in, of, my, do, me,* and *so* are all two-letter words; *there* and *that* both begin with the digraph *th; and, after,* and *along* all begin with the letter *a.*

3. Build new sentences with the words. Knowledge of all the words is not needed to begin to build sentences. Suppose Frannie learns these words:

a
lion
lived
in
cage
my
I

She can write sentences like the following:

A lion lived.
A lion lived in a cage.
A lion lived in my cage.
My lion lived in a cage.
My cage lived in a lion.
I lived in a cage.

Since all of the words are on cards, Frannie does not even need to write the words. All that is required is to place the cards in a sensible sequence:

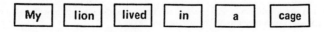

My   lion   lived   in   a   cage

Other benefits come with language-experience reading. A child learns that a word remains the same whether it is typed or written on the chalkboard. *Cage* remains *cage* no matter how large or small the letters are. The child also is learning, in sentence building particularly, that words string together to form either sentences or incomplete thoughts. *I lived* is a complete thought Frannie might write with her cards. *I lived in a lion* is another thought she might write. She begins to learn that the thoughts she writes—and reads—can be funny or nonsensical or truth or fiction.

Children also learn important listening skills when working with language-experience stories. The author has seen a group of children pay rapt attention to another child who was telling a flannel board story by manipulating the figures and disclosing the action. And the discussion following the telling confirms their attentiveness. They note nuances of expression, personalities of the figures, and actions that took place. When listening to their retelling of the story, it is astonishing to note the wealth of detail and accuracy of accounting that most children are able to supply.[41]

Finally, the stories a child dictates to a teacher or tutor offer materials for writing. Perhaps a child has learned the sentence:

I see a lion.

These words are on cards, and the cards help the young reader recognize that words are units and do not run together in writing in the same way they do in speech. Teachers know that one of the first tendencies of the young child is to run written words together so that they look like this:

Iseealion.

The cards help him establish the separateness of words, and in writing he can duplicate what he sees on the card, either on another card or on a chalkboard or newsprint.

In preparing cards for the child to write on, the teacher can help establish left to right movement by simply placing a tiny dot on the far left of the card and informing the child that it is there he begins his word.

WORD ATTACK SKILLS

How do children learn words? Traditionally, we have described several techniques by which a word may be recognized:

Sight Words

This is the look-say of word recognition and simply means that the person recognizes the word because he has seen it a number of times before. What that

---

41.   It is also interesting to note how few children, when given a choice, will retell a story told to them. They would much prefer to make up their own stories.

number is, however, remains open for question. If the word is an exciting one, like *ghost* or *kiss* or *elephant*, the number of repetitions required before the word is in the sight vocabulary of the child is few. If, however, the word is one like *there* or *were* or *was*, then the number of repetitions needed skyrockets. There are many of us who have seen *through-though* hundreds of times and still confuse them.

Phonics

Phonics instruction is based on the sounds associated with letters. Once a child learns a number of these associations she can use this knowledge to aid in reading. For this reason, much beginning reading instruction is concerned with categorizing words that begin with like sounds that rhyme, that end with the same sound, and that contain "long" and "short" vowels.

Phonics programs accompany almost all basal reader programs. The word study section of beginning lessons help children listen for like sounds or for rhyming words. Children learn to observe both the sound and graphic patterns in words. They are given opportunities to build words by substituting beginning consonants or blends of two consonants. A "word wheel"—as illustrated in Figure 6.1—is often used. This is used to teach the basic pattern part of the word—for example, *eet, ack, ake, ing*—as well as the sounds and letter representations that begin the words.

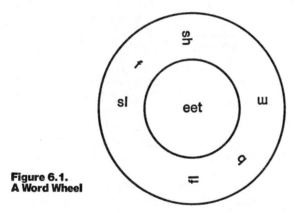

Figure 6.1.
A Word Wheel

The point of phonics instruction is twofold: The child should learn what sound may be attached to a letter or combination of letters, and when the child hears a series of sounds put together to form a word, he should be able to recognize it as a word he knows (a word he uses in his speech and whose meaning he understands). The shortcoming of this approach is that most sounds are represented by different letters in different words. On the other hand, phonics knowledge is a help to most children in attempting to decode or "unlock" a printed word, particularly if this is combined with knowledge of word structures and skill in using the content to gain meaning.

In addition to the phonics in a basal program, some teachers also use programs that give specific attention to phonics. The value of some of this material is debatable, but one such program will be described briefly. The word *song* is used to illustrate the instructional procedure teachers may use:

s   o   n   g

In the word *song*, what letter makes the "ssss" sound?
In the word *song*, what letters make the "ong" sound?
In the word *song*, what sound does the letter *s* make?
When put together, what sound do the letters *o, n, g* make?
If I took off the *s*, what sound would be left?
What is the whole word?[42]

The author of this material recommends that if a teacher is working with more than one pupil, it is best to begin instruction by using choral response—all children answering together. Once a pattern of response has been established, then the teacher can call on individual children. Glass describes the use of "A Challenge," in which one child attempts to answer all the questions about the word.[43]

The purpose of this so-called perceptual conditioning is said not to be to teach the identification of a word. Words are used presumably to help the child form perceptional conditioning habits regarding attaching sound associations to specific letter clusters. A lesson is not considered complete when a child can identify all the words by sight that he has been taught using this technique. A lesson is considered successful when a child can, within the *gestalt of a word*, consistently identify letter clusters and give the sounds they represent when asked.

Structural Analysis

This is a word recognition technique needed by a reader to help her to decode a word; that is, to get its meaning. This approach is based on knowledge of prefixes, suffixes, syllables, and the various rules for affixing, compounding, and syllabication.

Such suffixes as *-ed, -ing, -s, -es* and such prefixes as *re-, pre-, pro-* are common in the language. Also, some *base*, or *root*, words occur frequently—for example, *port* in *report, import, transport, portable* or *direct* in *direction, indirect, directory, redirect*. Rules about dividing words into syllables, such as between adjacent consonants *(les/son, com/pound, clus/ters)* or between bases and affixes *(in/direct, common/ly, end/ing)* are also a part of structural analysis.

Structural analysis is usually used in conjunction with phonetic analysis and

42.   Gerald G. Glass, "Perceptual Conditioning for Decoding: Rationale and Method," *Learning Disorders*, vol. 4 (Seattle: Special Child Publications, 1971).
43.   The reader is reminded that a *letter makes no sound* (there'd be quite a clatter here if this were not so!). Also, it is important to remember that isolating a letter and attempting to say it "has" a particular sound distorts the actual sound the letter represents in a word.

other means for gaining clues to the unknown word. For example, knowing that a word such as *happier* consists of a suffix *(er)* added to a base word, that *y* should be changed to *i* when a suffix beginning with a vowel is added, and that the sound of the single vowel between the consonants is "short," the reader should be able to pronounce the unknown word. Children are often interested in words with prefixes and suffixes, particularly those with multiple ones. For example, *antidisestablishmentarianism* is such a word and a good one to use in illustrating the virtues of structural analysis as a means of decoding a word.

The beginning reader needs to grasp the concept of prefixes and suffixes in order to use this technique, which is not too difficult, but overemphasis on structural analysis may make a heavy demand on the young reader. Learning the meanings of various prefixes and suffixes is a difficult task for the child. Syllabication is also not easy, as is shown by the adults who go to the dictionary to check on word syllabication when a division of a word must be made at the end of a line of type. And so, while structural analysis does aid the beginner, it is, unfortunately, most helpful to the more advanced reader. The beginning reader makes better use of phonics, sight words, and context in determining unknown words.

MEANING AND BEGINNING READING

Sometimes giving teaching attention to phonics and structural analysis results in too little or no emphasis on word meaning. Indeed, with such activities as those identified as "perceptual conditioning," it may be that a child will "read" words like *entirely* and *forgetfulness* without knowing their meanings.

Meaning is the sine qua non of reading. If reading is done without understanding, if no images are aroused, no ideas fermented, what is the use of reading? "Barking at print"—the purposeless reading of words—is a waste of time.

What can the teacher do to develop in the beginning reader a tendency to seek meaning in what he is reading? Reading one's own story, of course, solves much of the problem in advance. This technique helps the child perceive the point of reading. The child *knows* that meaning exists in her story. Frannie has, lodged in her mind, a lion (tiger), a butcher, and a puppy. To Frannie, those "little dried herbals," which have been penciled on a page to record her story, are wriggling with life. She has only to unlock those words, and her story, recorded faithfully for her, can be told again and again.

The ability in experience reading to understand that words tell a story, give directions, elucidate facts, or do all these at the same time may carry over to book reading. Reading in beginning basal materials continues to explore meaning. If, for example, a story like the following one is read, there may not be a great deal of meaning to explore:

Page 1: Tom
Page 2: Mary
Page 3: Tom and Mary
Page 4: "Tom, Tom!"
Page 5: "Oh, Mary. Oh! Oh! Oh!"

But there is picture meaning. What is Tom doing on this page? What is Mary doing? Why does Mary call to Tom? Other reading/meaning skills that may be taught are the use of quotation marks to show that someone is talking. And why are exclamation marks used? The period? The commas? Reading aloud and showing how Mary would say, the words "Tom, Tom!" or how Tom would say, "Oh, Mary. Oh! Oh! Oh!" also aid in deriving meaning. True, these may seem like crude beginnings to the glory of meaning, but they need to be learned, and each day a little more can be added on. But it may be that the real first thrill of meaning comes from the stories a child tells and the teacher writes down. These stories the child shares with others. And, to a great extent, that is one of the purposes of gaining the meaning of what is read—to share thoughts and ideas with others.

Reading and Questioning

In basal reader instruction, the teacher asks the children questions concerning the story. The asking of questions serves as the prime method in ascertaining whether or not a child has understood a passage. But another function of questioning is to help the child learn. It can be a basis for the dialogue method of teaching, in which children and teacher come together to discuss material that has been read.

Increasingly, attention is being paid to the types of questions asked. Beyond the basic factual and recall questions, teachers are more and more using inferential questions that help a child move away from specificity toward curiosity and speculation.

One new way of looking at questioning is contained in the work of Norris M. Sanders.[44] Using Bloom's *Taxonomy of Educational Objectives* as a beginning point, Sanders proposes that the teacher learn to question pupils in the following categories:

1. *Memory.* The pupil is asked to recall or recognize information. (What was the color of Tom's wagon?)
2. *Translation.* The pupil is asked questions that help him change information into a different symbolic form or language. (Tell what happened in the story, putting it in your own words.)
3. *Interpretation.* The pupil discovers relationships among facts, generalizations, definitions, values, and skills. (Compare the way Tom behaved when he was frightened with the way John acted in the story we read last week. How were they the same? How were they different?)
4. *Application.* The pupil is asked to solve a real-life situation requiring the identification of the problem and the use of appropriate generalizations and skills. (Now that you have finished reading *The Cat in the Hat*,[45] imagine that a stranger came to your house and began to change things all around. Your mother was not at home. You had to decide what to do on your own. What would you do? Tell why you would do each thing.)

44. Norris M. Sanders, *Classroom Questions, What Kinds?* (New York: Harper & Row, 1966).
45. Theodor Seuss Geisel, *The Cat in the Hat* (New York: Random House, 1957).

5. *Analysis*. The pupil is asked to solve a problem after knowing the parts and forms of thinking. Thus he has to begin to understand inductive and deductive thinking, semantics, and have an awareness of fallacies. (A pig is not a good pet. Why do you think this is true or not true? Use facts you have found to support your answer.)

6. *Synthesis*. The pupil solves a problem that requires original, creative thinking. (Now that you have finished reading the story, write or name, in five minutes, as many interesting titles for the story as you can.)

7. *Evaluation*. The pupil is asked to make a judgment of good or bad, right or wrong, according to standards he designates. (Who was your favorite person in the story? Why?)[46]

The preceding points are an oversimplification of Sanders's questioning technique, but they do suggest the richness and complexity of questioning that is available and can be used, even with the beginning reader. William H. Burton points out that teachers were found to ask, on the average, 150 questions per class hour.[47] Obviously, with that number of questions, there is little time for thoughtful or inventive discussion. Instruction tends to be at the level of memory of fact and detail. Thus if "thinking" readers are to be developed, it is best to begin in the early grades to ask children questions that stimulate them to read in a deeper and broader sense.

Reciprocal Questioning and Reading

One new technique for developing meaning in reading is through the use of reciprocal questioning (ReQuest).[48] In this procedure, the teacher and child take turns asking questions. Essentially, the procedure works like this:

1. The child reads a sentence.
2. She asks the teacher a question about what she has read.
3. The teacher answers the question.
4. The teacher asks the child a question about the same sentence.
5. The child answers the question.
6. The process is repeated until there is no more content for discussion in the sentence, and then another sentence is read.

In practice, a dialogue between teacher and pupil might go as follows:
(The pupil reads a sentence: "The big lion said, 'I will eat you for supper.'")
Pupil: "What did the lion say?"
Teacher: "I will eat you. What sort of lion was it?"
Pupil: "A big lion. When was he going to eat the person?"

---

46. These categories and the related discussion made extensive use of Sanders, *Classroom Questions*, p. 3.

47. Cited in Amelia Melnik, "Questions: An Instructional-Diagnostic Tool," *Journal of Reading* 2 (April 1968): 509.

48. A.F. Manzo, "The ReQuest Procedure," *Journal of Reading* 13 (November 1969), p. 123.

Teacher: "For supper. Why did the lion say he would eat him?"
Pupil: "The sentence didn't tell me. It must be that he was hungry. What is the first word that the lion said?"
Teacher: "*I* is the first word. What word in the story means *am going to?*"
Pupil: "*Will.*"

Clearly, some of these questions are "better" than others, but the more important goal here is to get pupils to ask questions. First questions may seem pretty silly:

How many words are there in the sentence?
What is the third word?
What is the last punctuation mark in the sentence?

On the other hand, there is a need to begin somewhere. Literal questions are easy to form. Beyond these, children can be taught to ask translation questions, analysis questions, and synthesis and evaluation questions if the teacher, by example, shows them how.

READING TO LEARN

In a sense, the discussion so far in this chapter has been about learning to read. But how does a person use reading to learn? The art of questioning, the techniques for experience writing, the use of SSR all are obviously related to learning—and reading is the strategy. In what other ways can reading skills be used to learn?

Nontextbook Reading

First of all, it is helpful that all reading does not come from school textbooks. College students were asked to maintain a list of what they read in one day. Among the large diversity of materials were beer ads, signposts, telephone books, graffiti on plywood fences, ads on the bus, newspapers, classified ads, magazines, lettering on police cars, television schedules, words on the television screen, and recipes. The point is that if these are the things people are reading, then they are, in part at least, what reading instruction should be based on.

It should be noted that pupils do not have to know every word that they meet in order to read newspapers and magazines. Mutual reading—the teacher and child sharing the reading task—can be done at any level.

Here are several ways in which a newspaper may be used:

1. Clip news stories, complete with headlines.
2. Separate the stories from the headlines.
3. Distribute the headlines to pupils.
4. Help pupils with any unknown words in the headlines.
5. Read the stories to the class, a sentence or two at a time.
6. For each story, ask which pupil has the headline that goes with it.

7. Ask for a justification if two persons think they have the headline that fits the story. (This happens more often than one would expect.)
8. Continue reading from the newspaper stories and asking questions, jumping from story to story, occasionally reading twice from the same story, until most of the content from each story has been pretty well explored.
9. Give the stories to the children for their own reading. If you feel it is necessary, use the underlining technique so that they may see how many words they can read from a newspaper.

The preceding activity may be modified for an analysis of commercial ads or a study of the classified ad section. Besides these, children may be engaged in many other activities that use newspapers. The same news story may be selected from two or three papers, and the pupils should note how nuances of meaning are conveyed by slight changes in wording. Fitting cartoons to captions used by the artist or writing captions and comparing them with the printed captions get children interested in how to condense thoughts into language.

Reading radio and television schedules will teach the pupils how to read across and down in graph form. Then they may locate critical discussion of upcoming programs and watch those programs. Class discussion may center around how their personal evaluations compare with the reviews they read.

Using a recipe to make something in class may provide a valuable lesson in direction following. One teacher made root beer by mixing together sugar, water, extract, yeast and then bottling and capping according to directions. Learning what ¾ *of an inch* means is much more interesting when pupils are following a recipe that says, ''Fill the bottles within ¾ inch of the top.'' The meaning of *five days* becomes apparent when the recipe says, ''Store bottles on their sides for five days before drinking.'' No five days ever seemed so long!

The same teacher and his class made ice cream. They pored over the recipe, cranked the mixture in an old-fashioned ice cream maker, and studied the effect of salt on ice as it supercooled the mixture. Root beer floats and reading go together.

Many school textbooks, other than basal readers, are known for their high level of reading difficulty. The teacher who individualizes or groups for reading instruction by placing children at a reading level commensurate with their ability may not show the same concern when faced with a social studies text or a math or science text. And yet, these are the materials that pupils encounter day after day and are a prime source for learning. What techniques does a teacher use to make materials from these books more available to pupils?

Reading together is a commonly used technique. Pupils take turns reading aloud, while others in the class listen. This is a simple procedure but not terribly effective. It is boring to both teacher and pupils. However, reading together permits discussion and clarification of meaning as children move through the material.

The teacher may also read aloud as pupils follow along in their books. A good model is set in this technique if the teacher can read aloud reasonably well. Also, there is opportunity for discussion. Unfortunately, everyone gets hooked to the same speed of learning and pupils are *not* reading.

Another technique used is the tape recording of lessons. Also, questions can be placed on the tapes so that pupils can answer them following the reading. Taping may be done by teacher aides or tutors, so that the process does not cut into the teacher's time. With use of listening post facilities, there is no noise distraction in the classroom.

Reading-Study Skills

Teaching children to use SQ3R or a version of that study technique is another important procedure in the reading curriculum. SQ3R stands for Survey, Question, Reading, Recite, and Review.[49] This technique was originated for use by college students, but since study procedures are needed at all levels there is no reason why a simplified version of it should not be used by primary and middle grade children. The procedure, which follows, is described as if a teacher were instructing pupil in its use:

1. *Survey* the entire assignment; read the first paragraph and the last paragraph carefully and note all the bold face type, the captions, and the illustrations.
2. *Question* the assignment; turn each bold-faced type statement into a question; jot these down in the briefest possible form.
3. *Read* to answer the questions posed; answer one question at a time. As soon as the answers to the questions are apparent, move on to the next step.
4. *Recite* by looking away from the book and see if you can answer the questions aloud, one at a time. Continue reading and reciting until the assignment is completed.
5. *Review* by going back and taking another look at the total chapter, trying to piece together all the bits of information you've collected into a meaningful whole.

Task cards, such as the ones illustrated on these pages are based on a teacher's reading of the material and deciding the important parts of the material to be read. Various tasks for the pupil to handle are noted. Task cards can help children read difficult material if they are put in simple terms and carefully done. For example, the teacher's reading may show that pages 13-17 can be safely omitted and that the really important material is on pages 12, 18, and 19. Thus, a task card can tell pupils which pages to study most closely. It is important that the card reads as if the teacher is talking. A typical card might look like the following:

Task Card: Pages 16-21, "Harvesting Food and Fuel from the Gulf"

This article tells about the harvesting of food from the Gulf of Mexico. It tells about the oil fields that exist in the Gulf. Do this:

1. Read page 17 carefully. Is there trouble between the people who fish and the oil companies?
2. Look at the pictures on pages 19-21. What is the author of the article trying to tell you with these pictures? Do you agree with the author?

---

49. This technique, together with the research relating to its use, is described in detail in Francis P. Robinson, *Effective Study* (New York: Harper & Row, 1946).

3. On page 23 the author quotes one of the people who fish as saying, "The oil companies and the people who fish need each other. I couldn't make a dime out there without diesel for my boat. And where's that going to come from if we ban the oil drillers?" What do you think the author is trying to get you to believe at this point?

4. On pages 22 and 23 there are nine pictures showing the fishing operation. Can you rearrange those pictures to tell the story better?

5. The article does not list any of the possible problems that might occur when the people who fish and oil companies use the same waters. Can you think of some of these problems?

A task card, such as the following, may simply contain tasks that involve reading:

Task Card: Making a World

1. Get a piece of string 3 feet long.

2. Take it outside the classroom. Put it on the ground so that it makes the largest circle possible.

3. The space inside the circle is your world to study.

4. Observe everything that happens in that world for 10 minutes.

5. Using drawings, words, maps, or models, prepare a report of that world. Be sure that others will be able to understand your report.

6. Scan Du Bois's The Twenty-One Balloons.[50] How does he describe the new world he finds?

MATCHING PUPILS WITH APPROPRIATE MATERIALS

Bringing children and books together in a comfortable match is sometimes not easy. While many children can select books that are readable at their level and yet are challenging, many others cannot. Discussed in this section are three procedures for helping children select books that are neither so difficult as to be incomprehensible nor so easy as to seem babyish. But the following procedures are not infallible. It may be that Karen is keen on learning about eye makeup. Somehow, no matter how difficult the reading material, she works her way through reading directions on the box. Daryl has no interest in the home life of drone bees in Africa. It doesn't matter how easy the book is; he won't understand it.

Obviously, some materials are more difficult to read than others. The Tale of Peter Rabbit[51] and Doctor Zhivago[52] are worlds apart. Why? Sentence length is one explanation. Longer sentences generally are harder to read than shorter ones. Long words tend to be more unfamiliar to a child. Complex sentence structure

50. William P. Du Bois, The Twenty-One Balloons (New York: Dell Publishing Co., 1971).
51. Beatrix Potter, The Tale of Peter Rabbit (New York: F. Warne, 1903).
52. Boris Pasternak, Dr. Zhivago (New York, Pantheon, 1958).

may make reading difficult. But these alone do not account for the readability of materials. Writing may have short sentences, little words, and simple syntax and still be complex. One reads: "To be or not to be, that is the question." Such simple words! Most of them are within the ken of a first grader. And yet, the idea expressed is a difficult one to grasp.

The readability of material is measured by sampling words and sentences in a selection, then applying the findings to a formula that takes into account such factors as the frequency of use of words, word length, and sentence and word structures. These formulas have been developed by various scholars and are generally used in the development of text materials used in schools. Thus, if subjected to check by such a formula, the content of third-grade basal readers will tend to show "third grade difficulty." In other words, all materials at a certain level are equally easy to read by all pupils. Inability to comprehend the content will probably mean that the individual child finds it difficult to understand the intended meaning because of "outside" reasons. Lack of interest, or dislike for a topic, or oversaturation of a topic (how many times some children have read about the Pilgrims!) can lead to lessened ability to comprehend in spite of what a readability formula may show.

So, considering the factors in readability implied in such formulas, here are three simple techniques to use in determining whether a child will be comfortable with his reading selection.

1. *San Diego Quick Assessment.* The San Diego Quick Assessment is a fast and easy way to locate an appropriate reading level for a child.[53] The test consists of a list of words, graded to range from preprimer through grade eleven (see Table 6.1). Procedures for administering the test are as follows:

1. Type out lists of ten words, with each list on a three-by-five-inch card.
2. Begin testing from a word that is two levels below the child's present grade placement.
3. Ask the child to read the words aloud from the list on that card. If she makes any mistakes, use easier lists until she reads with no errors. This is her independent level of reading.
4. Continue with the list, advancing the difficulty until the child makes three errors on a list. This is her frustration level. Her instructional level will be shown by the list in which she misses no more than two words.
5. Write down all incorrect responses, using a phonetic transcription. This list can be used in determining what word attack skills need to be taught.

Table 6.1. The SDQA List

Preprimer	Primer	1
see	you	road
play	come	live
me	not	thank
at	with	when
run	jump	bigger

---

53.   Margaret La Pray and Ramon Ross, "The Graded Word List: Quick Gauge of Reading Ability," *Journal of Reading* 12 (January 1969,)-305-307.

go	help	how
and	is	always
look	work	night
can	are	spring
here	this	today

2	3	4
our	city	decided
please	middle	served
myself	moment	amazed
town	frightened	silent
early	exclaimed	wrecked
send	several	improved
wide	lonely	certainly
believe	drew	entered
quietly	since	realized
carefully	straight	interrupted

5	6	7
scanty	bridge	amber
business	commercial	dominion
develop	abolish	sundry
considered	trucker	capillary
discussed	apparatus	impetuous
behaved	elementary	blight
splendid	comment	wrest
acquainted	necessity	enumerate
escaped	gallery	daunted
grim	relativity	condescend

8	9	10	11
capacious	conscientious	zany	galore
limitation	isolation	jerkin	rotunda
pretext	molecule	nausea	capitalism
intrigue	ritual	gratuitous	prevaricate
delusion	momentous	linear	risible
immaculate	vulnerable	inept	exonerate
ascent	kinship	legality	superannuate
acrid	conservatism	aspen	luxuriate
binocular	jaunty	amnesty	piebald
embankment	inventive	barometer	crunch

Source: Margaret La Pray and Ramon Ross, "The Graded Word List: Quick Gauge of Reading Ability," *Journal of Reading* 12 (January 1969): 305-307. Used with permission of International Reading Association.

The following list shows the record of a third grader, Samuel, reading from the SDQA:

Level 1: No errors

Level 2: No errors

Level 3: *improve* for *improved*

Level 4: *amaze* for *amazed*

        interrupt for *interrupted*

Level 5: *kertenly* for *certainly*
discuse for *discussed*
a-kented for *acquainted*
exscape for *escaped*

Samuel, even though a third grader, is able to read at the fourth grade level according to the SDQA; that is, he made only two errors. His instructional level is probably fourth grade. Independently, he ought to be able to enjoy second and third grade books, reading them with ease. Fifth grade level materials are going to be difficult, and if he can read them it will only be with considerable frustration and dismay. Incidentally, Samuel seems to need some work with endings; he omitted the -*ed* in *improved, interrupted, discussed,* and *escaped.* When *ce* is used initially, it has a soft sound. Samuel gives it a hard sound. He also does not seem to understand the sound *qu* generally represents. These and other bits of word attack information come out when the SDQA is given by a teacher.

2. *The GFT.* A variation in testing readability is to teach the child to administer, for himself, the GFT (Greasy Finger Test).[54] In this test, the child selects a page from a book he wants to read. He begins reading to himself and when he finds a word he doesn't know, he puts a finger on it. For the next unknown word, another finger. The child continues reading until he has read the entire page. If he hasn't used all the fingers of one hand, the book is about right. If he needs more than five fingers, then the book is probably too hard.

3. *The Cloze Technique.* The Cloze technique is another way in which children can test for themselves whether or not material is too difficult. The procedure for a child to use is as follows: Choose a partner to help with the test. Ask the partner to mask, using tiny bits of colored construction paper, every fifth word in a selection of about one hundred words. Thus, a selection might look like the following:

Slowly Amber struggled to ▮▮▮▮ feet, dragging
wet strands ▮▮▮▮kelp behind him. The ▮▮▮▮
was dark, and behind ▮▮▮ the surf muttered, still
▮▮▮▮ but quieter now. He ▮▮▮▮ his hand
to wipe ▮▮▮ hair from his eyes. ▮▮▮ sticky,
warm darkness pulsed ▮▮▮ the palm of his
▮▮▮ . Blood? Had he cut ▮▮▮ . When? There
was no ▮▮▮▮ of pain. . . .

Now, try to fill in the words missing. In general, if one is able to give exact word replacements for fifty percent or more of the blocks, the passage is not too hard. Below that percentage the material is probably too difficult. A pupil will find it frustrating. Incidentally, here are the replacements for that passage:

	his	of	shore	him	threatening	
raised	his	A	from	hand	himself	feeling

54.   Frank Greene, McGill University Reading Centre, Montreal, Canada.

One may use Cloze in a variety of ways, deleting every tenth word, every one hundredth word, substituting synonyms, blocking out entire sentences, reading aloud and asking the listener to guess the next word. Used in these ways, this technique serves to develop comprehension and improve grammatical and semantic sensitivity. It helps pupils develop an ear for the "just right" word.

EXERCISES FOR THOUGHT AND ACTION

1. What is your definition of reading? In answering this question, consider the following: At what point can a child be said to know how to read? When he knows fifty words? When he can read a passage aloud without any errors in pronunciation? When he can give the meaning of a passage, even though he mispronounced or misread thirty percent of the words?
2. What is meant by *readiness*? How do readiness activities in the early grades differ from those in the later grades? How are they alike?
3. With a five-year-old child, go for a walk in your neighborhood, study the contents of a refrigerator, or visit a supermarket. Ask her to identify as many words as she can. Ask her what helps in identifying those words. Categorize the words as to those dealing with food, with transportation, with clothing, with television shows. What seem to be the qualities that help a word come into a child's cognizance?
4. Think back to your own experiences with learning to read. What aspects do you recall most clearly? Are affective or cognitive aspects most vivid? If you could change one part of that experience, what would it be?
5. In your view, what are the five most essential skills for a beginning reader? Rank these in order and then discuss them with others in your group. Try to reach a consensus. Repeat this process for a mature reader.
6. A number of ways in which reading instruction may be organized are suggested. Try visiting schools at which these or alternate programs are in effect. Which method of teaching reading appears best fitted to your perception of yourself as a teacher?
7. Try the ReQuest technique with a friend, using reading material that is unfamiliar to both of you. What benefits do you note as a result of this technique? What difficulties arise?
8. A ten-year-old girl in your class said that she could not read, hated reading, and was incapable of reading. What would your response be?

SELECTED READINGS

Barrett, Thomas C. "The Relationship Between Measures of Prereading Visual Discrimination and First Grade Reading Achievement: A Review of the Literature." *Reading Research Quarterly* 1 (Fall 1965): 51-76.

Bond, Guy L., and Dykstra, Robert. *The Cooperative Research Program in First Grade Instruction*. Washington, D.C.: U.S. Department of Health, Education, and Welfare, February 1967.

Chall, Jeanne. *Learning To Read: The Great Debate.* New York: McGraw-Hill, 1967, pp. 141-149.

Durkin, Delores. "What Does Research Say About the Time To Begin Reading Instruction?" *Journal of Educational Research,* October 1970, pp. 52-56.

Fay, Leo, and Anderson, Paul S., *Young America Basic Reading Program,* Level 12. Chicago: Lyons & Carnahan, 1972.

Fay, Leo; Ross, Ramon; and La Pray, Margaret. *Young America Basic Reading Program,* Level 1 and 2. Chicago: Lyons & Carnahan, 1972.

Fry, Edward. *Reading Instruction for Classroom and Clinic.* New York: McGraw-Hill, 1972.

Glass, Gerald G. "Perceptual Conditioning for Decoding: Rationale and Method." *Learning Disorders,* vol. 4. Seattle: Special Child Publications, 1971.

Goodman, Kenneth S. "Reading: A Psycholinguistic Guessing Game." In *Readings on Reading,* edited by Albert Harris and Edward Sipay, p. 54. New York: David McKay Co., 1972.

Harris, Albert J. "Evaluating Reading Readiness Tests." In *Problem Areas in Reading—Some Observations and Recommendations,* edited by Coleman Morrison, p. 11. New York: Oxford University Press, 1965.

Kucera, H., and Francis, W.N.. *Computational Analysis of Present Day English.* Providence, R.I.: Brown University Press, 1967.

Labov, William. "Academic Ignorance and Black Intelligence." *Atlantic,* June 1972.

La Pray, Margaret. *Teaching Children To Become Independent Readers.* New York: Center for Applied Research in Education, 1972.

La Pray, Margaret, and Ross, Ramon. "The Graded Word List: Quick Gauge of Reading Ability." *Journal of Reading* 12 (January 1969): 305-307.

La Pray, Margaret, and Ross, Ramon. "Visual Perception and Beginning Reading." Paper read at California Educational Research Association Meeting, Spring 1964.

Lee, Dorris M., and V. Allen, R. *Learning To Read Through Experience.* 2nd ed. New York: Appleton-Century-Crofts, 1963.

McCracken, Robert, and McCracken, Marlene J. *Reading is Only the Tiger's Tail.* San Rafael, Calif.: Leswing Press, 1972.

McKee, Paul. *A Primer for Parents.* Boston: Houghton Mifflin Co. 1971.

Melnik, Amelia. "Questions: An Instructional-Diagnostic Tool." *Journal of Reading* 2 (April 1968): 509.

Orme, Lillian. "Building Readiness for Reading in First Grade Children Through Special Instruction." *National Elementary Principal* 35 (September 1955): 43-46.

Robinson, Francis P. *Effective Study.* New York: Harper & Row, 1946.

Robinson, Helen M. "Perceptual Training—Does It Result in Reading Improvement?" In *Some Persistent Questions on Beginning Reading,* edited by Robert C. Aukerman, Newark, Del.: International Reading Association, 1972, pp. 135-150.

Ross, Ramon R. "Frank and Frannie and the Flannel Board." *The Reading Teacher,* October 1973, pp. 43-47.

Sanders, Norris M. *Classroom Questions, What Kinds?* New York: Harper & Row, 1966.

Sartre, Jean-Paul. *The Words.* New York: Fawcett World, 1964.

Smith, Frank. *Understanding Reading.* New York: Holt, Rinehart & Winston, 1971.

Sullivan, M.W., et. al. *Programmed Reading.* Manchester, Mo.: McGraw-Hill, Webster Division, 1968.

Warner, Sylvia Ashton. *Teacher.* New York: Simon & Schuster, 1963.

The focus of this chapter is not only on literature as an enjoyable experience that provides children with inspiration, insights into human behavior, and knowledge about our literary heritage but also on literary selections and how they may be used in other areas of the language arts and in social studies, mathematics, science, art, music, health, physical education, and safety. Any conception of children's literature as something to be experienced only in a "free reading" period during the school day will certainly disappear as this chapter is read.

This broad view of literature coincides with the emphases in the beginning chapters on individualizing learning activities and giving children opportunities for making choices as to what they study, read, or work on.

W.T.P.

Children's Literature Throughout the School Day

Paul C. Burns

7

Literature takes form through three main categories—picture books, prose, and poetry. Picture books may be fiction or nonfiction, as may prose. Prose fiction may be classified as realistic or fantasy (fable, myth, or legend), while nonfiction prose may be informational or biographical. Poetry includes categories such as Mother Goose, narrative, lyrical, and specialized forms (haiku, cinquain, limerick, and sonnet).

Each of these types of literature is appropriate for the elementary school child, and although not every child will respond with equal enthusiasm to every type, deliberate efforts should be made to provide children with as many experiences as possible.

CURRENT OBJECTIVES

Some of the major objectives of the literature program are to:
1. Provide enjoyment
2. Bring new perspectives through vicarious experiences

3. Develop insight into human behavior and wisdom
4. Provide beauty and inspiration

In achieving these goals, a good literature program will provide knowledge about the literary heritage (classics, authors and illustrators, types of literature and the like; teach skills of literary analysis; develop language skills; and stimulate creative activities. The ultimate objective, however, is the enjoyment of literature as a means for developing children's reading tastes so they will appreciate fine reading materials throughout their lives. Only if this last goal is achieved can the child become a fully functioning individual—creative, imaginative, responsible.

CURRICULUM CONTENT

The objectives of a program determine the selection of content. Goals for a particular group of pupils must be suited to their needs and abilities; be child centered, not teacher centered; and be flexible enough to provide for individual differences. Such goals cannot be reached by using previously established content and telling pupils what they are to like and what they are to gain from the materials. For example, unless reading is a pleasurable experience for children, they will read little but what is required of them, and thus the major goal of the program will not be reached. Therefore, the teacher must study himself and his class; discover needs, interests, experiences, and abilities; and then plan an appropriate program.

Children need balanced, sequential experiences throughout their school years. Pupils will experience literature in various ways—listening, reading, discussing. They will interepret literature in different forms—oral and written expression, creative art, dramatics. There will be experiences emphasizing enjoyment and experiences designed to instruct. Both spontaneous and planned instruction will be utilized. Analysis of a work will include the relation of its meaning to the life of the reader. There will be a balance between the old and the new in literature, prose and poetry, fiction and nonfiction, realism and fantasy, and historical fiction and fiction with contemporary settings.

Taking into account the needs and interests of the children, the teacher must select a basic list of material that provides these balances. Curriculum guides can provide excellent suggestions for the program.[1] In the final analysis, however, the classroom teacher must make the final decisions in the selection, development, and use of the suggestions.

One example from the field of poetry should help clarify the ideas presented above. Too often, a teacher is unable to give a satisfactory answer when asked:

---

1. For example, see University of Nebraska, *A Curriculum for English and Poetry for the Elementary Grades* (Lincoln: University of Nebraska Press, 1966) and *Teaching Literature in Wisconsin* (Madison, Wis.: Department of Public Instruction, Wisconsin English-Language Arts Curriculum Project, 1965).

"What is your poetry program?" A planned poetry program should include a balance of poems that illustrate a variety of the following elements, content topics, and forms:

1. Elements	2. Content topics	3. Forms
action	everyday happenings	ballads
fantasy	the family	free verse
humor	interesting people	narrative verse
imagery	weather and the seasons	lyrical
mood	animals	limerick
rhythm		sonnet
plot		
characterization		
contrasting pictures		
theme		

Besides aiming for a balance in a poetry program, the teacher needs to consider other factors. She may first need to combat pupil prejudice against poetry. Also, the particular group must be considered in finding suitable poems—including poetry by and about minorities. Ways of presenting poems must be considered. She must decide which elements of poetry should be brought to the children's attention: comparison; condensation; contrasts; imagery (sense, simile, metaphor, allusion, personification); mood; repetition; rhyme and sound (alliteration, assonance, onomatopoeia); rhythm; suggestion; symbolism. The teacher may need to turn to specialized poetry textbooks for help.[2]

In addition to general anthologies, the classroom or school instructional center should have poetry anthologies containing poems that deal with a single subject, that are based on folklore, and that are collected from around the world. Besides anthologies, Mother Goose books, source books for nursery rhymes, books by one poet, and books with a single poem should be available. A most helpful source for choosing books of poetry is the *Index to Children's Poetry*.[3] Not to be overlooked are the many fine poetry collections for young readers now available in paperback (for example, *The Secret Place and Other Poems*)[4] and the volumes of poetry written by children for children (for example, *It Is the Poem Singing into Your Eyes*).[5]

The primary purpose of the literature program has been and still is the enjoyment of prose and poetry. However, as noted earlier in this chapter and in the preceding two chapters, children need to acquire knowledge and skills in order to enjoy and increase their appreciation of literature, to heighten their levels of

---

2. For example, see May Hill Arbuthnot and Shelton Root, *Time for Poetry*, 3rd ed. (Chicago: Scott, Foresman & Co.: 1967) and Louis Untermeyer, *The Golden Treasury of Poetry* (New York: Golden Press, 1959).

3. John and Sara Brewton, *Index to Children's Poetry* (New York: H.W. Wilson Co., 1942). Also see the three supplements, 1957, 1965, and 1972, to the *Index*.

4. Dorothy Aldis, *The Secret Place and Other Poems* (New York: Scholastic Book Services, 1971).

5. Arnold Adoff, ed., *It Is the Poem Singing into Your Eyes* (New York: Harper & Row, 1971).

understanding, and to help them make wise choices for independent reading. This does not mean there should be literary analysis of every book or poem read by the child, but it does suggest that some order of inquiry and study may be needed to help children in these areas.

For example, in a study of poetry as a type of literature, questions like the following may be asked:

What do you think the author said in this poem?

How does this poem make you feel?

Why do you think the poet used the words he did?

What senses does the author appeal to in this poem?

What picture does this poem bring to your mind? Sounds? Smells?

What do you notice about the way in which rhyme is used in this poem?

How would you compare this poem with others on the same topic?

Some analysis of prose will help children to understand and enjoy what they will be reading. The following elements lend themselves to study by elementary school children:

1. *Genre.* Children should profit from knowing the different major types of literature, since such knowledge will permit them to pursue a particular preference and apply the appropriate criteria for evaluation. One way to categorize pieces of literature is by genres, or types. Other frequently used classification systems are based on motifs, uses of literature, reading levels and age groups, and topical divisions.

2. *Plot.* The plan of the story is referred to as its plot. Questions such as "What are the conflicts or problems in the book?" or "How do the events build to a climax?" may be asked by the teacher to evaluate the child's understanding of plot.

3. *Setting.* The setting answers the questions of when and where. To draw attention to setting, such questions as the following may be asked: "Does the story capture the feeling of the place or the age?" and "How does the author reveal the setting?"

4. *Theme.* The theme refers to the author's purpose in writing the story. Questions about the theme may include "What is the 'big idea' of the story?" or "What do you think the author is trying to tell the reader?"

5. *Characterization.* Questions such as "How did the author reveal the characters in the story?" will help to discover the way in which the characters are brought to life by the writer.

6. *Style.* The author's selection and arrangement of words is known as "style." Questions such as the following may be used to direct attention to the style of the writer: "From what point of view does the writer tell the story?" and "What can you say about the way the author wrote? How does he use language? Symbolism? Dialogue?"

7. *Format.* Features of the book itself, such as size, shape, design of pages, illustrations, typography, paper and binding, comprise the format. Questions such as these may develop sensitivity to such aspects: "How is the format related to the story?" and "Why are the particular colors used in the illustrations?" Children should also be made aware of the major dif-

ferences in types of illustrations, format, and printing techniques in children's books published before and after the seventeenth century.

Besides having an understanding of these elements, children need to recognize that each type of literature has a separate evaluation criteria. For a modern fantasy tale, the child may be asked: "How does the author make the story believable?" For information books, the child may consider: "Are differing viewpoints presented?" Knowledge gained from answering such questions helps children recognize the differences among types of literature and to evaluate the quality of writing among books on the same subject or written by the same author. The child grows in the ability to evaluate literature as she recognizes features of a well-constructed plot, effectiveness of setting, significant themes, qualities of convincing characterization, and appropriateness of style of writing.

Children also need to learn about authors and illustrators. What child would not more fully enjoy *April's Kittens*[6] or *Mittens*[7] if she knew the influence of drawing and cats on the life of Clare Newberry? Of if she knew about Robert McCloskey's detailed research on Mallard ducks as evidenced in the illustrations in *Make Way for Ducklings?*[8] Or if she heard the story of Maurice Sendak's Jennie, who appears in *Where the Wild Things Are?*[9]

Some teachers have found it profitable to read from (or possibly rewrite for pupils) the biographical sketches found in *Junior Book of Authors*[10] or *More Junior Authors.*[11] Biographical sketches of illustrators may be found in *Illustrators of Children's Books, 1744-1945*[12] and *Illustrators of Children's Books, 1946-1965.*[13] Other sources include *The Story Behind Modern Books,*[14] *Writing Books for Boys and Girls,*[15] *Newbery Medal Books, 1922-1955*[16] *Caldecott Medal Books, 1938-1957,*[17] and *Newbery and Caldecott Medal Books, 1956-1965.*[18] Additionally, *Elementary English* (now entitled *Language Arts*) and *The Horn Book Magazine* regularly publish essays about writers and illustrators of children's literature.

6.   Clare Newberry, *April's Kittens* (New York: Harper & Brothers, 1940).

7.   Clare Newberry, *Mittens* (New York: Harper & Brothers, 1936).

8.   Robert McCloskey, *Make Way for Ducklings (New York: Viking Press, 1941).*

9.   Maurice Sendak, *Where the Wild Things Are* (New York: Harper & Row, 1963).

10.   Stanley J. Kunitz and Howard Haycraft, eds., *Junior Book of Authors,* 2nd ed. (New York: H.W. Wilson Co., 1951).

11.   Muriel Fuller, ed., *More Junior Authors* (New York: H.W. Wilson Co., 1963). The most recent addition to this series on authors is Doris De Montreville and Donna Hill, eds., *Third Book of Junior Authors* (New York: H.W. Wilson Co., 1972).

12.   Bertha A. Mahony et al., *Illustrators of Children's Books, 1744-1945* (Boston: The Horn Book, 1946).

13.   Bertha A. Mahony et al., *Illustrators of Children's Books, 1946-1965* (Boston: The Horn Book, 1958).

14.   Elizabeth Rider Montgomery, *The Story Behind Modern Books* (New York: Dodd, Mead, 1949).

15.   Helen Ferris, ed., *Writing Books for Boys and Girls* (New York: Doubleday & Co., 1952).

16.   Bertha Mahony Miller and Eliner Whitney Field, eds., *Newbery Medal Books, 1922-1955* (Boston: The Horn Book, 1955).

17.   Bertha Mahony Miller and Eliner Whitney Field, eds., *Caldecott Medal Books, 1938-1957* (Boston: The Horn Book, 1957).

18.   Lee Kingman, ed., *Newbery and Caldecott Medal Books, 1956-1965* (Boston: The Horn Book, 1965).

Children should share stories and poems that have delighted generation upon generation of children. They will delight in exploring myths;[19] epics (as the *Illiad* and the *Odyssey*); folk and fairy tales (by Perrault, The Brothers Grimm, Asbjornsen, and Joseph Jacobs); fables (as Aesop, Jataka Tales, La Fontaine); and other fanciful literature (by Hans Christian Anderson, Andrew Lang, Charles Kingsley, Lewis Carroll, Kenneth Grahame, Beatrix Potter, Rudyard Kipling, and Wanda Gag).[20] Folktales of various ethnic origins that have similar plots may be discussed for differences in style, characters, and incidents; and traditional tales may be compared with selections from modern fanciful literature. Innumerable rhymes that children have sung for many, many years as well as other poetic forms continue to have strong appeal for children. The works of William Blake (1757-1827), Christina Rossetti (1830-94), Edward Lear (1812-88), Walter de la Mare (1873-1956), Robert Louis Stevenson (1850-94), and A. A. Milne (1882-1956) can be compared with the verses of contemporary poets writing for children. Another activity might involve comparing the illustrations of several distinguished artists of contemporary children's books with those of earlier artists, such as Tenniel (1820-1914), Randolph Caldecott (1846-86), Walter Crane (1856-1915), and Kate Greenaway (1846-1901).

Children also acquire knowledge and skills related to literature through less direct means. As discussed in Chapters 4, 5, 6, and 8, activities such as reading, listening, storytelling, oral interpretation, discussion, creative drama, reporting, and written composition are often based on literature. How each of these aspects is related to literature will be discussed in the following section.

INSTRUCTIONAL PRACTICES

There are components of the literature program other than those alluded to earlier in this chapter. Opportunities for free silent reading are provided frequently at every level of the elementary school. Children need opportunities to browse through books and magazines in the classroom or the instructional materials center to find reading materials that interest them and then to read silently. Because this practice involves the opportunity for free selection by the pupil, the materials provided by the school must meet the highest standards of literary quality.

Some teachers have found it helpful to have a regularly scheduled recreational reading period, one that is separate from the instructional reading time, the

---

19. For example, see Anne Terry White, *Gold Treasury of Myths and Legends* (New York: Golden Press, 1959).

20. For some good examples of fanciful literature, see Lewis Carroll, *Alice in Wonderland* (New York: Macmillan Co., 1950); Wanda Gag, *Millions of Cats* (New York: Coward-McCann, 1928); Kenneth Grahame, *The Wind in the Willows* (New York: Charles Scribner's Sons, 1961); Charles Kingsley, *The Water Babies* (New York: John C. Winston, 1930); Rudyard Kipling, *Just So Stories* (New York: Doubleday, 1909); and Beatrix Potter, "Four Little Rabbits."

free reading time, and the literature time. During the recreational reading session, teachers may introduce new books to the class, discuss books that the pupils are reading, and provide information about authors and illustrators. A portion of the period may be devoted to helping pupils who are slow in starting to read or who need help with words. However, those who are progressing successfully should not be interrupted. During the final minutes of the class time, some ideas may be shared.

Some schools use literature readers, or anthologies. These readers should, however, serve only as an introduction to the literature program; they should not *be* the program. The short selections can serve as springboards to good oral discussions, creative drama, and creative writing. Also, if the selection is interesting, the child may be motivated to read the complete work. (Pupils must not be left to think they have read *Henry Huggins* when they have encountered only a brief excerpt.)[21] There are several series of literature readers that are commercially available. The following is a representative listing:

Best of Children's Literature. Indianapolis: Bobbs-Merrill, 1960. (Grades 1-6).

Literature Readers. New York: Harcourt, Brace & World, 1968. (Grades 4-6).

Prose and Poetry Series. Boston: L.W. Singer Co., 1960. (Grades K-8).

Reading Caravan. Boston: D.C. Heath & Co., 1964. (Grades 1-6).

Sounds of Language Readers. New York: Holt, Rinehart & Winston, 1966. (Grades K-6).

Treasury of Literature. Columbus, Ohio: Charles E. Merrill Books, 1966. (Grades 1-6).

Wide Horizons Series. Chicago: Scott, Foresman & Co., 1966. (Grades 2-9).

Children's literature programs are constantly expanding as educators become more aware of the value of trade books. (Trade books are aimed at a more general audience than are textbooks and usually deal with one long plot as opposed to the short selections of a reader.) The reading/language arts center has taken on a fuller meaning as it is no longer used only for free reading. Reading and the other language arts, social studies, mathematics, science, art, music, health, physical education, and safety can be more fully developed when each is enriched with trade books.

Reading

As the author of Chapter 6 has stated—and as reemphasized here—the delightful world of children's literature should be an integral part of good reading programs, which include those using basal readers for skill development purposes. Exploring literature permits the child to acquire additional reading skills and to practice reading skills that are being taught in a good, developmental,

---

21. Beverly Clearly, *Henry Huggins* (New York: William Morrow & Co., 1950).

sequential reading program. Trade books particularly lend themselves to the development of reading skills. For example, common reading errors are humorously presented in *Olaf Reads*.[22] Compound words abound in *Mouse House*,[23] and numerous rhyming words are found in *Mop Top*.[24]

Attitudes toward reading are significant factors associated with children's literature. If the child likes what he reads, he will continue to read more. Children's trade books, which are necessary instructional tools and so should be made a regular part of any good reading program, contain highly enjoyable stories. And what teacher can get along without *Good Reading for Poor Readers*, with its information on readability and interest levels?[25] The real reason for the teaching of reading in our schools is to produce readers, not children who just know how to read.

Individualized, or "personalized," reading involves the use of trade books, which cover a wider range of personality, emotion, and action factors than that generally found in basal readers. The use of the more individual approaches to reading instruction has accelerated the production of commercially packaged literature programs, such as the following:

Classroom Library Packet. Oklahoma City, Okla.: The Economy Co., n.d. (25 books for the primary level).

Invitation to Story Time and Personal Reading. Chicago: Scott, Foresman Co., 1966. (16 books for pre-first grade; 25 books per set for grades 1-6).

Macmillan Reading Spectrum. New York: Macmillan Co., 1964. (30 books for grades 1-6).

Owl Books. New York: Holt, Rinehart & Winston, 1965. (20 books for preschool-grade 1; 40 books for grades 1-2; 40 books for grades 2-4; and 20 books for grades 4-6).

Treasure Chest. New York: Harper & Row, 1966. (36 books for the primary level).

Listening

Children of all ages enjoy listening to well-selected and well-presented prose and poetry. The listening may focus on (1) gaining appreciation (enjoying the development of a story; listening for pleasing rhythm; reacting to the mood set by an author); (2) receiving information (listening for the answer to a specific question; listening to follow directions, follow sequence, and get the main ideas); and (3) reacting critically (discriminating between fact and fantasy; detecting prejudice and bias; sensing the writer's purpose).

Teachers of very young children frequently use literature as a means to listen for sequence ("Goldilocks and the Three Bears") or for rhyming words ("Jack be

22. Joan Lexau, *Olaf Reads* (New York: Dial Press, 1961).
23. Rumer Godden, *Mouse House* (New York: Viking Press, 1957).
24. Don Freeman, *Mop Top* (New York: Viking Press, 1955).
25. George Spache, *Good Reading for Poor Readers* (Champaign, Ill.: Garrard Publishing Co., 1970).

nimble; Jack be quick; Jack jump over the candlestick"). Several trade books focus on the value of listening to sounds, words, letters, and sentences: *Ounce, Dice, Trice,*[26] *Do You Hear What I Hear?*[27] *The Listening Walk,*[28] and *Listen! And Help Tell the Story.*[29] Besides the teacher or pupil as reader or storyteller, literature is presented in many ways by television, radio, motion pictures, and recordings. Each of these media develops in the listener habits of concentrated attention. There are many films, filmstrips, records, and tapes that can be used in the literature program and that demand sharp listening skills. For example, Encyclopaedia Britannica has produced such records as *Hans Christian Anderson Fairy Tales, Just So Stories,* and *You Know Who.* The National Tape Recording Repository contains tapes, such as *Stories Are Fun, Open the Door,* and *Land of Make Believe.* Films for listening produced by Encyclopaedia Britannica include *The Loon's Necklace, The Bear and the Hunter,* and *Morning Star.* (See the "Audiovisual Aids" listing at the end of this chapter for information on securing appropriate media for use in the classroom.)

Storytelling

Even someone as young as the preschool child often wants to retell a story or recite a poem to a friend. If the child is fortunate, she will come in contact with many teachers, who, through storytelling, will acquaint her with much literature and present a model for her own storytelling. The child who tells a story to the class or to a small group is developing poise and skill as a speaker as well as the ability to organize events in proper sequence. Pupils soon learn that there are characteristics of a story that make it a good one to tell: interesting, perhaps episodic, plot; realistic characterization; appropriate mood and literary style. All types of stories appeal to children: realistic, nature, and animal stories; traditional and contemporary fairy tales; folktales; fables; cumulative stories; as well as nonsense stories. The following list illustrates some good collections of stories for telling aloud:

Bailey, Carolyn S., and Lewis, Clara M. *Favorite Stories for the Children's Hour.* New York: Platt & Munk, 1965.

De LeMare, Walter. *Tales Told Again.* New York: Alfred A. Knopf, 1959.

Gurenberg, Sidonie M. *More Favorite Stories Old and New.* New York: Doubleday & Co., 1960.

Jablow, Alta, and Withers, Carl. *The Man in the Moon.* New York: Holt, Rinehart & Winston, 1969.

Mathon, Laura E. and Schmidy, T. *Treasured Tales.* New York: Abingdon Press, 1960.

Untermeyer, Louis. *The World's Great Stories: 55 Legends that Live Forever.* Philadelphia: J.B. Lippincott, 1964.

---

26.   Alastair Reed, *Ounce, Dice, Trice* (New York: Atlantic Monthly Press, 1958).
27.   Helen Borton, *Do You Hear What I Hear?* (New York: Abelard, 1963).
28.   Paul Showers, *The Listening Walk* (New York: Thomas Y. Crowell, 1961).
29.   Bernice W. Carlson, *Listen! And Help Tell the Story* (Nashville, Tenn.: Abingdon Press, 1965).

Oral Reading

The teacher who reads a story aloud is using one of the best ways of presenting literature to children. Oral reading often may need to be preceded by some background information or followed by informal discussion. Books such as *Mike Mulligan and His Steam Shovel*,[30] *Whistle for Willie*,[31] and *Charlotte's Web*[32] are examples of good books for reading aloud at the primary level. For the intermediate years, such books as the following may be used: *Caddie Woodlawn*,[33] *Just So Stories*,[34] *Amos Fortune, Free Man*.[35] (For a comprehensive listing of suggested "read-aloud" books, see *Let's Read Together*.)[36]

At times a child may read his favorite story to the class or to a small group of children, and at other times the teacher should encourage children to share general-interest stories with the group. A brief story that is new to the class and presented with visual aids has a good chance of being a successful experience for the child and his audience. Older children reading well-prepared stories to younger children can be an activity highly beneficial to both age groups. When children start to read poetry orally to other members of their class, the emphasis should be on the enjoyment of having a delightful poetic experience. Unless the child has difficulty understanding the structure of the vocabulary in the poem, she should be allowed to read the poem chosen in her own way. Only on the upper elementary school level should rhythm and critical interpretation of the content of a poem be stressed.

Choral activities (discussed in Chapters 4 and 5) provide children with the opportunity to experience literature in interesting ways. Most beginning choral work makes use of the refrain, such as those found in Robert Lewis Stevenson's "The Wind." Question-and-answer types of poems, such as "Baa, Baa, Black Sheep," lend themselves to antiphonal, or two-part, choral arrangements. Line-a-child arrangements, such as "Monday's Child," can be used with young children. Unison speaking—sequence and cumulative—may use such poems as Rachel Field's "Roads" (sequence) and Beatrice Brown's "Jonathan Bing" (cumulative).

Discussion

There are many opportunities throughout the school day for discussion of literature. When the same piece of literature has been read by a number of class members, a small "group talk" may be held. The discussion need not be concerned exclusively with details of the plot but may also bring out such aspects as the way in which the characters react to the events of the story, how they change

---

30. Virginia Burton, *Mike Mulligan and His Steam Shovel* (Boston: Houghton Mifflin Co., 1939).
31. Ezra Keats, *Whistle for Willie* (New York: Viking Press, 1964).
32. E.B. White, *Charlotte's Web* (New York: Harper & Row, 1952).
33. Carol Brink, *Caddie Woodlawn* (New York: Macmillan Co., 1936).
34. Rudyard Kipling, *Just So Stories* (New York: Doubleday, 1909).
35. Elizabeth Yates, *Amos Fortune, Free Man* (New York: Alladin Books, 1950).
36. *Let's Read Together*, 3rd ed. (Chicago: American Library Association, 1969).

as the story progresses, and how the book or poem relates to the child's own experience. Such questions as the following may be used to prompt discussion:

Have you ever seen anything like this happen? When?
Has anything like this ever happened to you? What did you do about it?
How are you like the people in the story?
Do you think that people really do these things? Why?
How did the story make you feel? Why?

In addition to group talks, round-table and panel discussions are worthwhile activities. Several books that lend themselves to such sessions are *Up a Road Slowly*,[37] *Onion John*,[38] *Across Five Aprils*,[39] and *I'll Get There, But It Had Better Be Worth the Trip*.[40] Conducting real or imaginary interviews with authors and illustrators is another interesting oral language experience.

Creative Drama

Chapter 5 presented the role of literature in drama and stressed that many kinds of literature—nursery rhymes, folktales, fables, fairy tales, myths—lend themselves to creative dramatics. Young children enjoy pantomiming nursery rhymes. (It's fun to be Jack and jump lightly over a candlestick!) Aesop's fables and fairy tales like "Little Red Riding Hood," "Sleeping Beauty," and "Rumplestilskin" are exciting to act out as are folktales such as *Dick Wittington and His Cat*[41] or *The Shoemaker and the Elves*.[42] Acting out "Cinderella" was suggested in Chapter 5. Another excellent selection for pantomime by older children is Robert Browning's poem "Pied Piper of Hamlin." To add variety, puppets may be used or the dramatization may be presented in the form of a shadow play. The most advanced pupils may try to dramatize a book such as *Bears on Hemlock Mountain*[43] or episodes from such books as *Homer Price*[44] or *Wrinkle in Time*.[45]

Reporting

A special form of reporting is the book review. By participating in this form of oral composition, the child learns how to share a book with others. The child should mention the title and the author of the book and give an indication of what the book is about; however, a full summary of the plot should be avoided. There are numerous ways in which children may report on books. Pupils may retell an exciting or funny part of the book, show an illustration, or read aloud a few

37. Irene Hunt, *Up a Road Slowly* (Chicago: Follett Publishing Co., 1966).
38. Joseph Krumgold, *Onion John* (New York: Thomas Y. Crowell, 1959).
39. Irene Hunt, *Across Five Aprils* (Chicago: Follett Publishing Co., 1964).
40. John Donavan, *I'll Get There, But It Had Better Be Worth the Trip* (New York: Harper & Row, 1969).
41. Marcia Brown, *Dick Wittington and His Cat* (New York: Charles Scribner's Sons, 1950).
42. Adrienne Adams, *The Shoemaker and the Elves* (New York: Charles Scribner's Sons, 1960).
43. Alice Dalgliesh, *Bears on Hemlock Mountain* (New York: Charles Scribner's Sons, 1952).
44. Robert McCloskey, *Homer Price* (New York: Viking Press, 1943).
45. Madeline L'Engle, *Wrinkle in Time* (New York: Ariel Books, 1962).

passages. They may think up new episodes for such books as *Lassie Come Home*[46] or share interesting topics, such as map making in *Journey Outside*.[47] The book may be compared with others on a similar topic or written by the same author. The details included will vary according to the type of book and the pupil's particular interests. Reviewing a book reinforces understanding of the setting, characters, and sequence of events; develops skills of analysis; and points out the differences between literary experience and real-life experience.

Creative Writing

It seems obvious that both listening and reading can spur creative written expression. Young writers are helped to become good writers by immersing themselves in literature that provides them with a stream of ideas; an increasing stock of words and language patterns; and knowledge of story structures, plot motifs, and elements of style.

Children at the primary level can write stories that draw on the repetition, magic, and enchantment of folktales. After hearing and reading *Just So Stories*,[48] children often like to tell or write their own accounts of "why" or "how." Paul Bunyan or Pecos Pete stories may provide intermediate level children with the incentive to create their own tall tales. Many children who have thoroughly enjoyed reading, discussing, and studying several stories of one type are apt to use that type in their own storytelling or writing. In the same way, individual stories can stimulate follow-up efforts: After reading *Pippi Longstocking*[49] or *When I Am Big*,[50] children may write about other things that happened to Pippi or may tell about what might happen to them when they grow up. Opportunities for creative responses abound throughout literature; children may create new beginnings and endings to stories or make up additional information about the characters.

Children's literature contains many models for the child's reference in writing her own stories. For example, a pupil who wants to write a story in the first person might profitably read or hear such stories as *Henry Reed, Inc.*,[51] *The Enormous Egg*,[52] or *Island of the Blue Dolphins*.[53] If a pupil is searching for a way to "invite" the reader into her prose, she might profitably study beginning sentences in such works as *Charlotte's Web* ("Where's Papa going with that ax?"),[54] *Roosevelt Grady* ("The Opportunity Class. That's where the bean pickers got put."),[55] or *It's Like This Cat* ("My father is always talking about how a dog can be very educational for a boy. That is one reason I got a cat.").[56] "Supposing" or

46. Eric Knight, *Lassie Come Home* (New York: Holt, Rinehart & Winston, 1954).
47. Mary Q. Steele, *Journey Outside* (New York: Viking Press, 1969).
48. Kipling, *Just So Stories.*
49. Astrid Lindgren, *Pippi Longstocking* (New York: Viking Press, 1950).
50. Paul Robert Smith, *When I Am Big* (New York: Harper & Row, 1965).
51. Keith Robertson, *Henry Reed, Inc.* (New York: Viking Press, 1958).
52. Oliver Butterworth, *The Enormous Egg* (Boston: Little, Brown & Co.; 1956).
53. Scott O'Dell, *Island of the Blue Dolphins* (Boston: Houghton Mifflin Co., 1960).
54. White, *Charlotte's Web.*
55. Louisa R. Shotwell, *Roosevelt Grady* (Cleveland, Ohio: World Publishing Co., 1963).
56. Emily C. Neville, *It's Like This Cat* (New York: Harper & Row, 1963).

"What if" types of books, like the following, can be used to encourage children to let their imaginations soar:

Belting, Natalie. *The Moon Is a Crystal Ball*. Indianapolis: Bobbs-Merrill, 1952.

Glasser, Milton, and Glasser, Shirley. *If Apples Had Teeth*. New York: Alfred A. Knopf, 1959.

Henderson, Le Gran. *The Amazing Adventures of Archie and the First Hot Dog*. New York: Abingdon Press, 1964.

Joslin, Sesyle. *What Do You Do, Dear?* New York: Young Scott Books, 1961.

Joslin, Sesyle. *What Do You Say, Dear?* New York: Young Scott Books, 1958.

Klein, Lenore. *What Would You Do If?* New York: William R. Scott, 1956.

Lobel, Arnold. *The Great Blueness and Other Predicaments*. New York: Harper & Row, 1968.

Regnier, Beatrice Schenk de. *What Can You Do with a Shoe?* New York: Harper & Brothers, 1955.

Reid, Alastair. *Supposing*. New York: Atlantic Monthly Press, 1959.

Shorpen, Liesel. *If I Had a Lion*. New York: Harper & Row, 1968.

Stolz, Mary. *Say Something*. New York: Harper & Row, 1968.

Zolotow, Charlotte. *Someday*. New York: Harper & Row, 1968.

Exploring the field of literature enables the child to develop a greater sensitivity to the use of language. Some books particularly lend themselves to an awareness of words and phrases. For example, the writings of Virginia Sorensen—especially her book *Miracles on Maple Hill*[57]—contain many descriptive phrases. Multiple meanings of words are explored in *If You Talked to a Boar*.[58] Words and phrases are used humorously in *The Phantom Toolbooth*[59] and used ironically and humorously in Mary Stolz's *Belling the Cat*.[60] Alliteration and personification are found in *Joji and the Fog;*[61] similes and metaphors, in *White Snow Bright Snow*[62] and *Backbone of the King;*[63] and idiomatic phrases, in *Strawberry Girl*.[64]

Similarly, a study of a variety of poems that contain vivid imagery or have appealing rhythm may encourage children to try to capture images of color and sound in writing their own poems.

Some poetry books that have been helpful in motivating children to write poetry include:

De Graztold, Carmen B. *Prayers from the Ark*. Translated by Rumer Godden. New York: Viking Press, 1962.

Howard, Caralie. *The First Book of Short Verse*. New York: Franklin Watts, 1964.

---

57. Virginia Sorensen, *Miracles on Maple Hill* (New York: Harcourt, Brace & World, 1956).
58. Michael Sage, *If You Talked to a Boar* (New York: J.B. Lippincott, 1960).
59. Norman Juster, *The Phantom Toolbooth* (New York: Random House, 1961).
60. Mary Stolz, *Belling the Cat* (New York: Harper & Row, 1961).
61. Betty Lifton, *Joji and the Fog* (Eau Claire, Wis.: E.M. Hale & Co., 1959).
62. Alvin Tresselt, *White Snow Bright Snow* (New York: Lothrop Lee, & Shepard Co., 1965).
63. Marcia Brown, *Backbone of the King* (New York: Charles Scribner's Sons, 1966).
64. Lloyd Alexander, *Strawberry Girl* (New York: Holt, Rinehart & Winston, 1964).

Joseph, Stephen. *The Me Nobody Knows*. New York: World Publishing Co., 1969.

Larrick, Nancy. *Green Is Like a Meadow of Grass*. Champaign, Ill.: Garrard Publishing Co., 1968.

Lewis, Richard. *Miracles*. New York: Simon & Schuster, 1966.

O'Neill, Mary. *Hailstones and Halibut Bones*. New York: Doubleday & Co., 1961.

Zolotow, Charlotte. *Some Things Go Together*. New York: Abelard, 1969.

Poems that ask questions, such as "Nancy Hanks" by Rosemary Carr and Stephen Vincent Benet or "What Is Pink?" by Christina Rossetti, often stimulate poetry writing. Children like to add their own stanzas to poems that repeat many words or phrases, such as Margaret Wise Brown's "Little Donkey Close Your Eyes," Eleanor Farjeon's "In the Week When Christmas Comes," Eve Merriam's "Catch a Little Rhyme," Evelyn Beyer's "Jump or Jiggle," and Laura E. Richard's "Kindness to Animals." Poems that may be used to encourage the use of metaphors in writing poetry include Langston Hughes's "Dreams," Emily Dickinson's "I Like To See It Lap the Miles," Dorothy Aldis's "Clouds," and Eve Merriam's "Metaphor." Merriam's poem "A Cliche" may help alert children to overworked expressions, while her "Simile: Willow and Ginkgo" may aid understanding of figurative language. Two books that may provide incentives to write haiku are *Cricket Songs*[65] and *In a Spring Garden*.[66] And children may wish to write their own limericks after reading *Laughable Limericks*[67] and *The Complete Nonsense Book*.[68] Many different types of poetry writing can be pursued following the reading and studying of various types and forms of literature: couplets, tercets, quatrains, free verse, ballads, narrative verse, lyricals.

One project developed by the Nebraska Curriculum Development Center (Lincoln: University of Nebraska) places literature as the central feature of each unit of work. Composition exercises, language explorations, and other writing activities are expected to grow directly out of the literature presentation. The English Curriculum Study Center (Athens: University of Georgia) has produced as a part of the project, "Use of Literary Models in Teaching Written Composition, Grades K-6."

Other Activities

Literature plays so many roles in the curriculum that it is impossible to comprehensively describe all of them. However, a few examples will show the importance of literature to other facets of the curriculum.

First, books are a prime source for vocabulary growth, particularly if they raise questions and provoke discussion. Children should be taught to become sensitive to word usage. What words in the selection can be interpreted by

---

65. Harry Behn, *Cricket Songs* (New York: Harcourt, Brace & World, 1964).
66. Richard Lewis, *In a Spring Garden* (New York: Dial Press, 1965).
67. Sara and John E. Brewton, *Laughable Limericks* (New York: Thomas Y. Crowell, 1965).
68. Edward Lear, *The Complete Nonsense Book* (New York: Dodd, Mead, 1912).

examining the context? Why are certain sentences interesting to read? What words or phrases seem particularly well chosen? What are some good descriptive words that have appeared in books recently read? The following are some books in which "words" comprise the major theme:

Asimov, Isaac. *Words from the Myths*. Boston: Houghton Mifflin Co., 1961.

Ernst, Margaret. *Words*. 3rd ed. New York: Alfred A. Knopf, 1954.

Funk, Charles. *Hog on Ice and Other Curious Expressions*. New York: Harper & Row, 1948.

O'Neill, Mary. *Words, Words, Words*. New York: Doubleday & Co., 1963.

Pervensen, Alice, and Pervensen, Martin. *Karen's Opposites*. New York: Golden Press, 1963.

Rand, Ann, and Rand, Paul. *Sparkle and Sin*. New York: Harcourt, Brace & World, 1957.

Reid, Alastair. *Ounce, Dice, Trice*. New York: Little, Brown & Co., 1958.

Van Gelder, Rosalind. *Monkeys Have Tails*. New York: McKay, 1966.

Two trade books that discuss the famous American dictionary maker are *Noah Webster, Boy of Words*[69] and *Noah Webster, Father of the Dictionary*.[70]

Second, children's books can be used to discover language patterns, such as changes in language over a period of time, familiar word usage, and geographical and social dialects. Some books that are conducive to such study include *Corn Farm Boy*,[71] *The Yearling*,[72] *Thee Hannah*,[73] and *Amos Fortune, Free Man*.[74] Among the books presenting the history of our language in readable form for elementary school children are *The Wonderful World of Communication*[75] and *The Language Book*.[76] There are several articles in *Elementary English* that have bibliographies citing other books which give a thorough overview of our changing language.[77]

Third, using literature to study the historical development of handwriting adds interest and increases appreciation for writing as a tool. Excellent books such as the following have been prepared on this topic:

Gourdie, Tom. *The Puffin Book of Lettering*. Baltimore, Md.: Penguin Books, 1961.

Hofsinde, Robert (Gray-Wolf). *Indian Picture Writing*. New York: William Morrow & Co., 1959.

Irwin, Keith Gordon. *The Romance of Writing*. New York: Viking Press, 1957.

---

69. Helen B. Higgins, *Noah Webster, Boy of Words* (Indianapolis: Bobbs-Merrill, 1961).

70. Isabel Proudfit, *Noah Webster, Father of the Dictionary* (New York: Julian Messner, 1942).

71. Lois Lenski, *Corn Farm Boy* (Philadelphia: J.B. Lippincott, 1954).

72. Marjorie K. Rawlings, *The Yearling* (New York: Charles Scribner's Sons, 1961).

73. Marguerite De Angeli, *Thee Hannah* (New York: Doubleday & Co., 1949).

74. Yates, *Amos Fortune*.

75. Lancelot Hogben, *The Wonderful World of Communication* (New York: Garden City Books, 1959).

76. Franklin Folsom, *The Language Book* (New York: Grosset & Dunlap, 1963).

77. See Paul C. Burns, "Elementary School Language Arts Library—A Selected Bibliography," *Elementary English* 41 (December 1964): 879-84; Maxine Delmare, "Language Books for the Library," *Elementary English* 45 (January 1968): 55-66; and Iris and Sidney Tiedt, "Linguistic Library for Students," *Elementary English* 45 (January 1968): 38-40.

Norling, Joe, and Norling, Ernest. *Pogo's Letter, A Story of Paper*. New York: Holt, Rinehart & Winston, 1946.

Russell, Solveig. *A is for Apple and Why*. New York: Abingdon Press, 1959.

Fourth, teachers often rely on literature in preparing "job sheets" or "independent study cards" for individual or small-group activities.

For example, a teacher may make the following assignments: (1) Look through the trade book *Heavens to Betsy*[78] on the language arts table to find some "old" words and some picturesque words; (2) prepare a short talk on different ways of talking. A good reference source is *Communication: From Cave Writing to Television* by Julie F. Batchelor;[79] (3) prepare to read a story (one of Aesop's fables or one of the *Just So Stories*)[80] to another class member.

Fifth, literature plays an important role in challenging the pupils, particularly those who are linguistically advanced. Some teachers supply the classroom with a variety of books, and the advanced pupils are allowed to read widely and are given considerable time for free reading. At times some pupils may be challenged to investigate specifically assigned topics, such as "What is the Newbery Prize?" or "What is the history of the word *shibboleth?*" or "What is *Roget's Thesaurus* and how is it used?" These activities encourage the use of the library, and children begin to acquire functional library skills. While browsing in the library, pupils will become familiar with the availability of hardbound books; paperbacks; magazines and periodicals *(American Girl; The Boy's Life; Child Life; Children's Digest; Cricket; Ebony, Jr.; Electric Company Magazine; Highlights for Children; Humpty Dumpty Magazine; Jack and Jill; Ranger Rick);* and newspapers (those written especially for the young as well as "regular" newspapers). Some children may wish to enroll in a book club. Membership is not as prohibitive as it once was, since some clubs now offer paperbacks exclusively.

Sixth, literature helps children to understand personal and social problems. There are many books dealing with a variety of problems that children may be trying to comprehend. For example, *Grizzly* is the story of a young boy reared by his mother after she is separated from the boy's father.[81] Some children can identify with *Queenie Peavy*, whose father is in prison.[82] In *The Empty Schoolhouse*, Lullah, a black girl, feels left out as her white friend plays on the swings in a segregated playground.[83] *A Certain Small Shepherd* gives some details of life in the Appalachian area.[84] In *A Promise Is a Promise*, the writer helps children understand the Jewish faith.[85] *Judy's Journey* is a story about migrants.[86]

Seventh, not to be overlooked is the incidental use of prose and poetry so that children may more fully enjoy everyday experiences. The teacher may relate literature to many different occasions. For example, when children catch sight of

---

78. Charles E. Funk, *Heavens to Betsy* (New York: Harper & Row, 1955).

79. Julie F. Batchelor, *Communication: From Cave Writing to Television* (New York: Harcourt Brace, 1953).

80. Kipling, *Just So Stories*.

81. Annabel and Edgar Johnson, *Grizzly* (New York: Harper & Row, 1964).

82. Robert Burch, *Queenie Peavy* (New York: Viking Press, 1966).

83. Natalie Carlson, *The Empty Schoolhouse* (New York: Harper & Row, 1965).

84. Rebecca Caudill, *A Certain Small Shepherd* (New York: Holt, Rinehart & Winston, 1965).

85. Molly Cone, *A Promise Is a Promise* (Boston: Houghton Mifflin Co., 1964).

86. Lois Lenski, *Judy's Journey* (Philadelphia: J.B. Lippincott, 1947).

the first robin of spring, any of the several robin poems in May Hill Arbuthnot's *Time for Poetry* may be introduced.[87] Or it's Betty's birthday today; it can be noted by reading an appropriate selection from *Birthday Candles Burning Brightly*.[88] For holidays, children may enjoy reading from *Poems for Seasons and Celebrations*;[89] and during particular seasons of the year, they may wish to read selections from *The Year Around*.[90] A cold morning when the classroom windows are frosted over is the time to experience David McCord's "Frost Pane."[91] And so the opportunities for the spontaneous introduction of literature into the school day become limitless.

CHILDREN'S LITERATURE STRENGTHENS ALL CURRICULUM AREAS

Children's literature is not a compartment in the school day. Surely this fact has been made clear in the preceding sections of this chapter as well as in many of the other chapters in this book. Unfortunately, children's literature is sometimes associated only with reading and other language arts areas and disassociated from mathematics, science, and social studies. This misunderstanding occurs because literature is sometimes viewed as being merely enjoyable, at the expense of being a source of information. The facts are, of course, that literature contributes to all these areas in virtually innumerable ways and must be made available throughout the school day.

Social Studies

In considering the social sciences, John Michaelis explains the role of literature in a social studies program:

> Literary selections are used in the social studies to heighten interest, deepen understanding, create moods and atmosphere, portray the diversity of ways of living and thinking among people in various cultures, stimulate imagination, give colorful backgrounds, promote more complete identification with others, provoke creativity, and give vivid impressions of ways of living.[92]

Trade books offer depth of meaning as they go beyond the skeletal facts offered in many social studies texts and reference materials. By reading realistic fiction, historical fiction, informational books, biographies, and folk literature,

---

87. May Hill Arbuthnot, *Time for Poetry*, 3rd. ed. (Chicago: Scott, Foresman & Co., 1967).
88. John and Sara Brewton, *Birthday Candles Burning Brightly* (New York: Macmillan Co., 1960).
89. William Cole, *Poems for Seasons and Celebrations* (Cleveland, Ohio: World Publishing Co., 1961).
90. Alice Hazeltine and Elva Smith, *The Year Around* (Nashville, Tenn.: Abingdon Press, 1956).
91. David McCord, "Frost Pane," in *Far and Few Rhymes of the Never Was and Always Is* (Boston: Little, Brown & Co., 1952).
92. John Michaelis, *Social Studies for Children in a Democracy*, 4th ed. (New York: Prentice-Hall, 1968), p. 476.

children can often gain more meaning from the intellectual concepts presented in the social studies program. For example, young children can gain a deeper understanding of occupations and careers by reading Lois Lenski's *Little Farm*[93] and *Cowboy Small*.[94] *Johnny Wants To Be a Policeman*[95] is another well written book on this subject.

A number of fine books about the procurement of food, clothing, and shelter are available—for example, *A House for Everyone*.[96] Biographies such as *The Columbus Story*[97] and *Lincoln: A Big Man*[98] give children the spirit of other times and enrich their comprehension of the past. Children see heroes as "real persons" in such books as *The One Bad Thing About Father*[99] and *George Washington's Breakfast*.[100] The westward movement is vividly related in *The Tree in the Trail*,[101] and the story of the first Americans is told in the *Book of Indians*.[102] Children learn about the history of medieval Europe in *Chivalry and the Mailed Knight*[103] and many interesting facts concerning Israel and its inhabitants in *This Is Israel*.[104] Children can learn more about particular regional areas by reading books such as *Blue Willow*.[105] A greater understanding of primitive life in different parts of the world can be gained by reading *Igloos, Yurts, and Totem Poles,* a collection of first person accounts.[106] And with emphasis in today's curriculum on non-Western studies, the school program should take advantage of the ever-growing list of fine books about Africa, China, India, Latin America, and Russia. Historical fiction can also be used in a social studies program, for books such as *Little House in the Big Woods*[107] and *Door in the Wall*[108] give children a flavor of particular historical periods.

Stories for holidays and other special days have provided one means for preserving much of the cultural and religious heritage of various peoples. The growing amount of quality material includes *The Littlest Angel*,[109] *Thee Hannah*,[110] and *Once upon a Holiday*.[111]

Another contribution to children's literature in recent years has been the publication of books based on original documents and journals, such as the *Russia, Adventures in Eyewitness History* series by Rhoda Hoff.[112] The series provides reports written by people who lived or traveled in the country. Other documentaries include:

---

93. Lois Lenski, *Little Farm* (New York: Oxford University Press, 1964).
94. Lois Lenski, *Cowboy Small* (New York: Henry Z. Walck, 1961).
95. Wilbur Granberg, *Johnny Wants To Be a Policeman* (New York: Alladin Books, 1951).
96. Betty Miles, *A House for Everyone* (New York: Alfred A. Knopf, 1958).
97. Alice Dalgliesh, *The Columbus Story* (New York: Charles Scribner's Sons, 1955).
98. Helen Kay, *Lincoln: A Big Man* (New York: Hastings House, 1958).
99. F.N. Monjo, *The One Bad Thing About Father* (New York: Harper & Row, 1970).
100. Jean Fritz, *George Washington's Breakfast* (New York: Coward-McCann, 1969).
101. Holling C. Holling, *The Tree in the Trail* (Boston: Houghton Mifflin Co., 1942).
102. Holling C. Holling, *Book of Indians* (New York: Platt & Munk, 1962).
103. Walter Buerk, *Chivalry and the Mailed Knight* (New York: G.P. Putnam's Sons, 1963).
104. Miroslav Sasek, *This Is Israel* (New York: Macmillan Co., 1968).
105. Doris Gates, *Blue Willow* (New York: Viking Press, 1940).
106. Frederick Boer, *Igloos, Yurts, and Totem Poles* (New York: Pantheon Books, 1957).
107. Laura Ingalls Wilder, *Little House in the Big Woods* (New York: Harper & Row, 1953).
108. Marguerite De Angeli, *Door in the Wall* (New York: Doubleday & Co., 1949).
109. Charles Tazewell, *The Littlest Angel* (New York: Children's Press, 1946).
110. De Angeli, *Thee Hannah*.
111. Lillian Moore, *Once upon a Holiday* (Nashville, Tenn.: Abingdon Press, 1959).
112. Rhoda Hoff, *Russia, Adventures in Eyewitness History* (New York: Henry Z. Walck, 1964).

Hays, Wilma P. *Freedom.* New York: Coward-McCann, 1958.

Meltzer, Milton. *History of the American Negro, 1916-1965.* New York: Thomas Y. Crowell, 1965.

Meredith, Robert, and Smith, E. Brooks. *The Coming of the Pilgrims.* Boston: Little, Brown & Co., 1964.

Sobel, Donald J. *An American Revolutionary War Reader.* New York: Franklin Watts, 1964.

Today's social studies program focuses on people—and problems of people. Reading the following books encourages discussion of "others":

Caudill, Rebecca. *A Certain Small Shepherd.* New York: Holt, Rinehart & Winston, 1965.

Hughes, Langston. *Black Misery.* New York: P.S. Erickson, 1969.

Keats, Ezra. *Goggles.* New York: Macmillan Co., 1969.

Scott, Ann H. *Sam.* New York: McGraw-Hill, 1967.

Udry, Janice M. *What Mary Jo Shared.* Chicago: Albert Whitman & Co., 1966.

Yaskima, Taro. *Crow Boy.* New York: Viking Press, 1955.

Two sources for more material about other people and their experiences and problems are *The Black Experience in Children's Books*[113] and *Multi-Ethnic Books for Young Children.*[114]

Some biographical series are suggested below; however, the teacher should evaluate the merits of each book within a series:

Beginning-To-Read Series. Chicago: Follett.

Breakthrough Books. New York: Harper & Row.

Childhood of Famous Americans Series. Indianapolis: Bobbs-Merrill.

The Discovery Books. Champaign, Ill.: Garrard Press.

Horizon Caravel Books and *American Heritage Junior Library.* New York: American Heritage (distributed by Harper & Row).

Initial Biographies. New York: Charles Scribner & Sons.

The Landmark Series. New York: Random House.

Lives to Remember Series. New York: G.P. Putnam's Sons.

North Star Books. Boston: Houghton Mifflin Co.

The See and Read Beginning-to-Read Biographies. New York: G.P. Putnam's Sons.

See and Read Biographies. New York: G.P. Putnam's Sons.

Step-Up Books. New York: Random House.

The following is a listing of geography series, but once again each book must be evaluated individually:

Enchantment of America. Chicago: Children's Press.

Getting To Know . . . New York: Coward-McCann.

Key to the City. Philadelphia: J.B. Lippincott.

---

113. Augusta Baker, *The Black Experience in Children's Books* (New York: New York Public Library, 1971).

114. Louise Griffin, *Multi-Ethnic Books for Young Children* (Washington, D.C.: National Association for Education of Young Children, 1970).

Let's Travel In . . . Chicago: Children's Press.
Let's Visit . . . New York: John Day.
My Village Is . . . New York: Pantheon Books.
Rivers of the World. Champaign, Ill.: Garrard Press.

A fine example of using children's literature in the teaching of social studies is given by Dewey W. Chambers and Margaret H. O'Brien.[115] Other helpful sources are *Literature and Music as Resources for Social Studies*,[116] *Children's Books To Enrich the Social Studies*,[117] and *American History in Juvenile Books*.[118] An excellent resource for the teacher's understanding and developing of social studies concepts is *Literary Time Line in American History*.[119]

Not to be overlooked is the use of poetry. *A Book of Americans*[120] and *America Forever New*[121] are representative of books of poetry that could be used in social studies. Richard Lewis's *The Moment of Wonder*[122] is a good collection of Chinese and Japanese poetry, and Leonard Doob's *A Crocodile Has Me by the Leg*[123] is a worthwhile presentation of African folk rhymes.

Mathematics

Trade books can contribute to children's understanding of mathematics. Counting books for the primary years suggest activities such as identifying like objects and enumerating and grouping. Several of the Mother Goose rhymes are counting jingles. The three books *Jeanne Marie Counts Her Sheep*,[124] *What Is One?*[125] and *Moja Means One*[126] help add meaning to numbers. Concepts of time and size are developed in *The Big Tree*[127] and *One Wide River To Cross*;[128] scale drawing is shown in *Understanding Maps*;[129] and an interesting portrayal of the history of geometry is found in *String, Straightedge, and Shadow*.[130] The new math is explained in several well written trade books, such as *Adler's Sets*.[131] And

115. Dewey W. Chambers and Margaret H. O'Brien, "Exploring the Golden State Through Children's Literature," *Elementary English* 46 (May 1969): 592-95.

116. Ruth Tooze and Beatrice P. Prone, *Literature and Music as Resources for Social Studies* (Englewood Cliffs, N.J.: Prentice-Hall, 1955).

117. Helen Huus, *Children's Books To Enrich the Social Studies* (Washington, D.C.: The National Council for the Social Studies, 1966).

118. Seymour Metzner, *American History in Juvenile Books* (New York: H.W. Wilson Co., 1966).

119. Patricia Cianciolo and Jean LePere, *Literary Time Line in American History* (Garden City, N.Y.: Doubleday & Co., 1969).

120. Rosemary and Stephen Vincent Benet, *A Book of Americans* (New York: Holt, Rinehart & Winston, 1961).

121. Sara and John E. Brewton, *America Forever New* (New York: Thomas Y. Crowell, 1968).

122. Richard Lewis, *The Moment of Wonder* (New York: Dial Press, 1964).

123. Leonard Doob, *A Crocodile Has Me by the Leg* (New York: Walker & Co., 1966).

124. Françoise Seignobosc, *Jeanne Marie Counts Her Sheep* (New York: Charles Scribner's Sons, 1951).

125. Nancy Watson, *What Is One?* (New York: Alfred A. Knopf, 1964).

126. Muriel Feelings, *Moja Means One* (New York: Dial Press, 1971).

127. Mary and Conrad Buff, *The Big Tree* (New York: Viking Press, 1963).

128. Barbara Emberly, *One Wide River To Cross* (New York: Prentice-Hall, 1966).

129. Beulah Tannenbaum and Myra Stillman, *Understanding Maps* (New York: McGraw-Hill, 1957).

130. Julia Diggins, *String, Straightedge, and Shadow* (New York: Viking Press, 1965).

131. Irving and Ruth Adler, *Adler's Sets* (New York: John Day, 1967).

Famous Mathematicians provides informative biographies of some of the great mathematicians.[132]

A number of poems have mathematics as a topic. The following are some examples:

Barnstone, Aliki. "Numbers." *The Real Tin Flower.* New York: Crowell-Collier, 1968.

Brown, Beatrice Curtis. "Johnathan Bing Does Arithmetic." In *Gaily We Parade,* edited by John E. Brewton. New York: Macmillan Co., 1964.

Read, Sir Herbert. "Equations." In *Catch Me a Wind,* edited by Patricia Hubbell. New York: Atheneum Publishers, 1968.

Sandburg, Carl. "Arithmetic." *Wind Song.* New York: Harcourt, Brace & World, 1960.

"There Was an Old Man Who Said Do." (Anonymous). In *Rainbow in the Sky,* edited by L. Untermeyer. New York: Harcourt, Brace & World, 1935.

A valuable list of trade books that can be used to supplement and enrich a mathematics program is found in *The Elementary and Junior High School Mathematics Library.*[133]

Science

Since reading for information is an important part of any science program, trade books should be an integral part of the program. Trade books offer material at various reading levels and can provide the reader with a greater understanding of various topics, excitement and delight, and information on new developments in science.

A good science program makes use of books dealing with concepts *(The World Is Round);*[134] identifications *(Junior Book of Birds);*[135] the life cycles of animals *(Sphinx, the Story of a Caterpillar);*[136] experiments *(Now Try This);*[137] scientific methods *(Let's Get Turtles).*[138] Also included should be biographies (of Thomas Alva Edison, Madam Curie, Albert Einstein, George Washington Carver, for example); independent activities books *(Science Teasers);*[139] and picture books *(A Butterfly Is Born).*[140] Trade books cover innumerable topics: birds; earth and sky; energy, matter, and machines; fish, reptiles, and amphibians; insects; mammals; oceanography; plants; and space. Well-written, accurate nonfiction trade books widen the child's vista of the real world and help to bring him an understanding of its secrets. Science books are also available in such series as *First*

---

132. Frances Benson Stonaker, *Famous Mathematicians* (Philadelphia: J.B. Lippincott, 1966).

133. Clarence Hardgrove, *The Elementary and Junior High School Mathematics Library* (Washington, D.C.: The National Council of Teachers of Mathematics, 1968).

134. Anthony Ravielli, *The World Is Round* (New York: Viking Press, 1963).

135. Roger Peterson, *Junior Book of Birds* (Boston: Houghton Mifflin Co., 1939).

136. Robert M. McClung, *Sphinx, the Story of a Caterpillar* (New York: William Morrow & Co., 1949).

137. Herman and Nina Schneider, *Now Try This* (New York: W.R. Scott, 1947).

138. Millicent Selsam, *Let's Get Turtles* (New York: Harper & Row, 1965).

139. Rose Wyler and Eva-Lee Baird, *Science Teasers* (New York: Harper & Row, 1966).

140. J.P.V. Eeckhoudt, *A Butterfly Is Born,* (New York: Viking Press, 1963).

Books (New York: Watts); *All About Books* (New York: Random House); and *True Books* (Chicago: Children's Press).

The science teacher is encouraged to have these three volumes of poetry ready for use:

Bramblett, Ella. *Sheets of Green.* New York: Thomas Y. Crowell, 1968.

Brewton, Sara, and Brewton, John. *Bridled with Rainbows.* New York: Macmillan Co., 1950.

Platz, Helen. *Imagination's Other Place.* New York: Thomas Y. Crowell, 1955.

A valuable source for choosing science books is *The AAAS Science Booklist for Children.*[141] The books on this list have been checked for scientific accuracy as have those reviewed in the monthly magazine *Science and Children.*[142] Other specialized listings are found in *A Guide to Science Reading,*[143] *Library Materials for Elementary Science,*[144] and *Growing Up with Science Books.*[145] Teachers should also be aware of award-winning science books. The Thomas Alva Edison Foundation Award is given annually in the categories of "The Best Children's Science Book" and "The Best Science Book for Youth."

Art and Music

Children's literature can play an important role in helping children develop a sensitivity to the arts. The beautiful work of Taro Yashima as found in *Crow Boy*[146] is an example of the fine artwork found in many selections of good children's literature, and such models should not be ignored in developing art appreciation in our schools. Trade book illustrations acquaint the child with many different art forms: realism *(American Indian Story);*[147] expressionism *(Charley Sang a Song);*[148] cubism *(Brian Wildsmith's 1,2,3's);*[149] collage *(Frederick);*[150] pointillism *(This Is New York);*[151] folk art *(The Nightingale);*[152] and cartoon art *(Horton Hatches the Egg).*[153] Opportunities to develop appreciation and understanding of

---

141.   Hilary J. Deason, *The AAAS Science Booklist for Children* (Washington, D.C.,: American Association for the Advancement of Science, 1963).

142.   *Science and Children* (Washington, D.C.: The National Science Teachers Association).

143.   Hilary J. Deason, *A Guide to Science Reading* (New York: Signet, 1964).

144.   Albert Hama and Mary K. Eakin, *Library Materials for Elementary Science* (Cedar Falls, Iowa: State College of Iowa, 1964).

145.   Julia Schwartz, *Growing Up with Science Books* (New York: R.R. Bowker Co., 1966).

146.   Taro Yashima, *Crow Boy* (Viking Press, 1955).

147.   May McNeer, *American Indian Story* (New York: Farrar, Straus, & Giroux, 1963). (Illustrated by Lynn Ward.)

148.   H.R. and Daniel Hays, *Charley Sang a Song* (New York: Harper & Row, 1964). (Illustrated by Uri Shulevitz.)

149.   Brian Wildsmith, *Brian Wildsmith's 1,2,3's* (New York: Franklin Watts, 1965). (Illustrated by author.)

150.   Leo Lionni, *Frederick* (New York: Random House, 1967). (Illustrated by author.)

151.   Miroslav Sasek, *This Is New York* (New York: Macmillan Co., 1960). (Illustrated by author.)

152.   Hans C. Anderson, *The Nightingale* (New York: Harper & Row, 1965). (Illustrated by Nancy E. Burkert.)

153.   Dr. Seuss, *Horton Hatches the Egg* (New York: Random House, 1940). (Illustrated by author.)

graphic arts are abundant in children's books, since they contain illustrations done in various media (watercolor, oils, tempera, pastels) and techniques (woodcuts, linocuts, wood engraving, scratch board).

Looking at Art[154] contains excellent reproductions of paintings and interpretative comments about composition and the way in which artists express their ideas. There are children's books that display photographs and drawings of prehistoric art *(The Caves of the Great Hunter)*[155] and discuss art in other lands *(The Art of the Eskimo).*[156] Many "technique" books, such as *Print Making with a Spoon,*[157] are available. A most useful source book is *A Bibliography of Children's Art Literature.*[158]

For experiencing music, there are books of folk songs that can be used to supplement the textbook material, such as *Folk Songs of China, Japan, Korea.*[159] Children may enjoy books that give information about instruments of the orchestra, such as *Horns.*[160]

Library shelves contain a host of trade books—biographies or informational books—on the fine arts. These include *The Book of Ballet;*[161] *The Story of Leonard Bernstein;*[162] *The Wonderful World of the Theatre;*[163] and *Gainsborough.*[164]

Almost any book of poetry can enhance the art and music curriculum, but the following are especially recommended:

Adshead, Gladys, and Duff, Annis. *An Inheritance of Poetry.* Boston: Houghton Mifflin Co., 1948.

O'Neill, Mary. *Hailstones and Halibut Bones.* Garden City, New York: Doubleday & Co., 1961.

Plotz, Helen. *Untune the Sky.* New York: Thomas Y. Crowell 1957.

Tolkein, J.R.R. *The Road Goes Ever On.* Boston: Houghton Mifflin Co., 1967.

Wilder, Alec. *Lullabies and Night Songs.* New York: Harper & Row, 1965.

Children's literature provides an excellent springboard for artistic activities, such as illustrating a favorite story and placing the illustrations on a roller movie for presentation. Other activities are mural painting; constructing dioramas, peep boxes, puppets and marionettes, bulletin board displays, mobiles, and wall hangings; clay modeling; and telling flannel board stories. Activities related to music include identifying appropriate background music for prose and poetry selections, composing of music, and moving rhythmically.

---

154. Alice E. Chase, *Looking at Art* (New York: Thomas Y. Crowell, 1966).
155. Hans Baumann, *The Caves of the Great Hunter* (New York: Pantheon Books, 1962).
156. Shirley Blubek, *The Art of the Eskimo* (New York: Harper & Row, 1964).
157. Norman Gorbarty, *Print Making with a Spoon* (New York: Reinhold Publishing Corp., 1960).
158. Kenneth Marantz, *A Bibliography of Children's Art Literature* (Washington, D.C.: National Art Association, 1965).
159. Betty Dietz and Thomas Park, *Folk Songs of China, Japan, Korea* (New York: John Day, 1964).
160. Larry Kettelkamp, *Horns* (New York: William Morrow & Co., 1964).
161. James Audsley, *The Book of Ballet* (New York: Frederick Warne, 1964).
162. David Ewen, *The Story of Leonard Bernstein* (Philadelphia: Chilton Books, 1960).
163. J.B. Priestly, *The Wonderful World of the Theatre* (Garden City, N.Y.: Doubleday & Co., 1959).
164. Elizabeth Ripley, *Gainsborough* (Philadelphia: J.B. Lippincott, 1964).

Health, Physical Education, and Safety

Many trade books are available that can be used to enrich these three areas of the curriculum: *The Human Senses*,[165] *Physical Fitness for Young Champions*,[166] *Modern Medical Discoveries*,[167] *The Human Body: The Heart*,[168] *The Wonderful Story of How You Were Born*,[169] *Drugs: Facts on Their Use and Abuse*,[170] *The First Book of Nurses*,[171] *Lifeline: The Story of Your Circulatory System*,[172] *Let's Find Out About Safety*,[173] and *Inside You and Me*.[174] Books on health and safety are frequently reviewed in *School Safety*, a magazine for elementary school teachers.[175]

Sports are an important part of children's lives, and this interest may lead them to read fiction *(Basketball Sparkplug)*,[176] biography *(Famous Negro Athletes)*,[177] and informational books *(Figure Skating)*.[178] Another book that children may enjoy reading is *Sprints and Distances,* which tells of "sports in poetry and the poetry in sport."[179]

EVALUATION AND DIAGNOSTIC TEACHING

In the literature program, overall aims may be translated into statements of pupil behavior for assessment and evaluation purposes. For an example, see "A Taxonomy of Literary Understandings and Skills" in *Children's Literature in the Elementary School*.[180] One pencil-and-paper test of literature appreciation for children in grades four, five, and six is found in *A Look at Literature*.[181] Another tool to determine children's knowledge and background in literature is given in "Get Children Excited About Books" in *Coordinating Reading Instruction*.[182] Two other excellent references include: "Evaluating Elementary Literature Programs"

165. Robert Antonacci, *The Human Senses* (New York: McGraw-Hill, 1962).
166. Jeanne Bendick, *Physical Fitness for Young Champions* (New York: Franklin Watts, 1968).
167. Iregarde Eberle, *Modern Medical Discoveries* (New York: Thomas Y. Crowell, 1963).
168. Kathleen Elgin, *The Human Body: The Heart* (New York: Franklin Watts, 1968).
169. Sidonie Gruenberg, *The Wonderful Story of How You Were Born* (New York: Doubleday & Co., 1959).
170. Norman Houser, *Drugs: Facts on Their Use and Abuse* (New York: Lothrop, Lee & Shepard Co., 1969).
171. Eleanor Kay, *The First Book of Nurses* (New York: Franklin Watts, 1968).
172. Herman Schneider, *Lifeline: The Story of Your Circulatory System* (New York: Harcourt, Brace & World, 1958).
173. Martha Shapp, *Let's Find Out About Safety* (New York: Franklin Watts, 1964).
174. Eloise Turner, *Inside You and Me* (New York: John Day, 1961).
175. *School Safety* (Washington, D.C.: National Safety Council).
176. Matt Christopher, *Basketball Sparkplug* (Boston: Little, Brown & Co., 1957).
177. Arna Bontemps, *Famous Negro Athletes* (New York: Dodd, Mead, 1964).
178. Sally Lindsay, *Figure Skating* (Chicago: Rand McNally & Co., 1963).
179. Lillian Morrison, *Sprints and Distances* (New York: Thomas Y. Crowell, 1965).
180. Charlotte S. Huck and Doris Y. Kuhn, *Children's Literature in the Elementary School*, 2nd ed. (New York: Holt, Rinehart & Winston, 1968), pp. 588-691.
181. *A Look at Literature* (Princeton, N.J.: Educational Testing Service, 1969).
182. Charlotte S. Huck, "Get Children Excited About Books," in *Coordinating Reading Instruction*, ed. Helen M. Robinson (Chicago: Scott, Foresman & Co., 1971), pp. 114-24.

in *Elementary English*[183] and "Evaluation of Children's Responses to Literature" in *Library Quarterly.*[184]

TRENDS OF THE FUTURE

There are some general trends that are very likely to influence the future of children's literature and the literature program at the elementary school level. It can be said with assurance that trade books will continue to reflect the changes in our culture and so will play a vital role in the curriculum. Language changes will be noted in children's books as language itself changes. Also, changes in life-styles and attitudes will be reflected in books for children. Some more specific trends in children's books include the following:

1. With the focus on early childhood education, there will be an increasing demand for picture books for two-, three-, and four-year-olds.
2. There will be experimentations with new media and art forms in picture books.
3. More informational books and biographies as well as trade books recognizing features of a pluralistic society will be available for children.
4. There will be more trade books that relate to contemporary curriculum areas. For example, trade books dealing with science will likely draw on our growing knowledge of outer space, biological principles, and underwater life. And those trade books dealing with social studies will likely focus on the traditionally neglected topics of anthropology, economics, and government.
5. More paperback editions will be available, including paperback picture books.

Some trends in the literature program may include the following:

1. Instructional materials centers, centralized libraries, and classroom libraries will expand as financial support is increased for the purchase of materials.
2. More sources of knowledge needed by the teacher of literature will become available. In part, this will be achieved through research on children's reading interests, preferences, and habits, particularly those of the urban and minority-group child. Classroom teachers will have a more substantial repertoire of children's literature—both prose and poetry—and more materials with information on authors, illustrators, and techniques for creative reading and telling of stories and poems. Information will be provided through professional materials, periodicals, and paperbacks.

183. Martha E. Irwin, "Evaluating Elementary Literature Programs," *Elementary English* 40 (December 1963): 846-49.
184. Doris Young, "Evaluation of Children's Responses to Literature," *Library Quarterly* 37 (January 1967): 100-109.

3. Literature will be recognized as a valuable discipline of study and as such will hold a more prominent place in the curriculum and will be planned more carefully to fit into the school program.
4. Audience reading, or oral interpretation of literature, will likely receive increased attention as a facet of the literature program.
5. Literature will be recognized for its contribution to the understanding of other disciplines. As such, there will be more overlap in the use of trade books and textbooks in terms of sources of information and means of learning. Teachers will reorganize instructional patterns to make maximum use of trade books.
6. Literature and media will become even more closely related, and ways of using audiovisual aids will be expanded in many directions.

EXERCISES FOR THOUGHT AND ACTION

1. Discuss "What is your read-aloud program?" in terms of the need for a balanced program.
2. Describe how you would introduce a particular author or illustrator to a group of children.
3. Interview a reading specialist in your school system. Ask this person to discuss the role of trade books in helping children learn to read.
4. Discuss significant features of several children's magazines and newspapers and indicate their possible uses in a school program.
5. Examine a social studies textbook to find areas that can be enhanced by children's literature.
6. Compile for a grade level of your choice a file of stories and poems suitable for a particular mathematics topic.
7. Develop a bibliography of children's trade books that will strengthen a specific science unit. Indicate how these books would be used in that unit of study.
8. Interview an artist (or a professor of art) on the importance of book illustrations to the art education of children.
9. Develop a list of desired behavioral characteristics in regard to literature at one school level of your choosing.
10. Preview some of the media cited in "Audiovisual Aids" and prepare a list of literary concepts associated with each.

SELECTED READINGS

I. *Specialized Reading Material*

A Curriculum for English and Poetry for the Elementary Grades. Lincoln: University of Nebraska Press, 1966.

A Multimedia Approach to Children's Literature. Chicago: American Library Association, 1972.

Arbuthnot, May Hill. Children and Books. Chicago: Scott, Foresman & Co., 1964.

Arbuthnot, May Hill; Clark, Margaret Mary; and Long, Harriet Geneva. Children's Books Too Good To Miss. Cleveland, Ohio: Western Reserve University Press, 1963.

Bamman, Henry A.; Dawson, Mildred A.; and Whitehead, Robert J. Oral Interpretation of Children's Literature. 2nd ed. Dubuque, Iowa: William C. Brown Co., 1971.

Boyd, Gertrude. Teaching Poetry in Elementary Schools. Columbus, Ohio: Charles E. Merrill Publishing Co., 1973.

Carlson, Ruth K. Enrichment Ideas. Dubuque, Iowa: William C. Brown Co., 1970.

———. Poetry for Today's Child. Danville, N.Y.: F.A. Owen Publishing Co., 1968.

Chambers, Dewey. Children's Literature in the Curriculum. Chicago: Rand McNally & Co., 1971.

Cianciola, Patricia. Illustrations in Children's Books. Dubuque, Iowa: William C. Brown Co., 1970.

Cohen, Monroe D., ed. Literature with Children. Washington, D.C.: Association for Childhood Education International, 1972.

Coody, Betty. Using Literature with Young Children. Dubuque, Iowa: William C. Brown Co., 1973.

Crosby, Muriel, ed. Reading Ladders for Human Relations. 4th ed. Washington, D.C.: American Council on Education, 1963.

Cullinan, Bernice E. Literature for Children: Its Discipline and Content. Dubuque, Iowa: William C. Brown Co., 1970.

Darton, F.J. Harvey. Children's Books in England. 2nd ed. Cambridge: Cambridge University Press, 1958.

Teaching Literature in Wisconsin. Madison: Wisconsin Department of Public Instruction, English-Language Arts Curriculum Project, 1965.

Development of Taste in Literature. Champaign, Ill.: The National Council of Teachers of English, 1963.

de Vries, Leonard. Flowers of Delight: An Agreeable Garland of Prose and Poetry. London: Dennis Dobson, 1965.

Eakin, Mary K. Good Books for Children, 1948-1961. Chicago: University of Chicago Press, 1962.

Fenwick, Sara Innis, ed. A Critical Approach to Children's Literature. Chicago: University of Chicago Press, 1967.

Georgiou, Constantine. Children and Their Literature. Englewood Cliffs, N.J.: Prentice-Hall, 1969.

Gillespie, Margaret. Literature for Children: History and Trends. Dubuque, Iowa: William C. Brown Co., 1970.

Guilfoile, Elizabeth. Books for Beginning Readers. Champaign, Ill.: The National Council of Teachers of English, 1962.

Hanna, Geneva R., and McAllister, Mariana K. Books, Young People, and Reading Guidance. New York: Harper & Brothers, 1960.

Haviland, Virginia. Children's Literature. Washington, D.C.: U.S. Government Printing Office, 1966.

Hopkins, Lee Bennett. Pass the Poetry, Please. New York: Citation Press, 1972.

Huber, Miriam Blanton. Story and Verse for Children. 3rd ed. New York: Macmillan Co., 1965.

Huck, Charlotte S., and Kuhn, Doris Y. *Children's Literature in the Elementary School*. 2nd ed. New York: Holt, Rinehart & Winston, 1968.

Johnson, Edna; Sickels, Evelyn R.; and Sayers, Frances C. *Anthology of Children's Literature*. Boston: Houghton Mifflin Co., 1959.

Kosinski, Leonard V., ed. *Readings on Creativity and Imagination in Language and Literature*. Champaign, Ill.: The National Council of Teachers of English, 1969.

Lamb, Pose, ed. *Literature for Children*. Dubuque, Iowa: William C. Brown Co., 1970.

Larrick, Nancy. *A Teacher's Guide to Children's Books*. Columbus, Ohio: Charles E. Merrill Books, 1961.

Lonsdale, Bernard J., and Mackintosh, Helen K. *Children Experience Literature*. New York: Random House, 1972.

Martignoni, Margaret, ed. *The Illustrated Treasury of Children's Literature*. New York: Grosset & Dunlop, 1955.

Meigs, Cornelia, et al. *A Critical History of Children's Literature*. New York: Macmillan Co., 1953.

Meeker, Alice M. *Enjoying Literature with Children*. New York: The Odyssey Press, 1969.

Montebello, Mary. *Children's Literature in the Curriculum*. Dubuque, Iowa: William C. Brown Co., 1972.

Morton, Miriam, ed. *A Harvest of Russian Children's Literature*. Berkeley: University of California Press, 1967.

Odland, Norine. *Teaching Literature in the Elementary School*. Champaign, Ill.: The National Council of Teachers of English, 1969.

Prescott, Orville, ed. *A Father Reads to His Children*. New York: Dutton, 1965.

Robinson, Evelyn R., ed. *Readings About Children's Literature*. New York: David McKay Co., 1966.

Root, Sheldon, ed. *Adventuring with Books*. New York: Citation Press, 1973.

Smith, James Steel. *A Critical Approach to Children's Literature*. New York: McGraw-Hill, 1967.

Smith, Dora V. *Fifty Years of Children's Books, 1910-1960*. Champaign, Ill.: The National Council of Teachers of English, 1963.

Wagner, Joseph A. *Children's Literature Through Storytelling*. Dubuque, Iowa: William C. Brown Co., 1970.

Whitehead, Robert. *Children's Literature: Strategies of Teaching*. Englewood Cliffs, N.J.: Prentice-Hall, 1968.

Witucke, Virginia. *Poetry in the Elementary School*. Dubuque, Iowa: William C. Brown Co., 1970.

II. *Reference Books*

Brewton, John E., and Brewton, Sara W., comps. *Index to Children's Poetry*. New York: H.W. Wilson Co., 1942. (Supplements in 1954 and 1965.)

Eakin, Mary K. *Subject Index to Books for Intermediate Grades*. 3rd ed. Chicago: American Library Association, 1963.

Eakin, Mary K., and Merrit, Eleanor, eds. *Subject Index to Books for Primary Grades*. 2nd ed. Chicago: American Library Association, 1961.

Eastman, Mary, comp. *Index to Fairy Tales, Myths, and Legends*. Boston: Faxon, 1952.

Fidell, Rachel, and Fidell, Estelle, eds. *Children's Catalog*. New York: H.W. Wilson Co., 1966.

Field, Carolyn W. *Subject Collections in Children's Literature*. New York: R.R. Bowker Co., 1969.

Gaver, Mary Virginia, ed. *The Elementary School Library Collection*. Newark, N.J.: Bro-Dart Foundations, 1967-68.

Sell, Violet, et al., comps. *Subject Index to Poetry for Children and Young People*. Chicago: American Library Association, 1957.

Snow, Miriam, et al. *A Basic Book Collection for Elementary Schools*. 7th ed. Chicago: American Library Association, 1960.

Subject and Title Index to Short Stories for Children. Chicago, Ill.: American Library Association, 1955.

III. *General Book Lists*

Bibliography of Books for Children. Washington, D.C.: Association for Childhood Education International, 1965.

Currah, Ann, ed. *Best Books for Children*. New York: R.R. Bowker Co., 1967.

Guilfoile, Elizabeth, ed. *Adventuring with Books: A Booklist for Elementary Schools*. New York: New American Library, 1966.

IV. *Periodicals*

The Booklist and Subscription Books Bulletin. Chicago, Ill.: American Library Association.

The Bulletin of the Center for Children's Books. Chicago: University of Chicago, Graduate Library School.

Childhood Education. Washington, D.C.: Association for Childhood Education International.

Language Arts. Urbana, Ill.: The National Council of Teachers of English.

The Horn Book Magazine. Boston: The Horn Book.

Saturday Review. 25 W. 45th St., New York, N.Y. 10036.

School Library Journal. New York: R.R. Bowker Co.

AUDIOVISUAL AIDS

I. *Reference Sources*

American Library Association. *Catalog*. 50 E. Huron St., Chicago, Ill. 60611.

Annotated List of Recordings in the Language Arts. Champaign, Ill.: The National Council of Teachers of English, 1964.

Caedmon Records. *Catalog*. 508 8th Ave., New York, N.Y. 10018.

Charles E. Merrill Publishing Co. *Catalog* (of tapes of stories and poems.) 1300 Alum Creek Dr., Columbus, Ohio 43216.

Churchill Films. *Catalog*. 662 N. Robertson Blvd., Los Angeles, Calif. 90069.

CMS Records. *Catalog*. 14 Warren St., New York, N.Y. 10007.

Coronet Film. *Catalog*. 65 E. Water St., Chicago, Ill. 60601.

Educator's Guide to Free Films. Randolph, Wis.: Educator's Progress Service. (Annual.)

Educator's Guide to Free Filmstrips. Randolph, Wis.: Educator's Progress Service. (Annual.)

Educator's Guide to Free Tapes, Scripts, and Transcriptions. Randolph, Wis.: Educator's Progress Service. (Annual.)

Encyclopaedia Britannica Educational Corporation. *Film Catalog*. 425 No. Michigan Ave., Chicago, Ill. 60611.

Films for Libraries. Chicago: American Library Association, 1963.

Folkway Records. *Catalog*. 121 W. 47th, New York, N.Y. 10036.

Grover Film Productions. *Catalog*. P.O. Box 12, Helotes, Tex. 78023.

Jam Handy Organization. *Catalog*. 2821 E. Grand Blvd., Detroit, Mich. 48211.

Library of Congress Catalogue: Motion Pictures and Filmstrips. Washington, D.C.: Library of Congress.

Miller-Brody Productions. *Catalog* (of records and filmstrips). 342 Madison Ave., New York, N.Y. 10017.

National Education Association. *National Tape Recording Catalog*. Washington, D.C.: Department of Audiovisual Instruction.

National Information Center for Educational Media. *Index to 16-mm Educational Films*. New York: R.R. Bowker Co., 1969.

Recordings for Children. New York: New York Public Library, Office of Children's Services, 1964.

Roach, Helen. *Spoken Records*. New York: Scarecrow Press, 1963.

Rufsveld, Margaret, and Guss, Carolyn. *Guides to New Educational Media*. 2nd ed. Chicago: American Library Association, 1967.

Society for Visual Education. *Film Catalog*. 1345 Diversey Pkwy., Chicago, Ill. 60614.

Spoken Arts. *Catalog*. 59 Locust St., New Rochelle, N.Y. 10801.

Sterling Films. *Catalog*. 316 W. 57th St., New York, N.Y. 10016.

Teaching Resource Films. *Catalog*. 86 East Ave., Norwalk, Conn. 16851.

Westinghouse Learning Corp. *Learning Directory* (A-V Reference Section), 100 Park Ave., New York, N.Y. 10017.

Weston Woods. *Catalog*. Weston, Conn. 06880.

II. *Filmstrips, Films, and Recordings*

1. *Filmstrips*

The Little Engine that Could. Society for Visual Education.

Make Way for Ducklings; Millions of Cats; Crow Boy. Weston Woods.

Stories from Other Lands series; *Hans Christian Anderson Stories*. Encyclopaedia Britannica Educational Corp.

The Three Bears; Three Billy Goats Gruff; Three Little Pigs; Heroes of Greek Mythology; Myths of Greece and Rome. Jam Handy Organization.

2. *Films*

The Camel Who Took a Walk and *Robert McCloskey*. Weston Woods.

Fire Flowers of Yet Sing Low. Sterling.

Hare and the Tortoise. Encyclopaedia Britannica Educational Corp.

The Little Engine That Could; The Midnight Ride of Paul Revere; Paul Bunyan Lumber Camp Tales; The Ugly Duckling. Coronet.

Poetry for Me and *Poetry to Grow On*. Grover.

Story of a Book. Churchill Films.

3. *Recordings*

An Anthology of Negro Poetry for Young People; Folktales from West Africa. Folkways.

Joy to the World; Poetry Parade. Weston Woods.

Mother Goose. Caedmon.

Star Maiden; Other Indian Tales. CMS Records.

Wheel on the School. American Library Association.

You Read to Me, I'll Read to You. Spoken Arts.

4. *Multimedia sets (book/record)*

Favorite Rhymes from a Rocket in My Pocket; Over in the Meadow; Selections from Faces and Places; Selections from The Arrow Book of Poetry. Scholastic Book Services.

5. *Picture sets*

Reproductions suitable for framing from the works of illustrators of children's books are available from the publishers.

Major instructional attention is given in this chapter to the development of organizational skill in writing as well as other composition skills. The discussion focuses on written expression, but much of what is said is applicable to speaking and other forms of expression.

This chapter is related in many ways to the rest of the book. For example, this chapter, as with all the others, gives much attention to children's thinking processes. Furthermore, suggestions on the writing first done by children reemphasizes the importance of an activity presented in Chapter 6—the use of experience charts in reading instruction. In addition, the writing of poetry and stories elaborates on some of the ideas presented in the chapter on children's literature. In some of the chapters that follow—those on social studies and science, for example—the learning processes stressed and the related activities provide for various kinds of writing.

W.T.P.

Children's Writing in Modern Classrooms

Walter T. Petty

8

Attempting to teach children to put their thoughts into written form is a prevailing task of schools, which begins with the child's first experiences in the classroom and continues through the freshman year in college and beyond. The consequences of this teaching effort are difficult to determine. Certainly many persons do learn to write their thoughts very ably, yet others demonstrate competence only in extremely limited situations, and still others show virtually no competence at all. How much effect the teaching effort has on a person's ability to write is not at all clear. At best, teaching children to write well is an elusive goal.

The fact that writing may be difficult to teach does not diminish its importance. Even in a multimedia world, the value of writing to individuals and to society is evident. Most of us write something every day, and all about us are the products of writers: books and magazines, newspapers, advertisements, legal documents, government reports, and so on.

WRITING: SKILLS, OBJECTIVES, EXPERIENCE

Writing is a personal act; it is a means for expression of the self. It is a process of thought and emotion that requires the use of certain skills and abilities if the final product is to accomplish the particular purpose. Because writing is a personal activity, the writer determines the purpose and judges the effectiveness of the product. As an expression of self, both the process and the product change as the individual changes. As the individual grows, as his or her background of experience enlarges, as he or she learns, the personal storehouse of knowledge and emotion for written expression becomes greater. Furthermore, as the individual grows, the ability to express ideas and feelings also grows, providing that the writer has learned or is learning the necessary skills and that the desire to voice these ideas and feelings is not stifled.

Many teachers as well as curriculum guides and language arts textbooks identify two types of writing. These are usually called "creative" and "practical," with factual, functional, expository, or utilitarian sometimes substituted for practical and with personal less frequently substituted for creative. However, making this distinction in types of writing is declining since educators are increasingly recognizing that if children are taught what they should be taught—that is, to write about what is important to them and to their personal communication needs—then writing becomes both personal and purposeful, or practical. Educators are becoming more and more aware that each child's writing is an individual matter and should reflect his or her feelings and thoughts as an individual. It is also recognized that the product will be satisfying to the individual only if the writer has a good command of compositional skills, style, and form.

Writing Skills

Writing involves many skills and abilities. The most fundamental of these are the thinking skills or abilities, which are basic to the expression of feelings and thoughts, whether the medium is speech, movement, art, or writing. In relation to writing, these skills include collecting and organizing data; classifying, comparing, and summarizing ideas and feelings; choosing the most appropriate words and phrases for conveying expressions; organizing these expressions into sentences that are clearly understandable; and sequencing the sentences into a meaningful whole. All of these thinking abilities are used to compose a piece of writing, with the effectiveness of any composition largely dependent on the quality of the thinking ability or skill of the composer. No written expression, not even a single sentence or a label or a short memorandum, will be effective expression unless it is well thought out.

In addition, of course, skill in forming letters and words, in spelling correctly, in punctuating sentences properly, and in those matters of form and custom in the appearance of various types of writing are also very much a part of effective written expression. And each of these general skills or abilities consists of specific lesser ones: in handwriting, the strokes needed to make the letters, spacing, rhythm of movement; in spelling, making sound and symbol associations, affixing, capitalizing; in punctuation, the strokes needed to form the punctuation marks. All of these skills require teaching and thorough practice so that they become automatic to writers and permit them to use full thinking power for composition.

Curriculum Objectives

As indicated in the preceding section, the skills and abilities to be fostered, taught, and developed in the elementary school writing curriculum are many and varied. Taking into account that writing is such a personal activity and that children have different rates of development, it is impossible to state that certain objectives will be achieved by specific times or by all children. The primary, overall objective is for each child to achieve effectiveness in as many of these skills and abilities as possible. It is important to consider, however, that the extent to which this general, overall objective is achieved largely depends on helping each child to accomplish the following:

1. Awareness of the various purposes and uses of written language
2. Satisfaction of personal and social needs through written language
3. Knowledge of the basic forms society prescribes for different types of writing
4. Freedom and willingness to experiment with all aspects of written language

Fundamental in meeting these general objectives is an environment that fosters interest in writing, gives opportunity for creativity and expression of self, and nurtures and develops learning. This environment cannot be achieved by the use of any set of materials or prescribed teaching plan or lesson or by any physical conditions of a classroom or building. A good classroom environment is almost solely the responsibility of the individual teacher, and those teachers who have a workable teaching plan and who make each child feel relaxed are most likely to achieve it.

Stated more specifically, the program should seek to develop each pupil's ability to:

1. Organize the content of sentences, paragraphs, and more extended discourse by such means as (1) time signals and order, (2) cause and effect relationships, (3) classification of elements, (4) comparison and contrast of information and ideas, and (5) development of generalizations through inductive and deductive approaches
2. Use basic sentence patterns with comparable ability to their use in oral expression
3. Choose words and phrases that are most appropriate to the purpose of the expression
4. Show unity and coherence by skillful use of ordering, linking ideas, making transitions, topic sentences, and the like
5. Use the processes of compounding, subordinating, and substituting in constructing sentences
6. Vary writing style, point of view, and tone

In addition, children need to learn the basic conventions for recording expression in written form, hence there are many objectives that are related to specific skills needed in this area. These objectives are stated in later sections of this chapter.

Writing and Experience

Adults generally recognize that they cannot write very effectively about something they really do not understand. Few of us could write about a chemical experiment without some background in chemistry, about how to direct a play without theater experience, or about a legal decision without studying law. This fact is an important clue to teaching written expression: Children will write about those things they know about, that they have experienced, or that have some kind of meaning for them. Furthermore, they will write in those forms that they have had experience with. That is, they will write letters if they know how letters are written; they will write reviews of books if they know the organization and form of reviews; they will write a story if they understand such matters as characterization, plot, and climax.

All children entering school for the first time have had many experiences. They have learned from these experiences and have many ideas based on them. Thus the bases for writing are present. But as suggested in the following section, children need to gain more experiences.

A vital writing program can exist only if the entire language arts curriculum—actually the total curriculum—is meaningful and challenging. If children have an abundance of ideas, written expression comes freely and naturally. Ideas may originate from working on a science project, taking a field trip as a social studies activity, learning a new musical number, discussing rules for a game played during recess, working out solutions to mathematics problems, or engaging in any one of a number of other activities that interest children and broaden their experiences.

Providing Input

The classroom should provide children with many opportunities to gain new ideas, new impressions, new feelings and to relate these to the experiences they have had. There is an almost infinite number of activities that teachers can provide to give children these experiences: reading aloud from a variety of materials; giving time to observe, appreciate, and talk about things; taking field trips; listening to recordings and television and radio programs; watching films and still pictures; providing books and opportunities to read them; and giving special attention to expressive words and apt phrases and how they may be used. The effective teacher plans for continuous input of this sort throughout the year.

To achieve expression that shows real imagination, vividness, and individuality, however, requires more than just providing activities and experiences from which children *may* gain input. Children need to be guided and encouraged to be observant of the things and feelings they encounter: the intricate weaving in the spider web found during a walk in the school yard, the metaphor in a selection read, the hardships encountered by sailors in a film about early explorers. The program of enriching children's experiences must recognize that the impressions made on children by what they see, hear, read, feel, and taste are often vague, and therefore children may lack the motivation to write and the experiences that would enable them to write well.

THE PERSISTENCE OF TRADITION

About ten years ago, the former executive secretary of the National Council of Teachers of English stated: "Writing is the disgrace of American education."[1] Perhaps this was not a point of view universally held then, nor possibly is it one that is true now. However, observation would indicate that there is some truth in this statement. And this causes a great deal of frustration, since much effort has always been directed at teaching writing.

Historically, much of our teaching effort has been misdirected and based on misconceptions, and it has continued in this manner in spite of the research evidence about ineffective practices.[2] The persistence of tradition is a fact of life though, and therefore this description of the elementary school curriculum in written expression is not one that is found in many school programs. It is a description of desirable practices, a favored curriculum—one that recognizes evidence from research and willingly ignores tradition when tradition perpetuates faulty practices.

The curriculum in written expression at both the elementary and secondary school levels has been—and, as suggested above, to a great extent, still is—based on the misconception that learners must be given facts about our language system in order to write effectively. To gain these facts they have been given textbooks that present, through exposition and exercises, a particular grammar system and various declarations about "good" English. For years the grammar presented was based on the Latin language, with an emphasis on definitions of parts of speech and terminology naming sentence elements. More recently the science of linguistics has led to the development of better descriptions of the language than the Latin-based grammar provided. However, the notion that children must be taught this system (or, more precisely, any *one* of the several newly developed descriptions of the system) continues in spite of the discovery by linguists that the child already shows a great deal of understanding and control of the language system at a very young age.

Related to this misconception is the continuing practice of marking "errors" in the written expression of the child.[3] This disregards much of what we know about motivation and the problems encountered by anyone in deciding just what comprises an error. It continues in spite of research evidence that shows marking errors does not result in better composition. Marking errors is related to instructional practices based on grammar in that most decisions regarding errors are based on the grammar system being taught. This is particularly true when traditional, or Latin-based, grammar is taught, since it is a prescriptive system that emphasizes "correct" usage rather than a descriptive system that would simply show how language works.

Some curriculums have separated the teaching of grammar from the teaching

---

1. James R. Squire, "The Teaching of Writing and Composition in Today's Schools," *Elementary English* 41 (January 1964): 3-14.
2. J. Stephen Sherwin, *Four Problems in Teaching English: A Critique of Research* (Scranton, Pa.: International Textbook Co., 1969), pp. 109-116.
3. Note that this statement finds fault with *marking errors* but not with correcting faults by teaching skills or by pupil self-diagnosis and correction.

of written expression—particularly if the latter is called "creative writing." Others have minimized the teaching of grammar altogether. Both types of curriculums arose in the 1940s, with some decline occurring in the late 1960s largely due to the acceptance by many teachers of linguistics as the godsend to their problems and to the postsputnik movement for "intellectual rigor." In either case, the focus of the curriculum was "learning to write by writing." The approach was simply to have pupils do much writing. The intent of the proponents of this practice was undoubtedly that writing skills would be taught and that pupils would be helped to think out their compositions. They wanted to avoid a grammar-based writing program and sensibly believed that a direct approach to writing was likely to be more productive than learning about writing without application. However, the result was that little teaching was done, along with the rise of the misconception that pupils simply need to write in order to improve.

Fortunately, changes that are advantageous to curriculums have been adopted from time to time by many schools. The most notable departure from tradition followed the publication in 1935 of *An Experience Curriculum in English*.[4] As the title suggests, the thesis of the curriculum proposal was utilization of pupils' experiences and a departure from formalized teaching. In 1954 this curriculum focus was continued in *Language Arts for Today's Children*, a publication that had a favorable influence on curriculums, although it may have had less impact than the earlier report, particularly in terms of changing teaching materials.[5] Elementary schools borrowing ideas from these publications are not limited by the misconceptions and false directions discussed previously. It is the curriculums in these schools that are the bases for practices described here.

LEARNING ACTIVITIES: THE FOCUS OF WRITING INSTRUCTION

Learning to write effectively is not accomplished by assigning writing tasks to children without regard to their interests, their experiences, and the value or lack of value they hold for the assignments. Children will be motivated to write, and to try to do their best, when the writing has a purpose that is theirs or that they understand and that makes sense to them. They will write when they have something to say and when they feel that someone will read and appreciate or learn from what is written. For instance, a child will willingly write a report if he or she feels that the information in it has not already been read by the other children and that it is information of interest. Certainly some children will write a report simply because the teacher assigns it, and they may even put forth their best efforts to please the teacher. Usually, however, these children are already fairly capable writers, who have learned much on their own and will probably continue to learn

---

4. The Curriculum Commission of the National Council of Teachers of English, *An Experience Curriculum in English* (New York: Appleton-Century, 1935).

5. The Commission on the English Curriculum of the National Council of Teachers of English, *Language Arts for Today's Children* (New York: Appleton-Century-Crafts, 1954).

more by themselves because they will have reasons of their own for writing. But those children who need more motivation to write will show little interest in completing assignments that are simply assignments. They will neither learn very much nor will they become personally involved, and their writing products will fail to reflect individuality and creativity.

The key to teaching children to write is the genuineness of the need for the writing task (see Chart 8.1). In other words, as Alvina Treut Burrows and her associates have suggested: "Ever since we began expecting children to write only when they had a genuine need or the earnest desire to do so, we have found them eager to write well. In that mood they have been sensitive to our guidance and suggestion."[6]

Chart 8.1. Writing Activities

Primary grades	Captions for pictures, bulletin boards, and charts
	Individual and group-composed "thank-you's" announcements, and simple informational notes
	Records of weather, classroom duties, books read, and the like
	Personal experiences—either composed by the group or by individual pupils
	The completion of a story dictated by the teacher or composed by the group
	Describing feeling related to touch, smell, and so forth
	Poetry and rhyme
	Library cards, permission slips, etc.
	Observations made on field trips
	Imaginative stories
	Riddles and limericks
Intermediate grades	Announcements, notices, and requests
	Personal letters
	Imaginative stories
	Social studies and science reports
	Directions for games and experiments
	Descriptions of objects, people, and so forth
	Diaries and logs of activities
	Autobiographies
	Summaries of science experiments and social studies units
	News items (chalkboard, chart, or dittoed "newspaper")
	Reviews of television programs and books
	Television and radio commercials
	Fables, myths, legends based on reading and listening

6. Alvina Treut Burrows et al., *They All Want To Write* (Englewood Cliffs, N.J.: Prentice-Hall, 1955), p. 3.

	Questions to answer in social studies reading Outlines Scripts for plays and skits Information in blanks List of words to learn to spell
Upper grades	Book reviews and reports Business letters Minutes of meetings Biographies Editorials Limericks, ballads, chants Imaginative stories Reports Bibliographies and footnotes Sympathy notes

Children's First Writing

Children in kindergartens—and more particularly in first grade— get much satisfaction from helping the teacher write a chart story about something they have experienced. Individually, a child's first writing may be that of copying the chart story on his or her own paper so that he or she can take it home to share with the family.

The first writing of children should be simple and not tax them beyond their abilities. Learning to form letters and words is a task that requires practice and to the young child is difficult. However, if the writing is purposeful—if the child wants to do it—it will be a good experience and one that will motivate practice in both composition and handwriting.

Chart stories written by the teacher and children usually precede or follow closely some group activity, such as a trip, a film, a party, a visit from someone, or even the sharing of a story or song—any activity that is a little different from the usual classroom events. (Frequently, chart stories are used to teach children to read [see Chapter 6]). Whatever the reason for the chart story, though, children must be involved in order to feel a need for copying the story or writing their own stories.

Effective programs in written expression provide for guidance in composition and for building on a base of oral language expressional skill. When a class writes a group composition about what was seen during a trip to a dairy, the teacher should guide the story's development with questions: "Where did we go first?" "Where are the cows kept?" "What does the milking machine do?" After the story is written, the teacher may need to say, "Let's go back over this to decide which sentences we need to keep in our story and to see if a different arrangment of them will help us tell the story in a better way." The effective teacher, of course, tries to make the final story the product of the children's thinking. However, when the classroom atmosphere is conducive to the stimulation of thinking and to the genuine exchange of ideas, and the teacher and children have a good rapport, then the children's story may be the same one the teacher would have written.

The writing of group compositions can gradually lead into independent writing. For example, a group story of two or three lines may be written on the board and copied by the children, with each child adding a line or two. Other independent writing that can be done by young children includes story titles, captions for pictures or charts, listing of names or tasks, and notes of one or two sentences.

Developing Writing Skills in Expressional Situations

As stated previously, a viable writing program will exist in a classroom in which the total program is meaningful and challenging. A good classroom atmosphere is conducive to the free and natural expression of ideas, and the traditional concerns related to writing assignments—and all the negative attitudes associated with them—become irrelevant. Writing in these effective modern programs stems from purposeful, often spontaneous, activities and is related to all subject areas. However, this does not mean that writing activities are haphazard or unplanned. On the contrary, they must be carefully planned if children are to improve their compositional skills as well as maintain their interest and motivation to write.

Experience Stories

Children are eager to talk about their experiences and many times wish to keep a record of them. One method that capitalizes on this interest while teaching composition skills is that of the individual child or a group of children dictating to the teacher what is to be written. Whether children simply relate their experiences or refer to their records, being able to dictate their thoughts and reactions frees them from concern about handwriting and other mechanical factors that may otherwise restrict their composition. While most primary teachers use this method, fewer teachers in the middle and upper grades do so. Yet teachers in the latter group should recognize that this practice gives primary attention to composition, where the emphasis in teaching written expression should be.

Letter Writing

Since letter writing is one of the most frequently used writing forms, it should receive at least some instructional attention in every language arts curriculum. It is a form of writing that can be taught to very young children. Primary children soon recognize a genuine need for letter writing: They are anxious to write letters to their parents or thank-you notes to the nurse or office clerk. Letter writing, then, is best taught in situations in which the need for the letter is real rather than manufactured. For example, invitations may be written to parents to attend a school activity, to the principal to visit, to another class to come to a party, or to a resource person to give a talk or demonstration. Likewise, many letters of reply, sympathy, greeting, application, complaint, and request stem from purposeful reasons.

An effective letter writing program recognizes that children "learn by doing."

When children write purposeful letters regularly, they begin to develop an awareness of the situations that call for letter writing, the ability to make letters interesting and natural-sounding, and an understanding of the courtesies and attitudes extended in good letters. They will also develop an awareness of appropriate writing materials, of the need to proofread, and of the importance of promptness in answering and mailing letters. The many matters of form that are particularly important to letter writing—the placement of parts of the letter, capitalization of particular items, abbreviations of various titles and names, wording for the salutation and complimentary closing—are also mastered through purposeful letter writing experiences.

Reports, Reviews, and Summaries

Many of the activities in the elementary school classroom almost demand the writing of some kind of report. Among the varieties of reports that may be written are summaries of the content or principal ideas in books, news articles, movies, talks, television programs, school and club meetings, and assembly programs; accounts of interviews, trips, and individual and group investigations of topics of interest; and descriptions of people, games, hobbies, and neighborhood activities.

The writing of reports should begin in the primary grades, with the children dictating to the teacher accounts of experiences and of things that interest them. This early practice will serve as a foundation for writing the reports that were previously suggested.

This form of writing has a special function for the very capable children who need to be challenged further. These children will often painstakingly search for information about topics that they are particularly interested in and that they think classmates will want to read about. Naturally there must be enough openness in the classroom to allow these children to pursue their interests and to permit other children to read and react to the report.

Minutes and Records

Many classrooms have one or more class organizations or clubs that need to keep minutes of activities. This type of writing has a real purpose in that it serves child and adult needs outside of school. Record keeping requires straightforward, factual writing that is not too taxing in length, thus providing opportunities for those children who have difficulty with more complicated forms of writing. Some records that may be kept involve the following:

1. Weather (forcasts, fluctuations in humidity and temperature)
2. Growth of plants in classroom
3. Classroom duties of class members
4. Height and weight records
5. Visitors to the classroom
6. Daily news items
7. Standards or rules agreed on by the class in regard to some activity
8. New words learned in various subjects and activities
9. Science and health experiments
10. Attendance

Writing Derived from Reading

Many of children's reading experiences may serve as bases for writing activities. Writing derived from reading not only provides opportunities to learn writing skills but also gives reinforcement of reading skills and helps to show the importance of reading. The following suggestions for writing activities illustrate opportunities to elaborate on reading experiences to develop expressional skills:

1. Book reviews that stem from a reaction by a reader
2. Advertisements
3. News items
4. Character sketches that focus on a behavior trait or that give a full, detailed description of a character
5. Biographies that are "made up" or based on facts read
6. Descriptions of objects, places, and so on using such devices as personification and simile
7. Letters to authors, librarians, or characters in books
8. Riddles about story characters or events
9. Diaries of imaginary experiences
10. Captions and other short forms of writing, such as labels, headlines, and titles

Other Activities

Practically every situation or activity in the elementary school may provide opportunities for writing. For example, children may write autobiographies, biographies of friends and persons they meet in various activities, and journals related to historical events. They will have need to write outlines for summaries and reports and as a means for helping them to remember what they read, to fill in blanks on various forms, to write announcements, and to engage in less "practical" writing as suggested in the following section.

Opportunities for Creative Writing

Opportunities for children to be creative and imaginative occur in many of the writing situations previously described. Imaginative biographies and autobiographies, hypothetical eyewitness accounts of historical events, and descriptions of characters in stories are some examples. The effective curriculum easily incorporates creative writing into any subject area, particularly if creative writing is viewed as more than writing stories and poetry. If all writing is recognized as a personal activity, then writing always reflects the individual's personality and imagination. Certainly some forms of writing require more imagination and less facts and information than others. These forms, some of which are described below, require the same use of composition and writing skills as other forms.

Poetry

As emphasized in Chapter 7, every child should have some experience with poetry—reading it, hearing it read, reciting it individually or as part of a group (see Chapter 5), and writing it. The author of Chapter 7 stresses that children should have many different experiences with poetry before trying to write their own poems. This procedure must not be overlooked. A particularly useful experience is the composing of poems by the class or part of the class. Teachers would select a particular form and then encourage the children to suggest topics, words and phrases, rhyming words (if applicable), and possibly entire lines. The children would discuss which word sounds best or fits the subject or rhythm best. In this way, they learn the process of creating a poem.

Children may use a number of poetry forms in writing their own poems. Generally suitable for elementary school children are couplets and triplets, cinquain, limericks, haiku, and free verse. While effective teachers of poetry writing take advantage of opportunities that arise spontaneously—the utterance of an apt bit of imagery or a unique expression—the curriculum should provide for the planned introduction of poetry forms and a sequence of experiences in writing. The emphasis in a planned program, however, should be on enjoyment rather than on poetry forms, writing skills, and the demand for full pupil participation.

Stories

Most people like to tell stories and to hear and read them; it seems to be a human tendency to dwell romantically and imaginatively on experiences and desires. Children are particularly anxious to tell about ideas and events—real or make-believe—and they are much less inhibited than adults in both the telling and reacting. Thus, it is comparatively easy for a teacher to motivate children to write stories, providing that each child's abilities are respected.

Even though children's minds may abound with imaginative ideas, motivation may be required to start the expression flowing. Many teachers depend largely on such remarks as "Can you write a different ending to the story you've just finished reading?" or "What does this picture make you think of? Write a story about it." An even less imaginative approach to motivation is the assignment of a topic. Too often topics such as "The Most Exciting Thing that Happened Last Summer" or "Life in a Spaceship" are assigned, possibly with no choice on the part of the pupil and with little or no discussion.

Certainly both topics and illustrations may motivate creative writing, although under the most desirable conditions—particularly those of openness and freedom of expression—children themselves will be able to think up more interesting topics and will gain ideas from their own experiences with illustrations and many other objects. On the other hand, if topics are provided, children should be given the opportunity to choose the one that is most interesting to them. Topics such as "The Easter Egg that Hatched," "The Year Santa Claus Was Lazy," or "What I Could Do if I Could Fly" may provoke more imagination than some of the more traditional ones. In using topics and illustrations to stimulate ideas, children will become more interested and will be able to think more clearly if possible story lines, characters, settings, action, and their own experiences are discussed before they begin to write.

Children are often encouraged to use their imaginations when they are given one or more frameworks for a story. For example, the teacher may hand out a printed slip of paper that states: "You were traveling on a wagon train from Independence, Missouri, to California. Many of the wagons were lost crossing the Colorado River. What happened the next morning?" And for those children who have real difficulty getting started, the teacher may wish to present them with a partial story, which is to be completed by the pupils.

MAKING WRITTEN EXPRESSION EFFECTIVE

All language expression is effective to the extent that sentences are well constructed, interesting, and arranged in such ways that the information and ideas are clearly conveyed. This is true in both oral and written expression. Therefore, the curriculum in written expression must give attention to selection of content, word and phrase choices, organization and style, and consideration of the potential reader.

Teaching Sentence Sense

The sentence is the principal unit in all communication; therefore, helping children learn to compose effective sentences should be a vital part of every elementary school program. Since a sentence is a means for expressing an idea, the teaching effort should focus on the idea and its expression in a way that is clear and exact. Sentences must make sense and should not contain unrelated ideas or too many thoughts.

There are no shortcuts to learning how to write good sentences. The most effective curriculums place emphasis on children expressing themselves orally; describing objects in one or two statements; dictating sentences to the teacher, who writes them down; and participating in many other activities involving sentence construction.

Sentence construction activities that result in the most learning stem from necessary communication situations, for motivation provided by purposeful activities cannot be matched by any other means. However, there are enjoyable learning activities and exercises that simply involve the arrangement of words and phrases to make sentences. These include the following:

1. Incomplete sentences (on charts, chalkboard, and dittoed sheets) for which the child supplies the missing words. Usually this activity should have a particular focus—learning to use pronouns, expressive adjectives, synonyms, and so forth.
2. Word cards—one set for each child—used for building as many sentences as possible, compound sentences, especially interesting sentences, and so on. Phrases or lexical units, instead of words, may be printed on the cards.
3. Word or phrase cards folded, hung on a string, and placed along a wall or held taut by two children. This arrangement is particularly conducive to group sentence-building activities.
4. Phrases that elicit mental pictures (a pile of clothes on the floor; wet

leaves on the sidewalk) written on the board. To construct sentences, the children combine the phrases, add to them, and so on.

5. Unpunctuated paragraphs presented to children for oral reading. This activity will show the children that punctuation helps to determine how material should be read and that reading in a natural manner generally shows where sentences begin and end.

These are only some of the many activities involving sentence construction. The advantages of such activities are that they may be done individually, by pairs of children, by small groups, or by the entire class and that most of them may be presented as games rather than as assignments.

Teaching Organization in Expression

An effective writing program attempts to teach children that the best way to present a thought or piece of information is through good organization and interesting and suitable sequencing. The first activities for helping children learn to organize their ideas in written expression include sequencing pictures related to a story, objects seen on a trip, or events of the day; assembling puzzles; classifying objects by size, color, shape; and telling how to play a game. As suggested in the discussion of sentence construction, the most effective learning occurs in situations related to actual communication needs. This is also true for organizing more extensive thoughts. At first, children may dictate to the teacher stories of two or more sentences. As children communicate with one another and with other persons encountered in their daily activities, they will write letters, reports, records, stories, and so forth.

Talking over ideas before attempting to write, with the discussion centering on communication objectives, helps children learn the importance of organization in their writing. Proofreading and editing and learning about various writing forms from studying models will also aid in good organization.

There are many activities that appeal to children while providing learning experiences in organizational skills. Children enjoy:

1. Looking at and discussing an illustration and then stating in one sentence the main idea conveyed. A variation of this activity is to choose a title for the illustration.
2. Choosing from a number of sentences those that can be arranged to form a complete paragraph
3. Unscrambling sentences to make a sensible paragraph
4. Supplying a beginning or ending sentence to make a complete paragraph
5. Crossing out sentences unrelated to the main idea or topic of a paragraph

Children should be encouraged to outline their thoughts before they begin to write. They should learn that an outline can be very informal (thought out but not necessarily written) rather than only learning to use the written outline form. (The latter practice usually has too much formality associated with it and consequently results in very little use of outlines.) The important point is that children should learn to think more effectively before they begin to write. This includes thinking about the purpose of the writing as well as clarifying, sorting out, and relating facts and ideas.

Developing Sensitivity to Words

Teachers should encourage discussion prior to writing activities to help children learn new words, new meanings, differences in pronunciation, and words appropriate for specific contexts. The discussion usually leads to activities such as writing words on the board or on charts, looking up meanings and pronunciations, and word building and word listing. Children enjoy words that rhyme, sound unusual, are new to them, or say something unusually well. They like to "collect" words for bulletin boards, notebooks, and charts and for use in particular writing activities.

Knowledge of words and sensitivity to them may also be developed by the activities of a creative and child-centered classroom. As children build an aquarium, construct a simple generator, trace a route on a map, discuss an interesting news item, visit city hall, or observe a bird's nest, new words and meanings will be discovered. Manipulative activities that involve handling various materials, tools, and equipment bring children into direct contact with objects and ideas and provide opportunities for learning new words and concepts and relating them to those already known. In fact, any part of the oral and written expression that is certain to occur in such classrooms provides opportunity for vocabulary development and growth in the sensitivity to words.

The various experiences also provide opportunities to learn about personification, simile, metaphor, hyperbole, and onomatopoeia. Children are usually interested in collecting and categorizing the words and expressions in these forms, in keeping charts and individual lists of those they want to use, and in immediately trying out new ones.

Self-Editing and Proofreading

An aspect of making written expression effective that too often is neglected is that of self-editing and proofreading. Children may recognize the need for writing in a situation; they may be presented with a model and decide on their own standards; they may have considerable understanding of errors to be avoided; and finally, they may actually write and then give the product to the teacher or to others to read without rereading it themselves or even giving a second thought to what they have written. Usually, pupils who do practice proofreading and self-editing have been taught to do so by teachers who have recognized the significance of these skills in improving written expression.

As with the teaching of other writing skills, simple proofreading should be taught when children first begin to write. In the first or second grade, children should be taught to read over what they have written to doublecheck such matters as capitalization of first words of sentences and periods at the end of sentences. But little learning will result from the teacher simply saying "Proofread what you have written." The emphasis needs to be on teaching—actually guiding children. This is important in later grades as pupils may begin to lengthen the list of items they check.

SPELLING IN THE WRITING PROGRAM

Every time children write they must spell. Therefore spelling is very much a part of the writing curriculum. While children need not always spell every word correctly, communication is often lost if there are too many spelling errors, and misspellings show a lack of concern for the reader. Learning how to spell words correctly has always been a concern of more than slight interest to parents and society generally, with expressions of concern, complaint, and frustration readily evident to most teachers.

The spelling curriculum in elementary schools varies from an informal, or perhaps incidental, approach to a systematic and direct one that generally includes the use of spelling textbooks or workbooks. Informal programs usually make use of a list of words for the children to learn, but study procedures and amounts of time devoted to spelling vary from program to program. In a spelling curriculum that gives only incidental attention to specific words on lists, the individual child learns to spell words as needed or as misspelled in writing activities.

The curriculum in most schools, and the one generally recommended, is systematic and functional. It focuses on the direct instruction of each child in learning to spell the words on a basic list. The systematic nature of this program is also shown by the planned study procedures, the fostering of positive attitudes toward spelling words correctly, and the development of useful work habits.

Goals of the Program

The basic objective of spelling instruction is to develop in children the desire and the ability to spell correctly all words that they write. It is not possible to teach the spelling of every word an individual may need to write, but a spelling program should—and most of them do—provide activities by which children learn to spell very frequently written words (numbering three thousand to four thousand in spelling programs for grades one through eight). In addition, a good spelling program emphasizes the necessity of correct spelling and develops in the children attitudes that recognize the importance of various practices for learning new words, of consulting the dictionary for correct spellings, and of proofreading for spelling errors.

Fundamental to these objectives is the ability to associate a written word with the same word as spoken or as remembered from reading or listening. This requires recalling the visual form of the complete word or the letter pattern or series of letter patterns associated with the sounds in the word. Thus, an effective spelling program teaches children to look at words carefully and to practice their recall as well as to associate letters and patterns of letters with corresponding sounds. The teaching of such associations, of course, has limitations. Thus, while some general rules may be taught, the lack of a high degree of correspondence of sound and symbol in the majority of English words requires that cautions about such sound-to-letter patterns must also be taught.

Instructional Plan

Spelling is most often taught in periods set aside for that purpose, and spelling books largely determine the words taught and the teaching and learning procedures followed. For this instruction, two general plans have been identified, and one or the other is typically used. These are the *study-test* and the *test-study*, with the latter most often recommended.[7] The test-study plan calls for testing the pupils prior to study to determine the specific words each pupil does not know how to spell and needs to study. The principal advantages of this plan are that individual needs are pinpointed and pupils who know how to spell many of the words will not lose interest in the lesson.

The test-study plan consists of these features:

1. A preliminary term or monthly test is given to determine the general level of spelling achievement of the class and of each child.
2. A test on each weekly (or other instructional period) assignment is given prior to studying. This test identifies the words that each pupil misspells and must study.
3. While studying, each child uses the procedures or steps developed by the class or suggested in the textbook, with modifications necessary to fit individual needs or learning problems.
4. A midweekly test is used to determine progress made since the pretest and to identify the words that need further study.
5. A final weekly or lesson test is given to measure learning achievement.
6. A final term or monthly test serves to measure the progress made since the first term test.

Sometimes this plan is modified prior to the pretest to include the teacher's pronouncing the words as the children look at them. This is generally not recommended except in the primary grades, where it may be used until the pupils become accustomed to the pretest procedure.

The major difference between the test-study plan and the study-test plan is the pretest; that is, in the study-test plan the children begin the lesson by studying all of the words on the list. Also, usually only two weekly tests—a midlesson test and a final—are administered in the study-test plan.

In addition to the features just described, an effective plan provides for each child to check his or her own tests, keep his or her own record of spelling achievement on a chart or similar device, and record words misspelled on the final lesson tests for later study and review testing.

---

7. Sherwin, *Four Problems in Teaching English.*

Pupils' Study Procedures

Modern spelling programs incorporate the findings of research in the procedures used for teaching children how to spell. These techniques focus on developing the child's ability to gain visual, auditory, and kinesthetic impressions of a complete word and its parts and to recall these impressions. The following procedure (presented as a series of steps for a child to follow) is representative of the systematic study plan that is needed.

1. Look at the word carefully and pronounce it correctly. If you are not sure of the pronunciation, look it up in the dictionary or ask someone who is sure to know. While looking at the word, say it slowly, naturally, and clearly.
2. Cover the word or close your eyes, pronounce it, and think about how it looks. Try to see in your mind just the way the word is written as you spell the word to yourself.
3. Look at the word again to be sure that you said it and spelled it correctly. If you did not, start over at step one.
4. Thinking carefully about how the word looks, cover the word and then write it. Check to make sure you spelled the word correctly.
5. If you misspelled the word, begin again at step one. If you spelled it correctly, go on to the next word.

These steps, which stress visual imagery, make use of the fact that most people try to recall how a word looks. For children who have difficulty in learning how to spell, the steps can be modified to give more attention to the gaining of auditory and kinesthetic impressions.

Most commercial spelling materials suggest study procedures similar to the one just described. However, it is recommended that a teacher and a class establish their own pattern that may or may not coincide with that used in commercial materials. Guiding children into thinking about how a word should be studied and organizing this thinking into a statement of procedure will result in much learning and the development of desirable attitudes toward spelling.

Linguistics and Spelling

Since the late 1950s there has been considerable interest in linguistics and its relationship to the several areas of the language arts. While some of this initial enthusiasm has declined, particularly that regarding the assumptions that linguistics is a panacea for language arts teaching problems, there has been continued interest in linguistics as related to spelling. In particular, educators pay special attention to linguistics as a method of determining how speech sounds are related to the letters used to represent them and how these relationships could affect the spelling curriculum.

The early interest in linguistics as related to the language arts program resulted in research showing that each speech sound (phoneme) is represented more frequently by one particular letter (or in some cases a group of two or more letters) than by some other letter. For example, one researcher reported that "the k sound is spelled with *c* 64.36 per cent and the *s* sound with *s* 71.19 per cent of the time."[8] More recent research has sought to bring the percentages of correspondence between sound and symbol higher by determining the most common spellings when sounds are in initial, medial, or final positions in syllables.[9] But the interest has not resulted in research regarding the teaching of such correspondences (or stressing the pupils' learning of them). This latter fact, unfortunately, has not prevented the advocacy of unwarranted instructional practices or the appearance of commercial materials that emphasize the teaching of sound-symbol regularity, spelling patterns, and the like.

Certainly there is some validity in making such associations. Some sounds (the *b*, for example) are represented with a great deal of regularity by a single letter or cluster or letters. But it is also true that other sounds (particularly vowel sounds) are represented by many different letters. The important point is that children should be taught to recognize both facts. A similar approach must be taken with the teaching of certain word patterns. For example, it is important for pupils to understand that *bed, red, fed,* and *led* fit into the same pattern. Thus, they should not write *bede, bead,* or *baid* for *bed.* But they must also learn that the vowel sound in *bed* also occurs in *head* and *said* but is represented differently.

In spite of the lack of evidence that should be the guide to curriculum and instructional decisions, there are some conclusions regarding the phoneme-grapheme correspondence issue that appear to be warranted:

1. Instruction in both the consistencies and inconsistencies of phoneme-grapheme relationships should be a part of every spelling program but should not dominate it.
2. Instruction in generalizations or "rules" concerning spelling patterns or sound-to-letter associations should focus on those that occur in a considerable number of words and have few exceptions.
3. Instruction in sound-symbol correspondences must recognize that there are dialect differences in many classrooms and that the pronunciation of many words, even by the same individual, varies with the context in which they are used.
4. Linguistic principles should be regarded as possible aids to learning to spell a number of words rather than as a substitute for studying the lesson words directly.
5. Most persons have learned to make application of many phoneme-grapheme correspondences from reading and spelling instruction that has not emphasized these correspondences.

Spelling and Creative Writing

While a major objective is to teach children to spell correctly all words that they write, it is even more important that they are taught to be *concerned* about

---

8. Ernest Horn, "Phonetics and Spelling," *The Elementary School Journal,* May 1957, p. 431.

9. Paul R. Hanna, Richard E. Hodges, and Jean S. Hanna, *Spelling: Structure and Strategies* (Boston: Houghton Mifflin Co., 1971).

spelling correctly. But when children write imaginatively and attempt to get their ideas on paper before they are forgotten, they frequently use—or want to use—words that they do not know how to spell. Every child faces this problem, and an effective language arts curriculum must help provide some solutions. Certainly it is more important for children to "capture" their expression on paper than to spell every word correctly. It only makes sense to permit children to do some of the things adults do when they are in a hurry to write their thoughts but do not know how to spell a word correctly. For example, children may write only the first letters of a word, draw a line to show where a word was left out, or attempt a spelling but place a question mark after it. However, if the child is so stymied by not being able to spell a word that creativity is impaired, the teacher should provide help. The teacher may encourage the child to try to spell it on scratch paper to see if he or she can recognize the correct spelling or may simply write the word on a slip of paper and give it to the child. Some spelling problems can be avoided, however, by listing on the board words that may be needed.

Many spelling problems encountered in writing are the result of poor teaching, testing, and reviewing as well as a program that is too limiting. Problems are also caused by not knowing and applying rules and generalizations that have some validity (affixing and compounding rules, for example), by a lack of understanding of the apostrophe, and by failure to capitalize properly or to use a dictionary properly. Certainly poor attitudes toward spelling, as well as low expectations on the part of the teacher, take their toll.

TEACHING HANDWRITING SKILLS

The teaching of handwriting has long been a part of the school curriculum, and the need for teaching this skill continues regardless of the widespread use of typewriters and mechanical speech-recording equipment. Traditionally, handwriting has been taught as a separate subject, even though handwriting enters into practically all written language activities in the school. Yet, in spite of the apparent need for handwriting instruction, there is some reason to believe that an increasing number of schools give little attention to it after the teaching of basic movements and letter forms. The great majority of schools do teach handwriting, however, and recent surveys show that this teaching is done in separate periods.[10]

In the early part of this century, handwriting instruction was dominated by particular systems—Spencerian, Roman, Palmer—that emphasize the specific forms of letters and the precise movements needed to reproduce them. Since the 1930s this formalism has declined, and greater freedom in individual styles has come to the fore. This change resulted from (1) a recognition that children often had difficulty performing the required movements of an excessively elaborate nature, (2) an increasing awareness of the differences in the growth and development of children, (3) the difficulty in reading the script produced by some of the

---

10.   Harry A. Greene and Walter T. Petty, *Developing Language Skills in the Elementary Schools,* 5th ed. (Boston: Allyn & Bacon, 1975), p. 433.

systems, and (4) a too-long-delayed understanding that handwriting as separated from its practical use is not a valuable skill.

Objectives of Handwriting Instruction

Handwriting is a major tool in written expression; for this reason it must be legible. Thus, the principal objective of handwriting instruction is to help the child write legibly. In consideration of this objective, there should be no use of meaningless drill; instead, there should be a stress on each pupil doing his or her best to achieve legibility in all writing products. Simply permitting children to write as they have the need is not enough, just as handwriting cannot be taught once and then dropped from the curriculum. Production of legible handwriting at a reasonable speed can be achieved and maintained only as a result of good initial instruction and constant and meaningful practice. A desirable program should be built around the following:

1. Encouraging pupils to express themselves through writing
2. Helping each child to discover how handwriting skill serves him or her
3. Encouraging pupils to strive for neatness and legibility with appropriate speed in all their writing
4. Analyzing the handwriting faults of each child and trying to correct them
5. Developing in each pupil a sense of personal pride in writing legibly and the desire and ability to improve
6. Establishing practice periods of adequate length at each grade or development level
7. Developing in pupils the correct posture and teaching them the proper use of writing tools

Instructional Considerations

As with other skills, handwriting is most effectively taught when (1) the attitudes of both the teacher and the children are favorable to its learning, (2) a level of readiness for the learning has been attained, and (3) the children are properly motivated.

In building desirable attitudes, teachers need to make sure that their own writing is neat and legible, with properly formed letters; that they write smoothly and rhythmically; and that they show good posture and hold the pen, pencil, or chalk correctly. Of major importance, also, is the assignment of writing tasks that are meaningful to the children and that require the handwriting to be legible so communication is not lost.

Readiness considerations in handwriting instruction should be similar to those commonly given attention in reading instruction. That is, for initial handwriting instruction, children need to have developed work habits and an attention span that are adequate for the learning task, know left and right directions, have an awareness of likenesses and differences in sizes and shapes of objects, and show an understanding of space relationships (depth, height, width, distance, comparative size). Most importantly, they need the neuro-muscular coordination required for forming letters properly and with ease. Readiness for handwriting, like readiness for reading, cannot be fostered for initial instruction only and then dropped. Attention to readiness must be continued as children develop their handwriting skills.

The need for handwriting instruction as well as for practice should grow out of the children's writing of stories, poetry, reports, summaries, diaries, and the many other products of writing suggested earlier. Although the primary purpose of writing activities is to help the child to communicate effectively through good composition, this does not mean that time should not be taken from such activities to teach children how to hold the writing instrument, place their paper, make the writing strokes, form letters and connect them, and develop handwriting rhythm and ease. After basic handwriting skills have been learned, continued direct and supervised practice is needed. Handwriting skill will simply diminish unless it is practiced, and this practice must include corrective work on factors that cause the writing to be illegible or cause it to be done awkwardly or in a tiring fashion.

First instruction is almost universally in printscript—probably more often called "manuscript." Printscript is a handwriting form that requires only simple curves (circles or parts of circles) and straight lines to form the letters and therefore is considered easier for children to learn than is the connected writing, or cursive form, that most people use. Manuscript form is also taught because it is typically more legible and can be done more rapidly by the beginning writer and because the letters are similar to those encountered in reading.

Most schools teach children the cursive form in about grade three. Some teach it in terms of its similarity to manuscript by slanting the manuscript letters and connecting these letters by simple strokes. Others teach the cursive form as an entirely new way to write, usually stressing that some skill in manuscript should be maintained also. School or district curriculum guides or commercial programs generally guide teachers in these decisions as well as in the specific instructional procedures used in first instruction, transitional instruction, or skill maintenance practice.

Research evidence indicates that ten to fifteen minutes of concentrated work each day is sufficient for learning and practicing handwriting skills. In the primary grades there is a need for daily handwriting periods, while a period of about five minutes on alternate days is adequate at the middle and upper levels for maintaining the skills learned. The fewer and shorter periods presuppose that attention is given to individual diagnosis of need and practice and to handwriting skills in all writing activities.

The materials for handwriting instruction include chalk, chalkboard, paper, crayons, pencils, pens, and usually commercial handwriting manuals. Most programs in the primary grades make use of chalk and crayons as well as beginners' pencils (these have soft lead that is thicker than the lead in ordinary pencils). There are differences in the characteristics of paper suggested for writing. For grade one, twelve-by-eighteen-inch newsprint is ordinarily used first. In the beginning this may be unlined, and when the child's abilities increase, lines may be made by folding the paper. Still later, paper with rules spaced one-inch apart is used. In grade two (usually), paper with lines three-fourths to one-half inch apart is recommended. After about grade three, three-eighths-inch space between rules is satisfactory for most children.

CONVENTIONS IMPORTANT IN WRITING

Since the major concern in teaching children to write is always the content or message and how it is organized to communicate most effectively, children should be made aware from the time they first begin to write that thoughts and feelings may be lost without attention to punctuation, paragraphing, capitalizing, margins, and similar matters of form and custom (as well as those discussed earlier—spelling and handwriting). They need to learn that a neat and attractive looking product, whether it is a letter, a report, an announcement, or a story, is a courtesy to the reader, helps to make the expression more effective, and in many instances is an absolute necessity for communication to occur.

Form and Appearance

While there are few set rules about the many factors that contribute to the appropriate appearance of a written selection, there are generally accepted customs about such matters as margins, paragraph identification, placement of titles and headings, and general tidiness. Curriculums that recognize the need for attention to form and appearance usually also are aware of the confusion that may arise due to the lack of absolutes regarding these customs. Thus, the curriculum guides for these programs include certain standards about form and appearance and suggestions for teaching them. Sometimes these standards are rather general so that each classroom may adjust them according to need.

Punctuation

Incorrect punctuation is the most frequent type of error among those made in the conventions, or mechanics, of writing. Studies have shown that the errors persist through all educational levels, which indicates that punctuation skill is either difficult to learn or is too little or too ineffectively taught. The difficulty seems to be the result of several facts: Many punctuation items taught are little used, many practices are arbitrary and often meaningless, and teaching of punctuation is frequently not related to the actual writing tasks that children perform.

In recognition of these facts, curriculum guides—and to some extent textbooks—are beginning to limit the number of different punctuation items to be taught and to show pupils that there are variations in uses (for example, the use or nonuse of a comma after the next-to-the-last item in a series). Teachers are urged to have pupils note punctuation items and differences in their uses and to base teaching on these.

There is increasing attention being given to the relationship between punctuation and speech intonation. However, while junctures in speech flow may signal the terminal punctuation of a sentence, it is a fallacy to assume that any pause or change in pitch requires a punctuation mark. Thus, effective programs relate intonation patterns of speech to some punctuation items but do not teach children to punctuate only according to speech signals.

The teaching of punctuation should begin in the primary grades. The first sentences that are written on the board or on a chart or are encountered in a reading textbook provide opportunities for beginning the teaching. This first teaching should be informal and focus primarily on making the children aware of the punctuation items used. In the intermediate grades, punctuation items are introduced and practiced as they are needed by the children in their writing.

Capitalization

Textbooks and curriculum guides list capitalization uses—often by grade level of introduction and teaching. However, the best way to find out about the needs of children in a particular class is by examining their spontaneous and assigned writing.

When children first begin to learn about letters, they discover that each letter has two forms: upper and lower case. As they write their own names, they learn to use capitals. Later, as they become involved with words and sentences written on charts and on the chalkboard or printed in their reading materials, they begin to learn when words should be capitalized. When children are making these observations, direct teaching—both group and individual—may begin with the copying of sentences and the closely associated independent writing. The objective of this teaching is to establish good habits so that later corrective work may be avoided. The problem of over-capitalization, which usually results from the desire to emphasize points, often occurs in the intermediate grades and if left uncorrected will require considerable reteaching later on.

EVALUATING WRITTEN EXPRESSION

Since evaluating any written expression is very often difficult and teachers are sometimes reluctant to criticize a child's creative efforts, little evaluation is done in many schools. However, since evaluation is one of the major elements in the total teaching-learning activity, it should be included in the curriculum in fairness to the children. Effective programs, particularly those that view evaluation from a positive perspective, acknowledge this fact. These programs recognize that evaluation need not be such a difficult process if its focus is realistic and instruction-centered rather than directed at giving grades, making red marks, and finding fault. In effective programs, evaluation is more often concerned with the programs themselves, their objectives, and the teaching procedures and materials used rather than with the products of children's writing attempts or even with the writing processes that children use.

Evaluating the Program

Program evaluation should be a continuing process, not simply an end-of-the-year reflection on what has taken place. In consideration of the total curriculum, program evaluation should become as specific as possible. Questions such as the following should be asked: What is really occurring? What are the children writing? What are their problems? Particular attention should be given to the reasons children may not write as well as expected. These may include lack of direction and guidance, fear of teacher and peer disapproval, stifled oral expression, inadequate vocabulary development, ignorance of the various writing forms, a deficiency of experience input, failure to consider potential and actual readers, a lack of knowledge of writing skills, drudgery approaches to teaching skills, inhibiting expression. Examination of these and other causes requires the teacher to consider such questions as the following:

1. What is the atmosphere of the classroom? Is it one in which each child feels free to express ideas and make contributions to projects and discussions? Is there anything that might tend to repress individual expression?
2. Does the physical appearance of the classroom reflect freedom, creativity, and purpose in expression (on the part of both teacher and children)?
3. Is there sufficient input of many kinds throughout the year and in all areas of the curriculum? Are ongoing experiences captialized on for writing activities? Do writing activities spring from many curriculum areas?
4. Do children have many opportunities to read and hear well-written stories, reports, letters, poems, and the like? Is there a real interest in words and the way they may be put together?
5. Do children have sufficient skill in the mechanics of writing so that they are able to express their ideas? Or is the emphasis on spelling, conventions, and the like so great that children are afraid to experiment with new words and new ways of expressing themselves?
6. Are motivation and preparation for writing adequate, or are children expected to write without really having a purpose or knowing what is expected of them? Do children help establish reasons for writing?
7. Does each child feel rapport with the teacher? Does he or she feel free— and have opportunity—to ask questions, try out ideas, seek help when it is needed, work independently? Does he or she know that his or her efforts in learning and helping others are appreciated?
8. Are expectations realistic? Do the children think that they are? Do children set their own standards?[11]

These, of course, are not all of the questions that could be asked. They do show, though, the major focus an effective curriculum gives to evaluation.

Evaluating Writing Abilities and Products

There are a number of instruments and techniques for evaluating children's writing, and these are briefly discussed below. It should be kept in mind that they present useful information only to the extent that they themselves are valid, reliable, and related to curriculum objectives. If these criteria are met, they then may be used in the context of instruction.

---

11. Adapted from Walter T. Petty, Dorothy C. Petty, and Marjorie C. Becking, *Experiences in Language: Tools and Techniques for Language Arts Methods* (Boston: Allyn & Bacon, 1973), chap. 12.

Standardized Tests

There are published tests that purport to measure ability in written expression or some aspect of it. However, these measures generally do not actually do what is often claimed. For example, a test may determine a pupil's knowledge of grammatical terminology or rules, but this kind of knowledge of grammar has nothing to do with writing ability. Identifying good and poor sentences, choosing acceptable words and expressions, and arranging words and sentences in order are other categories found in these published tests. Again, measuring these abilities on a test may have little relationship to performance in actual expression.

Checklists

The most satisfactory means for evaluating writing performance is by the use of checklists based on pupil-teacher established standards for particular writing products. Depending on the form of the written expression and the objectives for teaching it, the standards will usually include statements about organization, content, appeal, vocabulary, spelling, and so on. Checklists often give too much attention to such matters as punctuation, margins, handwriting, and the like and too little to compositional elements. For checklists to be genuinely effective, they need to be developed with children and understood and used by them.

Group Evaluation

Among the several types of group evaluation procedures used in elementary school programs are (1) the child reads his or her paper (or distributes copies of it) to the class, and the other children evaluate it according to content and organization; (2) children work in small groups to read papers and make suggestions for improvement; and (3) the opaque or overhead projector is used to show papers, and the children make corrections and suggestions. The third technique can be a valuable evaluation procedure if papers are preread so that those selected for viewing will illustrate weaknesses common to many children or will show especially good vocabulary choices, organization, or development of ideas.

Many teachers prefer to tell children before writing begins if there is to be class or group evaluation. Other teachers prefer to read papers themselves instead of having children read them. When the projector is to be used, some teachers have names put on the backs of papers rather than the front. However, these approaches tend to regard evaluation in a negative sense rather than in a positive one. The teacher will find, of course, that the development of a positive approach to evaluation is difficult to establish but that respecting the wishes of each child and making efforts to avoid individual embarrassment and inhibition will be the central focus of any effective evaluation technique.

Pupil Self-Evaluation

Pupils should participate in the process of evaluation and assessment of learning needs. The curriculum should provide children with opportunities to:
1. Make and keep their own checklists of errors (spelling, punctuation,

capitalization, and so forth), faults in composition, and unacceptable word usages

2. Keep progress records of number of words spelled correctly on tests, new vocabulary learned, book reviews written, and so forth
3. Compare the forms of their letters and other types of written work with models
4. Use a handwriting scale and a chart of handwriting faults and diagnostic procedures
5. Keep folders of written products
6. Check their own spelling tests and evaluate their own written products based on standards they have established

Teacher Marking of Papers

The marking or "correcting" of papers is perhaps the most commonly used procedure for evaluating children's writing. Often the purpose of this marking, however, is to assign grades rather than to assess children's expression for the purpose of identifying instructional needs. This persists even though it is generallly known that the sight of red marks usually causes the child to destroy his or her paper or at least conceal it from classmates and parents. Children do not learn from this kind of marking, since it supplies little information of a specific nature concerning those items needing further instructional emphasis. This practice and children's reaction to it can be avoided in a number of ways. For example, only the grossest errors might be marked or occasionally papers might be marked only for one type of error. Such marking can be combined with the use of checklists and conferences with pupils. Many teachers have also begun to use the red pencil in a more positive fashion by pointing out commendable aspects of the writing—good word choices, apt expressions, appropriate margins, good organization, and so forth. This practice, again combined with the use of checklists and conferences, is probably the most effective evaluation procedure.

EXERCISES FOR THOUGHT AND ACTION

1. Make a list of factors that may cause children of a particular grade level to write less well than might be expected.
2. Work out a plan for improving the attitudes of children in a specific class toward spelling correctly all words that they write.
3. Try your hand at creative writing. Pick a topic based on an object, a picture, or the like. When you have written your poem or story, consider the process you engaged in. What were your major problems? What was your sequence in thinking?
4. Make an informal survey of the handwriting of children in a particular classroom. Collect papers and analyze them for specific handwriting faults. Also note evidence of such matters as the amount of writing done, postures, and types of assignments and relate these to the handwriting skills shown.

5. Report on the content of a set of commercial language materials (textbooks, for example) for one particular grade level. Do these materials contain all that you would need to teach written expression? What do they contain that seems extraneous to you?
6. Demonstrate to the class how you would help a class of first graders to write a group composition.
7. Plan for creative writing activities related to a unit in social studies or science.

SELECTED READINGS

Arnstein, Flora J. *Poetry and the Child.* Urbana, Ill.: The National Council of Teachers of English, 1971.

Braddock, Richard, et al. *Research in Written Composition.* Urbana, Ill.: The National Council of Teachers of English, 1963.

Burns, Paul C. *Diagnostic Teaching of the Language Arts.* Itasca, Ill.: F.E. Peacock Publishers, 1974.

Burrows, Alvina, et al. *They All Want To Write.* 3rd ed. New York: Holt, Rinehart & Winston, 1964.

Greene, Harry A., and Petty, Walter T. *Developing Language Skills in the Elementary Schools.* 5th ed. Boston: Allyn & Bacon, 1975.

Hennings, Dorothy Grant, and Grant, Barbara M. *Content and Craft.* Englewood Cliffs, N.J.: Prentice-Hall, 1973.

Horn, Thomas D., ed. *Research on Handwriting and Spelling.* Urbana, Ill.: The National Council of Teachers of English, 1966.

Logan, Lillian M., and Logan, Virgil G. *A Dynamic Approach to Language Arts.* Toronto: McGraw-Hill Company of Canada Limited, 1967.

Marksberry, Mary Lee. *Foundations of Creativity.* New York: Harper & Row, 1963.

Moffett, James. *A Student-Centered Language Arts Curriculum, Grades K-13: A Handbook for Teachers.* Boston: Houghton Mifflin Co., 1968.

Personke, Carl and Yee, Albert H. *Comprehensive Spelling Instruction.* Scranton, Pa.: International Textbook Co., 1971.

Petty, Walter T. and Bowen, Mary. *Slithery Snakes and Other Aids to Children's Writing.* New York: Appleton-Century-Crofts, 1967.

Rodgers, Mary C. *New Design in the Teaching of English.* Scranton, Pa.: International Textbook Co., 1968.

Sherwin, J. Stephen. *Four Problems in Teaching English: A Critique of Research.* Scranton, Pa.: International Textbook Co., 1969.

Tidyman, Willard F., et al. *Teaching the Language Arts.* 3rd ed. New York: McGraw-Hill, 1969.

The title of this chapter genuinely reflects what the author emphasizes. As he points out, contemporary social studies attempts to help children confront and more adequately cope with the social realities that they encounter every day. But what is social studies, and what should be taught in a social studies program? The author recognizes that the problem of defining social studies is essentially one of determining the content of a social studies program. He advocates a social studies thrust that emphasizes ecological awareness; activism; decision making; and the affective areas of beliefs, attitudes, values, and moral development.

The author suggests that activity-oriented social studies programs, which rely only minimally on textbooks, are increasingly being used and that modern social studies can only be taught by the teacher who attempts to know the issues and trends with respect to content and procedures. The comprehensive review of social studies developments in the sixties and early seventies as well as the descriptions of desirable programs for today will aid the reader in understanding these issues and trends and in developing an effective social studies program in an elementary school.

(Sections of this chapter are taken from the author's forthcoming book Elementary Social Studies as a Learning System, *a methodology text, soon to be published by Harper & Row.)*

W.T.P.

Social Studies and the Social World of the Child

Peter H. Martorella

⑨

Reflect a moment on your past experiences with social studies in elementary school. What do you remember? Are your memories happy or unhappy ones?

Perhaps a series of dates and capitols and maybe even a few explorers flash through your mind; certainly, a war or two must be mixed in. And don't forget all those community helpers! Were those periods exciting or a seemingly never-ending string of dry, pointless facts? Whatever you conjure up from those long forgotten moments, chances are they bear little resemblance to what social studies has to offer in the 1970s.

You still would recognize many of the old topics: home life, the school, and the community. But the activities that are associated with these labels, the instructional methods, and the materials have been radically altered. Scan the sample lesson on pages 218-19 as a case in point. It is taken from the teacher's guide of the first grade component of a forthcoming K-7 social studies program. Contemporary social studies, as we shall see, attempts to help children confront and more adequately cope with typical social realities they encounter every day. The knowledge it seeks for pupils is highly functional as well as significant.

Sample Lesson: What Is a Family?

General objectives

1. To identify the wide range of family types that exist in the United States
2. To allow children to identify with family types as a way of clarifying their own family structure
3. To identify the basic characteristics of a family

Materials

The People Book (Student Manual)

Commentary

Unfortunately many of the characterizations of families that young children encounter are often stereotypes or offer, at best, a limited view. This activity is designed to expose them to a wide range of different family types that can be found in the United States. Families come in different sizes, colors, and groupings, and whichever one the children in our classes belong to should be represented in their discussions. Accordingly, twenty different types of families are presented to the children. At least one, and possibly several families, should be similar to that of every child in your class.

For your summarization of this activity, keep in mind these characteristics of a family. A family is a group of two or more people who

1. Live together at least part of the time
2. Satisfy each other's needs in some way
3. Are either related by blood, marriage, adoption, or agreement

The concept of family is a complex one, and social scientists have defined it in many different ways. While not all would agree with the definition used here, it does seem to cover the basic points that you would want to consider.

Suggested procedures/Questions

Start the discussion by asking: "How many of you belong to a family?" This question should focus attention on the topic and on the fact that every member of the class belongs to a family. Follow with a question such as: "Why do we have families?" Accept whatever plausible responses the students offer and gently challenge any that are not.

Be sure that each child has a pencil. Call attention to appropriate pages in *The People Book* by announcing that the class is to hear about many different kinds of families. To explain the meaning of the house outline, point out the numbers beneath each family group in *The People Book* and that each of the people in a family live in the same house. Then proceed to tell the class about each family, referring to the numbers as you read. Tell the children to circle the families that most seem like their own.

1. This is the Martinez family. It is made up of Mrs. Martinez and her son.
2. This is the Agronski family. It is made up of Mr. and Mrs. Agronski and their five children.
3. This is the Patterson family. It is made up of Mr. Patterson and his daughter.
4. This is the Cordasco family. It is made up of Mr. and Mrs. Cordasco and their daughters.
5. This is the Choy family. It is made up of Mr. and Mrs. Choy and Mr. Choy's mother and father.
6. This is the Grier family. It is made up of Mr. and Ms. Grier.
7. This is the Redbird family. It is made up of Mrs. Redbird and her children.
8. This is the Stevens family. It is made up of Mr. and Ms. Stevens and three children whom they adopted. (Check to see if everyone knows what *adopted* means.)

9. This is the Jackson family. It is made up of Mrs. Jackson and her two children.
10. This is the Pagano family. It is made up of Mr. and Mrs. Pagano and their three children, Mr. Pagano's mother and father, and Mr. Pagano's aunt and uncle.

Stop at this point to see if the children are following along, are circling families with which they identify, or have questions about any of the families described.

11. This is the Wong family. It is made up of Mr. and Mrs. Wong.
12. This is the Juarez family. It is made up of Mr. Juarez and his granddaughter, whose parents have died.
13. This is a Commune family. It is made up of Mr. and Mrs. Larson and their children, Mr. Carbo, Mr. and Mrs. Jolson, Mr. and Mrs. Peterson and their children, and Mr. and Mrs. Goldberg.
14. This is the Heller family. It is made up of Mr. and Mrs. Heller and their three children. They belong to a religious group called the Amish who try to live as people did long ago.
15. This is the Rainwater family. It is made up of Mr. and Mrs. Rainwater and their three children.
16. This is the Thomas family. It is made up of Mr. and Mrs. Thomas and Mr. Thomas's nephew, who has come to live with them.
17. This is the Battaglia family. It is made up of Mrs. Battaglia and her child.
18. This is the Rodriguez family. It is made up of Mr. and Mrs. Rodriguez and their child.
19. This is the Diaz family. It is made up of Ms. Diaz and her child.
20. This is the Chinn family. It is made up of Mr. and Mrs. Chinn and their four children.

At the conclusion, ask if anyone would like to tell which families they circled as most like their own. As the pupils respond, try to give everyone who volunteers a chance to name at least one family. If a child does not volunteer, do not call on him. You may want to check the books of the nonrespondents at a later time to note their choices.

In the next phase of the discussion, ask: "In what ways were all of these families alike?" and "In what ways were they different?"

Conclude and summarize by stating the three basic characteristics of a family cited in the "Commentary."

WHAT IS SOCIAL STUDIES?

Surprising as it may seem, the returns are not yet in on the answer to this question. Prior to the nineteenth century, the term *social studies* did not even exist. Children studied "history" and "geography." In the early twentieth century, the term came into use, taking the name of a committee that was established to expand the curriculum of the schools. In its report, the Committee on Social Studies defined *social studies* broadly to mean all subject matter dealing with the growth and structure of human society. The committee went on to posit the cultivation of good citizenship as a major goal of social studies and, in turn, to define good citizenship in terms of noble and lofty social responsibilities.[1]

---

1. Committee on Social Studies, "The Social Studies in Secondary Education," Bureau of Education, Bulletin no. 28 (Washington, D.C., 1916).

Over the years, "good citizenship" has been translated in many ways in the social studies curriculum. In less-enlightened times, good citizenship has represented the inculcation of children with the dominant sociocivic mores of the controlling culture. A countertrend has skirted the ideological weaknesses of this position to argue that knowledge of the *social sciences* of itself could produce the good citizen. (This view of social studies sees the subject matter as a composite of appropriate items selected from the various social science disciplines.) Advocates of this latter approach saw a definite relationship between the social sciences and the social studies curriculum, and this association was further cemented in the late 1960s, after the advent of a series of federally initiated projects lumped under the label "Project Social Studies."

While not all scholars agree on the makeup of the social sciences,[2] there is consensus on a basic nucleus comprised of the following disciplines:

Anthropology
Sociology
Political Science
Economics
Geography
History
Psychology

Much of the 1960s was preoccupied with a search for the underlying structures of the social sciences, which in turn might be used as the bases for the social studies curriculum. This move was occasioned in part by Jerome Bruner's influential little book *The Process of Education,* which many educators viewed as a plea for discovering structures and, in part, as a reaction against seemingly endless progressions of irrelevant facts in the curriculum. The alternative advanced was to have students learn the basic *concepts* and *generalizations* that made up each of the various disciplines. In so doing, it was argued, the pupil would learn information that could transcend periods and revisions in data, and at the same time would acquire a cognitive structure or framework on which new knowledge could be organized.

While social scientists never were able to agree on definitive structures, a number of alternative possibilities were outlined in various studies, books, and conference reports published during the period.[3] The ramifications for curriculum development were that concepts and generalizations became one of the key organizing structures for the scope and sequence of social studies programs. Programs frequently would list in their overview the concepts and generalizations to be taught as well as the related social sciences that were to be incorporated into

2. For example, see D.L. Sills, ed., *The International Encyclopedia of the Social Sciences* (New York: Crowell, Collier & Macmillan, 1968).

3. For a sampling of the discussion, see I. Morrissett, ed., *Concepts and Structure in the New Social Science Curricula* (New York: Holt, Rinehart & Winston, 1967); M. Feldman and E. Seifman, eds., *The Social Studies: Structure, Models and Strategies* (Englewood Cliffs, N.J.: Prentice-Hall, 1969); and Bernard Berelson et al., *The Social Studies and the Social Sciences* (New York: Harcourt Brace Jovanovich, 1969).

each grade level. Some of the fruits of this developmental process—the various textbook series of the late sixties and early seventies, for example—reflect this pattern.

Even the process of arriving at what was meant by a social science *concept* or *generalization* was a long and tedious one, and in some instances these terms still remain a source of confusion.[4] Most social studies educators today, however, will recognize the following as concepts:

social change
power
island
mountain
election
role
income tax
culture

Similarly, the following statements are regarded as generalizations:
1. The family exists in every known human society.
2. People prejudiced against one ethnic group tend to be prejudiced against others.
3. As urbanization increases, employment opportunities tend to be concentrated in a limited number of regions.

This view of the social studies as being heavily dependent on the social sciences is reflected in some of the recent curriculum requirements written into law by various states. Witness sections of the Pennsylvania and California codes as examples:

> A planned course in the social studies shall be taught in each year of the elementary school. The content of this program shall include anthropolgy, economics, geography, history, political science and sociology. These may be combined into one general area known as social studies. (Section 20211, based on Section 1511, School Laws of Pennsylvania, 1968)
>
> The adopted course of study for grades 1 through 6 shall include instruction, beginning in grade 1 and continuing through grade 6, in the following areas of study . . . (c) Social sciences, drawing upon the disciplines of anthropolgy, economics, geography, history, political science, psychology, and sociology, designed to fit the maturity of pupils. (Article 2. *Course of Study of Grades 1 through 6;* Areas of Study: 8551, California Code)

Not all educators subscribe to the social-studies-as-the-social-sciences position, however. A recent past president of the National Council for the Social Studies leveled the following criticism of the position in his presidential address:

---

4. P.H. Martorella, *Concept Learning in the Social Studies: Models for Structuring Curriculum* (New York: INTEXT, 1971).

We, of the profession, have not immediately and clearly grasped this distinction between Social Science and Social Studies. We have devoted our major energies, including our efforts in the "new" Social Studies, to making the Social Sciences alone suffice for the broader needs of citizenship education. In this vein, we have tried to organize the teaching of the Social Sciences in all kinds of orders, sequences, and cycles; we have tried to organize teaching around concepts, generalizations, problems, and values; we have tried fusion, integration, and correlation of the social science disciplines; we have tried cases, projects, and contracts as organizing principles; we have prettied up our textbooks with maps, pictures, diagrams, graphs, charts, and a dozen other paraphernalia; we have thrown in audio-visual aids; we have "Brunerized" the subjects and made inquiry our god. These attempts to fit square pegs into round holes have never been entirely successful. It should be apparent that the social science disciplines, by themselves, do not constitute the whole of citizenship education. The effort to force citizenship education into a strict social science mold either does violence to Social Science, asking more of it than it has to offer, or it neglects the ethical component of citizenship altogether.[5]

The 1970s, then, have ushered in still different emphases concerning what the social studies should comprise. These newer thrusts emphasize ecological awareness; activism; affective concerns of beliefs, attitudes, values, and moral development; decision making; and generally a broader view of what knowledge is germane to social and individual concerns. Which notion of the nature of the social studies will ultimately prevail is not clear at this time. Certainly any definition is likely to include an important relationship with the social sciences. For purposes of our discussion, we will identify with this more recent, broader, and more yeasty view of the nature of social studies.

THE DESIGN OF THE K-6 CURRICULUM

While it would be impossible to specify all the variations of social studies curriculum designs that exist across the United States, one could predict with surprising accuracy the general structure of K-6 programs. This interesting phenomenon stems from the widespread impact of the "expanding-communities-of-men" notion of social studies curriculum design popularized by Paul Hanna.[6] The model, Hanna notes:

... starts with the oldest, smallest, and most crucial community—the family placed in the center of the concentric circles—and progresses outward

5. S.H. Engle, "Exploring the Meaning of the Social Studies," *Social Education* 35, no. 3 (March 1971): 280.
6. P.R. Hanna, "Revising the Social Studies: What Is Needed?" *Social Education* 27, no. 4 (April 1963).

in ever widening bands through the child's neighborhood community; the child's local communities of city, county, and/or metropolis; the state community; the regions-of-states community; and the national community.[7]

In spite of the fact that there are many ways to construct a curriculum sequence, each with its own defensible logic, the Hanna pattern dominates, representing virtually a national curriculum design.

> Though all textbook series do not follow precisely the theoretical approach espoused by Hanna, the general concept of expanding communities has been so popular throughout the United States that most textbook series follow some variation of that overall theme. As a result, that approach represents almost a national curriculum design for elementary social studies.[8]

Translated to K-6 grade level themes, the expanding horizons approach usually has resulted in the following basic pattern:

K-1   Family and School Community
2   Immediate Community
3   Towns and Cities
4   Regions of States
5   American History
6   World Cultures/Other Countries

CURRICULAR THRUSTS OF THE 1960s and 1970s

While a dominant pattern emerges in the design of the curriculum, considerable variation exists in the actual curricular materials that have been developed. The 1960s and early 1970s have been a period of growth for the social studies, during which both the shape and scope of materials and practices have broadened and diversified. Much of the shift was occasioned by what came to be identified as "Project Social Studies." Initiated in 1962 as part of the attempt of the United States Office of Education to bolster curriculum in the areas of science, mathematics, and foreign language, it was a belated response of our country to the Soviet challenge of Sputnik.

Project Social Studies encouraged experimentation in curriculum development and teaching practices as well as more effective teacher education programs. Many of the initial projects were based at university centers and concentrated on the task of building a total scope and sequence for a series of grades; others examined a specific social science focus for a course or courses; and still others analyzed some dimension of curricular improvement that could cut across grade levels. While the initial funding in most cases came from the federal gov-

---

7. Hanna, "Revising the Social Studies," p. 192.
8. R.M. Thomas and D.L. Brubaker, *Decisions in Teaching Elementary Social Studies* (Belmont, Calif.: Wadsworth Publishing Co., 1971), p. 125.

ernment, subsequent curriculum development often was supported by local and state, university, and foundation grants.

The net effect of this thrust by the Office of Education was to spur on many other centers of innovation in social studies, funded and nonfunded. Literally hundreds of large and small curriculum innovations of all shapes and sizes sprang up across the United States during the sixties. Those that were widely disseminated or were taken over by major commercial publishers have come to be considered as "national" projects, although there exists no formal definition of the term. Perhaps it is surprising to those who are familiar with parallel periods of growth in other areas of curriculum development, such as science education, that social studies educators in no way coverge on which developments are superior or even desirable for all schools across the United States!

This phenomenon has been both a source of strength and weakness for the social studies curriculum. The "bad news" is that it tends to produce confusion and strikes terror in the hearts of teachers, administrators, and curriculum adoption committees who must make pressured decisions with only meager resources at their disposal. "Just tell us what is considered to be the best program!" they cry in desperation. The "good news" is that lack of convergence on any one program or group of projects has promoted diversity in curriculum planning and has focused attention where it should always be—on the objectives of each school or district and the indigenous needs of the children it serves. Social studies curriculum development, no matter how exciting and innovative it may be, has not reached, if it ever will, the stage of sophistication and comprehensiveness at which a preassembled K-6 program can deal adequately with the social diversity and rapidly changing events in our country, let alone attend to the highly complex social needs of *each* child.

In the 1970s, evaluation of the legacy of the sixties is still ongoing, and with it concurrently, a recharting of what yet needs to be done (or undone) in the field. Due to the time lag that seems to attend all curriculum development, many teachers are still finding out about the results of the prior decade. Dissemination and diffusion, necessary accompaniments of development, are time-consuming and expensive processes. Moreover, the actual business of consolidating all of the constructive gains of the sixties has taken considerable time, since no national information retrieval center for curriculum developments in the social studies existed during this period.

In addition to its traditional role of dissemination and diffusion, the National Council for the Social Studies, the professional organization of teachers of social studies of both the elementary and secondary levels, has begun to assume some responsibility for curriculum evaluation. One of its ongoing activities has been the publication and updating of *Curriculum Guidelines*. (The latest revision was published in 1975.) In the seventies, the federal government also established the Educational Resources Information Center (ERIC)/Clearinghouse for Social Studies/Social Science Education (ChESS). ERIC/ChESS was commissioned to catalog, abstract, and index relevant documents in its subject area. It transmits findings of ongoing research in social studies as obtained from papers presented at educational conferences and progress reports of researchers. Many of these papers are never published in journals and might not ever be made available to a wide audience otherwise. In addition, ERIC/ChESS publishes a newsletter, bulletins, bibliographies, and commissions studies of special interest topics, such as environmental education.⁹ To date, ERIC/ChESS has largely devoted its energy to the dissemination and, to some extent, diffusion, rather than to the evaluation of the material it receives.

Much of the recharting in the 1970s has been preoccupied with the affective education movement as it relates to social studies instruction. The movement has emerged under many labels, including humanistic education, open education, intergroup education, personalizing education, valuing, and value clarification. But irrespective of the labels, there is a common focus: a persistent and underlying concern for individual and personal decision making. In some cases, affective education has emerged as a set of prescriptions that flow from a clearly defined theoretical framework; in others, it has been an eclectic potpourri of exercises abstracted from successful classroom experiences. Final results are not yet in, but they are certain to reflect in the social studies curriculum a turning inward to focus on the self—how it is shaped and perceives and reacts to the social world.

THE CURRICULAR LEGACY OF THE 1960s

This section is not an extensive analysis of the hundreds of curricular products produced during the 1960s, since such a discussion is obviously beyond the scope of this chapter. The reader, however, may already be familiar with quite a few of these projects, since many of them have been translated into basal textbook series. Yet for those who are interested in gaining a more complete view, various summaries of these products may be consulted.¹⁰ To coincide with the purpose of this chapter, brief synopses of three of the more visible and representative programs are offered to suggest the flavor of the products. Included with each program profile is a source address, at which more information on the materials may be secured. In many cases, the local instructional materials center or educational library will have copies of the programs.

Much more than the programs and materials are part of the legacy of the sixties, but they are its most visible elements. They constitute the tangible reflections of the excitement, ferment, debate, and discovery that repeatedly characterized the social studies curriculum during that period. Whether the momentum can be sustained and where it finally leads remain to be seen.

Man: A Course of Study (MACOS)

Probably no other single social studies program has been so lavishly funded and publicized as MACOS. It has been hailed as the embodiment of Jerome

---

9. The reader may write to ERIC/ChESS at 855 Broadway, Boulder, Colo. 80302, and ask to be placed on the newsletter mailing list.
10. For a comprehensive listing of projects and materials, see *Social Studies Curriculum Materials Data Book, I* and *II* (Boulder, Colo.: Social Science Education Consortium, 1973). Evaluations of twenty-six major social studies projects are found in *Social Education*, vol. 36.

Figure 9.1.

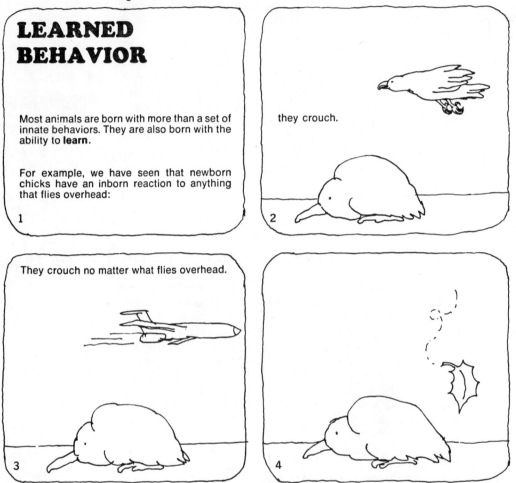

LEARNED BEHAVIOR

Most animals are born with more than a set of innate behaviors. They are also born with the ability to **learn**.

For example, we have seen that newborn chicks have an inborn reaction to anything that flies overhead:

1

they crouch.

2

They crouch no matter what flies overhead.

3

4

Source: Reprinted from *Innate and Learned Behavior,* part of the upper elementary school course *Man: A Course of Study,* developed by the Social Studies Program of EDC under a grant from the National Science Foundation. Text copyright © 1967, 1968, Education Development Center. Used with permission.

Bruner's curricular ideas as represented in *The Process of Education* (Bruner helped spawn, nurture, and oversee MACOS); vilified by groups of fundamentalists, since it accepts evolution as a scientific principle; attacked by equal rights groups who claim its title and focus are sexist; loved by thousands of teachers and pupils who note its novel and exciting content and material configuration (it employs many films, charts, records, games, different sized books, pamphlets, and posters—but no textbooks); and currently the object of Congressional scrutiny. Indeed the history of its development, dissemination, and diffusion comprises an interesting and complex story in itself.

The less-passionate details of the program are that it is a year-long course of study for the fifth grade or one of the other middle grades; was produced by the Educational Development Center (15 Mifflin Place, Cambridge, Mass. 02138); and was designed to answer three basic questions:

1. What is human about human beings?
2. How did they get that way?
3. How can they be made more so?

The materials are designed to allow children to derive conclusions about the human species through the study of salmon, herring, gulls, baboons, and the Netslik Eskimo (see Figure 9.1). Many of the materials in the course, such as the films and the diaries, represent actual field data gathered by social scientists.

Michigan Elementary Social Science Education Program

This program attempts to teach children in the intermediate grades how to investigate human behavior and values, using a modified form of techniques employed by social scientists. Organized flexibly into seven different units, the program is designed to supplement a basic social studies curriculum. The units may be spread over grades four, five, and six or studied in one year. Each of the seven units employs a project book consisting of thirty pages. In addition, a core resource book is used with all of the units. Basically, the pupils analyze and learn from a series of behavior specimens provided either in the project books, the core resource book, by the teacher, a recording (provided on an optional set of records), or role-play enactments. The project books include exercises and activities. The teacher is given a comprehensive guide and supplementary background readings to help orchestrate the various components and activities. A complete set of materials, available from Science Research Associates (259 E. Erie St., Chicago, Ill. 60611), then would include the following:

Teacher's Role in Social Science Investigation (background readings)
Teacher's Guide
Five-Record Set (optional)
Social Science Resource Book
Project Books:
   Learning To Use Social Science (Unit 1)
   Discovering Differences (Unit 2)
   Friendly and Unfriendly Behavior (Unit 3)
   Being and Becoming (Unit 4)
   Individuals and Groups (Unit 5)
   Deciding and Doing (Unit 6)
   Influencing Each Other (Unit 7)

A sample of the material, an activity sheet from *Discovering differences,* is shown below. The program's commercial title is *Social Science Laboratory Units,* and it does involve pupils in activities similar in general structure to those done in college and university social science laboratories.

Activity Sheet: Interviewing Dos and Don'ts

Directions: This exercise will help you to recall some of the things you learned about interviewing in Unit 1. Below are examples of dos and don'ts for successful interviews. Put a check (✔) in the space in front of the sentences that only describe *don'ts.*

_____ 1. Always wear a smile.

_____ 2. State the questions exactly as they are written on your schedule.

_____ 3. During the interview, be sure to tell the person what your answers would be.

_____ 4. Explain in a friendly manner what the interview is all about.

_____ 5. If you don't understand the answer given, go on to the next question.

_____ 6. If you can't write fast enough, finish recording the answers the next day or later.

_____ 7. Ask the person you are interviewing if he would be willing to help you by answering a few questions.

_____ 8. If the person you are interviewing wants to talk about something else, stop asking questions and listen.

_____ 9. When the person you are interviewing says he doesn't know how to answer, help him by telling him how other people have answered.

_____ 10. Ask the questions in the exact order listed on your interview schedule.

_____ 11. Record the answers to your questions exactly as they are given.

_____ 12. If the answer is not clear, repeat the question. You might say, "I'm sorry, I didn't understand you."

_____ 13. If you are interviewing sixth-grade boys, it's faster if one sixth-grader answers for his friends, too.

_____ 14. When the interview is over, thank the person you have been interviewing.

Source: Ronald Lippitt, Robert Fox, and Lucille Schaible, *Project Book 1/Social Science Laboratory Units, Learning To Use Social Science.* © 1969, Science Research Associates. Used with permission of the publisher.

The Minnesota Social Studies Project

The Minnesota Project differs from the other two in several important respects. For one, it is a K-12 articulated program. The themes for each grade level are as follows:

K	The Earth as the Home of Man
Grades 1 and 2	Families Around the World
Grade 3	Communities Around the World
Grade 4	Communities Around the World: Their Economic System
Grade 5	Regional Studies
Grade 6	United States History: From Community to Society
Grade 7	Man and Society
Grade 8	Our Political System
Grade 9	Our Economic System
Grade 10	American History
Grade 11	Area Studies
Grade 12	Value Conflicts and Policy Decisions

Unlike the other programs, this one does not include materials for the pupils but rather is largely a series of teaching and resource units. Each unit specifies teaching strategies and related objectives, along with a series of materials that are needed to complete the activities. From four to seven resource units are included in each grade sequence to allow for considerable flexibility in using the materials. In addition, there are a series of background papers that explain much of the theory and rationale of the program.

A major trademark of the program is its identification of social science concepts, generalizations, skills, and attitudes in a continuous and sequential K-12 strand. This construction produces a spiraling effect: It reintroduces more complex dimensions of the same general structure at each grade level. The program materials were never published in commercial form, but a duplicated version is available from the Green Printing Company (631 8th Ave. North, Minneapolis, Minn. 55411).

THE PROMISE OF THE 1970s

The 1970s emerged in many shapes for social studies educators. The plight of minorities and women, long a festering concern of the social activists within the social studies field, spilled over into curricular practices and programs. Some significant benchmarks were the creation of the Committee on Racism and Social Justice of the National Council for the Social Studies, one of whose tasks was to screen all Council activities; the growing impact of equal rights groups in redressing sexism in curricular materials; and the emergence of two significant Council yearbooks, *Teaching About Life in the City* and *Teaching Ethnic Studies,* both eloquent and powerful arguments for social concern in the classroom.

On another front, guidelines for eliminating sexism from publications are being adopted by major publishers of curricular materials. The following is an excerpt from a pamphlet published by McGraw-Hill:

Sexist Examples	*Suggested Alternatives*
Arthur Ashe is one of the best tennis players in America today and Billie Jean King is one of the best women players.	Arthur Ashe and Billie Jean King are among the best tennis players in America today.
The candidates were Bryan K. Wilson, president of American Electronics, Inc., and Florence Greenwood, a pert, blonde grandmother of five.	The candidates were Bryan K. Wilson, president of American Electronics, Inc., and Florence Greenwood, credit manager for Bloominghill's Department Store OR . . . Bryan K. Wilson, a handsome, silver-haired father of three, and Florence Greenwood, a pert, blonde grandmother of five.
Write a paragraph about what you expect to do when you are old enough to have Mr. or Mrs. before your name.	Write a paragraph about what you would like to do when you grow up.
Al listened patiently to the ladies chatter.	Al listened patiently while the women talked.

In New England, the typical farm was so small that the owner and his sons could take care of it by themselves.	In New England, the typical farm was so small that the family members could take care of it by themselves.
A slave could not claim his wife or children as his own because the laws did not recognize slave marriages.	Slave men and women tried to maintain family relationships, but the laws did not recognize slave marriages.[11]

Similarly, many communities across the United States are beginning to include citizen's groups sensitive to sexism and racism in the curriculum evaluation process.

More general affective concerns, as indicated earlier, permeate the newer curriculum materials and the practices in many classrooms. This phenomenon merits our extended analysis because it has various interpretations and because it is increasing its impact. Affective growth always has been an important, albeit frequently neglected, objective in the social studies curriculum. Today, however, it seems to have taken on a new urgency.

Affective learning, for our purposes, refers to those dimensions of learning concepts, conclusions, and generalizations that emphasize the identification, analysis, and clarification of self-concerns. In turn, self-concerns deal with subject matter that focuses on the personal choices and opinions of a pupil. There are a number of ways of categorizing the instructional activities that touch on self-concerns. Partly because of the imprecision in the social studies literature dealing with self-concerns and largely because many aspects of self defy easy classification, various practices frequently emerge under different labels. Mainly as a matter of the author's convenience, our discussion will be organized under the headings of "Self-Concepts," "Values," and "Moral Development."

Self-Concepts

As the child moves through developmental stages in acquiring knowledge, he or she also is forming the "self."

> The self is something which has a development; it is not initially there, at birth, but arises in the process of social experience and activity, that is, develops in the given individual as a result of his relations to that process as a whole and to other individuals within that process.[12]

As the child organizes the attitudes of others toward him or her, the youngster does so through his or her own special perceptual filters, which vary from child to child. Consider one incident in a series in which two children are beginning to organize the attitudes of others toward them. A boy and girl in the second

---

11. "Guidelines for Equal Treatment of the Sexes in McGraw-Hill Book Company Publications" (New York: McGraw-Hill, 1974).
12. G.H. Mead, *Mind, Self and Society,* ed. C.W. Morris (Chicago: University of Chicago Press, 1962), p. 135.

grade are the first ones to arrive in their classroom. They are neatly and brightly garbed, and the teacher immediately takes notice. "My, don't you two look pretty today!" Tanya filters this response as: "I am the kind of person who looks pretty and that is good, because I want to be viewed as pretty." Juan processes the same comment as: "I am the kind of person who looks like a sissy and that is bad, because I don't want to be seen as a sissy."

The self is truly social in that it both derives from society and helps shape it in some measure. A class bully not only is forming a notion of self that says : "I am the kind of person who can hurt other people and control them" but also is affecting the self of each peer that child confronts. The importance of self to the affective concerns of social studies teaching are nicely expressed by D.E. Hamacheck:

> It is through the door of the self that one's personality is expressed. How the self is expressed is a complex phenomena meaning different things to different people. It is one person's brashness and another person's shyness; it is one person's sympathetic giving and another person's selfish hoarding; it is one person's trusting nature and another person's suspiciousness. An individual's image of himself is constructed from his conception of the "sort of person I am." All of us have beliefs about our relative value and our ultimate worth. We feel superior to some persons but inferior to others. We may or may not feel as worthy or as able as most other individuals, and much of our energy is spent trying to maintain or modify our beliefs about how adequate we are (or would like to be).[13]

Analyzing and clarifying self-concerns is a lifetime process that requires some attention at every level of the social studies curriculum. Each person's self-concept constantly undergoes refinement and testing. By providing children with repeated opportunities to clarify and discover positive aspects of self, teachers help them resolve self-concerns. The task is one of eliminating unwarranted negative perceptions of self and maximizing chances for honest positive impressions of self.

There are many social studies activities that can help children deal constructively with self-concepts. A sample activity involves the use of Q-Sorts techniques. These require a child to sort a variety of statements or items into piles along some continuum. Applied to self-concepts, the Q-Sorts may be used to compare characteristics of self to those of an idealized self or of another person, such as a parent or loved one.

An illustration of this strategy involves two sets of cards similar to those shown on the facing page. The child sorts each set of adjective cards into five piles. One pile represents "what you would most *like* to be"; the other piles are arranged in a line, with the fifth being "what you would least *like* to be"; and the other piles show various stages in between. After the child has sorted all the cards, he or she turns them over. The child then sorts the second set of cards in similar fashion, but this time the first and fifth piles represent "most like the *real* me" and "least like *real* me." He or she then turns over the first set of piles and compares

---

13.   D.E. Hamachek, *Encounters with the Self* (New York: Holt, Rinehart & Winston, 1971), p. 8.

the similarities and differences in the two piles. Discrepancies represent the extent to which the person is not accepting of his or her existing self-concept or goals for self-development. *The Q-Sorts generally should be done privately, with pupils being asked to discuss their reactions and feelings on a voluntary basis.*

Q-Sort Adjective Cards

BOSSY	MEAN	FRIENDLY	SMART
DISOBEDIENT	LAZY	HAPPY	LIKABLE
SELFISH	SHY	CLEVER	STRONG
DUMB	BORED	HONEST	SENSE OF HUMOR
WEAK	JEALOUS	FEELINGS EASILY HURT	FAIR
STUBBORN	CONFUSED	CAREFUL	NICE
FORGETFUL	WORRIED	GOOD-LOOKING	HELPFUL
FRIGHTENED	UNCOOPERATIVE	QUIET	TRICKY

Values

Values teaching, however conceived, always has been an important concern of the schools. Historically, this concern often has been expressed through an emphasis on "good citizenship" and "desirable sociocivic behavior." While the meaning of these terms were often the subject of considerable debate, the dominant interpretation emphasized the support and promotion of existing norms of behavior. The implication was that learning to be a good citizen involved being inculcated with the dominant social, economic, and political views of society.

Over the years, however, there has been a serious reappraisal of this view. The increasing resistance of minority groups to the norms and mores advocated by majorities, the growing influence of the social sciences on the total curriculum, and the rise of the inquiry movement all have contributed to a reaction against efforts to inculcate values in schools. The traditional approach to values education has created particularly serious problems in schools in which pluralistic value systems were the norm or in which a subculture held values at odds with those of the dominant culture. (Examples of the latter would be Amish and native American schools.)

Perhaps the most serious challenge to the validity of the values inculcation position is the charge that it provides no direction for action in situations involving conflicts between cherished values. Learning loyalty and honesty as desirable absolute values gives no clue as to how to behave when it is impossible to hold both values simultaneously. A presidential assistant, for example, who discovers that his employer has committed some transgression is torn between what the value of honesty may compel him to reveal and what his value of loyalty may compel him to suppress. Both are desirable values, but in the case cited, some stratagem beyond mere value maintenance is required for decision making.

For our purposes, values may be regarded as basic end-states of feelings concerning matters of worth; these undergird all of our choices and decisions in life. In effect, they function as a first line of filtering that allows us to interpret and organize reality according to its worth and importance to us. Our values not only determine how we shall encounter reality but also predispose us to perceive selectively what is around us.

Assessing and analyzing these primary filters of reality are likely to yield the most pregnant information about self-concerns. Not surprisingly, values also are the most difficult dimensions of self-concerns to accurately diagnose and observe. At best, in classroom situations a teacher is dealing with verbalizations or paper-and-pencil reflections of values. Neither actions nor statements by an individual, considered separately, may be accurate indicators of what a person actually values. This fact should not discourage teachers from dealing with values but rather caution them to avoid easy judgments concerning a pupil's values.

Milton Rokeach has devised a *Value Survey* that assesses an individual's value system. It consists of two sets of eighteen values per set. Values are designated as instrumental (mode of conduct) and terminal (end-state).[14] Instrumental values are self-controlled, courageous, ambitious, forgiving, cheerful, capable, imaginative, intellectual, logical, loving, obedient, responsible, independent, honest, polite, broad-minded, clean, and helpful. Terminal values consist of a comfortable life, an exciting life, a sense of accomplishment, social recognition, national security, freedom, mature love, inner harmony, a world of beauty, happiness, equality, family security, a world at peace, pleasure, salvation, self-respect, true friendship, and wisdom. In Rokeach's *Survey*, respondents are given some explanation for each of the terms and then asked to rank them in order of perceived importance. Criteria for choices are to be personal, and an individual establishes his or her own list of priorities. According to Rokeach:

> A value is an enduring belief that a specific mode of conduct or end-state of existence is personally or socially preferable to an opposite or converse mode of conduct or end-state of existence. A value system is an enduring organization of beliefs concerning preferable modes of conduct or end-states of existence along a continuum of relative importance.[15]

Through the raising of an individual's value system to the level of consciousness, a person generally can learn a great deal about his or her own value preferences. Correspondingly, through the sharing of results and rationale for choices with others, reciprocal insights result.

Another possible application of the *Value Survey* approach is to try to translate some relevant cluster of values from the *Survey* into an exercise that requires the application of the values to social planning. The product would be a series of statements that reflect the abstract values. The pupils would then rank these statements in order of perceived importance in relation to some social issue or problem. Let us consider such a possible translation and application that might be

---

14. M. Rokeach, *The Nature of Human Values* (New York: Free Press, 1973).
15. Rokeach, *Nature of Human Values*, p. 5.

appropriate for very young children, possibly even at the primary level. The cluster of abstract values to be translated into a social context is taken from Rokeach's set of terminal values.

Freedom
Salvation
Wisdom
National security
A comfortable life
Equality
Family security

An activity sheet similar to the one below would be distrubuted to each member of the class, read aloud, and explained. Each child would complete the task individually. Every one of the seven statements is an attempt to reflect, at a child's level, the corresponding values of freedom, salvation, wisdom, national security, a comfortable life, equality, and family security. After each child completes the activity sheet, he or she is asked to share his or her rankings with others and the rationale for such choices. The children should be allowed to offer alternatives and to raise questions about one another's reasons.[16]

Activity Sheet: Building a New City

A number of new cities are being planned for the United States. Many of our cities just grew without anyone really planning them. In the new cities, most things will be carefully planned: where people will live, where they will shop, work, go to school, and have fun.

One new city being planned will be in Minnesota. It will be called Jonathon. How do you think Jonathon should be planned?

Below are some things that planners will have to think about. Put a 1 in front of the thing you feel is the most important for the planners to think about. Put a 2 in front of the second most important thing and so on until you have numbered everything from 1 to 7.

_____ People should be free to buy a house any place they like.
_____ There should be plenty of churches and temples built.
_____ There should be enough schools and colleges so that everyone can learn.
_____ A police department should be set up.
_____ People should have things to do that they really like.
_____ All people should be treated equally.
_____ There should be jobs for everyone who wants them.

Moral Development

Moral development basically is the process by which a child is able to decide that a certain course of action is right or wrong. Over the past twenty years, Lawrence Kohlberg and his associates have developed, refined, and tested a

---

16. Other applications of this approach to values are discussed in P.H. Martorella, "Valuing as a Teaching Strategy," 1975 Yearbook of the National Council for Geographic Education, on press.

theory of moral development based on Piaget's notions of hierarchical stages. The Kohlberg findings from research conducted on children in this and other countries reveal six stages of moral reasoning through which all individuals move:

Stage 1:   *Orientation to Punishment and Obedience.* The physical consequences of an action determine whether it is good or bad.

Stage 2:   *The Instrumental Relativist Orientation.* Right action consists of that which instrumentally satisfies one's own needs and occasionally the needs of others.

Stage 3:   *Good Boy-Nice Girl Orientation.* Seeking approval of others; to gain approval or avoid disapproval. Conforms to stereotype of majority or natural role behavior.

Stage 4:   *Law and Order Orientation.* Adherence to established rules for their own sake. "Doing one's duty" and evidencing respect for authority constitute right behavior.

Stage 5:   *Contractual Legalistic Orientation.* Recognition of an arbitrary element in rules for the sake of agreement. Duty is defined in terms of contract, and respecting the rights of others and the will of the majority. Right tends to be determined in terms of what has been agreed upon by the whole society or more general principles such as "the greatest good for the greatest number."

Stage 6:   *Conscience or Principle Orientation.* Looking to one's own conscience as a directing agent and to mutual respect and trust. Right is defined by the decision of conscience in accord with self-chosen ethical principles that appeal to logic. "At heart, these are universal principles of *justice*, of the *reciprocity* and *equality* of the *human rights*, and of respect for the dignity of human beings as *individual persons*.[17]

Like Piaget, Kohlberg argues that each successive stage builds on the preceding one and that no stage may be skipped. Stage movement for each individual occurs in developmental fashion, which may be accelerated or retarded. With training in the use of coding protocols, it is possible to diagnose the dominant stage of an individual's moral reasoning. Kohlberg maintains that most adults never move beyond stage 3 or 4. While the dominant stage of moral reasoning *may vary for an individual* in a given classroom, the probabilities are that most elementary pupils will be at stages 1 and 2, with some at stage 3; and most secondary students will be at stages 3 and 4, with some at 2 and a few at 5.

Empirical evidence also has been collected by Kohlberg's associates to support the notion that stage acceleration may be engendered by providing moral reasoning at *one* stage above that of the child. Individuals tend to be influenced by arguments representing one stage higher than their own, are unable to understand (though they prefer) arguments representing *more* than one stage above

---

17. L. Kohlberg, "Stage and Sequence: The Cognitive-Developmental Approach to Socialization," in *Handbook of Socialization Theory and Research,* ed. D.A. Goslin (Chicago: Rand McNally & Co., 1969), pp. 347-480.

their own, and reject those representing lower stages. By engaging in dialogues with others at stages above your own, Kohlberg assumes, fixation at a lower stage of reasoning will be prevented and upward movement facilitated.

Kohlberg's approach to moral development allows the school to participate in an important area of the child's self-growth, while avoiding the pitfalls of moralizing. Children may be aided in growing in their capacity for better moral reasoning without being conditioned to believe in a *particular* moral course of action. In effect, then, Kohlberg's moral development strategies provide a third alternative to the other moral inculcation and laissez-faire ("do your own thing") positions.

Moral dilemmas of the variety that Piaget and Kohlberg presented to children offer a novel opportunity for teachers to involve their pupils of any age in crucial issues and data and at the same time to make a contribution to the children's moral development. A basic instructional stratagem devised and refined by Kohlberg and his associates is to present students with moral dilemmas centering around real or hypothetical issues and to provide an opportunity to discuss them in groups. Typical dilemmas center around issues such as rights; justice, or fairness; and rules. The following example is taken from the materials used by Kohlberg and his associates in their attempts to study moral development in young children.

> Gladys has waited all week to go to the movies. On Saturday, her parents gave her some money so she can see a special movie in town that will only be there one day. When Gladys gets to the movie theatre, there is already a long line with many children waiting to buy tickets. Gladys takes a place at the end of the line.
>
> All of a sudden, a big wind blows the money out of Gladys' hand. Gladys leaves the line to pick up her money. When she gets back, there are lots more people in line and a new girl named Mary has taken her place. Gladys tells Mary that she had that place and asks Mary to let her back in line. If Mary does not let Gladys in line, Gladys will have to go to the end of the line and there may not be enough tickets left and she won't get a chance to see the movie.
>
> 1. Should Mary let Gladys back into the line?
> 2. Why do you think that is what Mary should do?
>
> *Probe Questions:*
>
> 3. Does it make a difference if Mary doesn't know why Gladys left the line?
> 4. How does Mary know whether or not Gladys is telling the truth?
> 5. Why is telling the truth important?
> 6. Gladys comes back and tells Mary that she left the line to chase after her ticket money which the wind blew out of her hand. Would you let Gladys in line if you were Mary? Why?
> 7. If Mary is Gladys' friend, should that make a difference? Why?
> 8. Suppose that instead of the wind blowing the money out of Gladys' hand, Gladys decided to leave the line to get an ice cream cone. If that is what happened, should Mary let Gladys in line when she comes back?

9. What's the difference between leaving the line to get some ice cream and leaving the line to chase some money?[18]

Guidance Associates has produced a series of filmstrips/records/cassettes kits built around moral dilemmas with which young children can easily identify.[19] Some of the kits use fantasy elements such as a wizard and "Cat Man," while others center around everyday contexts that children are likely to recognize.

A POTPOURRI OF COMMERCIALLY PRODUCED MATERIALS

Since any thorough, systematic listing of materials available would be an impossible task to handle within the confines of one chapter, our discussion will center on a random assortment of items that will suggest the broad range of what is available to a teacher of social studies.

Many new textbook series have been produced for the social studies, and most, if not all, reflect some of the characteristics discussed in preceding sections. Like most commercial products, these series vary in quality, size, and cost. And like all basic texts, they suffer from the limitations that two hard or soft covers impose. Most of the larger publishing companies also have ancillary media components to accompany the series. Frequently, these consist of filmstrips, records/cassettes, and large photocards (the latter usually for the kindergarten level).

As state-adoption guidelines become more flexible, permitting more non-textbook adoptions, the makeup of the series package is likely to change. Several companies have initiated rather conservative moves in the direction of more activity-oriented basal social studies series. These changes include less reliance on the textbook. Perhaps bolder moves are on the horizon.

Myriad supplementary materials, programs, and kits exist for those who wish to "build their own" programs or enrich a basal series. A fine source of information on a limited range of materials is the *Social Studies Service Catalog,* which is available free on request (as of this writing) from the Social Studies Service (10,000 Culver Blvd., Culver City, Calif. 90030). The items listed for sale in this catalog of almost two hundred pages include filmstrips, transparencies, simulations and games, filmloops, records, maps, and the like.

Commercially developed simulation games cover a wide scope of historical events and deal with a variety of social decision-making processes. For our purposes, "simulation games" refer to any gamelike activities that are designed to provide participants with lifelike problem-solving experiences. Its elements comprise a more or less accurate representation of some *real* phenomena. These characteristics distinguish it from a simple game, which has little relationship to the realities of daily living.

Probably the most comprehensive source of information concerning simulation games is *The Guide to Simulation/Games for Education and Training* by

18. L. Kohlberg and associates, "Moral Judgment Interview for Subjects 6-10: Preliminary Draft" (Cambridge, Mass.: Harvard University, n.d.), pp. 7-8.

19. *First Things: Values* (Pleasantville, N.Y.: Guidance Associates, 1972).

David W. Zukerman and Robert E. Horn. It is distributed by Information Re-
sources (P.O. Box 417, Lexington, Mass. 02173) and contains the following
information on each game:
Age level
Objective
Number of players
Playing time required
Roles
Components
Costs
Producer and address

A sampling of the simulation games listed and available is as follows:
Population: A Game of Man and Society
Extinction
Pink Pebbles—A Game About How Money Began
Market
Where Do We Live?
Down with the King
Discovery
Crisis

Not all games listed in the guide are of equal quality, nor are they appropriate
for all grade levels. Very few simulation games are designed for primary children,
since it is very difficult to simplify social variables sufficiently to make rules and
issues clear without so distorting the actual event represented as to make the
activity meaningless.

Three simulation games that this author has found to work effectively with
children and that are relatively inexpensive or easy to explain are *Powderhorn*,
The Road Game, and *Explorers I* and *II*. *Powderhorn* deals with the distribution
and manipulation of power, as reflected in the setting of a frontier society. *The
Road Game*, through the vehicle of having teams compete to construct roads
through areas, allows pupils to examine behavior that occurs when power and
status are at issue. *Explorers I* and *II* give pupils an experience in simulating the
early explorers of North and South America in encountering uncharted lands.

Several excellent sources of information exist on how to organize and conduct *role-playing* activities, including suggested scenarios and activities.

> Basically, role playing calls for a student's stepping outside the accus-
> tomed role that he plays in life, relinquishing his usual patterns of behavior
> in exchange for the role and patterns of another person. This other role
> may be that of a real person or may be entirely fictitious. . . . The student
> assumes the role of another person in the present or at a different time and
> place. He attempts, as far as possible, to speak like the other person, to
> behave like the other person, and to feel like the other person; this is the
> key to successful role playing.[20]

---

20. M. Chesler and R. Fox, *Role-Playing Methods in the Classroom* (Chicago: Science Research
Associates, 1966), p. 3.

Role-play enactments may begin with a simple story, problem situation, or scenario and may even employ props. Drama (frequently high drama!), a mainstay of role playing, accounts for much of the children's enjoyment of this activity, but drama should never be allowed to overshadow or supplant the objectives of role playing. It should be remembered that role playing is a vehicle for instruction; it is not an end in itself.

The compact, highly readable volume *Role-Playing Methods in the Classroom* provides a fine introduction to the topic and outlines a number of important procedural considerations.[21] It also has a helpful index, with entries interestingly arranged according to questions teachers usually ask. *Role-Playing for Social Values* is a more comprehensive study.[22] It contains a copious number of stories organized around problem themes of interest to children. The authors of this study also have produced a series of media materials (published by Holt, Rinehart & Winston) to be used along with role-playing techniques: *Words and Action: Role-Playing Photo-Problems for Young Children; People in Action: Role-Playing and Discussion Photographs for Elementary Social Studies;* and *Values in Action: Role-Problem-Situations for the Intermediate Grades.*

The *People in Action* series, for example, has four levels of large black and white photographs; each successive level represents an increasingly older group of children and events and concerns relevant to that age. Activities for the photographs include role-play activities. One group of photographs portrays open-ended problems (ones that may be resolved in a variety of ways), such as three children standing in front of a library looking apprehensive, with one boy holding a book with a torn cover. The accompanying teacher's guide presents a twelve-step strategy for introducing the problem and moving into role playing and follow-up discussions.

The Fitzgerald Publishing Company has published a series of stories about prominent black historical figures in an inexpensive color-illustrated comic-book format entitled *Golden Legacy.* The publisher notes: "*Golden Legacy* is not a comic magazine, but it is a new approach to the study of history. The intention of our publication is to implant pride and self esteem in black youth while dispelling myths in others."[23]

Two multimedia programs that are designed to be used across several grade levels to help children develop a better awareness and acceptance of self are the *Focus on Self-Development* series and the *DUSO* kits. The former consists of pictures for discussion and role playing, records, filmstrips, and student booklets.[24] Three levels of the *Focus on Self-Development* series are available, generally keyed to the first three levels of the Taxonomy of Educational Objectives, Affective Domain. The authors describe the program in this fashion:

> Its overall objectives are to lead the child toward an understanding of self, an understanding of others, and an understanding of the environment and

21. Chesler and Fox, *Role-Playing Methods.*
22. Fannie and George Shaftel, *Role-Playing for Social Values* (Englewood Cliffs, N.J.: Prentice-Hall, 1967).
23. "The Life of Robert Smalls," vol. 3, *Golden Legacy* (New York: Fitzgerald Publishing Co., 1970), p. ii.
24. *Focus on Self-Development* (Chicago: Science Research Associates, 1970). (There are three levels with corresponding kits in the program: *Awareness, Responding,* and *Involvement.*)

its effects. Its purpose is to bring out the child's ideas and feelings and to get him to think about them and act on them.[25]

The DUSO (Developing Understanding of Self and Others) program comes in kits I and II, which roughly correspond to preschool-primary and intermediate grade levels.[26] Kits contain storybooks, sets of recordings, posters, puppets and related activity cards and props, role-play cards, and other materials for discussion. Both humorous and talking nonhuman figures (for example, DUSO the Dolphin) are used in the activities. A series of strategies are built around typical children's problem situations.

A program built around a basic reader/workbook and supplemented with activity charts and ditto-master handouts is called *Dimensions of Personality*.[27] Student materials mainly consist of series of work activities to be preceded by some brief commentary and instructions concerning the tasks. The pupils produce some behavior specimens related to the unit theme and then analyze them in groups of four. The basic instructional cycle is to read a short passage, respond by supplying some personal data aloud or in writing, and share the results within the groups.

PLUGGING IN TO THE FUTURE OF THE SOCIAL STUDIES

"Plugging in" to the future of the social studies requires gaining access to communication networks that intersect with social studies developments. This is a pragmatic need for every teacher of social studies, especially the elementary teacher whose impossible assortment of subject-matter demands consume precious time. Beyond the college/university-course route and workshop sessions, affiliation with a related professional organization and monthly examination of a few key journals will help keep you abreast of social studies ferment. Two organizations specifically focused on the social studies and their addresses are National Council for the Social Studies (1201 Sixteenth St., N.W., Washington, D.C.) and National Council for Geographic Education (115 North Marion St., Oak Park, Ill. 60301).

Both councils publish a monthly journal and an annual yearbook focusing on a timely theme in social studies, and each holds an annual conference lasting several days and highlighting all the recent developments in the profession. Their respective journals are *Social Education* and *The Journal of Geography*. An independently published journal, *The Social Studies*, also follows the state of the profession and is issued monthly.

Finally, and perhaps most obviously, every teacher needs to take an active interest in society, whether it is at the local, state, national, or international level. As a teacher consciously intersects personally and vicariously with the ongoing social drama that surrounds us all daily, he or she begins to *live* social studies and

---

25. *Focus on Self-Development, Stage One: Awareness* (Chicago: Science Research Associates, 1970), p. 6.
26. *DUSO* (Circle Pines, Minn.: American Guidance Services, 1970).
27. *Dimensions of Personality* (Dayton, Ohio: Pflaum/Standard, 1972).

to enhance his or her teaching potential. Become an actor or a viewer, but get in on the show!

EXERCISES FOR THOUGHT AND ACTION

1. Identify some important social concern about which you feel strongly. Write it down, along with what you feel you can do about it this month. Then do it.
2. There are many worthy objectives for the teaching of social studies. What, however, do *you* consider to be *the* primary objective of teaching social studies?
3. Refer back to the example of the self-concept activity discussed on pages 232-33. Construct your own set of adjective cards and do the activity yourself.
4. Collect a group of five or six kids and a tape recorder. Use the moral dilemma cited on pages 237-38, along with the probe questions, and record the children's discussion. As you listen to the playback, try to assess the ways in which the arguments differ.
5. Locate the social studies curriculum guide for a school in your area. How does it compare with the expanding-horizons model of Hanna? Where does it differ?
6. Try your hand at being an SD (sexism detector). Refer to the illustrations of sexism given on pages 230-31 and also think of some others. Locate a newer social studies textbook series and examine several grade levels for instances of sexism. You will be surprised!
7. Locate in your educational library or materials center any of the materials listed in this chapter and examine them. Make a list of what you consider to be the strengths and weaknesses of them and why.

SELECTED READINGS

Ball, John M., et al., eds. *The Social Sciences and Geographic Education: A Reader.* New York: John Wiley, 1971.

Banks, James A., and Clegg, Ambrose A., Jr. *Teaching Strategies for the Social Studies.* Reading, Mass.: Addison-Wesley, 1973.

Chesler, Mark, and Fox, Robert. *Role-Playing Methods in the Classroom.* Chicago: Science Research Associates, 1966.

Clements, H. Millard, et al. *Social Study: Inquiry in Elementary Classrooms.* Indianapolis: Bobbs-Merrill Co., 1966.

Engle, Shirley, and Longstreet, Wilma S. *A Design for Social Education in the Open Curriculum.* New York: Harper & Row, 1972.

Estvan, Frank J. *Social Studies in a Changing World: Curriculum and Instruction.* New York: Harcourt, Brace & World, 1967.

Feldman, Martin, and Seifman, Eli, eds. *The Social Studies: Structure, Models and Strategies.* Englewood Cliffs, N.J.: Prentice-Hall, 1969.

Fraser, Dorothy McClure, ed. *Social Studies Curriculum Development: Prospects and Problems.* Washington, D.C.: National Council for the Social Studies, 1969.

Goldmark, Bernice. *Social Studies, A Method of Inquiry.* Belmont, Calif.: Wadsworth, 1968.

Greer, Mary, and Rubinstein, Bonnie. *Will the Real Teacher Please Stand Up?* Pacific Palisades, Calif.: Goodyear, 1972.

Jarolimek, John. *Social Studies in Elementary Education,* 4th ed. New York: Macmillan Co., 1971.

Jarolimek, John, and Walsh, Huber, eds. *Readings on Social Studies in Elementary Education.* New York: Macmillan Co., 1969.

Joyce, Bruce R. *New Strategies for Social Education.* Chicago: Science Research Associates, 1972.

Lyon, Harold C., Jr. *Learning to Feel–Feeling to Learn.* Columbus, Ohio: Charles E. Merrill Publishing Co., 1971.

Martorella, Peter H. *Concept Learning in the Social Studies: Models for Structuring Curriculum.* New York: INTEXT, 1971.

———. *Elementary Social Studies as a Learning System.* New York: Harper & Row, 1975.

———. *Social Studies Strategies: Theory into Practice.* New York: Harper & Row, 1975.

McClendon, Jonathon C., et al. *Readings on Elementary Social Studies: Emerging Changes.* 2nd ed. Boston: Allyn & Bacon, 1970.

Michaelis, John U. *Social Studies for Children in a Democracy.* 5th ed. Englewood Cliffs, N.J.: Prentice-Hall, 1972.

Michaelis, John U., and Keach, Everett T., Jr. *Teaching Strategies for Elementary School Social Studies.* Itasca, Ill.: F.E. Peachock, 1972.

Morrissett, Irving, ed. *Concepts and Structure in the New Social Science Curricula,* New York: Holt, Rinehart & Winston, 1966.

Shaftel, Fannie R., and Shaftel, George. *Role-Playing for Social Values: Decision Making in the Social Studies.* Englewood Cliffs, N.J.: Prentice-Hall, 1967.

Social Studies Curriculum Materials Data Book, I and *II.* Boulder, Colo.: Social Science Education Consortium, 1973.

Thomas, R. Murray, and Brubaker, Dale L. *Decisions in Teaching Elementary Social Studies.* Belmont, Calif.: Wadsworth, 1971.

Thomas, R. Murray, and Brubaker, Dale L., eds. *Teaching Elementary Social Studies: Readings.* Belmont, Calif.: Wadsworth, 1972.

The most striking feature of this chapter is the inclusion of many explicit examples and problem-solving processes. These are presented in the sequence that they should be dealt with in an effective mathematics program and are based on a scope and sequence chart that details the contents of such a program, including the grade placements of concepts, functions, and operations. The chart itself should also be of major importance to any elementary teacher interested in developing a comprehensive, modern mathematics program.

The author concludes the chapter with some predictions for the future of mathematics education, which, as he points out, are the same as or very similar to those that might be stated for any other elementary school curriculum area.

W.T.P.

Mathematics for Today's World

Klaas Kramer

10

Recent advances in science have had two important results: an increase in the body of mathematical knowledge and a more extensive use of mathematics in technology and in society. Today's citizen needs more competence in mathematics than did his counterpart of an earlier day in order to understand his environment and meet its demands. As a consequence of this need, institutions of learning face an increasing responsibility. Such institutions include the elementary school, which is responsible for laying the basic foundations of mathematics, teaching skill in computation, and developing in pupils the ability to solve verbal quantitative problems.

Dissatisfaction with the results of mathematics teaching was clearly expressed during the late 1950s. An increased need for mathematics skills was realized, and, consequently, mathematicians, educators, and psychologists searched for ways to improve programs. Committees formulated goals and proposals, and experimental materials were prepared and tested. Exploratory programs were developed. These projects, such as the School Mathematics Study Group (which was phased out in 1972), the Madison Project, and the University of Illinois Arithmetic Project, were often funded by the federal government or private agencies. The Nuffield Mathematics Teaching Project (which originated in England in the mid-1960s and has received attention in the United States and Canada) also has an exploratory focus.

All of these projects created much interest in the elementary school mathematics program and affected the curriculum in many ways. In fact, the results from the new emphasis on mathematics have been generally benefical: Useful content has been added; several topics are now introduced at earlier levels; creativity has been encouraged; and teachers are more highly trained and have developed better attitudes toward the subject. In addition, a variety of approaches to teaching and learning mathematics (including some of those advanced before the 1950s and 1960s) have been proposed and tested. These include programmed instruction, teaching by machine, discovery techniques, the activity approach, and computer-assisted instruction. Efforts have also increasingly been made to correlate mathematics and other subjects. Yet the curriculum changes and the promising values of several techniques and approaches have not resulted in total satisfaction. Certainly there is need for additional well-controlled research.

PROGRAM OBJECTIVES

The teacher of elementary school mathematics needs to keep in mind specific objectives for each class period, know the major objectives for the grade level or age of children whom he will be teaching, and be able to describe the general purposes of the program for the entire school.

To assist in the formulation of the objectives of mathematics education in the elementary school, the following points are presented for consideration and discussion. These concern long-range goals: development of understanding, building a body of functional knowledge, anchoring skills, fostering positive attitudes, and promoting self-confidence in the pupils.

1. *Understanding.* In a good program, every possible effort is made to help the child understand what she is doing and to enable her to see the principles that underlie basic mathematical processes. The focus of these efforts is to encourage the child to discover concepts on her own.

2. *Knowledge.* Several matters are not subject to discovery by the child; thus some knowledge must be supplied by the teacher or by printed material. For example, such matters as terminology, symbols, names of figures, how graphs are interpreted, and how various measures are used generally require direct teaching.

3. *Skill.* Skill must be developed in interpreting and building patterns, in computing, in estimating, and in using acquired techniques to solve verbal quantitative problems.

4. *Attitudes.* The skillful teacher stimulates curiosity, incites discussion, and develops questioning attitudes in the pupils in an effort to elicit intrinsic motivation and to foster positive feelings toward mathematics.

5. *Confidence.* The building of the child's confidence in his ability to reason

independently is an important goal. The good teacher realizes that each child should always experience some success and that success should be felt as often as possible.

PROGRAM CHARACTERISTICS

Some of the characteristics of a good elementary school mathematics program are described below. Illustrations of content and procedures that may be used to assist such programs are also presented. These reflect the teaching techniques and concern for the child's growth described in earlier chapters.

1. *Discovery is stressed.* The best learning takes place when the pupil is actively engaged in the learning process. Therefore, the teacher should establish an environment in which the child can work on her own. This means that the pupil is presented with situations that challenge her to explore, find answers, and discover rules. It means that she is encouraged to think critically, to use various methods of solutions, and to prove conclusions. Both the process and the product should be emphasized. It is anticipated that the discovery approach will better prepare the child to solve difficult problems that she will encounter outside the classroom.

The teacher necessarily plays a major role in the learning process because he guides the pupils by asking pertinent questions. Therefore, the process is usually one of directed discovery. However, the time element involved and the ability of some pupils make it difficult or impossible to use this approach at all times.

Example: A number trick

a. Select a number.	6
b. Add 3.	$6 + 3 = 9$
c. Subtract 2.	$9 - 2 = 7$
d. Multiply by 2.	$2 \times 7 = 14$
e. Subtract 2.	$14 - 2 = 12$
f. Divide by 2.	$12 \div 2 = 6$
g. Subtract the number you started with.	$6 - 6 = 0$

The pupils should discover why the answer is always zero. To assist them, the teacher may suggest that they replace the first number by ☐ and proceed as follows:

$$\square$$
$$\square + 3$$
$$\square + 3 - 2, \text{ or } \square + 1$$
$$2 \times (\square + 1) = 2\square + 2$$
$$2\square + 2 - 2 = 2\square$$
$$2\square \div 2 = \square$$
$$\square - \square = 0$$

2. *A sequential program is offered.* The program reflects the idea that a new concept is most effectively developed by building on previously acquired knowledge. Therefore, material must be provided that is properly sequenced.

Example: A possible sequence for subtraction cases with sums from 20 to 100.

    a. Subtraction with multiples of ten
       $60 - 20 = \square$

    b. Subtraction of a 1-digit number from a 2-digit number without regrouping
       $36 - 3 = \square$

    c. Subtraction of a multiple of ten from a 2-digit number
       $46 - 10 = \square$

    d. Subtraction with two 2-digit numbers without regrouping
       $46 - 13 = \square$

    e. Subtraction of a 1-digit number from a multiple of ten
       $40 - 7 = \square$

    f. Subtraction of a 2-digit number from a multiple of ten
       $60 - 27 = \square$

    g. Subtraction of a 1-digit number from a 2-digit number with regrouping
       $36 - 8 = \square$

    h. Subtraction with two 2-digit numbers with regrouping
       $46 - 18 = \square$

It should be noted that case *d* is a combination of cases *c* and *b*.

$$\begin{aligned}
46 - 13 &= 46 - (10 + 3) \\
&= (46 - 10) - 3 \\
&= 36 - 3 \\
&= 33
\end{aligned}$$

Similarly, case *f* is a combination of cases *a* and *e*, and case *h* is a combination of cases *c* and *g*.

3. *The spiral plan is followed.* The content is organized in a spiral sequencing plan so that learnings are introduced, maintained, and extended at successive levels. The objective of this organization is to refine concepts that were previously learned in their basic forms.

Examples: Probability

Primary grades: A spinner is used to develop simple concepts. Terms such as *more likely, less likely,* and *just as likely* are introduced to the children.

Intermediate grades: Coins are tossed and dice are rolled; possible outcomes are listed; and results are checked.

Upper grades: Pascal's triangle may be used in the study of the topic.

4. The child is guided through stages of development. In early number experiences most children need to be guided through the concrete and semiconcrete stages of development to the abstract stage. During the concrete stage, manipulative materials are used. Children at the semiconcrete stage work with representations such as pictures, drawings, and dots. Thus, these materials and activities should prepare pupils for the abstract stage, at which they work only with mathematical symbols.

Example: Find the missing addend in $7 = 4 + \square$.

Depending on which stage the child has reached, he may:
a. Use a balance scale. He places 7 new pencils on one scale and 4 on the other, and then he determines how many pencils are needed to make the scales balance.
b. Use a number line as shown:

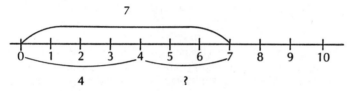

c. Find the missing addend without using aids.

5. In introducing a new topic, the teacher guides pupils in their attempts to find methods of solution, assigns needed practice, and provides children with opportunities to apply their acquired skills. Provide children a sufficient amount of meaningful practice exercises to anchor the particular skill. Children should gradually become able to perform needed computations with reasonable skill and accuracy as well as use such skills to solve verbal quantitative problems.

The following example shows one way of introducing and developing a new topic. It is not intended to be a recipe but only a frame of reference.

Example: Multiplying a 2-digit number by a 1-digit number

a. Situation: There are 3 piles of books. If there are 13 books in each pile, how many books are there in all?
b. Mathematical sentence: $3 \times 13 = \square$
c. The children are asked to find the answer. Since they can add 13 three times, some will probably find the answer by vertical or horizonal additions:

(1) $13 + 13 + 13 = 39$ (2) $\begin{array}{r} 13 \\ 13 \\ +13 \\ \hline 39 \end{array}$

In addition, the following ways of solving the problem may be found by pupils who have acquired skills in multiplication or may be suggested by the teacher through a class discussion:

(3) Since $13 = 10 + 3$,

$3 \times 13 = 3 \times (10 + 3)$

$= (3 \times 10) + (3 \times 3)$

$= 30 + 9$

$= 39$

(4) $13 = 10 + 3$

$\underline{\times\ 3 =\qquad 3}$

$30 + 9 = 39$

The discussion is continued and, with the help of the teacher, other algorisms are explored:

(5) 13
$\underline{\times\ 3}$
9, or 3×3
$\underline{30}$, or 3×10
39

(6) 13
$\underline{\times\ 3}$
39

The solutions are considered and it is agreed that algorism (6) is the shortest form of column multiplication.

    d. The textbook is studied to refine and reinforce learning.

    e. Practice exercises from the book are completed and, if necessary, are supplemented by exercises provided by the teacher.

    f. The newly acquired skill is tested by solving word problems in which the skill is to be used.

    6. *Individual differences are recognized.* The wide range in ability that usually exists among the pupils in a classroom makes it mandatory for the teacher to select the best form of organization for her class and to plan for each mathematics lesson with great care. Techniques that provide for individual differences include: planning remedial work for the slow learner and special activities for the advanced pupil; suggesting enrichment exercises for both the slow and the fast learner; assigning exercises of varying levels of difficulty; requiring different amounts of practice; grouping; and providing mathematics laboratories.

    A pupil who has mastered a topic can extend her knowledge by studying a different method of solution. As an example, after the child has learned how to solve $53 - 25 = \square$ by using the decomposition method (which employs the common algorism), she may then enrich her knowledge by using the equal-additions method to solve the same kind of problems.

Example:

Decomposition method: Regroup 1 ten of the 5 tens as 10 ones. The result is 4 tens, 13 ones. Subtract 5 ones from 13 ones, and subtract 2 tens from 4 tens.

$$\begin{array}{r} ④⑬ \\ 5\!\!\!/\,3\!\!\!/ \\ -25 \\ \hline 28 \end{array}$$

Equal-additions method: Add 10 ones to the 3 ones in the minuend. To keep the difference between the minuend and subtrahend equal, add 1 ten to the 2 tens in the subtrahend. Then subtract.

7. *Verbal problem solving is emphasized.* Children encounter verbal quantitative problems in school subjects other than mathematics as well as in daily life. And, as they get older, they are confronted with an increasing number of these problems. Thus, one of the main goals of mathematics education is the development of the ability to use acquired computational skills to solve verbal problems. Still the complaint is often made that elementary school children do not perform well in this area. This may be partly due to the insufficient coverage of this topic in textbooks and to inadequate teaching of the skills needed. Good programs stress verbal problem solving and offer a variety of techniques to assist children in developing their skills. Such techniques include:

a. Using pictures to illustrate numerical data
b. Showing pictures and asking the children to devise problems
c. Presenting in a verbal problem some information that is not needed and having the pupils identify such information
d. Presenting a verbal problem that needs additional information and having the children supply it
e. Presenting a mathematical sentence and having the children construct a verbal problem that fits the sentence
f. Estimating answers to verbal problems
g. Supplying a statement including numerical data and having the children formulate one or more number questions about it
h. Having children construct verbal problems
i. Supplying problems without numbers and having the children determine which operation would solve the problem if numbers were given
j. Providing brain teasers

Example: Quantitative verbal problem solving

a. Read the word problem below.
b. Tell what other information is needed before the problem can be solved.
c. Find the information that is needed.
d. Solve the problem.

Word problem: Mr. Groves plans to drive from Chicago to San Francisco. His car travels about 15 miles on a gallon of gasoline. The estimated average cost of a gallon of gasoline is $.61. About how much money will Mr. Groves need to pay for all the gasoline that will be used during the trip to San Francisco?

8. *A sequential program in mental computation is offered.* Because of the great need in daily life for competency in performing simple mathematical operations without the use of paper and pencil, the good mathematics curriculum presents a planned, well-organized program in mental computation. In this program, the pupils are encouraged to perform operations without using writing materials whenever possible. Also, they are invited to estimate the answer to a problem when the exact answer is not needed. Such instruction begins in the primary grades and continues through the elementary school years.

Example: Solve $9 \times 35 = \square$ with using paper and pencil.

   a. Rename 9 as $10 - 1$.
   b. Multiply 35 by 10 and then by 1.
   c. Subtract the products.

$$9 \times 35 = (10 - 1) \times 35$$
$$= (10 \times 35) - (1 \times 35)$$
$$= 350 - 35$$
$$= 315$$

9. *Mathematics skills are used during the school day.* Throughout the school day, numerous situations involving the use of numbers present themselves. The resourceful teacher uses such situations to the children's advantage. Money is counted; the temperature is read; the time is told; the number of absent children is determined; the calendar is used; records are kept; statistics are interpreted; and so on.

Mathematics activities become more meaningful for children when they are made a part of other subject areas. The laboratories, which are usually conducted in informal settings, appear to hold much promise for effective correlation of subjects.

Example: An open-ended question

Determine how much it costs a person to make a 3-minute telephone call. The pupils decide that in order to determine the cost, questions such as the following must be answered first:

   a. Between which two cities is the call to be made?
   b. Does the call require assistance from the operator?
   c. Is the call station-to-station or person-to-person?
   d. Is the call a collect call?
   e. What time of the day or what day of the week is the call made?
   f. What is the standard rate for making a call at this particular time?

10. *Content is selected to satisfy the mathematical and the social aims.* To serve the mathematical aim, the curriculum emphasizes such mathematical understandings as the structure of the number system, fundamental operations, principles, relationships, and logical reasoning. To assist the child in her application of these concepts, skills such as these are emphasized: written and mental computation, making change, solving word problems, and interpreting statistical data.

Example: You buy an article that costs $.48. You pay with a one-dollar bill.

a. How much change do you get?
b. If you get 8 coins, what are the coins?

SCOPE AND SEQUENCE OF TOPICS

An example of a possible scope and sequence of topics is shown in Figure 10.1, which is an adaptation of a chart prepared in the mid-1960s for California schools.[1] The material is from a guide that resulted from a study of current trends in mathematics and an examination of textbooks adopted by California.

Figure 10.1. Scope and Sequence of Mathematics Topics

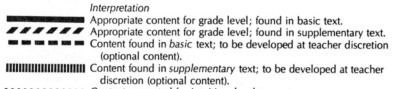

Interpretation

▬▬▬▬ Appropriate content for grade level; found in basic text.
🗡🗡🗡🗡 Appropriate content for grade level; found in supplementary text.
▬ ▬ ▬ ▬ Content found in *basic* text; to be developed at teacher discretion (optional content).
‖‖‖‖‖‖‖‖ Content found in *supplementary* text; to be developed at teacher discretion (optional content).
•••••••••• Content suggested for intuitive development.

TOPIC 1: SETS (COLLECTIONS)	Grade K 1 2 3 4 5 6
One-to-one correspondence and matching	
One-to-two correspondence	
One-to-many correspondence	
Classification of sets:	
Equal (identical) and equivalent	
Nonidentical and nonequivalent	
Subset	
Empty	
Disjoint	
Not disjoint	
Finite	
Infinite	
Operations on sets:	
Union	
Intersection	
The number of a set (abstracting the idea of number from equivalent sets)	
n-notation	
Operations on numbers developed from sets:	
Addition explained from union of disjoint sets	
Subtraction explained from set separation	
Equivalent sets to develop multiplication	
Division interpreted as set partitioning	
Properties of operations:	
Commutativity	
Associativity	
Distributivity	

---

1. J. Briggs, F. Mettler, and R. Denholm, *Implementing Mathematics Programs in California, A Guide K-8* (Menlo Park, Calif.: Pacific Coast Publishers, n.d.) pp. 17–38.

Grade

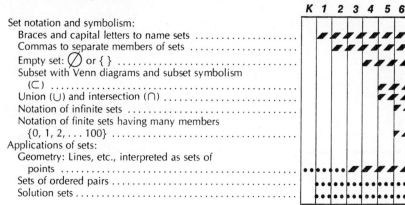

Set notation and symbolism:
Braces and capital letters to name sets ....
Commas to separate members of sets ....
Empty set: Ø or { } ....
Subset with Venn diagrams and subset symbolism
(⊂) ....
Union (∪) and intersection (∩) ....
Notation of infinite sets ....
Notation of finite sets having many members
{0, 1, 2, . . . 100} ....
Applications of sets:
Geometry: Lines, etc., interpreted as sets of
points ....
Sets of ordered pairs ....
Solution sets ....

TOPIC II: NUMBER

Grade

Abstracting the idea of cardinal number from
equivalent sets ....
Understanding sets of numbers:
Counting: one through ten ....
Whole (positive integers and zero)
Zero through one hundred ....
One hundred one through nine hundred
ninety-nine ....
One thousand through ninety-nine thousand,
nine hundred ninety-nine ....
One hundred thousand through millions ....
Ten millions through hundred millions ....
One billion through hundred billions ....
Fractional numbers (positive rational) ....
Decimals ....
Negative integers.......................................
Ordinal numbers (position in a series):
First through third ....
First through tenth ....
Eleventh through thirty-first ....
Beyond thirty-first ....
Number sequences:
Counting by tens, twos, fives, ...
Odd and even numbers ....
Rounded numbers ....
Prime numbers and factors ....
Composite numbers ....

TOPIC III: NUMERATION SYSTEMS

Grade

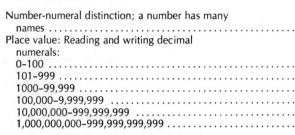
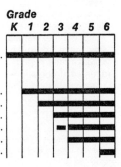

Number-numeral distinction; a number has many
names ....
Place value: Reading and writing decimal
numerals:
0–100 ....
101–999 ....
1000–99,999 ....
100,000–9,999,999 ....
10,000,000–999,999,999 ....
1,000,000,000–999,999,999,999 ....

	Grade						
	K	**1**	**2**	**3**	**4**	**5**	**6**
Expanded notation of decimal numerals:							
Two-place numerals		▬					
Three-place numerals			▬				
Four-place numerals				▬			
Five-place numerals					▬		
Six-and seven-place numerals						▬	
Exponential notation						▬	▬
Roman numerals:							
I, V, X			▥	▨			
L, C				▬			
D, M					▬		
Reading and writing decimal numerals:							
Through .999					▬		
Through .99999						▬	
Place value system in other bases:							
Base five						▨	
Base six							▬
Historical development of numeration	•	•	•	•	•	•	•

TOPIC IV: ADDITION AND SUBTRACTION

Note: In the basic texts for grade 1–3, "regrouping" is referred to as "carrying" in addition and "borrowing" in subtraction.

	Grade						
	K	**1**	**2**	**3**	**4**	**5**	**6**
Sets to develop addition and subtraction	▬						
Addition and subtraction combinations, sums through 18		▬	▬	▬	▬	▬	▬
Mathematical sentences (horizontal notation)		▬	▬	▬	▬	▬	▬
Addition and subtraction algorithms (vertical notation)		▬	▬	▬	▬	▬	▬
Addition table (grid)		▬	▬	▬	▬	▬	▬
Number line		▨	▨	▨	▨			
Cross Number Puzzle		▨	▨	▨	▨	▨	▨
Properties of addition:							
Commutative		▬	▬	▬	▬	▬	▬
Associative		▬	▬	▬	▬	▬	▬
"Zero" as the identity element for addition and for subtraction when "zero" is the subtrahend		▬	▬	▬	▬	▬	▬
Inverse relation of addition and subtraction		▬	▬	▬	▬	▬	▬
Addition and subtraction without regrouping (two-place)		▬	▬	▬	▬	▬	▬
Three-place			▬	▬	▬	▬	▬
Four- through seven-place			▬	▬	▬	▬	▬
Addition and subtraction with regrouping							
Two- and three-place		▬	▬	▬	▬	▬	▬
Four- through seven-place, regrouping in various places			▬				
Column addition		▬	▬	▬	▬	▬	▬
Addition with fractional numbers, sums not greater than "one"				▬	▬	▬	▬
Addition and subtraction:							
With denominate numbers			▬	▬	▬	▬	▬
Of fractional numbers, sums and minuends less than "two"					▬	▬	▬
Of fractional numbers without limiting sums and minuends in horizontal and vertical form					▬	▬	▬

	Grade K	1	2	3	4	5	6
Of decimals through thousandths						■	■
Of integers							■

TOPIC V: MULTIPLICATION AND DIVISION

	Grade K	1	2	3	4	5	6
Multiplication and division defined from set union and through set partitioning			■	■	■	■	■
Multiplication as repeated addition; division as repeated subtraction			■	■	■	■	■
Multiplication in rows and columns (arrays and Cartesian products)			■	■	■	■	■
Multiplication and division combinations:							
Products through 25			■	■	■	■	■
Products through 81				■	■	■	■
In mathematical sentences (horizontal notation)			■	■	■	■	■
Conventional multiplication algorithm (vertical notation)			■	■	■	■	■
Multiplicative property of "zero" and impossibility of division by "zero"			■	■	■	■	■
Multiplication table (grid)			■	■	■	■	■
Number line	▨	▨					
Cross Number Puzzle	▨	▨	▨	▨	▨	▨	▨
Properties of multiplication:							
Commutative			■	■	■	■	■
Associative				■	■	■	■
Distributive property of multiplication over addition				■	■	■	■
Distributive property of division over addition (only dividend may be renamed)			▨	■	■	■	■
"One" as the identity element for multiplication and for division when "one" is the divisor			■	■	■	■	■
Inverse relation of multiplication and division			■	■	■	■	■
Multiples of tens and hundreds as used in multiplication and division				■	■	■	■
Vertical form and subtractive method of division				■	■	■	■
Conventional division algorithm			▨	▨	■	■	■
Multiplication with one-place multipliers and three-place multiplicands, division with one-place divisors and two- and three-place dividends				■	■	■	■
Multiplication with two-place multipliers and three-place multiplicands					■	■	■
Two-place divisors ending in 1, 2, 3, and 4					■	■	■
Two-place divisors in subtraction form and in the conventional algorithm					■	■	■
Quotient estimation by rounding divisors downward and upward						■	■
Remainders expressed in fractional form						■	■
Multiplication with three- and four-place factors						■	■
Division with three-place divisors							■
Prime factorization						▨	▨
Multiplication and division with fractional numbers							■
Removing common factors before multiplying (cancellation)							■

	Grade
	K 1 2 3 4 5 6

Multiplication and division:
  Of decimals ....
  With denominate numbers ....
Equivalent ratios ....
Percents as ratios...
Exponential notation to express multiplication ....

TOPIC VI: PROPERTIES OF THE OPERATIONS

	Grade
	K 1 2 3 4 5 6

Commutativity:
  Explained from union of sets ....
  Of addition: ....
    Of whole numbers ....
    Of fractional numbers ....
    Of decimals ....
    Of integers ....
  Of multiplication: ....
    Of whole numbers ....
    Of fractional numbers ....
    Of decimals ....
Associativity:
  Explained from union of sets ....
  Of addition: ....
    Of whole numbers ....
    Of fractional numbers ....
    Of decimals ....
  Of multiplication: ....
    Of whole numbers ....
    Of fractional numbers ....
    Of decimals ....
Distributivity:
  Of multiplication over addition
    (whole numbers) ....
  Of division over addition (whole numbers;
    only dividend may be renamed) ....
  Of multiplication over addition (fractional
    numbers and decimals) ....
Inverse relations:
  Addition and subtraction as inverses
    explained from set union and set
    separation ....
  Addition and subtraction as inverses ....
  Multiplication and division as inverses ....
Identity:
  "Zero" for addition and for subtraction when
    "zero" is the subtrahend ....
  "One" for multiplication and for division
    when "one" is the divisor ....
  Multiplicative property of "zero" and
    impossibility of division by "zero" ....

TOPIC VII: ORDER, RELATIONS, AND MATHEMATICAL SENTENCES

	Grade
	K 1 2 3 4 5 6

Order in sets of numbers ....
One-more, one-less concept ....

Grade

K 1 2 3 4 5 6

Comparing whole numbers using sets and numerals ....
Number sequences (odd, even, . . .)........................
Symbols:
  Relationship
    =, >, < ....
    ≠ ....
  Grouping
    Parentheses ....
  Unknown number, operation, or relationship ....
  Letters as variables ....
Operations in mathematical sentences:
  Adding and subtracting whole numbers ....
  Multiplying whole numbers...........................
  Dividing whole numbers ....
  Adding fractional numbers ....
  Subtracting fractional numbers ....
  Adding and subtracting decimals ....
  Adding and subtracting integers ....
  Multiplying and dividing fractional numbers and
    decimals ....
Mathematical sentences involving:
  Equalities, inequalities; open, closed ....
  True, false...

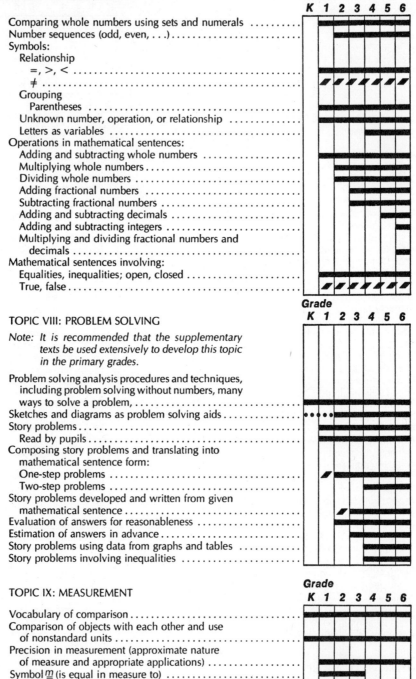

TOPIC VIII: PROBLEM SOLVING

Grade

K 1 2 3 4 5 6

*Note: It is recommended that the supplementary
texts be used extensively to develop this topic
in the primary grades.*

Problem solving analysis procedures and techniques,
  including problem solving without numbers, many
  ways to solve a problem, ...
Sketches and diagrams as problem solving aids ....
Story problems.....................................
  Read by pupils....................................
Composing story problems and translating into
  mathematical sentence form:
    One-step problems ....
    Two-step problems ....
Story problems developed and written from given
  mathematical sentence ....
Evaluation of answers for reasonableness ....
Estimation of answers in advance.......................
Story problems using data from graphs and tables ....
Story problems involving inequalities ....

TOPIC IX: MEASUREMENT

Grade

K 1 2 3 4 5 6

Vocabulary of comparison...............................
Comparison of objects with each other and use
  of nonstandard units ....
Precision in measurement (approximate nature
  of measure and appropriate applications) ....
Symbol $\underline{m}$ (is equal in measure to) ....
Measurement:
  Money...
  Liquid ....
  Weight ....

Time:
    Clock ....
    Calendar ....
    Time zones ....
Length:
    Foot, inch, ...
    Using ruler (inch, foot, yard, . . .) ....
    Map reading and scale drawing ....
    Perimeter ....
Temperature:
    Fahrenheit ....
Area ....
Angle ....
Operations with denominate numbers ....

TOPIC X: GEOMETRY

Geometric shapes in environment ....
Geometric designs ....
Two-dimensional shapes (circle, square, triangle,
    rectangle) ....
Shape characteristics (measurement, inspection) ......
Spatial relationships (distances) ....
Comparing sizes, shapes, distances ....
Construction of plane figures ....
Interior and exterior regions ....
Points, lines, points on a line ....
Diameter concept ....
Point in space ....
Line, line segment ....
Right angle ("square corner") ....
Three-dimensional shapes (cube, sphere, . . .) ....
Ray and angle ....
Plane ....
Intersection (lines, planes, . . .) ....
Simple closed figures ....
Area and perimeter ....
Arc degrees ....
Use of protractor ....
Symbolism:
    Line ($\overleftrightarrow{AB}$) ....
    Line segment ($\overline{AB}$) ....
    Ray ($\overrightarrow{AB}$) ....
    Arc ($\overarc{AB}$), triangle ($\triangle$) ....
    Angle ($<$) ....
Parallels and perpendiculars (lines, planes) ....
Construction of three-dimensional figures ....
Congruence (angles, triangles, line segments) ....

TOPIC XI: GRAPHING—STATISTICS

Tally marks ....
Charts for reference, comparison, and
    record keeping ....
Grids:
    For record keeping by pupil ....
    Addition table ....

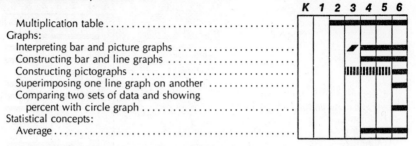

	Grade						
	K	1	2	3	4	5	6
Multiplication table							
Graphs:							
Interpreting bar and picture graphs							
Constructing bar and line graphs							
Constructing pictographs							
Superimposing one line graph on another							
Comparing two sets of data and showing							
percent with circle graph							
Statistical concepts:							
Average							

Source: J. Briggs, F. Mettler, and R. Denholm, *Implementing Mathematics Programs in California, a Guide K-8* (Menlo Park, Calif.: Pacific Coast Publishers, n.d.), pp. 17-38. Used with permission.

ILLUSTRATION OF TOPICS

On the following pages, examples of possible activities for selected items from the scope and sequence chart are suggested. For each part, three examples—usually one each for the primary, intermediate, and upper levels—appear in order of difficulty. An effort has been made to include content and procedures that reflect differences between traditional and contemporary programs. It will be noted that the first two parts of the scope and sequence chart have been combined.

Sets and Numbers

1. *One-to-one correspondence*
Draw lines to see if there are the same number of objects in both sets.

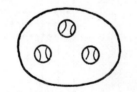   

2. *Odd numbers*
Write the set of odd numbers greater than 1 and less than 15.

3. *Prime numbers*
Write the set of prime numbers greater than 10 and less than 30.

Numeration Systems

1. *Expanded notation*
Complete: a. $15 = 10 + \square$ b. $32 = 30 + \square$ c. $24 = \square + 4$

2. *Roman numerals*
There are 16 chapters in a book. Use Roman numerals to write the number of each chapter.

3. *Base five*
Solve: $4_{five} + 3_{five} = \boxed{}_{five}$
The addends are shown on the number line; then the sum is obtained.

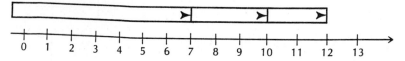

$$4_{five} + 3_{five} = 12_{five}$$

Addition and Subtraction

1. *The number line*
Solve by using the number line: $7 + 5 = \boxed{}$

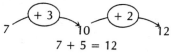

Think: First go to 10: $7 + 3 = 10$
How many more to add?
$5 = 3 + 2$
Add 2 more.

$$7 \overset{+\,3}{\longrightarrow} 10 \overset{+\,2}{\longrightarrow} 12$$
$$7 + 5 = 12$$

2. *A mathematics laboratory: rolling sugar cubes*
The children form groups of two. Each child gets two sugar cubes. The faces of one cube are marked *2, 4, 6, 8, 10, 12.* The faces of the other cube are marked *1, 3, 5, 7, 9, 11.* Each child rolls his two cubes and observes the numbers on the top faces of the cubes. He subtracts the smaller number from the larger, and his partner writes that number down. After each player takes his turn, his partner adds the number to the player's running score, and the addition is checked by the player. The child who first gets a sum of 50 or more wins the game.

3. *Magic squares*
In a magic square the sum of the numbers in each horizontal, vertical, and diagonal row is the same.

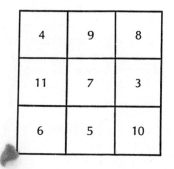

4	9	8
11	7	3
6	5	10

a. Find out whether the number square on page 261 is a magic square.

$4 + 9 + 8 = \square$ $4 + 11 + 6 = \square$ $4 + 7 + 10 = \square$

$11 + 7 + 3 = \square$ $9 + 7 + 5 = \square$ $6 + 7 + 8 = \square$

$6 + 5 + 10 = \square$ $8 + 3 + 10 = \square$

b. Make a new addition square by adding 5 to each of the numbers in the first square and placing the resulting numbers in corresponding cells of this square. A few have been done already. Check to see if this number square is a magic square.

9	14	
		15

c. Make a fraction square by dividing the numbers in the first square by 12. Add the fractional numbers in each horizontal row, in each vertical row, and in each diagonal row. Is the square a magic square?

4/12		
11/12		
	5/12	

Multiplication and Division

1. *Introduction to multiplication*
Solve: $3 \times 2 = \square$

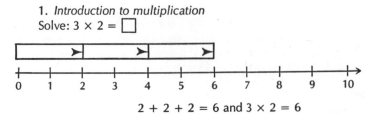

$2 + 2 + 2 = 6$ and $3 \times 2 = 6$

2. *Beginning division with a 2-digit quotient*
Solve $28 \div 2 = \square$ by first subtracting 10 twos and then subtracting as many more twos as possible.

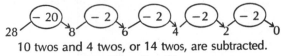

10 twos and 4 twos, or 14 twos, are subtracted.

$28 \div 2 = 14$

3. *Division algorisms*

a. In this procedure—the subtractive method of division—the child subtracts the divisor repeatedly. He uses acquired subtraction skills.

```
6 )24
   6 1
  18
   6 1
  12
   6 1
   6
   6 1
   0 4
```

b. The subtractive way of division is gradually refined. In this presentation the pupil shows that she knows the multiplication fact 2 × 7 = 14.

```
7 ) 35
   14 2
   21
   14 2
    7
    7 1
    0 5
```

c. The product of the divisor and 10 is subtracted twice. It is anticipated that after additional practice, the pupil will see that at least 20 threes are contained in 72.

```
3 ) 72
   30 10
   42
   30 10
   12
   12  4
    0 24
```

d. This is another form of expanded division. The value of each digit in the quotient is shown.

```
        5
       30  35
5 ) 175
   150
    25
    25
     0
```

e. The standard algorism is used. The pupil should now realize that, in this example, 28 stands for 28 tens.

```
      43
7 ) 301
   28
   21
   21
    0
```

Properties of the Operations

1. *Commutative property*
Show that 3 + 5 + 3 is a true statement.

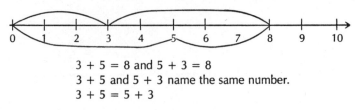

$$3 + 5 = 8 \text{ and } 5 + 3 = 8$$
3 + 5 and 5 + 3 name the same number.
$$3 + 5 = 5 + 3$$

2. *Inverse operations*
Write a multiplication and a division sentence for the model.

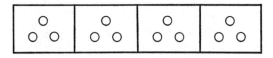

$$4 \times 3 = 12 \text{ and } 12 \div 4 = 3$$

3. *Distributive property*
Solve 78 ÷ 6 = ☐ by using the distributive property of division.
$$78 \div 6 = (60 + 18) \div 6$$
$$= (60 \div 6) + (18 \div 6)$$
$$= 10 + 3$$
$$= 13$$

Order, Relations, and Mathematical Sentences

1. *Sequence*
Complete: 5   10   15   ☐ ☐ ☐

2. *Number sentences*
Write =, >, or < to make a true statement.
a. 17 + 12 ◯ 30   b. 75 ◯ 100 − 29   c. 5 X 15 ◯ 3 X 25

3. *A number pattern*
Find the pattern and complete the sentences.

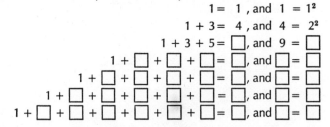

Problem Solving

1. *Method of analysis*
Problem:
   Kathy had 36 trading cards. She gave 7 cards to her friend. How many cards did Kathy have left?

Solution:
   a. Find the facts: Kathy had 36 cards. Kathy gave 7 cards to her friend.
   b. Find the question: How many cards did Kathy have left?
   c. Write the number question: $36 - 7 = \square$
   d. Answer the question: $36 - 7 = 29$
   e. Label the answer: Kathy had 29 cards left.

2. *Estimation*
Problem: About how many days are there in 10 months?

Solution:
   A month has 28, 29, 30, or 31 days. Since $10 \times 30 = 300$, there are about 300 days in 10 months.

3. *Problem construction*
Assignment:
   Write a problem that fits this number question: $(3 \times 49) + 12 = \square$

Possible solution:
   Ray has 49 marbles. Tom has 12 more than 3 times as many marbles as Ray has. How many marbles does Tom have?

Measurement

1. *Unstandardized unit of measure*
How many paper clips long?

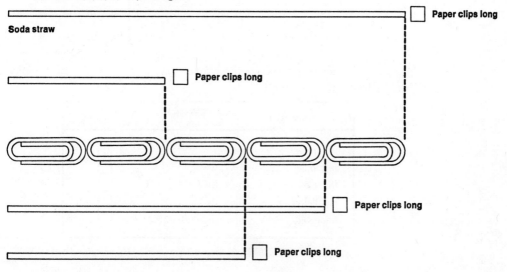

Paper clips long

Soda straw

Paper clips long

Paper clips long

Paper clips long

2. *Inches and centimeters*
Find the length of your desk both in inches and in centimeters.

3. *A device*
Measure the length of the school hall.
Needed equipment: a trundle wheel

   a. Measure the circumference of the trundle wheel.
   b. Roll the wheel from the beginning of the hall to the end and count the number of rotations.
   c. Find the length of the hall by multiplying the measure of the circumference of the wheel by the number of rotations.

Geometry

1. *Figures*
Find objects in the room that suggest geometric figures.

2. *Symmetry*
Print five capital letters that have symmetry. Draw lines through the letters to show the symmetry.

3. *The geoboard*
Secure a geoboard or construct one as shown. Note that the nails or pegs are one unit apart.

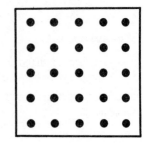

   a. Construct on the geoboard the following figures. Find the area of each figure in square units.

Figure	Dimensions in units	Area in square units
square	s=2	☐
rectangle	1=3; w=3	☐
triangle	b=4; h=2	☐
parallelogram	b=3; h=2	☐
trapezoid	b_1=3; b_2=1; h=2	☐

b. (1) Construct the figures shown.

(2) The area of figure ABCD is ☐ square units.

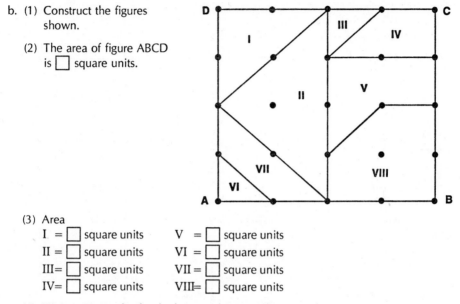

(3) Area

I   = ☐ square units   V   = ☐ square units
II = ☐ square units   VI = ☐ square units
III = ☐ square units   VII = ☐ square units
IV = ☐ square units   VIII= ☐ square units

(4) How can you check whether you have made a mistake in exercise (3)?

c. Construct on the geoboard a figure that you like and find its area in square units.

Graphing/Statistics

1. *Picture graph*
Make a picture graph to show for each day of a school week the number of children that are absent.

2. *Average*
On five mathematics tests Ellen made these scores: 25, 29, 31, 24, and 26. Find the average of Ellen's scores.

3. *Positions*
Twenty flags are displayed on the next page. We will locate the position of a flag by using ordered number pairs.

To identify the point at which the flag of the United States is placed, we go from the bottom left 2 across and 3 up. We write (2,3). The order of the numbers is important.

To find the flag that is placed at the point identified by (3,2), we go 3 across and 2 up. (3,2) names the point at which the flag of Norway is placed.

The numbers that identify the position are called "coordinates."

a. Name the country whose flag is placed at:

(1,2)   (4,0)   (0,3)   (2,0)
(0,0)   (1,1)   (0,2)

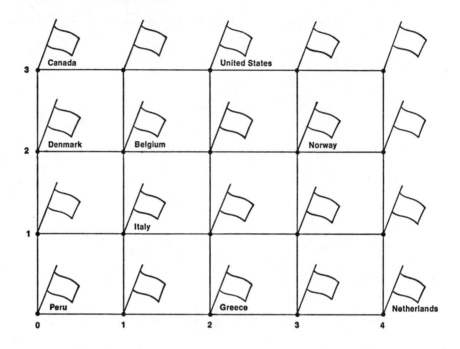

b. Tell how the positions (0,2) and (2,0) differ.
c. The coordinates for flags of other countries are given here. Write the name of the country under its flag.

Iceland	(3,0)	France	(2,1)
Poland	(4,3)	Turkey	(4,2)
Spain	(1,3)	Sweden	(1,0)
Hungary	(4,1)	Russia	(3,1)
Luxembourg	(2,2)	Japan	(0,1)
Portugal	(3,3)		

TEACHING TOOLS

This section illustrates a few of the many kinds of teaching tools (printed materials, machines, and various other tools) for use in a mathematics program.

Counting Frame

The counting frame has been used for a long time. In primary classrooms a frame with 10 rows of 10 beads each is an effective, easy-to-use device. In beginning instruction a child may work with a frame of 2 rows of 10 beads each. The frame is used for counting, multiple counting, and performing simple operations. For example, $8 + 7 = \boxed{}$ can be solved with the frame by first going to 10:

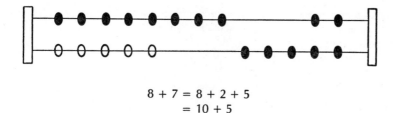

$$8 + 7 = 8 + 2 + 5$$
$$= 10 + 5$$
$$= 15$$

In higher grades the counting frame is helpful when a different number base is introduced. For base five, 5 rows of 5 beads each are used. The illustration shows numerals in base five.

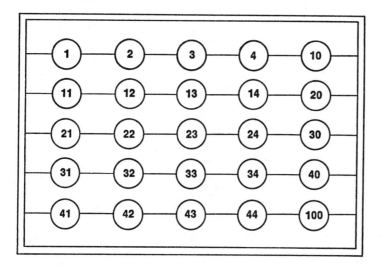

Abacus

The abacus is a very old device that has proven its value. The teacher may choose one from among the different models available or may construct one of her own. The illustration shows a type of abacus that the teacher can make. She needs to have only 9 beads available for each rod.

The device is helpful in teaching the concept of place value. In the illustration below, the number 234 is represented.

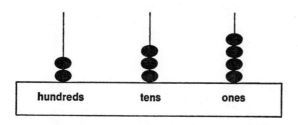

Computations can become more meaningful when performed with the help of an abacus. In the following presentation, an abacus is used that is different from the one just described.

Problem: 37 + 25 = ☐

Solution:

a. 37 = 30 + 7, or 3 tens 7 ones
    3 tens and 7 ones are isolated.

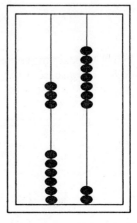

b. 25 = 20 + 5, or 2 tens 5 ones
    First, 5 ones are added.
    7 ones + 5 ones = 12 ones,
    or 1 ten 2 ones
    2 ones beads are isolated and
    1 ten is moved up on the tens rod.
    The abacus shows 4 tens 2 ones,
    or 42.

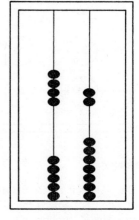

c. 20 must be added.
    2 tens beads are moved up.
    The abacus shows 6 tens 2 ones,
    or 62.
    37 + 25 = 62

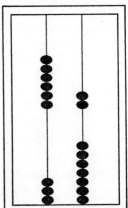

Calculator

Recently desk and pocket calculators have been introduced in elementary schools. It is obvious that they serve a purpose when answers must be checked. They also appear to be useful when mathematical principles are being explored. For example, the fact that the multiplication of an even number by an odd number yields a product that is even can be determined by children multiplying large as well as small numbers without spending a great deal of time. Unfortunately, while the expense involved in furnishing classrooms with desk calculators limits the use of this tool, the availability of pocket calculators may make their use possible.

Paper

Useful tools and models may be constructed from inexpensive material that is readily available: paper. It can be used to prepare:

1. *A folded paper model*

The resourceful teacher will be able to employ the folded paper model in various operations. One example is presented.

Problem: $13 - 7 = \square$

Solution:

    a. First go to 10. $13 - 3 = 10$

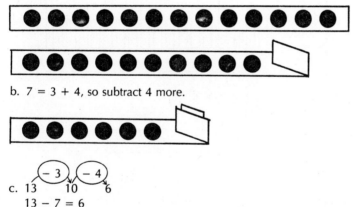

    b. $7 = 3 + 4$, so subtract 4 more.

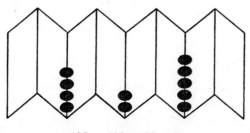

    c. $13 \overset{-3}{\longrightarrow} 10 \overset{-4}{\longrightarrow} 6$

       $13 - 7 = 6$

2. *An abacus*

A sheet of paper is folded as shown. Counters are placed in the folds. In the illustration the number 425 is represented.

$$425 = 400 + 20 + 5$$

3. A pocket chart

A pocket chart aids in the teaching of the place-value concept and assists children to understand renaming in addition and subtraction.

Problem: $43 - 18 = \square$

Solution:

a. $43 = 40 + 3$

Place 4 tens in the tens pocket and 3 ones in the ones pocket.

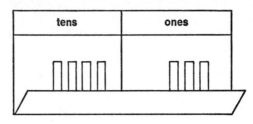

b. $18 = 10 + 8$

There are only 3 counters in the ones pocket. Remove 1 ten and place 10 ones in the ones pocket.

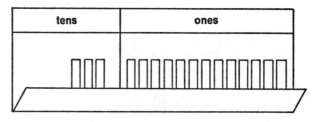

c. Remove 8 ones from the ones pocket and 1 ten from the tens pocket.

$43 - 18 = 25$

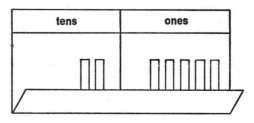

d. *Geometric figures*

The teacher can easily construct a variety of geometric forms by folding or cutting paper.

Cuisenaire Rods

The Cuisenaire rods were devised by George Cuisenaire, a Belgian teacher, who was later assisted by Caleb Gattegno, an English mathematician. The rods, also known as "Numbers in Color," are made of wood one square centimeter in cross section and varying in length from one to ten centimeters. Each rod has a specific color: the 1-centimeter rod is white and its letter symbol is *w;* the 2-centimeter rod is red *(r);* the 3-centimeter rod is light green *(g);* the 4-centimeter rod is purple *(p);* and so forth.

The child first engages in free play with the rods. Then the teacher directs some activities. After that stage, symbols are introduced and sentences such as *w* + *w* = *r* and *r* − *w* = *w* are written. Finally the pupil deals with the rods as models of numbers. For example the drawing

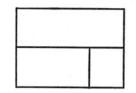

suggests the sentences:

$$3 = 2 + 1; 3 - 1 = 2; 3 = 1 + 2; 3 - 2 = 1$$

Any rod can be selected as the basic measuring rod. For example, if the purple rod is the measuring rod and is called one, then the red rod is called ½ and the white rod ¼.

Stern Blocks

The Stern blocks were devised by Catherine Stern, a student of Max Wertheimer, the founder of the Gestalt psychology.[2] Stern believed that working with visual perceptual structures will lead to the development of mental structures. In this system, the wooden blocks are segmented into unit cubes. The blocks fit into grooves. The child is to discover into which groove each block fits and to realize that there is a sequence of block length. Experimentation with the blocks should lead to the discovery of fundamental operations.

The *counting board,* illustrated in Figure 10.2 on the next page, has ten grooves into which ten blocks of different sizes fit. The child has to fit the blocks into the grooves. This activity, then, is a self-corrective one. Gradually the child should develop an awareness of the sequence of block lengths in the series. After this aim has been achieved, the counting board is equipped with a number guide that shows the symbols 1 to 10, which stand for the blocks. The child is to match symbols and blocks.

The *pattern boards,* which are introduced after the counting board, fit ten different patterns, one each for the numbers 1 to 10. The child has to place on each board the required number of cubes to become familiar with the characteristic configurations, or patterns.

---

2. The description of the Stern blocks is based on C. Stern, *Structural Arithmetic* (Boston, Mass.: Houghton Mifflin Co., 1965) and on C. Stern, "The Concrete Devices of Structural Arithmetic," *The Arithmetic Teacher,* April 1958, pp. 119-30.

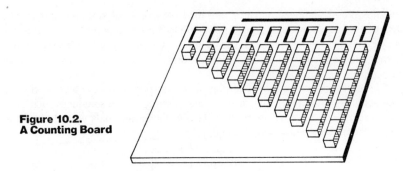

**Figure 10.2.
A Counting Board**

Source: Catherine Stern, *Structural Arithmetic* (Houghton Mifflin C0., 1965). Used with permission.

Figure 10.3 is an illustration of the *unit box*. The child uses the box first to match block pairs. Then the "story of 10" is introduced and the pupil is encouraged to make statements such as "the 7 needs 3 to make 10." Finally the child begins to use the plus and equal signs. The number sentence 6 + 2 = $\square$ is solved by combining a 6-block and a 2-block and selecting the single block of the same total length.

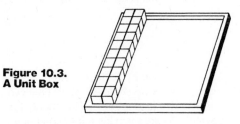

**Figure 10.3.
A Unit Box**

Source: Catherine Stern, *Structural Arithmetic* (Houghton Mifflin Co., 1965). Used with permission.

The *number track* shows the numerals 1 to 10, and the 10-block just fits into it. As an example: the 6-block needs the 4-block to reach 10. If the 4-block is removed again, the 6-block remains. Thus subtraction "undoes" addition. Sections of the track are joined for more advanced work.

Other Aids

A great variety of teaching tools and materials dealing with their use is available. These include films, filmstrips, tapes, games, puzzles, records, mathematics kits, and pamphlets or books on the use of bulletin boards and media. A list of selected aids would be too long to include in this chapter. The reader is referred to catalogs of book companies that produce such aids. One way to keep abreast of new developments is to read *The Arithmetic Teacher*. This magazine, published by the National Council of Teachers of Mathematics (1201 Sixteenth St., N.W., Washington, D.C. 20036), identifies and often evaluates new ideas in mathematics education; offers practical suggestions for classroom teaching; and, through advertisements, makes the reader aware of available teaching tools.

LOOKING AHEAD

This chapter has presented and demonstrated several changes that have been made in recent years in the elementary school mathematics curriculum. Experimentation and discussion is continuing and will result in additional improvements. Several mathematics educators have speculated on what may be in store. For commentary on possible trends, the reader is referred to the articles written by R.B. Davis, E.G. Gibb, D.A. Johnson, and J.R. Major, that are identified at the end of this chapter.

In general, predictions for the future are similar to those suggested in other curriculum areas and include the following:

1. Teacher education will be improved by the provision of greater attention to specific objectives and classroom procedures.
2. Instruction will be more individualized.
3. The approach to classroom instruction will be more pupil-centered.
4. Creativity will be emphasized.
5. Physical materials will be used more extensively.
6. More research in mathematics education will hopefully result in the identification of improved mathematics curriculums for the slow learner, the average pupil, and the gifted child.
7. More mention of mathematics in conjunction with other subjects will make mathematics more relevant to the child.
8. Evaluation of teaching and learning will be improved.

EXERCISES FOR THOUGHT AND ACTION

1. Describe what you consider to be the most important long-range goals for mathematics education in the elementary school.
2. List some characteristics that an elementary school mathematics program should possess.
3. Describe and illustrate some techniques that can assist the child in developing her skills in verbal-problem solving.
4. For a P.T.A. meeting, outline a talk on the topic "new approaches and techniques in elementary school mathematics."
5. React to this statement: Children themselves should discover everything they learn.
6. Explain what is meant by the spiral plan in the presentation of mathematics topics.
7. Prepare an outline of a lesson designed to teach a number property.

Select the number property yourself. Identify the grade level for the lesson.

8. Prepare a mathematics bulletin board for a particular grade level.
9. If Cuisenaire rods are available, present to a of group children a lesson in which you use the rods.
10. Visit a curriculum library and get acquainted with mathematics books, devices, filmstrips, and games.
11. Suggest some techniques that provide for individual differences in a mathematics program.
12. Select a mathematics book for a grade level of your interest. Examine the book. Pay attention to such matters as exposition, practice exercises, enrichment materials, provision for individual differences, readability, length of chapters, and testing program. Study the accompanying teacher's manual to determine if a sufficient amount of help is provided for the teacher. Write a report of your findings and/or present the results to the class.

SELECTED READINGS

Briggs, J.; Mettler, F.; and Denholm, R. *Implementing Mathematics Programs in California.* Menlo Park, Calif.: Pacific Coast Publishers, n.d.

Brownell, W.A. "Arithmetic Abstractions—Progress Toward Maturity of Concepts under Differing Programs of Instruction." *The Arithmetic Teacher,* October 1963, pp. 322–29.

Buckeye, D.A., and Ginther, J.L. *Creative Experiments in Mathematics.* San Francisco: Canfield Press, 1971.

Copeland, R.W. *How Children Learn Mathematics.* New York: Macmillan Co., 1970.

Davidson, J. *Using the Cuisenaire Rods–A Photo/Test Guide for Teachers.* New Rochelle, N.Y.: Cuisenaire Company of America, 1969.

Davis, R.B. *Committee on the Undergraduate Program in Mathematics.* Report No. 13, April 1966, pp. 27–31.

Deans, E. *Elementary School Mathematics.* Bulletin no. 13. Washington, D.C.: U.S. Department of Health, Education, and Welfare, 1963.

Dumas, E. *Math Activities for Child Involvement.* Boston: Allyn & Bacon, 1971.

Dumas, E.; Kittell, J.; and Grant, B. *How To Meet Individual Differences in Teaching Arithmetic.* San Francisco: Fearon Publishers, 1957.

Educational Development Center. *Goals for School Mathematics.* Boston: Houghton Mifflin Co., 1963.

Gibb, E.G. "The Years Ahead." *The Arithmetic Teacher,* May 1968, pp. 433–36.

Heddens, J.W. *Today's Mathematics.* 2nd ed. Chicago: Science Research Associates, 1971.

Johnson, D.A. "Next Steps in School Mathematics." *The Arithmetic Teacher,* March 1967, pp. 185–89.

Kidd, K.P.; Myers, S.S. and Cilley, D.M. *The Laboratory Approach to Mathematics.* Chicago: Science Research Associates, 1970.

Kramer, K. *Teaching Elementary School Mathematics.* 3rd ed. Boston: Allyn & Bacon, 1975.

Lucow, W.H. "Testing the Cuisenaire Method." *The Arithmetic Teacher,* April 1961, pp. 164-67.

Madden, R. "New Directions in the Measurement of Mathematical Ability." *The Arithmetic Teacher,* May 1966, pp. 375-79.

Major, J.R. "Issues and Directions." *The Arithmetic Teacher,* May 1966, pp. 349-54.

Marks, J.L.; Purdy, C.R.; Kinney, L.B.; and Hiatt, A.A. *Teaching Elementary School Mathematics for Understanding.* New York: McGraw-Hill Book Co., 1975.

The Revolution in School Mathematics. Washington, D.C.: The National Council of Teachers of Mathematics, 1961.

Passy, R.A. "The Effect of Cuisenaire Materials on Reasoning and Computation." *The Arithmetic Teacher,* November 1963, pp. 439-40.

Piaget, J. *The Child's Conception of Number.* Translated by C. Gattegno and F.M. Hodgson. London: Routledge & Kegan Paul, 1961.

Platts, M.E., ed. *PLUS: A Handbook for Teachers of Elementary Arithmetic.* Stevensville, Mich.: Educational Service, 1964.

Polya, G. *How To Solve It.* Garden City, N.Y.: Doubleday & Co., 1957.

Riedesel, C.A. *Guiding Discovery in Elementary School Mathematics.* New York: Appleton-Century-Crofts, 1967.

Spitzer, H.F. *Enrichment of Arithmetic.* St. Louis, Mo.: Webster Division, McGraw-Hill Book Co., 1964.

_____. *Teaching Elementary School Mathematics.* Boston: Houghton Mifflin Co., 1967.

Stern, C. "The Concrete Devices of Structural Arithmetic." *The Arithmetic Teacher,* April 1958, pp. 119-30.

Stern, C., and Stern, M.B. *Children Discover Arithmetic: An Introduction to Structural Arithmetic.* New York: Harper & Row, 1971.

Swenson, E.J. *Teaching Mathematics to Children.* 2nd ed. New York: Macmillan Co., 1973.

Underhill, R.G. *Teaching Elementary School Mathematics.* Columbus, Ohio: Charles E. Merrill Publishing Co., 1972.

Welch, R.C., and Edwards, C.W. "A Test of Arithmetic Principles, Elementary Form," Bulletin of the School of Education, vol. 41, no. 5. Bloomington: Indiana University, Bureau of Educational Studies and Testing, September 1965, pp. 69-79.

Williams, J.D. *Teaching Technique in Primary Maths.* London: National Foundation for Educational Research in England and Wales, 1971.

Traditionally, a good many elementary school teachers do little about teaching science. And among those who do include science in the curriculum, many simply have the children read their science textbooks. Although there are many reasons for so little effective science teaching, one important one may well be that too few teachers have had the opportunity to learn the specifics of content and methods that are included in this chapter. Many recently published books that deal entirely with teaching methods in the science curriculum offer much less real help to teachers than is given in this single chapter.

The author is a strong advocate of the open informal classroom and adds much to discussions in preceding chapters about learning in such an environment. In relating science learning to most other curriculum areas, she suggests many science activities that require the use of language arts skills and that correlate with social studies, mathematics, and creative art activities.

W.T.P.

Science in the Elementary School Classroom

Betsy Davidson Siegel

11

Every child wonders, speculates, and asks why. In fact, from the beginning of time, individuals of all ages have been curious: They have tried to find out how something works, what causes actions, and why a thing is like it is. This curiosity has driven men and women to find answers and to organize the facts and theories that they discover. These facts and theories are what is known as the body of science knowledge.

Because of this innate motivational catalyst, curiosity, science learning fascinates children unless, of course, a teacher fails to capitalize on this curiosity or unthinkingly permits the formalism of some materials and program guides to obscure what learning about science entails.

SCIENCE AND SCIENCE EDUCATION

Science has both structure and function. As stated previously, the functional roots of science lie in the urge of individuals to discover pattern, to bring order out of disarray, to perceive selectively, to seek cause for effect, to explain the mysterious, and to utilize discoveries to satisfy practical purposes. The finding of possible answers results in a structural hierarchy of interrelated conceptual schemes that human intellect has evolved to explain phenomena observed and experienced. The concepts of modern science represent neither truth nor certainty but rather human ideas about the world, human interpretations of reality.

Children touch and wonder and imagine; they see and feel and enjoy. Only if these powers in children are respected and an environment provided that encourages their use can their potential be realized. Without the activities and materials that stimulate and encourage children's natural tendency to wonder, to explore, and to discover, they will not continue to do so. If children's sensitivities are to be developed, their senses must be given play. If a child's intellectual powers are to grow, he must be allowed to organize his own experiences into a pattern of meaning for him. This is learning.

The concepts children form from discovery activities and experiences will not be adult concepts; the processes they use in arriving at concepts will not be adult processes. Therefore, children cannot be trained to think and act like adult scientists, or to "learn the behaviors of scientists."[1] However, the processes and concepts of children are the bases from which emerge more complex concepts and processes. Children continually build and rebuild their concepts, integrating each into one more complex. They use the mental powers available at a given age, and through this use new and more complex intellectual powers emerge.

OBJECTIVES OF SCIENCE EDUCATION

Historically, science education has been a stepchild in the elementary school curriculum, and it continues to be, for its prime importance is not yet recognized by many program developers and classroom teachers. Even when appropriate materials are available, the learning strategies necessary for developing understandings of science concepts are rarely practiced in classrooms. Science objectives, in the minds of most teachers, continue to exist in terms of acquiring information or facts, yet the prime objectives of science education cannot be stated in terms of facts. Rather they must be stated in terms of the intellectual characteristics that an effective science program should foster and develop.

Science education in the elementary school should contribute to the development of each child's ability to:
1. Think logically, critically, and creatively
2. Recognize and define problems
3. Produce and verify new ideas and solutions to problems
4. Comprehend abstract conceptual schemes

---

1. *Science, A Process Approach* (American Association for the Advancement of Science, 1968), p. 7.

5. Interpret phenomena within these conceptual schemes
6. Be self-directive
7. Resist collective thought and propaganda
8. Enjoy the excitement of mystery and discovery
9. Appreciate the beauty and complexity of the natural world
10. Understand and respect the equilibrium in nature
11. Have compassion and respect for all life on earth

The greatest asset society has for its betterment is the individual, creative mind of the human being. Creativity is a human resource that is found in abundance in young children. Science education can be an efficient vehicle to protect this resource by promoting creativity and independence in children, who then will be able to resist effectively the kind of regimentation that tends to deaden individual critical and creative potential into a still and silent quiescence.

CONTENT AND PROCESS IN SCIENCE LEARNING

The focus of the objectives on thinking processes, attitudes, and values does not negate the fact that content must be thought about and examined. Values must be considered and certain attitudes toward content must be taken. The need for balance between content and process in a social studies program as suggested in Chapter 9 is applicable to a science program as well.

The content of a science program may be placed in three related strands: physical science concepts, life science concepts, and concepts common to both areas (see Table 11.1 on the following page). To deal with these concepts, certain classificatory and seriative skills will be learned during the elementary school years (see Table 11.2 on page 283). Thus, the program is one of engaging children in learning activities involving these concepts, and this process results in the acquisition of certain concept-related skills.

Since children's interests are different and their abilities and levels of development vary, it should not be assumed that every child who completes the elementary school science program will have, or even should have, a complete understanding of all the concepts listed. In fact, only a few of the most intellectually mature children at the uppermost grade levels will be able to handle or be much interested in such concepts as evolution, natural selection, or genetic change. Furthermore, few elementary school children will have developed sufficient intellectual maturation to deal abstractly with such concepts as volume, speed, acceleration, energy, momentum, force, work, and time. However, all children should be provided with concrete experiences related to these concepts so that they will eventually be able to understand them in the abstract.

Consideration of children's interests is of prime importance in an effective science program. It is important to recognize that some children will be enticed by one aspect of the content and show relative disinterest in another area. Certainly all of these concepts can be built by a variety of appealing activities. The

Table 11.1. Concepts in Elementary School Science Programs

Physical Sciences	Common Concepts	Life Sciences
Substance	Measurement	Characteristics of
Inertia	Time	organisms
Weight	Length	Organization
Volume	Distance	Growth
Density	Area	Development
	Volume	Metabolism
Space	Weight	Reproduction
Length	Force	Responsiveness
Distance	Work	
Area	Energy	Survival techniques
Volume		of organisms
Interior	Change	Adaptation
Occupied	Physical systems	Structural
Displaced	Organisms	Physiological
	Communities	Behavioral
Time	Ecosystems	Community
Motion	Motion	Food chains
Speed	Position	Ecosystems
Acceleration		Change
Momentum	Relativity	Evolutionary
	Motion	Natural Selection
Energy	Position	Geological
Mechanical		Genetic
Chemical	Causality	
Thermal		
Electrical	Equilibrium	
Nuclear	Physical systems	
	Organic systems	
Force	Communities	
Mechanical	Ecosystems	
Gravitational		
Frictional	Interaction	
Magnetic	Physical systems	
	Organic systems	
Work		
Levers	Systems within systems	
Inclined Planes	Physical	
Wheels	Organic	
Pulleys		
Adaptations		

child should be allowed to explore a given concept as thoroughly as her motivation and intellectual maturity permit, and it is undoubtedly more intellectually useful that the child cover fewer concepts in depth than many of them in a superficial manner.

There is a very definite sequence to the placement of the concepts within the curriculum, and this order is determined by developmental considerations (see Table 11.2). Those concepts that are available perceptually, such as substance, can be investigated and understood at least on a basic level by younger children; whereas a concept that is not available perceptually, such as time or acceleration, and which results from the interaction of many variables, may be grasped only by adolescents or adults. Sequencing concepts demands an understanding of what each concept is and of how concept development takes place.

Table 11.2. Development of Classification and Seriation Skills

Description of Skill	Approximate Age Attained
Matching two objects from an assorted group	4–5
Setting up two aligned groups by matching process	4–5
Discerning one-to-one correspondence in two aligned groups	5–6
Discerning one-to-one correspondence in two nonaligned groups	6–7
Making several consistent sorting decisions before switching to some other property	5–6
Sorting all objects from an assorted group according to a single criterion	6–7
Ordering objects in one direction according to one property	5–6
Ordering two groups of objects in opposite directions according to a single property	6–7
Discovering that an object can belong in more than one class	7–8
Forming new groups from an assorted group so that objects are placed in more than one class	8–9
Forming classes or groups into a vertical organization with superordinate and subordinate classes	9–10
Seriating objects along two axes according to two properties	11–12
Categorizing objects or properties within a matrix in the cells of which two properties converge	12–13

Source: Partially derived from Ellen Kofsky, "A Scalogram Study of Classificatory Development," *Child Development* 37 (1966): 191–204; Barbet Inhelder and Jean Piaget, *The Early Growth of Logic in the Child* (London: Routledge & Kegan Paul, 1964), pp. 100–118, 142–145, 176–88, 25–60; Jean Piaget, *The Child's Conception of Number* (New York: W. W. Norton & Co.), pp. 85–95, 147–57, 198–202; and Jean Piaget, *Psychology of Intelligence* (London: Routledge & Kegan Paul, 1966), pp. 129–53.

HOW SCIENCE EDUCATION HAS EVOLVED

In the minds of curriculum designers and authors of textbooks, elementary school science teaching has changed considerably in recent years. Much that has been done by scientists, psychologists, and curriculum developers has had a definite impact on programs. Present programs, while perhaps being somewhat different from those of a decade or so ago, actually vary so considerably that no single definition of a modern science program is possible.

Religious Beginnings

In the early schools of America, children were taught to read, to cipher, to spell, and sometimes to write. The school program had strong moral overtones.

The first readers used contained references to nature, but nature was always presented as the handiwork of God. Furthermore, every reading lesson was accompanied by some moral exhortation.

Benjamin Franklin and Thomas Jefferson expressed in their writings the practical need for the people of frontier agricultural communities to become more educated in the applications of science, since people needed to know husbandry to care for their plants and animals as well as some of the principles of mechanics to make and repair their tools. In the common school, however, science was an incidental part of the instruction, and what the pupil learned about science depended to a great extent on what the teacher happened to know. The texts were moralistic and only a few trade books on science topics at the juvenile level were published.

Object Teaching

About the mid-1850s, faculty psychology came into educational vogue. This view held that certain pursuits developed particular "faculties" of the brain. About the same time, the Swiss educator, Pestalozzi, influenced American schools with his idea of "object teaching." Under this aegis, texts in which each lesson focused on a specific object were published. A verbal presentation of the object was given, after which the children carefully observed it and memorized its name and characteristics.

The aim of this pedagogical approach was not so much to acquaint children with the objects as it was to improve their faculties of observation to science education as well as memory. Moral overtones permeated the object-teaching texts.

During the last decades of the nineteenth century, a few states passed legislation that added science to the school curriculum; but in many instances this meant in actual practice that science was combined with literature, and science instruction carried more of an emotional than a conceptual approach to reality. Nature was romanticized rather than analyzed, and the beauty and moral excellence of rural life was extolled. In short, science education during this period was directed toward mind training, aesthetic appreciation, or religious and moral development.

Nature Study

At the beginning of the twentieth century, nature study was introduced into the curriculum. Children studied the life cycle, environment, and characteristics of plants and animals. However, children did not learn about nature by taking hikes through fields and forests or by gathering and examining specimens; rather they looked at pictures of plants and animals and listened to stories about them. Sometimes the children drew or modeled the plant or animal while looking at an illustration of it. No attention was given to problem solving or to the development of thinking abilities. Schools and communities developed their own curriculum guides to supplement the teacher's scanty knowledge.

Social Needs and the "Scientific Method"

By 1920 the rapid industrial expansion and the advent of technology stimulated an increased interest in the technological applications of science to society. This trend, combined with John Dewey's philosophy of education and Gerald Craig's research on children's interests,[2] gave still a new direction to science education. This period saw the publication of texts that contained units of study directed toward practical and social needs. The so-called scientific method (formation of hypothesis, experimentation, observation of data, conclusions) was introduced into the classrooms, and the children performed the "experiments" as suggested in the texts. This meant that children went through the routine steps of the prescribed method, arriving at the "right" answers.

This approach was subject to criticism because of the lack of a conceptual framework and the absence of any real problem solving. Furthermore, it perpetuated a fundamental misconception about methodology in science. This view considered the scientific method to be a prescribed series of steps that were used to reach conclusions; whereas in reality what was called the "scientific method" in these texts is actually only the format used by scientists in reporting their research results. The approach also overlooked the fact that scientific knowledge results from intuition, bold hunches, or imagination as often as from carefully controlled laboratory experimentation.

The Unit Approach

After World War II, children continued to "learn" about science by reading science readers, which were rapidly proliferating at this time. Every publishing company that serviced schools had one or more science series to offer. School systems developed their own guides to supplement the texts and to bolster the wavering courage of their poorly prepared teachers, who could see little continuity or structure to the science they were expected to teach.

There were bright spots in classrooms here and there. These were classrooms in which creative teachers were beginning to build their own science programs, using some of the excellent and beautifully illustrated trade books being published as well as focusing on the objects and animals that the children brought into the classroom. The books intrigued the children and did much to further understanding in specific areas. One such book, *The Little Island,* is an excellent example because it proceeds from the child's perceptual idea of an island to the actual structure of one.[3]

The science texts of the forties and fifties were organized according to the spiral pattern, which repeated a given topic at each grade level in ever-increasing depth (or so the advertisers claimed). The unit approach was used, but conceptual relationships between the content of succeeding units was not apparent to

---

2. Gerald Craig, *Certain Techniques Used in Developing a Course of Study in Science for the Horace Mann Elementary School* (New York: Columbia University, Teachers College, 1927).
3. Golden MacDonald and Leonard Weisgard, *The Little Island* (Garden City, N.Y.: Doubleday & Co., 1946).

teachers and children. Activities were specified and "experiments" suggested, but the conceptual strands of the discipline were not examined, and no distinction was made between science and technology.

Science Programs of the 1960s

About 1960, two new currents of thought appeared to influence the course of science education. The processes and concepts of science were the focus of both schools of thought.

The behaviorists, drawing from the work of Edward L. Thorndike, John B. Watson, Clark L. Hull, B. F. Skinner, and others began to produce programs that attempted to train children in the "skills of the scientist."[4]

Those who understood child development, on the other hand, drew on the philosophy of John Dewey and the research and theory of Piaget to produce programs that focused on concept development and creativity as well as on the development of intellectual processes of logical thought.[5] These programs tried to match the content of the program to the intellectual development of the child and provided activities that gave the child practice in the process he was perfecting or the concept he was building.

The Elementary School Science Project focused in depth on one topic.[6] This project encouraged children to observe phenomena, raise questions, make predictions, and experiment to prove or disprove their guesses.

Also developed in the midsixties were the materials issued by the American Association for the Advancement of Science. These were incorporated into the program *Science—A Process Approach.*[7] This program, which is widely used in school systems at the present time, is based on behaviorist learning theory and does not recognize developmental considerations to any perceivable extent. The materials are highly prescriptive: They provide exact terminology that the teacher must use, with exact responses expected from the children. The processes of science give the program its structure, a structure derived by constructing a hierarchy of behaviors (specific overt actions and verbal responses), with a terminal behavior depending on the acquiring of certain subordinate behaviors. The processes are carried down to the simplest kinds of behavior. Precise assessment of behavior is provided at the end of each lesson. In spite of these deficiencies in the program, many of the activities suggested are excellent and could be used in a different manner than prescribed in the teachers' guides.

The *Elementary Science Study* (ESS) program is based on the developmental theory of Piaget.[8] The technique used is almost exclusively that of discovery. The program consists of many unrelated units that are all highly creative in nature.

---

4. Association for the Advancement of Science, *Science.*
5. Robert Karpus et al., *Science Curriculum Improvement Study* (Berkeley, Calif.: D.C. Heath & Co., Lexington, Mass., 1966).
6. *Elementary School Science Curriculum Project* (Urbana, Ill.: University of Illinois, 1965).
7. Association for the Advancement of Science, *Science.*
8. Eleanor Duckworth, "The Elementary Science Study Branch of Educational Services, Inc.," *Journal of Research in Science Teaching* 2 (1964): 241–43.

There is no articulation between units and no particular sequence within the program. Children are supplied with material kits, and teachers are provided with guidebooks. Verbalization is not stressed, but there is emphasis on discovery and creativity in language as well as in thought and action.

The *Science Curriculum Improvement Study* (SCIS) also has its roots in Piaget's theory.[9] The structure of the program is based on the conceptual development of the child, and therefore the subject areas of the program are closely related to the concepts the child is structuring at a given age level. The two strands of the program, the physical sciences and the life sciences, are closely correlated in this conceptual orientation. For example, the physical-strand booklet, *Material Objects,* and the life-strand booklet, *Organisms,* are designed to help the six-to-seven-year-old child in his construction of the substance concept.

The long-range goals of the SCIS program are to contribute to the development of logical thought processes and to increase functional understanding of basic science concepts. The teacher functions as a diagnostician, as a guide, and infrequently, as an expositor. There is no behavioral assessment of either processes or concepts, based on developmental psychology postulates that intellectual processes develop integratively and observed behavior is not an accurate indicator of understanding.

Environmental and Ecological Considerations

Since the dimensions of the environmental crisis have become so apparent in the last few years, there are now new materials and texts available that encourage investigation of ecological relationships and provide a structure of concepts as well as suggested activities for studying the environment and the social issues that are related to various environmental questions. Most of the programs published in the seventies have included at each level a unit on environmental problems.

ORGANIZING LEARNING EXPERIENCES IN SCIENCE

The reader will have judged from the preceding sections that science programs in schools today are apt to be quite varied. It is also fair to say that most of these programs are heavily dependent on commercial materials. But although the materials are important, they are only a part of an effective science education curriculum.

Elementary school children cannot learn science concepts through verbal means only. Language—oral or written—can enrich experience, but it cannot substitute for it. For children to achieve the objectives stated earlier and to learn fundamental science concepts, attention must be given to children's development

---

9. Karplus, *Science Curriculum Improvement Study.*

and their interests and experiences as well as to the organization of activities for maximizing learning.

Children's Development and the Science Program

The child entering school for the first time comes into the classroom with many perceptions and feelings relating to his movement in space and to the movement of objects. He operates intuitively by a trial-and-error method. His thinking is based on action, and everything is seen from his own perspective.

The five- or six-year-old child normally can focus on only one aspect of an object or event at a time, without seeing the changes that may take place in an object. Since her perception dominates, she must judge by the appearance of an object at a given moment. If, for instance, she is shown two balls of clay, identical in shape and size, she will acknowledge the equal amount of substance in the balls of clay. But even if she watches someone elongate one of the balls of clay into a sausage shape, she will deny the equality of amounts. Depending on her perception of the size of each shape, she will insist that either the sausage or the ball contains more clay.[10]

For children of this age, and up to about age seven, science activities should allow for much grouping and sorting of objects and for attention to characteristics of plants and animals and to properties of objects. The concepts of substance, time, length, distance, and relative motion may be explored, and intuitive ideas of speed, force, and work can be strengthened. Children of this age will be deeply interested in their own growth and development as well as that of the plants and animals familiar to them. Some aspects of adaptation, community, metabolism, and reproduction may be explored. Measurement, change, relativity, interaction, and the relationship of parts to the whole (systems within systems) may also become a part of the science curriculum in kindergarten and the primary grades.

Between the ages of eight and twelve, logical thinking comes into play and perception ceases to dominate the thought processes. For example, the children would simply assert that the amount in the two balls of clay is the same, since nothing was added or taken away.

Children in this age group now see that a whole is made up of its parts, that objects can belong to many different classes, and that some classes will include other classes. During this period, children stabilize the concepts of substance, distance, length, area, weight, and measurement. They may begin to investigate the more complicated concepts of speed, time, acceleration, force, and work as long as one of the variables in the interaction remains constant so that children can see the remaining two variables in operation.[11] In regard to the life sciences, children may delve more deeply into the characteristics of organisms and will be able to begin to understand some of the relationships involved in adaptation, community, and change.

---

10.   Jean Piaget, *Psychology of Intelligence* (London: Routledge & Kegan Paul, 1966), pp. 146–47.
11.   Betsy D. Siegel and Ronald Raven, "The Effect of Manipulation on the Acquisition of the Compensatory Concepts of Speed, Force, and Work," *Journal of Research in Science Teaching* 8 (1971): 4.

However, there is one important limitation: Children in this age group think logically in solving problems dealing only with concrete objects, things that they can see and feel and touch. Children in the intermediate grades are realists, and they are able to deal only with real problems that exist before their eyes. Their thinking still depends on action and imagery.

Organization of Classroom and Materials

Many teachers have wondered why curriculum and methods have been made separate entities in teacher education programs, since those who deal extensively with children in the classroom know that the two are inextricably interwoven. What children will learn is determined by how and why they learn. The child is the active learner, and the teacher provides materials and organizes the classroom so that learning can take place.

The classroom must be a consciously organized environment that offers a wide variety of materials for the children's use. These offerings should have a learning potential suited to the developmental levels of the children. The richer the materials and the better their organization, the more effective the program will be.

In order to evaluate the learning potential of materials, the teacher must keep in mind the learning strategies a group of children will likely have at their command or will be ready to employ. The teacher must also actually use the materials to find out through experience what the children can learn from them and how this may be accomplished. The materials should invite manipulation, aid in concept formation, and force children to make certain generalizations after working with them. Optimally, the materials should entice children to practice the particular skills and thought processes under consideration.

Teachers may wish to make question charts and activity cards to help children explore materials more productively. Such charts and cards should be attractively printed and illustrated, sturdily constructed, and perhaps laminated or covered with acetate or clear contact paper for protection.

An uncluttered and selective arrangement of materials placed on surface areas is necessary, and not too many materials should be displayed at one time. Few people, either adults or children, can think or work purposefully in the midst of disorganization and clutter. Materials that have served their purpose should be removed, for materials used too long no longer challenge, and objects visible too long are not longer seen. Humans tend to perceive only that which interests them. Perception rejects monotony.

Many of the materials used in classrooms are commercial products prescribed for a certain use, directed toward a stated objective, and too often intended to be used by each child in the same way. What is needed, however, are teacher and pupil created materials that demand contact and manipulation and can be used in many ways. Such materials encourage the individual to put something of himself and his ideas into whatever he is working on. The significant point is that there is no one right way to use these materials and no one answer to be found from using them. Their purpose is to encourage investigation and thinking and not to elicit correct responses.

On the other hand, children do need to learn the correct use and purposes of such instruments as projectors, tape recorders, and microscopes. For children who are six or seven years old or older, charts presenting the information can be placed near the instrument. With younger children, oral instructions can be given to the group or to individuals. As some children become proficient in operating the equipment, they may help others to learn the operation. Children in the first grade are quite capable of threading a projector, adjusting the focus, and running and rewinding the film.

There should be large table and floor working surfaces as well as wall areas in classroom and corridors for the display of children's products. Sometimes it is necessary to arrange groups of four or six desks as tables so that the children are working face-to-face for increased communication and interaction. The grouped desks may be covered with masonite or plyboard and oilcloth or linoleum to provide a smooth and easily cleaned working surface.

Clear passageways around work areas are essential for safety and flexibility of movement. The placement of furniture, equipment, and materials should take into account the health and safety of the children. Storage facilities for materials used in a particular working area should be readily accessible to children.

Besides the responsibilities of selecting, arranging, and changing the materials, furniture, and other equipment, the teacher needs to guide the children in their use of reference materials and in their care of living things in the classroom. The teacher should also help children to establish responsible housekeeping habits and to care for all the materials by using them properly and putting them back in the same condition and place in which they were found.

Yet guidance should not be overdone. The golden mean of moderation and good sense must be exercised. The teacher should not state ideas or explain processes before they can be explored, nor seldom should an idea be introduced verbally before it is viewed in operation. Children need to discover characteristics and operations for themselves by manipulating materials, asking questions of themselves and others, seeing what happens in an experiment, and drawing their own conclusions.

Reference Materials

One area of the classroom should be reserved for reference materials, which may be read, viewed, and/or listened to. This reference center should be stocked with late editions of one or two encyclopedias; many substantive and attractive trade books of varying reading levels, dealing with science topics or scientists; and dictionaries of several levels of difficulty. Some publishing companies are now producing slim, individual books, each of which covers a specific topic, such as heat, weather, or climate.[12] Several copies of each of these books should be available.

This center should contain the projector, filmstrip viewer, tape recorder, record player (and the films, filmstrips, tapes, and records to be used with them),

---

12. *Exploring and Understanding Series* (Westchester, Ill.: Benefic Press, 1969).

as well as the individual listening devices now on the market. Tape recordings and books made by the children as well as their chart displays, exhibits, models, paintings, and other such products should be a part of the reference center. Of course, many of these objects should be placed throughout the classroom and corridors as well.

Carpentry Materials

Another storage and work area might focus on carpentry activities. Much can be learned about physical science concepts through the creation and use of such devices as axles, pulleys, wagons, balances, inclined planes, electric circuits as well as cages for classroom animals and containers for plants and marine life. Depending on the age of the children, materials such as the following can be used: short pieces of boards and doweling; hammer, nails, tacks, and screws; vises and saws; nuts, bolts, wire, twine, and string; springs, wheels, and pulleys; a folding rule, screwdriver, and pliers; and a hand bit and drills.

Materials for Classification and Seriation of Objects

In order for children to learn the process of classification and seriation, they need to explore an assortment of many collections of objects that differ in several characteristics, such as shape, size, color, composition, and function. These collections may include spools, pieces of cloth, cubes and blocks, beads and buttons; fossils and shells, driftwood, acorns and chestnuts, pebbles and rocks; two- and three-dimensioanl shapes made of paper, cardboard, wood, Styrofoam, or other material; marbles, bottle tops, different-sized bottles, jars, cans, and boxes.

Other items intended to show seriation and classification can be made by the teacher. These include various games and charts as well as a collection of flannel shapes and pictures mounted on flannel.

Materials for Making Projects

Another area for storage and for activities should provide the materials necessary for making books, displays, models, charts, and exhibits. In this area, pupils may engage in simple bookbinding, different kinds of printing, and making plaster models. Children should have access to the following materials: Oaktag; drawing, construction, and chart paper; printing sets and typewriter; clay, Plasticene, plaster of Paris, and materials for making papier-mâché; paste and glue; stapler, paper punch, and scissors; crayons, paints, pens, and felt-tip markers; and lined and unlined writing paper.

Measurement Materials

In a measurement center are materials for measuring length, area, volume, and time. These include balance and spring scales; six- and twelve-inch rulers, yardsticks, and meter sticks; clocks, toy clocks, stopwatches, egg timers, and hourglasses; cubes, blocks, different-sized squares of linoleum and wood, geometric figures of two and three dimensions; cartons, shoe boxes, bottles, jars, measuring cups and spoons, cylindrical containers like oatmeal boxes and coffee cans; pendulums and balances; sieves and funnels; sand, beans, water, and other such materials to use in measuring volume.

Miscellaneous Materials

Other materials will be needed as activities are created. For example, children who wish to build an aquarium will need a pan; goldfish, snails, guppies, polliwogs, or other animals requiring water environments; dirt, sand, pebbles, and rocks; a fish net; and a floating thermometer. A terrarium would require a pan or deep dish and glass; seeds or plants; dirt or sand; and a watering can to care for the plants.

The materials that can be used to aid in concept formation are almost limitless: a tub or dishpan with objects to investigate flotation, density, and water displacement; mirrors and prisms to study light refraction; small carts, toy cars and trucks, assorted balls and marbles to experiment with speed and acceleration; hand lenses, a microscope, slides, and a medicine dropper to investigate specimens; liquids and solids, such as borax, baking soda, sugar, salt, vinegar, and oil to investigate mixtures.

Many of the materials need not be purchased for the activities; rather the teacher and children can bring them from home. The more that parents are encouraged to participate in class activities, such as by providing materials, visiting the classroom to see their children at work, and giving demonstrations in a field of their expertise, the firmer will be the bond of understanding between teacher and parents regarding the progress of the children and the concerns and goals of the instructional program.

CONCEPTS AND ACTIVITIES IN THE PHYSICAL SCIENCES

Table 11.3 lists the concepts in the realm of physical science to be explored and understood by elementary school children. These concepts are discussed in the following section, and activities that help children to build the concepts are suggested.

Substance Concepts

Substance concepts include the idea of substance itself and the related areas of inertia, weight, and density. To investigate these concepts, children will need to use classification and seriation processes as they sort, group, and order concrete materials and to engage in measurement processes involving such space concepts as length, area, and interior volume. Table 11.3 indicates the approximate ages at which particular physical science concepts may be understood by children who have had sufficient experiences in concrete activities involving these concepts. Ordinarily, children should be taking part in these kinds of preliminary activities two years before they reach the ages shown in the table.

Substance is the amount of matter contained within an object. Inertia is the resistance of an object to having its velocity changed. In order to measure substance, its inertia must be analyzed to determine the force necessary to move it. The more substance an object has, the greater the gravitational pull on it relative to its distance from the earth. This gravitational pull can be translated as weight. Therefore, a simple way of determining substance is in terms of its weight.

Children can be helped to define substance by presenting to them two identical containers filled with different substances, one light, one heavy. The children should be asked to identify the box with more substance. Since young children will not be familiar enough with the concept of substance to discern similarities and differences by visual means, they will discover through trial-and-error investigation that substance can be identified through pushing, pulling, lifting, or weighing. To discover exact differences in substance, weighing is necessary. Objects similar in appearance but different in density are particularly useful for defining substance.

Table 11.3. Understanding and Conservation of Physical Science Concepts

Age	Substance Concepts	Space Concepts	Time Concepts	Motion Concepts
12	Interior volume	Displaced volume Occupied volume	Coordinated time	Momentum Energy Work Force Acceleration Speed
10	Weight			
8	Substance	Measurement: area, length Distance	Conservation of time	
6			Perception of simultaneity of starting and stopping	Relative motion
4				
2	Object permanence	Spatial notions	Temporal notions	Motoric knowledge

Source: Adapted from Jean Piagnet and Barbel Inhelder, *The Child's Conception of Space* (London: Routlege & Kegan Paul, 1956); Jean Piaget, *The Construction of Reality in the Child* (New York: Basic Books, 1954); and Kenneth Lovell, *The Growth of Basic Mathematical and Scientific Concepts in Children* (London: University of London Press, 1966).

Children discover properties of substances by manipulating and changing the shapes of substances. They enjoy squeezing, rolling, or flattening Plasticene; stretching rubber bands; blowing up, squeezing, and pricking balloons; and pouring liquid and granule substances from a container of one shape to one of another shape. Children may investigate the similarities and differences among substances by sorting, or ordering objects according to some criterion, such as size, shape, color, texture, odor, composition, or use. Older children may classify and seriate objects, pictures, words, and ideas in more complex arrangements with guidance provided by game boards developed for these purposes.

Older children may also examine substances in the light of change by distinguishing between physical and chemical changes. They may work with mixtures, solutions, and suspensions to determine how different substances have been combined and how they can be separated into the original ingredients. Children should learn that a mixture is not formed through chemical change; it is a combination of elements and /or compounds that do not unite. A solution is a mixture in which particles of solid, liquid, or gas are dissolved in a gas or a liquid. A suspension is a mixture in which the particles have not dissolved and are visible under a microscope. Slides of such matter as muddy water, salt water, furniture polish, or vinegar may be viewed under a microscope to determine in which category each of these fall.

Children may make collections of various materials formed by chemical change and manufacture, such as iron nails, copper wire, table salt, water, marble, sugar, and baking soda. They then may investigate the composition of these by inspecting them and using reference works. Minerals and ores such as diamonds, carbon, and quartz may be examined under a hand lens, and the degree of their hardness may be ascertained by finding out what each of these substances can scratch and what can scratch it.

To investigate weight, inertia, and density, children may push or hold two objects similar in size and shape but different in density. After this initial sensory investigation, they may weigh the objects and record the data. Children will gain experience in estimating density and weight by participating in activities involving flotation. However, since a number of variables operate in buoyancy as well as density, the teacher must provide some control of variables so that incorrect conclusions will not be drawn.

The equal-arm balance and scales may be used to show children the weight concept in terms of quantity. Children may make ounce and pound and five-pound weights by filling cloth bags with the right amount of sand and sewing them closed. Metric weights may be introduced at the intermediate grade levels.

Space Concepts

The space concepts are length, distance, area, and volume. Each of these is tied closely to a measurement process. Length is the filled space between two points; distance, the unfilled space between two points; and area, the filled or unfilled space within a perimeter formed on more than two points. Volume has three aspects: Interior volume is the amount of space within the surfaces of an object; occupied volume, the space taken up by the object; and displaced volume, the amount of space taken up by the substance displaced by the object (for example, water displacement). Understanding of each of these concepts is dependent on acquiring knowledge of the previous one.

Distance is the space concept first understood by children, and this understanding slowly evolves. About the age of five, a child's idea of distance is confined to only that part of a distance on which she focuses. Later, she believes that a distance becomes less when an object is placed between the two end points. A child understands the concept of length when she is able to see that the site occupied by an object remains the same when the object is removed and that the length of an object does not change as its position changes.

The child's first attempts at gaining an understanding of measurement will be made in terms of his own body. For children who are five to seven years old, only trial-and-error measurement exists, and therefore it is futile to impose on children tasks that require the use of tools for measuring or to teach them any specific measurement terms. Children who are seven years of age or so will begin to develop the ability to work with units of measure as related to the concepts they are forming.

Early investigations of space should focus on qualitative assessments rather than on quantitative measurements. Young children may lay two objects side by side to determine which one is longer. They may use dominoes or blocks or other objects to construct two equal and parallel rows that align at both ends. They then may rearrange one row by removing an object from one end and placing it at the other or by making a zigzag formation. Young children will mistakenly discern a change in length or distance as the overall arrangement changes. Gradually, however, children will realize that the change in appearance does not alter the length or distance. Once this occurs, children have stabilized their understanding of the concept.

Area measurement may be introduced by the use of one-inch or one-foot squares placed on a given area or of different-sized squares drawn on graph paper. Only after children understand the concept of area in terms of units that can be manipulated should they attempt computation of area. Children should be led through the thinking that culminates in computation rather than asked to learn a formula by which area is computed. Area computation will not be understood before children reach nine years of age.

Conservation of area can be determined by placing identical small objects on each of two identical two-dimensional shapes. However, the objects should be clustered together on one of the shapes and placed in a scattered arrangement on the other. When children acknowledge that the unoccupied space in both shapes is equal and can explain why, they have attained understanding of the concept.

The understanding of interior volume can be facilitated by activities in which containers of varying shape and size, such as shoe boxes, coffee cans, cartons, are measured by the use of one-inch or one-foot wooden or plastic cubes or by volatile substances that can be poured, such as sand or water. Cubes may also be used to build layered rectangular shapes that contain varying numbers of cubes in their bases but have the same number of cubes in their total shapes and therefore contain the same volume. Children will soon see that area is affected by a horizontal addition of cubes and that volume is increased by a vertical addition of each layer of area. The construction of these structures in water and subsequent measurement of rise of water level in the container will contribute to an understanding of both occupied and displaced volume.

Older children may work with more abstract ideas of space by constructing models of the solar system, either in the form of mobiles or mounts, using scale measurement for the diameter of the planets and their distances from the sun. They may use the Celestial Globe, the telescope, and the Trippensee Planetarium to study the constellations, the movement of the planets, solstices, equinoxes, and eclipses of the sun and moon, as well as to investigate stars, double stars, nebulas, and the craters and seas of the moon. Other activities children enjoy are making constellation maps and illustrations or three-dimensional models of the phases of the moon. Children may also wish to research the advances in this area from the time of the ancient astronomers to present-day space exploration.

Time Concepts

Time is measured in intervals, each of which has a starting point, a stopping point, and an interval between. A time interval may be illustrated by one swing of a pendulum (its period). If the pendulum is made from a thirty-nine-inch piece of string with a weight attached, its period will be one second. As it swings, children can see and feel the rhythm and flow of one second into another. They may count successive seconds needed to time actions and to measure time durations.

Young children cannot perceive simultaneity and nonsimultaneity in the starting and stopping points of two or more events. They judge time in terms of the space covered by moving objects or in terms of what was accomplished during the time interval. They do not see the compensation operating between frequency of swings or revolutions and speed in a pendulum or in angular speed, or between time and speed in linear comparisons, in which one variable increases as the other decreases to achieve the same result in the third component. Children may develop more acute perception of starting and stopping times of an interval by participating in activities that involve clear beginnings and endings to an interval, such as two raps, a jump, the dripping of water, or by playing with objects, such as cars or dolls, that are made to traverse different distances at varying speeds but are started and stopped simultaneously. Consistent questioning should accompany the activities. Depending on whether or not the child can read, questioning may be accomplished verbally or through the use of activity cards.

In order to ascertain whether or not children have achieved the ability to perceive time elements, they may watch the teacher use two equal amounts of water to fill simultaneously two containers of different shapes so that the liquid does not appear to be equal in the containers. Children should then be questioned to determine whether they were able to tell that the flow of water into both containers started and stopped simultaneously and that it took an equal amount of time to fill the containers, despite the perceptual distortion of the amounts of water in the containers.[13]

It is helpful to use children's own experiences in devising activities that strengthen relative concepts of time, such as the day before, the day after, a week

---

13. Kenneth Lovell, *The Growth of Basic Mathematical and Scientific Concepts in Children* (London: University of London Press, 1966), pp. 84–85.

from today. Teachers can aid children in their understanding of the calendar by associating dates with events in their lives and by having children make their own calendars for recording these past and future happenings.

Telling time by the clock should be taught first with the aid of the pendulum coordinated with a large electric clock that has a second hand or with a play clock manipulated by the teacher. Later, play clocks and alarm clocks may be manipulated by the children to demonstrate the passage of hours, then half hours, then five minute intervals, minute intervals, and finally second intervals. The additive aspects of telling time should be presented last of all.

Children should be encouraged to experiment with stopwatches, egg timers, hourglasses, sundials, and shadow sticks, all coordinated with mechanical timepieces with which they are already familiar. Older children like to explore the methods by which prehistoric men and women kept track of time and to discover how navigational and mechanical means of measuring time evolved.

Motion Concepts

Table 11.3 identifies six concepts of motion (speed, acceleration, force, work, energy, momentum) that most children will not understand until the latter years of elementary school or even later. However, children should have experiences with these concepts before adolescence if they are to understand them eventually. These concepts result from the interaction of substance, space, and time. Speed plays a part in understanding the other five concepts, and therefore children first need to understand the concept of speed.

Speed

Speed is the distance covered per unit of time. Some activities for investigating speed involve the comparison of linear or angular motion of two objects moving along parallel tracks or around concentric circles. Linear comparisons can be made by using inclined planes to provide gravitational force for the movement of the objects or by placing objects on a horizontal surface, attaching weighted strings to them, and then hanging the strings over the edge of the surface to provide the force for movement. By varying the height of the inclined planes or the amount of the weights attached to the strings or the mass of the objects themselves, differences in speed may be compared.

Children can gain an understanding of angular speed by moving two objects abreast of each other and around parallel circular tracks made on Oaktag; by taping two coins to a record, one at the outer and one at the inner circumference, and then playing the record; and by taping one coin to the larger wheel of a windlass and another coin to the smaller wheel. The speeds of the coins may be compared in terms of both angular and linear measurement.

Acceleration

Acceleration is the rate at which speed changes, or it is a change in the direction of speed. An object in uniform motion has no acceleration, whereas an object whose speed changes by the same amount during equal successions of a given time period has uniform acceleration. Acceleration may be investigated most successfully in the classroom by the use of inclined planes or revolving wheels. The speed of an object on an inclined plane is determined by the height of the plane, whereas acceleration is determined by the slant of the plane. The acceleration of an object traveling down an inclined plane will be uniform. The plane may be marked off in equal distance intervals in order for children to see that speed is greatest in the last interval and the longest amount of time occurs in the first interval.

Force

Force is a pressure. It can affect motion by producing, preventing, changing, or balancing it. Force can affect substance by stretching or compressing it.

Force can be investigated by pushing or pulling objects of varying weights over horizontal surfaces or up inclined planes and then measuring the force by using a spring scale. Force can also be assessed qualitatively by allowing two objects to descend inclined planes and strike two identical objects at the foot of the planes. The amount of force can be discerned by the effect it produces on the objects.

Friction is a counterforce set up by the movement of an object over a surface. Differences in frictional force correspond to the force with which the object presses, which is related to its weight. Lighter objects press with less force on the contact surface and therefore cause less frictional counterforce than do heavier objects that would press with more force. The smaller the area of the contact surface between objects producing friction, the less friction will result. Another factor that affects friction is the texture of the surfaces in contact: Rough surfaces produce more friction than smooth surfaces.

Differences in frictional force may be observed and compared by noting the speed of movement of various objects on an inclined plane. Some appropriate items for this activity include a block, a domino, a billiard ball, a tennis ball, a toy car with big, thin, or tilted wheels. Children may compare the texture of the surface of the objects, the amount of contact surface involved, the mass of the objects, and whether the motion is a sliding or rolling motion. The friction produced by rolling wheels is less than the friction created by objects sliding on a nonrevolving surface. Pupils may wish to figure out methods to reduce the contact surface of an object by providing wheels or runners or by lubricating the contact surface.

Children should be encouraged to evaluate the positive and negative aspects of friction. Friction is necessary for movement. Braking requires friction. Heavily treaded tires increase friction and hasten the stopping and starting of wheels. Friction is necessary in the locomotion of human beings and animals. In machines, however, friction reduces efficiency, and lubrication is used to offset this effect.

Children may investigate magnetic force by using magnets that have been purchased or by using ones they have made. Some activities involving magnetic force include: magnetizing materials by taking a piece of iron or steel and stroking it in one direction with one end of a magnet, experimenting with objects to discover which ones are attracted to magnets and which are not, investigating the attracting and repelling features of magnetic poles. Children also enjoy making circuits by using a dry cell and a nail with wires attached to the dry cell. They may then note the magnetic quality of the nail in attracting objects when wires are attached to both terminals of the dry cell and the result when a wire is removed from one of the terminals.

Work

When force moves through distance, work is produced. A force applied and moving through a distance is the input that accomplishes work. There is work output as an object is moved through a distance. Input and output forces may be unequal if the distance over which the input force travels is greater than the distance the output force is required to travel. The operation of the human body incorporates this principle. The use of such simple machines as levers, pulleys, inclined planes, and wheels is based on this principle, and these devices are the foundations of all the complex machinery operating within our culture.

Use of the windlass can contribute to an understanding of the work concept. A windlass is an axle with wheels attached to each end and is used to lift weights. This device can be utilized to enhance understandings of not only work but also circumference, diameter, area, angular speed, linear speed, and force. Weights or objects can be lifted a specified distance, with children first turning and counting the revolutions of the smaller wheel, and then repeating the process with the larger wheel. The force exerted on each wheel can be compared, and the concept will be realized operationally and perceptually. Pulleys can be used to demonstrate the same principle, for the greater the distance of the hand on the rope from the object to be lifted, the less must be the force of the hand's pull on the rope, since the pulley is a form of wheel.

The lever can also be used to demonstrate the concept of work. In the lever, the greater the distance of the point at which pressure is exerted from the fulcrum, the less that force must be to equal the force of the weight to be lifted on the arm on the opposite side of the fulcrum. There are several kinds of levers, each determined by the position of the fulcrum in relation to the forces operating. Some objects children may manipulate to aid their understanding of the principle of the lever are a crowbar, a claw hammer, a manual can-opener, and scissors (double levers, with the fulcrum being the screw that holds the two cutting edges together). Children should be encouraged to examine these objects to determine the operating forces and the positions of the fulcrums. Other levers they will be familiar with are pliers, nutcrackers, oars, fishing rods, and various parts of the body.

Inclined planes can illustrate work most successfully. Children may pull the same object up planes of varying lengths and elevations and then contrast the force needed in each case to lift the object. Older children may measure distance and force extended. Work may also be illustrated by allowing objects to roll down inclined planes so that they move other stationary objects at the foot of the planes. Taking into account the mass of the objects, the amount of work accomplished can be assessed by measuring the distance the stationary objects were moved.

Energy

Energy is the ability to do work or to create an effect. Since energy is a capacity, it is not always realized. Potential energy is the capacity contained within the mass of a motionless object not yet put into use. When the object begins to move, potential energy becomes kinetic energy. Kinetic energy becomes energy-in-transition when the effect is being produced and the flow of energy is being transferred to another object.

To illustrate potential, kinetic, and energy-in-transition phases in mechanical energy, a ball may be rolled down an inclined plane so that it strikes another object at the foot of the plane. Children may make dry-cell batteries and construct electrical circuits by using fuses made from small pieces of aluminum foil. Too much current flowing through the electrical circuit will cause a short circuit, and the foil will melt. Children may take apart such devices as radios, flashlights, and doorbells and then reconstruct them so that they will operate.

Momentum

Momentum is produced by the interaction of the same variables that produce energy. It can be regarded as a form of energy that dissipates as the object displays its tendency to keep moving. Many illustrations of momentum can be provided within the classroom. Two balls, varying in mass, may be rolled down a table at the same speed and parallel to each other. The places at which they touch the floor as they leave the table may be marked. As the mass of the ball increases, its momentum increases, and therefore the ball with more mass will touch the floor farther from the table than the ball with less mass. Manipulating the variables so that speed is kept constant may be achieved by placing two objects of different mass, such as a quarter and a dime, in a container and pushing it, on its side, down a table. The objects will continue their motion after the container has stopped. The article with the most mass travels farther and displays the most momentum.

CONCEPT FORMATION IN THE BIOLOGICAL SCIENCES

All of the physical science concepts discussed operate within the life sciences, within each living cell, and within the organization and behavior patterns in the life cycle of an organism.

Concepts that identify the characteristics of organisms and that are related to the survival of and change in organisms and groups of organisms are discussed in this section. Classroom activities that aid children's understanding of these concepts are presented in a later section.

Growth and Development

Growth is quantitative change in the structure or the appearance of an organism, whereas development is qualitative change in these aspects. For growth

and development to occur, the potential must be within the initial organization of the species. Actualization of the potential depends on the maturation of the organism. A plant stem that increases in height and thickness represents growth, whereas the appearance of leaves represents development.

Metabolism

Metabolism is the process by which an organism takes materials from the environment and then transports them throughout the structure to serve its energy needs. The unusable materials are then returned to the environment through excretion.

Reproduction

Reproduction and death produce the equilibrium of control of an organism in the balance of nature. Organisms produce a large enough number of offspring so that the species will continue in spite of death but not so large that the particular species will override its place in the balance of species necessary for the equilibrium of food chains, communities, and ecosystems. Predator-prey relationships, life-cycle factors, as well as population questions are closely related to reproduction.

Two kinds of reproduction, asexual and sexual, exist in the organic world. In asexual reproduction, the parent organism simply divides. In sexual reproduction there is a fusion of two independent sexual cells into one cell that contains the genetic characteristics of each parent cell. Ultimately, the new cell develops into a separate individual that contains the general species factors as well as individual genetic characteristics transmitted by its parents.

Most of the characteristics that distinguish male from female in the different species are related to the sexual role, either for attraction during the mating process (petals of flowers, bright colors of male birds) or for the rearing of the offspring (antlers of buck for protection, secreting organs of female mammals that produce food for the young).

Responsiveness and Adaptation

All organic life reacts to its environment. A species copes with its environment by making changes that enhance its survival prospects. Birds respond to weather patterns by migration. When a change in environment occurs, the organism experiences a change because it is sensitive to and responsive to its environment.

All species have adapted to the habitat in which they are found, for if they have not made such adaptation they would not have survived in that environment. Habitats are constantly changing too. Therefore the organism must make continual adjustments to remain in equilibrium with its environment. This struggle continues until the death of the organism.

Over a long period of time, species evolve certain structures and methods that help the members to operate optimally within their environments and enhance survival possibilities. These adaptations are structural (feet of birds), physiological, or behavioral. The inherited fitness of an organism to a particular environment determines its place in a community and its chances to survive within that community.

Community

No organism exists alone. It depends on an outer environment for its food supply and protection, and it contributes to that environment by acting as a link in the food chain and by exhibiting behavioral patterns that help to protect others of its species.

A community is composed of different kinds of organisms as well as the inorganic substances necessary for the fulfillment of the life cycles of the organisms within it. Within a community there is an association among all of the differing organisms and the nonorganic material. A community provides for the passage of materials and the transformation of energy for the life purposes of the organisms and the preservation of the nonorganic material.

Food Chains

The food-and-energy cycle within a community derives from the energy of the sun combined with nutrients from water, soil, and air. These nutrients are converted by green plants into a substance stored in their tissues. Herbivorous animals consume this substance, and it is transformed into animal tissue. Species of carnivorous animals consume the animal tissue of the herbivorous animals, and this matter is converted into the energy needed to sustain the carnivores. When mortality occurs, certain microorganisms transform decaying plant and animal tissue once more into the elements essential to the first level of the food chain, so they may again be combined into plants.

Equilibrium

Within a community there is competition for the use and consumption of the elements needed by organisms for survival. The intense competition results in predator-prey relationships and in mortality of the least fit. But the death of organisms is balanced by the overproduction of new individuals. And unless there is interference from some external force, such as the introduction of a new species or the extinguishment of an established species, the community is kept in equilibrium.

Ecosystems

Sub-communities exist within communities. This relationship between and among communities is called an ecosystem. A simple example of this concept is the complex of a community that includes a pond surrounded first by cattails and then by grasses. On the shore of the pond might be bushes zoned by trees that are surrounded by a thicket, which in turn merges into a forest. Each of the communities within this system supports a different balance of species. The flow of energy within ecosystems over a period of time leads to a conclusion of biotic succession. Communities and ecosystems change and decay. Sometimes they are destroyed altogether by forces such as flood, tornado, or war. The planet earth is one giant ecosystem.

Change

Change is continually evident in nature. The earth itself has changed. This has occurred over long spans of time by such events as glacial erosions producing or erasing land masses and over short periods of time by such forces as earthquakes or erupting volcanoes.

Fossil remains are an evidence of such earth changes, for they indicate that aquatic animals once occupied certain portions of land that centuries later are occupied by land animals.

ACTIVITIES TO DEVELOP LIFE-SCIENCE CONCEPTS

The most important element in a good school science program is having many living things in the classroom for the children to observe and to interact with. Terrariums, aquariums, tadpole nurseries, dish gardens, guppies, tortoises, rabbits, hamsters, guinea pigs, and chicks may all be cared for in a classroom. Children may also collect and care for invertebrates, investigate microorganisms, study flowers, birds, and leaves, and gather fossils for study and display.

It is not recommended that children in elementary school dissect any species of animal. Therefore, the best means of observing metabolic functions, such as respiration, digestion, and circulation, are through the use of the many commercial models depicting these processes in humans and animals. Children may be made aware of the similarity of functioning in all living organisms by participating in activities involving plants. For example, they may make ink prints of various kinds of leaves. The venation of the leaves may be examined, and the leaves may be classified as to type of venation. The function of the veins in a leaf may be compared to that of the veins in a human being.

Studying Marine Life and Plants

Children may choose to have one aquarium for the class, and some may wish to make their own individual aquariums. The container for an aquarium must be able to hold a rather large volume of water. The aquarium should be covered with glass most of the time and placed so that it will receive only an hour or so of sunlight a day. In the preparation of an aquarium, the sand must be washed several times. The bottom of the tank is then lined with sand at least one inch deep. The plants are placed in the sand so that the roots are covered securely. Water that has been left sitting for two days should be allowed to flow over the hand as the tank is filled so as not to displace the plants. After a day or so, the fish as well as snails and perhaps another scavenger, such as a catfish, may be added.

Goldfish will survive better in classroom temperatures than will tropical fish. Care should be taken as to the kinds of fish used, since some fish will eat other varieties. Fish should be fed every other day and given only the food that they can consume in ten minutes. Fish in any given aquarium should be about the same size, and a good rule of thumb is a length of one inch of fish for every gallon of water in the aquarium.

Children may make a tadpole nursery by collecting amphibian eggs from a pond and a quanity of the pond water. Eggs of frogs, toads, and tree frogs are suitable. Toad eggs appear in long strings; salamander eggs, in clusters with a mass of jelly around them; frog eggs, in clusters with no jelly around them. Children may watch the eggs and keep records of the changes in the animals after they hatch and develop and of the time periods involved. Some of the microorganisms in the pond water may be examined under a microscope.

A terrarium container may be made by taping pieces of glass together and placing the four-sided glass frame into a pan. If children are interested, they may each make their own individual terrariums. Plants for a terrarium should be gathered from the same environment, or they will not survive. The soil should also be brought from that environment. The amount of moisture given the plants should be gauged by the amount they would have received in their natural habitat.

Dish gardens are small terrariums planted in dishes, but only plants that survive in shallow soil can be used. Care should be taken so that dish gardens do not receive too much sun, for the soil is not deep and will dry out very quickly.

The relation of flowers to their habitat may be observed in many ways. Bulbs of the tulip, the daffodil, the hyacinth, and the narcissus may be planted in early spring within the classroom and "forced" into bloom. These forced flowers can then be compared to a control group in an outdoor garden. Flower specimens may be gathered from different kinds of habitats and compared as to likenesses and difference as well as classified within their subordinate and superordinate classes. These specimens may be preserved by enclosing them in waxed paper pressed along the edges with a warm iron.

Flowers in different habitats can be staked off in early spring, and children may observe and record the kinds of flowers found in each habitat and bring back to the classroom specimens of each type of flower. They may keep records of the dates on which different varieties bloom and die as well as descriptions of the habitats. Some likely habitats might be a shady spot, a sunny spot, a wooded area, a meadow, along a country road, a riverbank. Children may wish to transplant a specimen from one habitat to another and keep a record of what happens. They may also make drawings of the specimens they bring back or construct a chart showing the classification of the specimens according to some criterion.

Other Living Things in the Classroom

Other animals and plants may become a temporary or a permanent part of the classroom. Any pets brought from home on a temporary basis should have a place set aside for them.

Guppies are an inexpensive addition to the classroom. Desert tortoises as well as other kinds of turtles make good pets, too. Turtles require containers with water and flat rocks protruding from the water on which they can rest.

Tame rabbits may be purchased at a pet store and kept in a carton placed on its side with newspapers in one corner for excretion. The newspapers should be changed daily, whereas the carton should be replaced every week or so. The rabbit is happiest if allowed to wander about the room. Different varieties require different diets, so the sales person at the pet store should be consulted on the most beneficial diet for the particular rabbit.

Hamsters, guinea pigs, white mice, and white rats may also be classroom occupants, but these should be kept in cages and fed according to the directions given by the dealer. Some of these animals bite, so children should be urged to exercise caution.

Silkworm eggs may be purchased and, subsequently, silkworms may be raised. Children enjoy watching the eggs hatch and the worms emerge. Silkworms will spin their cocoons, from which silk thread is obtained. Their diet consists of mulberry leaves.

Chicks may be hatched and raised in the classroom. The class may purchase or make an incubator or buy a hen and a setting of fertile eggs.

Investigating Invertebrates

Invertebrates (animals without bony skeletons) fall into classes such as crustaceans (for example, crab, clam, crayfish), insects (grasshopper, praying mantis, honeybee, dragonfly, ladybug), and spiders. Specimens may be gathered and kept in appropriate habitats within the classroom. Fruit flies, a form of invertebrate, may be raised by putting a piece of ripe fruit in a glass jar and covering it. Crickets, grasshoppers, and katydids may be kept in a terrarium. Children will enjoy watching grasshoppers as they lay eggs, molt, and eat. A hand lens is useful in examining these animals without having to touch them. Children may keep records of each type of invertebrate and of all their observations. They may draw illustrations of them and use these pictures or the names of the invertebrates to make a chart that shows their classification.

Investigating Microorganisms

Microorganisms must be viewed through a microscope. This class of organisms includes both plants (for example, mold, mildew, yeast, bacteria) and animals (amoeba, paramecium). These organisms enrich soil, cause decay and disease, and help to create foods such as cheese, bread, and alcohol.

These organisms may be raised in the classroom by setting aside a slice of potato for a few days, by gathering several samples of pond water (some from the bottom and some from the top for comparison purposes), or by making a mixture, such as that made by placing an overripe banana in water mixed with some vacuum cleaner dirt and allowing the solution to set for a week. After a few days, slides containing each of these mixtures may be examined under a microscope.

Microscopic examination demands both wet mounts and dry mounts. Microorganisms require wet mounts. Some of the liquid in which the specimens are living may be drawn up in a medicine dropper, which is held vertically for a second or so to allow the protozoa or bacteria to fall to the bottom. After a drop of the liquid is placed on the slide, the cover is carefully placed on the specimen. Wet mounts for molds require one part each of alcohol and water. Solids require dry mounts. A thin section of the solid should be sliced off with a single-edged razor. The slice should be thin enough for light to pass through. This can then be placed in the center of the slide and the cover placed on it.

There are other activities involving microorganisms that can be devised. For example, children may examine specimens under a hand lens or a microscope before and after exposing them to nutrient agar. Children should be encouraged to read about the life and discoveries of Louis Pasteur as well as other great microbiologists.

Bird Watching

Before going on a bird-watching expedition, each child should consult an encyclopedia and make index cards listing information about the birds in the particular area. There should be an index card listing the various characteristics of each species of bird: type of bill, type of feet, colors, general outline, how the bird flies, wing movements, position of feet when flying, type of birdcall, nesting places. When the child sees a bird, he notes on the card where and when it was seen and what it was doing. When considerable data have been gathered on a particular bird, a report may be written and illustrated. These reports may be compiled into a book and added to the reference section of the classroom until the end of the school year.

Investigating Fossils

Fossils may be the remains of animals, tracks, prints, or casts left in stone. Fossils reveal much about the change that has taken place over centuries on the earth and about the kinds of animals that once inhabited certain areas.

A group of children may go fossil hunting after they have consulted encyclopedias and know approximately what they are looking for. The main classifications of fossils are brachiopods, amphibians, and trilobites. After children bring back their specimens, they may check the identification again and make an illustration of the fossil or of the way they think the earth might have looked when the fossils they found were imprinted. As part of an exhibit, they may wish to make a chart that shows classification of the fossils.

Children may make imitation fossils that will illustrate to them the process by which fossils are formed. For example, seashells coated with Vaseline may be placed in a pan of creamy plaster shallow enough so that the shells are not totally immersed. The surface of the hardened plaster is also coated with Vaseline, and more creamy plaster is poured into the container until the shells are covered. When this layer of plaster is hardened, the plaster is split at the point at which the Vaseline was placed, and the seashells are removed.

EVALUATION IN THE SCIENCE PROGRAM

Much that has been stated on evaluation in other chapters equally applies to the science program. That is, evaluation is an intrinsic part of learning, and the objective of all efforts toward effective evaluation is that of getting the individual to assess his or her own learning.

Certainly an overall assessment of the effectiveness of a science program may be determined by the eagerness with which children engage in activities and by their absorption while participating in them. Evaluation of individual concept-formation can perhaps best be done by talking with the child and probing his thoughts. In order to ascertain whether the child really understands the concept under consideration, he may be given a sample problem and asked to predict the outcome and then solve the problem.

As suggested throughout this book, anecdotal records of each child should be kept. In science education, these records should include the activities the child participates in, his reactions when successful or frustrated, and the quality of the displays or exhibits he produces. The child, too, should keep an ongoing record of his science activities. He may include the date of the activity, the procedure used, and the results obtained. Young children cannot keep such a record, but from seven years of age on, record keeping should be part of the evaluation process.

Piagetian tasks can be used to evaluate the child's understanding of physical concepts. An excellent source of information on this area is *The Growth of Basic Mathematical and Scientific Concepts in Children*.[14] Checklists for recording specific logical thinking tasks and seriation and classification skills may also be used.

Every effort should be made by teachers to delve beneath the child's behavior and his answers to questions to discover the route by which he arrived at his action or response. The child's thought processes rather than the response should be the teacher's concern.

As has surely been noted from considering the activities included in this chapter, science cannot be realistically separated from the other curricular areas. Science activities demand reading, listening, writing, speaking, and mathematics skills as well as knowledge of art, music, and social studies. Thus, in studying the chapters that discuss these areas, the reader will gain greater understanding of science education and will begin to see the possibilities for aiding children in the integration of all learning.

EXERCISES FOR THOUGHT AND ACTION

1. For children of a specific age level, devise a manipulative game that will provide practice in the development of classification or seriation skill.

---

14. Lovell, *Growth of Basic Mathematical and Scientific Concepts.*

2. Make a set of activity cards and gather the necessary materials for children to use in investigating one of the concepts stated in this chapter.
3. Collect materials from some of the science programs currently on the market and evaluate them.
4. Make an annotated bibliography of trade books on science topics or on the lives of scientists that would be of interest to children of a particular grade level.
5. Make a list of the noncommercial science materials you would like to have in your classroom and investigate their cost.
6. Make a three-dimensional scale model of a classroom arrangement that would accommodate individual and small-group investigation in the science area. Model your approach on the "centers" concept.
7. Bring from your home materials that could be useful in a creative science program. Organize these into collections and write corresponding directions for their use.

SELECTED READINGS

Bruner, J.R. *Toward a Theory of Instruction*. New York: W.W. Norton & Co., 1966, chaps. 3 and 6. Develops theories on how learning takes place and on the nature of instruction. These theories take into account the child's desire to learn.

Jacobson, Willard J. *The New Elementary School Science*. New York: Van Nostrand Reinhold Co., 1970, chaps. 1-5 and 19-21. An overview of elementary science education as related to child development, to approaches to learning, and to the nature of science. A look at available science programs and materials as well as methods of evaluating science learning.

Karplus, R. "The Science Curriculum Improvement Study." In *Piaget Rediscovered*, edited by R. Ripple and V. Rockcastle. An evaluation of the SCIS program by its author and a detailing of the goals of the program in terms of today's society.

Lovell, K. *The Growth of Basic Mathematical and Scientific Concepts in Children*. London: University of London Press, 1966, chaps. 1 and 5-10. An explanation of how concept formation takes place and specific tasks to evaluate concept formation in the areas of substance, space, time, weight, length, measurement, area, and volume.

Piaget, Jean. *Science of Education and the Psychology of the Child*. New York: Viking Press, 1971, part 1, chaps. 4 and 8; part 2, chaps. 1 and 2. An explanation of various types of teaching methods and of the origination and basis of the new methods as related to educational principles and psychological findings.

Wartofsky, M. *Conceptual Foundations of Scientific Thought*. New York: Macmillan Co., 1968, chaps. 11-15. Attention is given to the explanation of causality, space, time, matter, organisms, mechanisms, and the relationship of science to human values.

Anyone who has attended many of the ever-increasing-in-number art exhibits is aware of the growing interest in art, in the willingness of more and more people to produce (and exhibit) the products of their creative efforts, and in the wide range of media used to produce works of art. Art is an "in" thing, and forecasters indicate that it will remain so.

The author of this chapter captures the essence of the art curriculum in the elementary school. She explores the content of programs, suggests many art-related activities, and guides the reader to other authors for more detail and ideas.

The principal focus of the chapter is on encouraging children to react to the environmental elements created by nature and by human beings; to sharpen their perceptions, which go beyond sensory reception; and to create art products. The importance of art as an discipline also receives attention. The author advocates that children should be allowed to discover for themselves and be taught directly facets of the discipline. As in other chapters, consideration is given to the development stages of children's growth and to procedures, media, and activities suitable to each stage.

The author of this chapter wishes to acknowledge the assistance of Professor Ivan Johnson, head of the Department of Art Education at Florida State University, in the development of this chapter.

W.T.P.

Creative Expression Through Art

Juanita G. Russell

12

There is a mosaic characteristic about the experiences a person has with the world—a mosaic created by the simultaneous interaction of sensations and perceptions. The multiple sights, sounds, and feelings of a New York City street can create an overall impression of joy or disgust. Gray skies, which threaten to add more snow to the already grimy slosh being spattered on pedestrians by noisy, erratic traffic, may depress the high spirits of a passerby; but the sunshine breaking through the overcast sky often restores his buoyant spirits.

Each individual reacts to the complex of an experience differently. Perceptually alert and aesthetically sensitive individuals respond to more than the total impression; they are aware of the components as well. They ask of themselves questions like the following: What shapes are present? Are they sharp-edged or fuzzy, light or dark, rough or smooth, dull or shiny, large or small? What colors contribute to the total emotional impression of happiness or gloom? Are there patterns of movement, sound, or smell? On the other hand, individuals who are less perceptually alert may react only to the total experience. They may perceive only that the day is dull and gray.

Perceiving is more than instinct. It is really seeing and identifying, not just looking; it is comprehending and assimilating, not just hearing. It is a total response to such sensations as rhythmic patterns of traffic, pulsating sounds of the city, cold splashings of rainwater from passing cars and from children running down the street, sounds of engines, of music, of language. Responses to these sensations are more than simple receptions of sensory inputs; they involve thinking and seeking to discover. In this manner, perceptions are made more acute, and individuals are able to more fully interact with their environment.

Teachers must seek to help children sharpen their perceptions, respond to aesthetic qualities, learn modes of inquiry for discovering patterns in the environment, and expand the nature of their actions and reactions. Most art educators claim they have not only advocated but also have done teaching that emphasizes art as a vehicle for sharpening perceptions and expanding reaction processes. Art teachers who are adequately trained have encouraged understanding and appreciation of the world of art by urging children to respond to works of art and by providing for individual expression in the various media.

CHANGES IN ART EDUCATION

Historically, art education in schools has reflected the economic needs of the country and the shifting view of the role art plays in the culture. As a result, art programs have grown in scope and depth, and children's experiences have become richer and their creative work more appreciated. Many art programs in elementary schools retain some practices related to earlier emphases. A look at the historical development of art education may serve to explain the presence of these practices.

Early Art Education

Prior to the midnineteenth century, art was a part of the cultural education provided in private schools for those young socialites who would have the leisure time to enjoy it. There was little time in the lives of children in public school for education in the fine arts.

Near the beginning of the twentieth century, the curriculum stressed the training of youth for an adult life of productive contributions to society. Part of that education included training in eye-hand coordination for legible handwriting, map making, and mechanical drawing. This "linear drawing" program emphasized perspective, classic proportion, and line. The prescribed subject matter included memorizing principles related to size, distance, and angles as well as learning, step by step, how to copy designs and objects. The teacher-planned activities were based on exercises for the pupil to copy so that she could reproduce such subjects as basic shapes and geometric designs, water pitchers and goblets, lines of railway tracks and telephone poles, color wheels, stereotyped designs of houses, animals, and people. The step-by-step lessons led to much uniformity of teaching and conformity by pupils who could be neither expressive nor creative. There was little coordination of art with other subjects. The blue-printlike precision learned in these activities was meant to be transferred to industrial work to further the development of the society. Children's personal experiences and contemporary situations were seldom integrated into the program. There was a striving for photographlike representation of objects rather than for the expression of impressions, feelings, and interpretations.

Child-Centered Curriculum

As noted in earlier chapters, the shift to a child-centered curriculum occurred about 1920. This new approach influenced the art program. There was a gradual increase in emphasis on self-expression, in which the child was encouraged to express his emotional reactions to daily life in visual form. Involvement in art meant emotional release and provided a means for developing creativity. The classroom was viewed as a laboratory for learning to live in the larger outside world. Teachers were encouraged to give children the freedom for natural growth, which purportedly would foster greater self-motivation and aid the development of intellectual abilities through problem-solving activities. Emphasis was placed on discovering how to learn the knowledge, skills, and strategies necessary for solution of immediate problems and of those problems anticipated in future adult life.

A "materials approach" to art education received increased attention. There was much experimentation with various materials that included scraps of cloth, string, paper, wood, vegetables, leaves and twigs, plaster of Paris, clay, sponges, and paint. This approach emphasized the idea that art is everywhere and that the individual could freely express herself through a host of materials.

Art textbooks continued to be used throughout the development of this movement. These books covered such topics as freehand drawing, perspective, and composition. Picture study was presented in booklets of gravure reproductions of so-called masterpieces. The reproductions were so reduced in size and lacking in color (although some were sepia-toned) that perspective and composition were generally the only topics that could be studied.

Attention to the child's creativity developed and increased markedly after World War II. The relation of psychology to art began to receive prominent attention. The influence of Viktor Lowenfeld (and his predecessor by a generation, Betty Lark-Horovitz, art teacher at the Cleveland Museum of Art) was felt.[1] Lowenfeld stressed that all children pass through certain recognizable periods and stages in their responses to art and in their expression of art. Their modes of artistic expression and production are identifiable and give the teacher clues to the developmental stage of each child and to his interests and skills. From those clues and from other information, the teacher can make some judgments about the strategies that may motivate and stimulate further growth and development of each child.

Lowenfeld also claimed that children fall into three categories: visual, haptic,

---

1. Viktor Lowenfeld and W. Lambert Brittain, *Creative and Mental Growth*, 4th ed. (New York: Macmillan Co., 1964).

nonidentifiable. Visual children closely observe their environment, and in re-creating it through their artwork, they give much information about their visual perceptions. Haptic children perceive themselves as the central actors in their environment. Their artwork reflects the amount of emotional value placed on various parts of that environment. The children who are labeled nonidentifiable are distinctly neither visual nor haptic.

More Recent Trends

The shift in curricular emphasis to the disciplines, with a focus being given to structure or logical order, was reflected in elementary school art programs. While the materials and activities approaches continued to be used because they appealed to the interests and needs of children, there was (and still is) an attempt to get the child to think and work as the artist does.

As in most curriculum areas, professional writing indicates the ideas and trends in art education, but the extent of each movement and the degree to which the application of the various techniques and ideas actually permeated elementary school art classes is less readily verified. Traditionally, time and money have not been allotted to art education because it has been viewed by most parents and by many educators as a low-priority concern. That belief still persists generally, and it is very likely that many schools have little, if anything, that may honestly be termed *art education*.

THE ELEMENTARY PROGRAM TODAY

Art programs in the elementary school curriculum today usually treat the nature of art as a discipline. The emphasis is on the learning of art principles: "Design is the structure of any art form" or "The elements of form or design are line, mass and space, light and shade, texture, and color." Technical ways of working with materials and tools are taught. Children learn to approach art as the serious artist does: They are encouraged to know what they want to communicate and to choose the media with which to say it. On the other hand, freedom of expression and open ways of seeing and working are recognized as necessary in the development of personal styles of learning and living. Through program procedures and teacher guidance, pupils learn to develop these styles. The child is also encouraged to apply her assimilated knowledge of the structure of other disciplines to discover through inquiry the structure and knowledge of art as a discipline.

While encouraging this discovery, the teacher also directly teaches facets of the discipline. There is no substitute for dealing directly with media, but children cannot learn all they need to know simply by working with a medium, such as tempera paint. From the very beginning of their involvement in the art program, children need some direct instruction on such topics as the attributes of the medium, such as its transparency or opaqueness and its permanency or temporality; various techniques for working with a particular medium; and examination of works of art created with the medium.

Discussion sessions after a work period are a necessary part of the process of learning about media, techniques, and elements of art. Children need a chance to describe how they went about producing their painting or other art object, the decisions they made regarding the use of a particular medium or a particular technique, what effects they tried to create, what—if anything—they were trying to show or say or represent. In a psychologically warm, accepting classroom environment, children will risk trying new things and talking about their efforts without fear of adverse criticism. The teacher is ultimately responsible for establishing and maintaining the appropriate learning climate.

Instruction and learning should spread beyond the confines of the classroom and the art room, or laboratory. Children should observe and study in many settings the works of designers, artists, architects, and urban developers. The place of visual form in all life should be stressed, but the art program should encompass other forms of the fine arts as well. Activities in many areas of the curriculum, such as social studies, science, and language arts, should reinforce concepts learned in the art program.

Planning the Art Program

Art is a special way of seeing, or knowing, and of presenting ideas, emotions, and dreams. As children develop perceptions about their world, they may learn some skills and acquire some knowledge without formal instruction. But art (like reading, for example) can be learned more efficiently and productively through an *organized* instructional program that is comprehensive and has long-range goals. Such a program should include:

1. The productive aspect, in which the child interacts with art media and communicates her feelings about the media, the world, and herself
2. The critical aspect, in which the child learns to evaluate her own creative efforts
3. The cultural-historical aspect, in which the child learns about her own heritage and that of other people

The Objectives of Art Instruction

The main purpose of education, according to some leading educators, is "the preparation of the individual to do in a better way all the desirable things he will do anyway."[2] Once enrolled in school, a child will continue to interact with his surroundings just as he did before stepping into the school environment. As the child progresses through the grades, he will continue to observe and to experiment with the objects, the materials, and the people around him; to absorb various sensations and perceptions and to assimilate them into his concepts of reality; and to communicate, through various means, his ideas and reactions to whatever he experiences.

The art program has a legitimate role in this process if, as many art educators

2. Harry A. Greene and Walter T. Petty, *Developing Language Skills in the Elementary Schools,* 4th ed. (Boston: Allyn & Bacon, 1973), p. 5.

advocate, it places great emphasis on art as the vehicle for improving a child's aesthetic perceptions and his contemplations about the world and for increasing his influence on the scheme of things. Likewise, the program is defensible if, as other art educators stress, the emphasis is on art as a vehicle for serving individual needs for emotional release, diversity of expression, enlightening the imagination and sensitivities, or developing the personality.

Regardless of the differences in emphases, art programs have some objectives in common. Most elementary school programs seek to assist children in:

1. Sharpening their perceptions and sensitivities to aesthetic qualities in the environment
2. Building mental structures for processing information so that they can better understand the world
3. Acquiring modes of inquiry and alternative approaches for problem solving
4. Developing ways of encoding and communicating visually
5. Studying the nature of art as a discipline
6. Learning art concepts, principles, and techniques for working with media and tools
7. Developing personal styles of learning and expressing
8. Understanding the contributions of artists, past and present, to the culture
9. Learning to respond to and engage in discourse about works of art[3]

Program Organizations

An effective art program has an overall plan, or design, to provide continuity and balance in content, processes, and media. There are many options open to elementary school art teachers in planning their programs and individual school-wide programs. Initially, teachers need to consider the particular grade or developmental level of the children. Next they should analyze and select the art concepts that might be suitable for the children to learn. They also need to analyze various processes for cognitive growth and determine whether the skills needed to manipulate the media are appropriate to the children's abilities.

Theme-Based Organization

In planning for the entire year, the teacher may relate art content, skills, media, and activities to a series of themes (for example, zoo animals, farm animals). The children may observe live animals, films about animals, and pictures of animals. In guided discussions, they would discover the shapes, sizes, colors, textures, and other characteristics of the animals. In representing what they have perceived and learned, the children should choose the media that would best express their feelings, that they felt most confident in using, or that they wished to experiment with in order to find out more about its particular properties.

---

3. For further information concerning objectives for elementary school art programs, see Elliot W. Eisner, *Educating Artistic Vision* (New York: Macmillan Co., 1972) and Warren H. Anderson, *Art Learning Situations for Elementary Education* (Belmont, Calif.: Wadsworth Publishing Co., 1965).

Unit-Based Organization

The teacher may plan a program around a series of units involving art content. The program may include units on color, forms, space and mass, design, model making, surfaces and textures, weaving, and printmaking. As an example, a unit of surfaces and textures may involve instruction and practice with different media, tools, and techniques that produce shiny surfaces; dull surfaces; bright surfaces; monochromatic or multichromatic surfaces; and smooth, wavy, or rough textures.

The activities should coincide with the children's interests and ability levels. Children in the third and fourth grades, for instance, may make clay and papier-mâché sculptures by using the additive and subtractive methods, create prints by using paint, and stitch with yarn to create designs. The works of past and present artists may be included in the art program so that children can examine, compare and contrast, and evaluate the ways in which various artists utilize colors, forms, or space and mass to express visually what they have tried to communicate.

Other Types of Program Organization

Other organizational options open to the teacher include planning the course content within the social studies, literature, music, or other programs. Or the program may focus on various media and would involve the techniques and tools for working in each medium.

Some art education books contain a suggested scope and sequence plan for an elementary school's total art program or a planned program for a particular grade level. These plans, which are often criterion-referenced, are based on the belief that children need to know the elements of art, some techniques and processes to use with various media, the language and vocabulary of art, and some knowledge of the contributions made by individuals in the fields of design, architecture, and other branches of art. Recently published textbooks for elementary school children contain lessons that can be used by a teacher who has a minimal background in art education. Thus, the recommended eighty to one hundred minutes of art instruction per week could be provided in a sequenced, comprehensive manner.[4]

An Example: One School's Art Program

Art in the Maryvale U-Crest School program is considered a manifestation of human expressive capability.[5] The purpose of the program is to expand each child's expressive capability without intimidation by self or group-imposed adult standards for her productions. This position is advocated by the school personnel, since the destruction of individual initiative results if the child feels that the scope

4. For example, see Guy Hubbard and Mary J. Rouse, *Art: Meaning, Method, and Media,* Books 1-6 (Westchester, Ill.: Benefic Press, 1972).
5. U-Crest Elementary Srhool, Maryvale District, Cheektowaga, N.Y.; Gulio Michienzi, art teacher; James Mancuso, principal.

of her expressive capability cannot be brought into favorable alignment with her perception of the accepted standard. Motivation for achieving the purpose of this program is shared by the art teacher and classroom teacher.

The physical environment consists of a studio that includes work centers that feature activities ranging from drawing and painting to printmaking and woodworking. None of the work centers is exclusive to any of the children, who range from first graders to fifth graders. The only requirement for access to any work center is the child's desire for involvement.

A primary pupil who wishes to work with wood is introduced to the nature and function of the tools with which she will be working. A child of this age would spend a good deal of the time in free exploration of the tools. In fact, the child generally consumes a great deal of energy by sawing, drilling, and nailing and often exhibits only a secondary interest in the completion of the product.

A pupil in one of the intermediate grades, more experienced in the use of materials and tools, will channel her efforts toward the development of specific products that usually involve more complex construction than those made by younger children. However, learning about the materials she needs to work with should not be neglected. Thus, her interest and desire to build a particular product may require her to learn about blueprints, for example, and to do considerable reading and research.

A unique feature in this kind of associated, or integrated, learning just described is the open access to the library resource center, a complex of rooms immediately adjacent to the studio. The card catalog in the library has a special section for each work center. The physical and philosophical joining of these two centers of activity provides a stimulating interplay between what sometimes appear to be separate factors of the learning process; that is, the academic aspect and the creative enterprise.

The Maryvale U-Crest School art program has work centers in graphics, painting, pottery, jewelry (including leather, metal embossing), weaving, fabrics (stenciling, design, and dyeing), casting (sand, clay, fresco preparation), model construction (including working models), and sculpture (wood, cardboard, paper, vermiculite, metal, plaster). Each work center contains displays of products, and music is played throughout the centers to add to the studio atmosphere.

EVALUATION OF ART PROGRAMS

Evaluation of art instruction is essential, but the nature of the fine arts as well as the imperfections in the methods of assessing the attainment of specific objectives often make this difficult. Art teachers should be capable of designing informal evaluative instruments for assessing their programs and the achievements of the children in those programs. They can develop tests on content taught; construct checklists, observation forms, and inventories; and prepare anecdotal reports to measure and record information about the children's learning. An example of a checklist for recording the progress of a child in a given medium is the first evaluation sheet on the facing page.

Evaluation Sheet

Name of Student _____   Medium _____

Date _____

Objective   Effectiveness

The child is able to:

1. List the characteristics of the medium

2. Use vocabulary appropriate to the medium; discuss the possible effects produced by use of the medium; and indicate the range of expression the medium may cover

3. Identify works done by artists who have used the medium

4. Choose appropriate processes and situations for using the medium

5. Select appropriate tools for working in the medium

6. Display appropriate and well-developed techniques when working in the medium

   Comments:

Another example is the evaluation sheet below. This list may be used for a total year's program. It is based on the curriculum developed by Guy Hubbard and Mary J. Rouse.[6]

Evaluation Sheet

Name _____
Date _____   Grade _____

Objectives   Effectiveness

Learning to perceive   (Circle One)

The child shows evidence that he:
1. Perceives familiar shapes as visual cues   +   √   —

2. Aurally recognizes music and perceives its effects on his art productions   +   √   —

3. Uses sense of touch to evaluate textures   +   √   —

4. Draws simple objects from memory   +   √   —

---

6. Hubbard and Rouse, *Art: Meaning, Method, and Media.*

Learning the language of art

The child shows evidence that he:

1. Is refining and expanding his knowledge of   +   ✓   –
   art concepts and vocabulary as he discusses
   the language of art and the elements of art

2. Is drawing parallels between the language of   +   ✓   –
   art and the language of music

3. Is learning the design ideas of:
   • symmetrical and asymmetrical balance   +   ✓   –
   • rhythm   +   ✓   –
   • dominance   +   ✓   –

4. Is learning art history terms and concepts,
   such as:
   • portrait art   +   ✓   –
   • landscape art   +   ✓   –
   • realism   +   ✓   –

Learning about artists in American history

The child shows evidence that he:

1. Knows the roles of painters, sculptors, and   +   ✓   –
   architects

2. Sees the effects of artists' backgrounds, en-   +   ✓   –
   vironments, and interests on their works

3. Recognizes art forms used by artists   +   ✓   –

4. Knows the contributions of artists to the   +   ✓   –
   progress of the nation

Judging and criticizing art
The child shows evidence that he:

1. Is verbally expressing his reactions to works   +   ✓   –
   of art

2. Is adding further objective criteria to his
   earlier understandings of:
   • balance   +   ✓   –
   • dominance   +   ✓   –
   • visual cues   +   ✓   –
   • rhythm   +   ✓   –
   • design   +   ✓   –
   • originality   +   ✓   –

3. Is discovering and interpreting the meanings
   of the artwork

Learning to use art tools and materials

The child shows evidence that he:

1. Is using tools and materials from previous
   learnings, such as:
   • crayons   + ✓ –   • scissors   +   ✓   –
   • papier mâché + ✓ –   • pencils   +   ✓   –
   • paste   + ✓ –   • paint   +   ✓   –
   • clay   + ✓ –   • yarn   +   ✓   –
   • templates   + ✓ –   • stencils   +   ✓   –

2. Is expanding uses of materials and tools,
   such as:
   • plaster for sculpturing   +   ✓   –
   • waxed paper for unusual effects   +   ✓   –

• ink and brayers for monoprinting	+	✓	−
• cardboard for scoring and making sculptures	+	✓	−

Building productive artistic abilities

The child shows evidence that he:

1. Is making more complex and interesting designs by using newly learned concepts	+	✓	−
2. Is making art projects, such as:			
• pictures expressing feelings	+	✓	−
• pictures distorting human figures	+	✓	−
• puzzle designs	+	✓	−
• "feelie" sculptures	+	✓	−
• monoprints	+	✓	−
• plaster shapes	+	✓	−

THE TEACHER'S ROLE IN TODAY'S ART PROGRAM

The classroom teacher is important to the success of any curriculum area in the school program. While some schools have special art teachers who either teach the art classes or serve as consultants—or do both—the classroom teacher largely sets the stage for effective teaching. More commonly, the classroom teacher has complete responsibility for the art program. How effective the classroom teacher is in either role depends on many elements.

One major factor is the teacher's attitude toward art and its place in a child's education. If the teacher views art as a worthwhile endeavor to be valued for itself and to be used as yet another vehicle to motivate and to teach children, art permeates the entire classroom curriculum and the various approaches taken to facilitate learning. Activities to develop art skills and knowledge are planned and sequenced to complement the entire classroom program.

Another important factor is the teacher's knowledge of art production and evaluation. A teacher who feels she is not "artistic" or "creative" may tend to de-emphasize art and may not be able to "squeeze it" into the schedule. This teacher may also resort to activities that involve the coloring of stereotyped pictures or to the tracing, coloring, cutting, and pasting of preprinted forms so that children march home at holiday time with identical Thanksgiving turkeys and Indian headbands. These affect art learning adversely.

The issues of space and materials, although somewhat less crucial, are also related to the effectiveness of an art program. While it is desirable to have a separate, fully equipped art room and an art teacher who is constantly available to the children, a teacher who is anxious to have an art program will find space in which children can work. Whether she incorporates art in the regular program or has a separate art program, she will utilize the children's regular desks, the hall, the classroom floor, or any other available space. She will request materials from administrators and will encourage children to help collect other art-related materials, such as cloth, shells, seeds, paper, dyes and other coloring media.

The classroom teacher is, of course, the person in the best position to know what each child's interests are, what level on the various concepts and skills continuums each child has reached, and how each child attacks problems and persists in seeking solutions.

MEDIA AND ACTIVITIES APPROPRIATE TO CHILDREN'S DEVELOPMENT

Children's growth and development have been discussed in Chapter 2 and referred to in the chapters discussing curriculum areas. Art educators have identified five stages of a child's growth and development as related to their study of art: scribbling, preschematic, schematic, dawning realism, and pseudonaturalism.[7] The attempts of a few children in the earliest primary grades may still take the form of random to patterned scribbles, but most of the children in the scribbling stage are in the age range of two to four years old. And since the vast majority of children in kindergarten through second grade will be in the preschematic stage, we will begin our discussion with this stage of development.

The Preschematic Stage

Children in the preschematic stage may use tempera paints to dabble with, to cover objects they have made or found, to paint pictures, and to make prints and designs. Finger paints and large crayons are also appropriate media for children in this stage. Clay of a nonmessy type to manipulate and to model is a good medium for children to work with as are all kinds of paper to paint on, to cut and tear, to weave, to paste things on, to fold, to crease and crumple and construct with, and to make papier-mâché objects. String and yarn are fun to twist, to weave, to stretch and knot, to decorate other objects with, and to hang things on.

Some suitable activities include drawing with wide, soft wax crayons; painting with tempera paints, broad brushes and sheets of paper at least as large as eighteen-by-twenty-four inches; finger painting, less for the artistic effect than for the fun of working with it; and various activities with paper used alone or with mixed media, such as cut-and-paste picture making or the making of sculptures, masks, and forms in space from crushed, rolled, stripped, and glued paper.[8] Making collages and mosaics of different materials also is appropriate as is simple modeling, sculpting, and printmaking. Monoprinting with a variety of paints, vegetable and stick printing, and stenciling using shapes and cutaway designs so that positive and negative forms are shown are instructive and satisfying activities for children in the lower primary grades.

---

7. Lowenfeld and Brittain, *Creative and Mental Growth.*
8. For an excellent resource, see Pauline Johnson, *Creating with Paper: Basic Forms and Variations* (Seattle, Wash.: University of Washington Press, 1958).

The Schematic Stage

In the schematic stage, which roughly includes children between ages seven and nine, the rudimentary forms used previously gradually take on more definite though stylized shapes. A person is drawn with more detail; a house is constructed with a roof and sides and with windows and doors; trees are made with trunks and tops. Base lines anchor objects, in a row, to the earth, and the sky often hangs at the top of the picture as the child attempts to organize and somewhat balance his picture or composition. Relationship of object sizes and perspective within the picture may have little to do with reality. There is an attempt to tell visually everything the "artist" knows about an object or situation. Interiors and exteriors of houses and airplanes are shown, and top views and side views of fire engines are blended in a single form. Objects or important parts of objects often are depicted in greater and somewhat distorted detail. A fishing pole may extend directly from a person's shoulder, for example. Color is used forcefully but usually in a single hue and in a somewhat stereotyped manner.

The media used are generally the same as those suitable for earlier stages. Clay continues to be an important modeling medium. Children enjoy using it to make various shapes and to mold or coil it into pottery. Colored chalk and pressed charcoal are sometimes added to the list of media. Children may wish to experiment with different-sized brushes to produce the details they desire.

Paper of all kinds—from thin and transparent to heavy cardboard—is especially useful. Activities with paper involve crumpling, twisting, folding, or ripping it. Scissors will be needed to cut and score paper in order to achieve clean, smooth edges and greater detail. Various other paper products, such as straws, and miscellaneous materials, such as buttons and toothpicks, can be used to add detail. Constructing paper box sculptures is especially appealing to children in this stage.

Wood of different sizes and shapes may be glued together, sanded, textured with files, weathered or antiqued by hammering bits of chain or other objects into it. Driftwood or wood from local trees also may be examined, discussed, and used in multimedia compositions or in rubbings. Children in this stage usually are not mature enough to use the tools or techniques for carving wood or other materials used for sculpture, such as soapstone, nor are they generally able to use oil-based paint in activities such as printmaking. Tempera and other water-based paints may be used for printmaking and stenciling with sponges, carrots, or potatoes, and sticks for printing on cloth and paper.

Some exciting new media are transparent acetate material and blank film leader material. Children may draw on these with felt-tipped marking pens, paint, and wax crayons. Acetate and glass for making 35-mm. slides may be used to make designs with liquid soap and to paint on. Colored cellophane, fingernail polish, and colored lacquers may be used by the most advanced children in this group.

The Dawning Realism Stage

The beginning of the realism stage often is characterized by children's attempts to depict natural objects and conditions. Children approach their tasks more cautiously and experiment with the media in a more restrained manner. They are more critical of their products and sometimes will throw them away and begin anew.

Children in this stage make collages, string designs, woven objects, and abstract sculptures in their efforts to produce realism. There is an attempt to show perspective and visual accuracy by overlapping forms and by varying the sizes of objects. A horizon begins to emerge and greater balance of composition is the evident.

Different hues and intensities of colors are used as the children mix paints of various types, or re-cover parts of areas previously colored (shading, accenting, and detailing various shapes and areas). Children's attempts at special texture effects are apparently more to depict reality than to serve aesthetic purposes.

Several resource books are available for the art teacher who desires more ideas for processes and media appropriate to children in this stage and for the general classroom teacher who wishes to learn and to assist pupils. *Creative Printmaking . . . For School and Camp Programs* explains several processes, such as stencil printing, photographic printing, planographic printing, intaglio printing, contour drawing, crayon etching, as well as preparation of linoleum and plaster blocks and woodcuts.[9] *Weaving on Cardboard, Simple Looms To Make and Use* contains ideas and instructions for weaving activities for children of many ages.[10] The author shows how to do card weaving, weaving on plastic soda-straws, weaving on preformed cardboard, and how to make belts, placemats, designs, and other objects. Another useful book is *Block Printing on Textiles: A Complete Guide,* which has a good chapter on helping children learn the rudiments of block printing.[11] *Forms of Paper* is another valuable book that helps the teacher and others to learn cutting, curling, bending, folding, scoring, and making paper forms.[12] Many of the ideas and the projects are also suitable for older children.

The Pseudonaturalism Stage

Children in the pseudonaturalism stage, associated with eleven to thirteen year olds, show evidence of increasing skill and success in depicting realism. Greater control of media permits the young artist to use it to serve his purposes. There may be more obvious messages and reactions to society and environment in his art products.

There is less emphasis on use of tempera paint, except for the purposes of creating special effects and for covering large areas. Also, there is less interest in making box sculptures from paper and doing printmaking with materials such as vegetables. Most of the other materials used previously, including shells and rocks, continue to be used. Added to these are water paints, inks, charcoal,

9.   Michael F. Andrews, *Creative Printmaking . . . For school and Camp Programs* (Englewood Cliffs, N.J.: Prentice-Hall, 1964).
10.   Marthann Alexander, *Weaving on Cardboard, Simple Looms To Make and Use* (New York: Taplinger Publishing Co., 1972).
11.   Janet Erickson, *Block Printing on Textiles: A Complete Guide* (New York: Watson-Guptill Publications, 1961).
12.   Hiroshi Ogawa, *Forms of Paper* (New York: Van Nostrand Reinhold Co., 1971).

pastels, different-sized lead pencils, acrylic and oil-based paint, wood and soapstone.

For painting activities, the child may mix his own paints and experiment with altered colors and tones. With the teacher's help, he learns to avoid using every possible color in one composition. He now begins to use color to show light and shadows, shapes, and space in a balanced design. More intricate or better-designed stabiles, mobiles, and other forms and sculptures are created. Linoleum block printing with nonwater-based paints is achieved by using tools that are too dangerous for the younger child to experiment with. A number of books by Ernst Rottger provide excellent help for the teacher in aiding children to use these processes.[13] Making films and slides and creating light shows with music and narration are especially intriguing for this age group. Books that might be helpful include *Understanding the Media*,[14] *Children as Film Makers*,[15] and *Moviemaking Illustrated*.[16]

ART FOR SPECIAL CHILDREN

"Special," or "exceptional," children have been described in various ways. Most often children so labeled include the gifted, the physically handicapped, the emotionally disturbed, and the learning disabled, or slow learner. While these children may or may not be in classrooms with "average" children, they do participate in art programs.

Perhaps the largest number of "special" children are those who are considered to be slow learners. It is these children who need the most assistance and require the most patience and understanding, and it is to this group that the following discussion is aimed. For further discussion of ways to help most special children, the reader is directed to a book entitled *Art for the Exceptional*[17] and the publications of the National Art Education Association.[18]

The Value of Art for Slow Learners

Art can be of great value to slow learners by providing many opportunities for various types of experiences. In order to develop concepts, these children need to

13. Creative Play Series (New York: Van Nostrand Reinhold Co.): Ernst Rottger, *Creative Paper Design* (1961); Ernst Rottger, *Creative Wood Design* (1960); Ernst Rottger, *Creative Clay Design* (1963); Ernst Rottger and Dieter Klante, *Creative Drawing: Point and Line* (1962); Rolf Hartung, *Creating with Corrugated Paper* (1961).

14. Kit Laybourne, ed., *Doing the Media: A Portfolio of Activities and Resources* (New York: Center for Understanding Media, 1972).

15. John Lidstone and Don McIntosh, *Children as Film Makers* (New York: Van Nostrand Reinhold Co., 1970).

16. James Morrow and Murray Suid, *Moviemaking Illustrated: The Comicbook Filmbook* (Rochelle Park, N.J.: Hayden Book Co., 1973).

17. Chester J. Alkema, *Art for the Exceptional.* (Boulder, Colo.: Pruett Publishing Co., 1971).

18. Task Force of Specialists in Elementary Art Education, Task Force Chairman, Paul Greenberg, *Art Education: Elementary* (Washington, D.C.: National Art Education Association, 1972).

spend more than the normal amount of time with objects and processes—time that the art program can provide.

Another value of the art program is the fact that its individual nature provides the teacher with the opportunity to gain much information about the children's personalities and their achievement and developmental levels. Through their art products and the methods they use in attacking problems they encounter, children often will indicate various learning problems. Art long has been recognized, of course, for its therapeutic value, and the behavior accompanying release of tension can be observed by the teacher. Slow learners seem to derive more than average pleasure from art. They spend much time in repetitive tasks but less time exploring and using new media and techniques. The art program gives these children the opportunity to experiment with one technique and with one medium until they gain some success and satisfaction.

Methods, Media, and Activities

While the "standard" these children hold of their artwork usually is lower than that of their "average" classmates (their products often lack unifying elements and balance in composition), some very interesting details may be present in the finished products. The absence of proper perspective and of the use of differentiation of object size to indicate distance and depth suggests that many of these children may still be utilizing the concepts and techniques of the "average" children in their earlier and less mature stages of development. Thus, much about an art program for slow learners suggests that it should be not much different from that for average and gifted learners. Because these children take longer to learn strategies for utilizing information, more guidance and more specific instruction may need to be given. However, no teacher who genuinely believes that *all* children differ from one another in many ways will try to categorize these children into a single group and to treat them as if they were all the same. In the elementary school, these children may engage in a wide range of art activities: painting, drawing with various materials, sculpting and molding with clay and with papier mâché, weaving with yarn or paper or raffia or cloth, stitching designe, making puppets, using watercolor and crayon-etching techniques, making box and other paper sculptures, stenciling on various materials with different media, and so forth.

THE VALUE OF ART EDUCATION IN THE SCHOOL PROGRAM

The models for art education that have been devised generally include attention to the child's readiness to respond to the stimulating physical environment that has been organized, in part by the teachers, and to the cultural and psychological interactions within the classroom society. Also included in the theories is the consideration of the individual child's modes of learning and his manner of processing and using information. How he responds ultimately through his own creations and methods and how he evaluates his efforts and the efforts of others are a part of the theoretical model, as is the child's readiness for subsequent activities as judged by his integration and application of his new knowledge and skills.

The behaviors advocated and nurtured by art teachere are those with high probability of aiding creative problem-solving. Those behaviors include visually perceiving and contemplating one's environment, imagining, reorganizing, designing, modeling, manipulating, and evaluating. Creativity is the attribute unifying all these behaviors into a set of productive ones. As an attitudinal characteristic developed and honed over time from many behaviors, creativity is the certain aura or sense of security gained from having useful and valued competencies and is the result of a stimulating yet psychologically supportive environment that helps to give children a set of successful skills and meaningful achievements. These factors allow those children to risk failure with new approaches, to trust their ideas, and to seek new configurations and solutions.

Creativity and the development of creative potential long have been within the ambit of the arts and art education. As educators and others seek ways to develop thinking skills and cognitive structures in children so they can deal creatively with the complexity and the volume of problems in the world, these people might do well to study some of the attitudes, theories, and the practices that art educators long have advocated.

EXERCISES FOR THOUGHT AND ACTION

1. Plan a year's art program for a class of children at a particular grade level. This may be team-planned with a partner. Use the "Unit-Based Organization" and attend to the three aspects: the productive, the critical, and the cultural-historical. Remember to include appropriate objectives, activities, and evaluation strategies.

2. Visit a local school and observe children in art classes. Obtain samples of artwork from children and categorize them according to the several maturational levels described in this chapter.

3. Develop a set of tasks by which pupils, individually or in small groups, could learn more about the shapes, textures, and surfaces in a designated area of the local environment. Describe how these tasks could be related to an art program.

4. Discuss ways to integrate art into the social studies and the literature programs. What knowledge and skills can be developed in such an integrated curriculum?

5. Become familiar with at least two of the media, such as tempera paint, paper, water colors, crayons, wood, cardboard, used in elementary art by (1) discovering the characteristics of each (its properties and limitations), (2) using at least two different techniques or processes while working with them, and (3) producing three objects. Employing appropriate vocabulary, discuss your efforts and results with the class. Suggest other activities that involve use of these media.

SELECTED READINGS

Anderson, Warren H. *Art Learning Situations for Elementary Education*. Belmont, Calif.: Wadsworth Publishing Co., 1965.

Arnheim, Rudolf. *Art and Visual Perception*. 4th ed. Berkeley: University of California Press, 1964.

Barkan, Manuel; Chapman, Laura H; and Kern, Evan J. *Guidelines: Curriculum Development for Aesthetic Education*. St. Louis, Mo.: Central Midwestern Regional Educational Laboratory, CEMREL, 1970.

Baumgarner, Alice A.D., Director. *Conference on Curriculum and Instructional Development in Art Education: A Project Report*. Washington, D.C.: National Art Education Association, 1966.

D'Amico, Victor. *Creative Teaching in Art*. rev. ed. Scranton, Pa.: International Textbook, 1966.

Eisner, Elliot W. *Educating Artistic Vision*. New York: Macmillan Co., 1972.

Gaitskell, Charles D., and Hurwitz, Al. *Children and Their Art: Methods for the Elementary School*. rev. ed. New York: Harcourt, Brace & World, 1970.

Hastie, W. Reid, ed. *Art Education*. Sixty-fourth Yearbook of the National Society for the Study of Education. Chicago: University of Chicago Press, 1965.

Hausman, Jerome J., ed. *Report of the Commission on Art Education*. Washington, D.C.: National Art Education Association, 1965.

Hauenstein, A. Dean. *Curriculum Planning for Behavioral Development*. Worthington, Ohio: Charles A. Jones Publishing Co., 1972.

Lark-Horovitz, Betty; Lewis, Hilda Present; and Luca, Mark. *Understanding Children's Art for Better Teaching*. Columbus, Ohio: Merrill, 1967.

Lowenfeld, Viktor, and Brittain, W. Lambert. *Creative and Mental Growth*. 4th ed. New York: Macmillan Co., 1964.

Luca, Mark, and Kent, Robert. *Art Education: Strategies of Teaching*. Englewood Cliffs, N.J.: Prentice-Hall, 1968.

McFee, June King. *Preparation for Art*. 2nd ed. Belmont, Calif. Wadsworth Publishing Co., 1970.

Packwood, Mary M., ed. *Art Education in the Elementary School*. Washington, D.C.: National Art Education Association, 1967.

Piaget, Jean. *Education and Art*. Edited by Edwin Ziegfeld. Paris: UNESCO, 1953.

Rueschoff, Phil H., and Swartz, Evelyn. *Teaching Art in the Elementary School*. New York: The Ronald Press Co., 1969.

Schwartz, Fred R. *Structure and Potential in Art Education*. Waltham, Mass.: Ginn-Blaisdell, 1970.

Task Force of Specialists in Elementary Art Education, Task Force Chairman, Paul Greenberg. *Art Education: Elementary*. Washington, D.C.: National Art Education Association, 1972.

Yochim, Louise Dunn. *Perceptual Growth in Creativity*. Scranton, Pa.: International Textbook, 1967.

The reader will quickly note the close relationship of this chapter to the preceding ones in terms of concern for the development of each child, and as in other chapters, for the provision of individualized learning activities. Considerable attention is given to creativity, to the informal classroom, and to the relationship of music to the dramatic activities in Chapter 5.

The amount of detail concerning music concepts is a striking feature of this chapter; certainly much more is presented than is generally included in a single chapter. These concepts are presented in the spiral framework discussed in several other chapters, with alternative strategies suggested for teaching each concept. The emphasis in these alternatives is the active role of the pupil in creating, performing, analyzing, evaluating, and responding to music. The cognitive aspects of the chapter are balanced by suggestions for providing affective experiences through music.

Since music is one of the curriculum areas that is sometimes taught by a specialist, sometimes by the regular classroom teacher, and sometimes by both of them, suggestions are given for maximizing the learning in each situation.

W.T.P.

Musical Environments for Every Child

T. Temple Tuttle

13

Music is a curricular area that has often been given only incidental attention in elementary school programs. Of course, schoolchildren have always sung as they sought to relax and enjoy themselves; they have also frequently accompanied their singing with rhythmic body movements and with instruments. However, a music program that goes beyond such singing and the related learning of new songs has often depended on the teacher's musical interest and talent. To a considerable extent this is still true, although most schools now indicate their intent to teach music, and some schools surpass these intentions by providing more than a minimal amount of music instruction.

It has also always been true that children of any age level have quite a wide range of experiences, interests, and talents in music, and this affects the music program. The uniqueness of each child—as has been stressed in earlier chapters in this book—emphasizes that learning is a highly personalized process, particularly the learning that is associated with programs reaching beyond minimal instruction.

A HISTORICAL GLANCE

Music, like most curricular areas, responds to the needs and emphases of each succeeding educational era. The changes that currently are being made in elementary school music programs involve its purpose, approach, content, facilities, and scheduling. Since these changes are coupled with a generation of music-oriented pupils, the prospects for music in today's schools are exciting indeed.

Traditional Music Programs

The prospects for the future of music in elementary schools have their basis in the historical past. Early in the history of music education in American schools, the goal was to produce competent hymn-singers. The Civil and World wars respectively stimulated an emphasis on patriotic songs and marching bands in the schools. The formation of the League of Nations led to the expanded use of the folk and patriotic music of foreign nations, particularly those countries in Latin America and Western Europe. American involvement in Southeast Asia increased the frequency with which music from this area was being included in textbook series. And the emergence of independent African nations demand greater coverage of their musical traditions. Thus, music has been a vehicle for the development of the social attitudes associated with loyal and informed citizenship.

More fundamentally, though, educators have generally shackled the educational possibilities of music by relying primarily on examples of so-called art music, Western European masterpieces of serious music written between about 1650 and 1900. When examples of folk or popular musics were included, the rhythm, melody, and harmony were frequently modified, or "acculturated," to conform with the art music tradition. And music of the present century, whether representing the art or popular tradition, has been included most frequently when it has reflected established musical practices of previous eras.

There has been a presumption that the body of art music represented what was best for all pupils to learn and that identical musical diets be force fed to succeeding groups of children. Beyond the primary grades, most general music instruction has been taught by the lecture method, which emphasizes the memorization of historical minutiae and of brief thematic excerpts. The more talented and motivated pupils have been sought out for bands, choruses, and orchestras. Although these children are allowed to perform, the selections played or sung are most frequently easy arrangements of the masterpieces, which have been musically homogenized, or school music compositions largely written in nineteenth-century styles.

On the other hand, since the earliest inclusion of music in American schools, educators have at least nominally tried to involve all pupils but have met two restricting forces: (1) The traditional art music literature is essentially aristocratic and is almost by definition not likely to be of vital interest to every pupil, and (2) pupils demonstrate a wide latitude in their musical performance abilities (singing, playing instruments, reading and writing music), which results in the problem of whether to focus the level of the class on the ablest, the average, or the slow learner.

Music Teaching

Staffing for music teaching in the schools has varied both historically and geographically. The principal participants have been the classroom teacher, whose interest in music and preparation for teaching it have ranged from poor to excellent, and the music specialist, who is generally well versed in a variety of aspects of music but is less knowledgeable than the classroom teacher in terms of general elementary curriculum and child development.

Although there is currently a great variation in staffing practices, from the earliest to the most modern arrangements, a general trend may be observed nationally. In the early American schools, the classroom teacher provided all the music instruction. Later, a music specialist supervisor from the district, county, or state aided the classroom teacher by providing materials, in-service training, or even daily lesson plans or teaching. With increasing frequency in recent years, due to teacher demands for released time for class preparation and personal reasons, the music specialist teachers have been employed to provide most or all the music instruction.

Thus, the primary purpose of music teaching has traditionally been social preparation. The content of the program has been predetermined by convention and tradition. The staffing has generally depended on administrative convenience, and the teaching approaches used have primarily appealed to the talented and interested few. It is no wonder that so many adults, including some elementary classroom teachers, have negative feelings about music instruction in the schools.

MUSIC EDUCATION OPPORTUNITY TODAY

Every generation of teachers, every decade of teaching, has its own unique opportunities and challenges. At present, teachers are confronted by new directions for education, by pupils who have unique interests, and by schools that evidence new styles of architecture and a new type of organization. Music has helped to mold these elements, and, in turn, music in the schools has been influenced by these forces.

Today, environmental education is ascendant, and music rightfully assumes an important role in this approach. The aural sense is a useful key to perceiving the nature of the environment, through the identification of sound generators (that which makes a sound) and through the analysis and classification of such musical variables as pitch, duration, rhythm, and intensity.

Human beings have always enhanced the auditory environment by organizing sounds and inventing new sound-generators. These aesthetic products will continue to be the focus of musical education, for they represent humanity's greatest achievements and traditions in modifying the auditory environment.

Increasingly, it is recognized that schools need to provide experiences in music other than art music, Western European music, or two-and-a-half centuries of music history. An effective program incorporates authentic folk music, rock and other popular styles, the musics of all cultures, and a historical spectrum from earliest times to the present. The criterion for selection of a particular work is the musical experiences, both cognitive and affective, that it may afford the child.

A school music program should provide every child with training regarding sound and its organization. The goal should be to make the child more aware of the auditory elements in his environment so that he will be able to perceive, identify, and compare sounds and to kindle in him a desire to make music an important part of his experiences both inside and outside the school.

The New Generation

Anyone involved with young people today is intensely aware that they constitute an audio-oriented subculture. The transistor radio has become virtually an appendage of the young, a veritable life-support system for youth away from the home stereo. This phenomenon, which was originally associated with college-age students, has filtered down through the secondary and elementary grades and can be observed to some extent even in preschool children.

This emphasis on sound is far from a superficial affectation. Music is used not just as a means to while away the hours but as a form of personal expression and communication. Although some of the current rock lyrics have surprisingly weighty sociological and philosophical implications, the basis of the communication in rock music is the organization of sounds, not the verbalization. This can easily be demonstrated by citing purely instrumental numbers and those pieces that employ primarily nonverbal (nonsense) vocal sounds, both of which frequently are among the most moving tunes. The facial expressions of young people as they listen to "their" music give evidence of the power of music to communicate emotion.

Even the youngest children exhibit more sensitivity to music than to verbalisms. Most can sing a half-dozen deodorant commercials with accurate pitch and rhythm long before they can state what the product is or how or why it is used. Before they can write their names, children compose chants to accompany their play activities.

One of the frequent criticisms of American education is that it lacks concern for experiences in the affective domain. Music, which is so important to today's children, helps to fill this gap by acting as an effective vehicle for meaningful school experiences involving feelings and emotions. By recognizing the importance of personal feelings, in many cases music has "turned on" pupils to school activities in general by developing more positive attitudes toward school personnel, fellow pupils, and the child himself.

New Teaching Practices

For generations the potential educative benefits of music training in the schools have been minimized by traditional school structures and procedures. There has been little accommodation to the wealth of individual interests and abilities in music. Inflexibility of scheduling and timing classes has been particularly harmful to music instruction. The only individualized scheduling provided has been for vocal and instrumental performance groups and instrumental lessons. Indeed, in no other curriculum area are the "specialists" so well accommodated. But even these pupils have suffered from inflexible scheduling and inefficient use of time.

Flexible scheduling would not necessarily provide *more* time but rather *more efficient blocks* of time. For example, a complete Beethoven symphony requires more than a single class to be listened to once, and its artistic balance is destroyed by any attempt to sythesize its elements to fit a conventional period. Also, longer blocks of time should be allowed for those musical activities that require the setting up of chairs or stands, the warming up of instruments or voices, and other essential preparatory activities.

New school practices, including those of the open school, can favor music instruction in several ways. Open classrooms may have a music area—supplied with instruments, environmental sound-generators, and electronic equipment—to encourage individual pupils to work independently in the exploration of sound. (Some commercial acoustical treatment of this area is desirable; however, the area may be boxed in by corrugated cardboard or fiber egg-cartons to lessen the expense.) As in other subject areas in which children contract for learning tasks, it should be possible for an individual pupil or a small group to select a music contract and work on it in the music area with minimal teacher supervision or assistance. A pupil who is interested in a particular area of music study should be provided with a sequence of contracts leading him to a greater understanding of that area. The contract approach should provide some form of evaluation of progress and an efficient method of recording the interest and achievement demonstrated by the individual pupil.

In addition, schools should have music laboratories—large rooms or areas having a greater variety of musical resources than a classroom music area can provide. Such a laboratory is staffed by a music specialist teacher and, ideally, by an aide, who may be a secondary school student or adult member of the community with an interest and some ability in music. The lab may contain fifteen to thirty or more stations, each concerning a particular area of music study. One area might deal exclusively with pentatonic (five-note) scale contracts, another with diatonic (seven-note), and yet another with chromatic (twelve-note). Other stations might offer projects in ethnomusicology (music of non-Western cultures), electronic music (with a small synthesizer), or jazz.

In music laboratories, cassette recorders have proven particularly useful for giving instructions, presenting a model performance, or providing additional music (such as an accompaniment part for a melody contract). Pupils in an open school may plan individual time in the music lab as their interest and progress dictate. Since it would be possible for not only an entire class but also for individuals from many classes in the school to be present in the music lab at any given time, the necessity of having an unusually large room and the desirability of an aide is obvious.

Emphasis on individualized instruction, open-classroom techniques, and creative projects is particularly appropriate for music education because music is a varied and unique medium. Highly motivating and self-generating activities are essential if music is to meet the challenge of relevance for each child.

The New Life

All present-day elementary school pupils can expect to live in the twenty-first century. By that time, economists predict, our present standard of living could be sustained by twenty percent of the work force working a forty-hour week. Even if such an estimate proves to be incorrect, it is likely that leisure time will be considerably extended. Certainly it seems now that the use of leisure time will eventually become a primary national concern.

In order to be constructive, leisure time must contribute to the self-actualization of the individual. Merely in the area of sense awareness, music contributes the auditory parameter. As appreciators of music, listeners add to their enjoyment of life. But listeners may also become creators, by choosing to compose, or interpreters, by choosing to perform. Any music training that the school can provide may produce valuable alternatives for present and future constructive use of leisure time.

Another concern for the future has to do with pollution. Noise pollution has been condemned with increasing fervor since the Industrial Revolution. There is the increasing possibility of deafness caused by such environmental factors as the rising noise levels in urban centers, not to mention the dangers of electronic overamplification of rock music. Noise pollution can be effectively combated by a concerned citizenry who are sensitive to both the dangerous excesses and the humanizing benefits of sound.

THE MUSIC STAFF IN THE MODERN ELEMENTARY SCHOOL

Since music teaching involves complex and extensive subject matter and essential individual motivation of pupils, deciding on the staff to teach the music curriculum is a complex problem. A music specialist, with years of training in the history, theory, and performance of the art, is barely able to keep up with the expanded curricular inclusions of modern music education. On the other hand, an elementary classroom teacher must employ a considerable repertoire of skills to motivate today's pupils, analyze their problems, and develop effective individualized teaching strategies.

The complexity of the instructional problem suggests that there are three possible solutions: (1) A music specialist provides all the music instruction, (2) a classroom teacher supplies all the music instruction as well as all other curriculum areas, or (3) a combination of the two ways. However, from further examination of the challenges of the program, the first alternative must be eliminated. When children are provided with only one or two periods a week with the music specialist, some continuing activities are essential to encourage retention of the musical concepts and skills and to prevent negative attitudes toward music. If the classroom is stocked with a variety of exciting projects for individual investigation and experimentation in language arts, mathematics, science, and social studies—but not in music—the pupils are learning a hierarchy of values that places music on the lowest level.

Another disadvantage of the "music specialist alone" solution involves the relationship between pupils and teacher. It is a rare schedule that allows pupils to meet their music specialist for even a half-hour a day. Much more typical is music instruction that takes place four to twelve times a month, and music lessons of twenty minutes duration are also commonplace. Considering the hundreds of pupils such a specialist sees in the course of a day, it is obvious that it is extremely difficult to learn all their names, let alone their individual musical interests and needs.

> No elementary music specialist, regardless of her ability, is able to plan and carry out a program of music for the elementary school entirely on her own initiative. The specialist may bring to the job good training, fine musicianship, and a genuine interest in boys and girls. However, she cannot possibly be aware of many of the possibilities for making music with a particular class during the limited time she is in the room.[1]

The specialist alone is not a viable solution. Therefore, the question is reduced to a matter of the *degree* of involvement of the classroom teacher.

The Classroom Teacher Alone

If it is hard for the music specialist to keep up with the demands of current trends in music education, this is even more true for the classroom teacher, who has many other pressing curricular responsibilities. The challenge for classroom teachers is to make the most of whatever music specialist help is provided, while improving their own musical knowledge and repertoire of music-teaching strategies.

In some districts, a classroom teacher may receive help from a music specialist who functions as a consultant or curriculum supervisor. This assistance may be as extensive as providing detailed lesson plans, occasional demonstration lessons, and suggestions and/or providing instructional materials and equipment.

Professional libraries in a school or in a district curriculum center often include helpful materials regarding music education. In many cases, if a need for additional materials in music is called to the attention of the administration, acquisitions will be made. The *Music Educators Journal* and other publications of the Music Educators National Conference are excellent resources.

The basic source of material for music classes has been the graded music series. Many schools provide a second series for supplementary materials and activities. Almost all publishers provide a teacher's edition of each book in the series. These editions include helpful teaching suggestions; piano accompaniments; suggestions for creative activities; and helpful reminders of the key note, number of beats, and starting note of each song. Most series are making increasing use of contemporary and non-Western music. Some also provide optional equipment, such as visual aids and recordings for listening activities, song accompaniments, and rhythmic movement activities.

Although in-service training is not as readily available as it was a decade ago,

1. Edward J. Hermann, *Supervising Music in the Elementary School* (Englewood Cliffs, N.J.: Prentice-Hall, 1965), p. 6.

similar experiences are available through government projects, graduate courses in music education, and workshops sponsored by manufacturers of musical products or music publishers. One of the great rewards of such study is that the teacher has not only better prepared herself to cope with instructional responsibilities but also has gained new personal insights and appreciation for music. In music, as in other curriculum areas, the mark of excellence in teaching is the instructor who is also learning.

The Classroom Teacher and Music Specialist Teacher Team

When a music specialist is used only for consultation or an occasional demonstration, he is functioning as a resource. When he teaches on a regular basis, even if only once or twice a month, the stage is set for a team-teaching approach. In this conformation, the specialist is the teacher, and the classroom teacher is the consultant, providing information about group and individual needs and interests, correlating music and other curriculum areas, and providing practice and reinforcement between the visits of the specialist.

The definition of the relationship between the specialist and the classroom teacher varies from school to school, depending on the abilities of the teachers, the interests of the children, and the degree of independent study employed. In all cases, careful planning for sequential pupil experiences is essential. The motto to follow is cooperation: working together to develop the aural awareness, the performance abilities, the creativity, and the genuine and abiding appreciation of music in all the pupils.

OBJECTIVES OF A MODERN PROGRAM

Every curriculum area has its own set of objectives that vary from time to time in content and relative emphasis. Music education has included such diverse emphases as learning to sing religious songs by rote, reading music, social adjustment through music, and the enhancement of patriotism. Some elements of each of these have been retained in spite of subsequent innovations and will likely be valued in the future for their contributions to a musical education. Thus, it is likely that pupils will continue to sing spiritual songs at Thanksgiving and the winter and spring holiday seasons. Music literacy will continue to have some role in good music curriculums. Individual and group experiences in music will always have some part in the social development of the participants. And it is almost inconceivable that an American child could attend a public elementary school without learning at least some verses of "America" and "The Star-Spangled Banner." These activities will be retained in some form, as they serve whatever curricular emphasis is current.

The present approach, sometimes known as the "environmental approach," stresses the aural development of the individual pupil in relation to his auditory environment. The goals are stated in terms of individual development: (1) of aesthetic sensitivity to aural stimuli; (2) of creative abilities in the organization and manipulation of sound; (3) of cognitive abilities in identifying and classifying musical elements; and (4) of psychomotor abilities, including the performance of vocal and instrumental music as well as reading, writing, and interpreting musical symbols. Wide differences in abilities of pupils are readily observable, but nearly all children are experienced to some degree in all four phases of the environmental approach to music education.

Teachers have a number of important tasks that relate directly to the success of the pupils in relating to music meaningfully. They must help the pupils to extend their experience with a variety of sounds and types of sound organization, to isolate and identify elements of sound for later manipulation, to utilize nonverbal sound as a form of communication,and to recognize and experience the affective meanings of organized sound.

Aesthetic Sensitivity

The most basic element of music instruction is making the pupil aware of aural stimuli (both environmental and musical sounds). An awareness of her auditory environment can give depth of meaning and emotion to her life. As pointed out in earlier chapters, some aspects of the child's perception of aural stimuli begin in infancy, as the child responds to voice tones long before she is aware of words. Likewise, fear and avoidance is associated early with harsh, unpleasant sounds. Later the child learns to control her vocal tones to communicate likes and dislikes nonverbally. She may compose short nonverbal tunes or chants to accompany her games and create rhythmic patterns by banging toys, food implements, or even her head against a bed or wall. The child learns to move her body and extends her limbs to convey emotion and to increase her sensory life-space.

This process of becoming functional with sound is a continuing one. Thus, it is essential for the teacher to establish an atmosphere of respect toward sound in the classroom. The teacher should provide a wide variety of auditory experiences. Serious or humorous, all sounds can become meaningful to children. Since children can turn their attentions elsewhere or try to be unaffected by aural stimuli, a certain willingness to become involved is essential. To encourage this, the teacher must permit a full spectrum of pupil-produced sounds to be used for consideration and analysis and must support individual emotional responses to sound, no matter how diverse.

To fully expand their sense experiences, children need to hear sounds that are new to them. The city child needs to hear the sounds a country child usually hears, and vice versa. The child who hears only rock music at home needs to hear Mozart and Beethoven. But equally important is exposure to Dixieland and contemporary art music and to the sounds of the Japanese koto, the sitar from India, and the African mbira.

Lest listening to music becomes a sonic bath, teachers must guide and direct the attention of their pupils to salient elements of the sound event. It is only at this point that interest becomes appreciation.[2] If the event is a single sound, is it high

---

2. David R. Krathwohl, Benjamin S. Bloom, and Bertram B. Masia, *Taxonomy of Educational Objectives, Handbook II: Affective Domain* (New York: David McKay Co., 1956), Figure 1, p. 37.

or low? Long or short? Loud or soft? Musical or environmental? What does the timbre (tone color) sound like? Does it come from a single sound-generator (voice, instrument, or object) or more than one? Is it localized or diffused?

For a series of sounds, there are questions to be asked in addition to those that apply to a single sound. Are the successive notes staying at the same level? If the notes are going up or down, what is the direction and is each note following one another by steps or are there skips? Is it a long or short series? Are the sounds even or uneven in length?

Affective states that can be communicated through sounds alone are multitudinous. Pupils need to be exposed to sounds that are sad and happy, that create moods, and that evoke pictorial representations. The sound's elements that create these affective states should be analyzed.

A music program that aims to develop sensitivity to sound should include the art and social music of all cultures and eras as well as many varieties of environmental sounds. It is important to provide musical listening experiences representing medieval times to the present. The musical performances should be as authentic as possible; that is, historically appropriate instruments and performance practices should be employed. Although the social music of an era may lack profundity, it can provide valuable insights to the human condition of the time. The music of African, Asian, and Latin American cultures, in addition to being fascinating auditory experiences, frequently is related intimately to unique social customs and ceremonies. Fortunately, good examples of the social and art music from many eras and different countries are readily available on long-playing records.

Even more accessible are the environmental sounds of the classroom, playground, community, and home. A ticking clock may be used as an example of a steady beat. An example of an electronic sound that is found in most classrooms is the fluorescent-light starter, which produces a sawtooth-wave sound that can be contrasted with the sine-wave sound of telephone circuit-switching tones. Whole compositions may be constructed by organizing a succession of classroom environmental sounds: tapping on desk tops and frames, slapping erasers together, banging on wastebaskets, and so on. To merely suggest such an activity to the children is to start them experimenting with the many interesting possibilities for producing and organizing sounds.

The use of environmental sounds tends to simplify the analysis of component elements, for these sounds have timbre, pitch (or if the sound has no specific pitch, a pitch range), duration, and volume; however, the complexities of scales and harmonies are absent from the sound. One practical value to studying these sounds is that there is no cost involved; no expensive instruments are required. But most significantly, the use of environmental sounds helps to relate the study of music to the life-space of the child, making the endeavor both vital and relevant.

The children should be made aware of the elements in all the sounds they hear and be able to recognize these elements. And they should be aware of how auditory experiences can affect themselves and others in terms of feelings and emotions. They should want to devote more of their time and energy to attending to sound events and should demonstrate increasing abilities to comprehend and be affected by music.

Creativity

Since elementary instruction needs to take into account the individual needs and experiences of the child, it follows that not only should the music program develop in the child an awareness of his auditory environment but also encourage him to use his creative abilities to manipulate sound and create auditory products. Creativity in music—as recent research has further indicated—does not require musical talent.[3] Many responses to music, such as moving or foot tapping, are not perceived by the teacher as creative responses, but in terms of an affective taxonomy, these are relatively high-level responses indicating satisfaction.[4]

All children are creative to some degree. It has been noted previously that preschool children create rhythms and sounds. When the creative response produces an independent product, such as a song or instrumental piece, the power of the creative approach is vividly seen. The creation involves the mind, body, and emotions of the child. Because music is an abstraction of reality, pupils, through their own compositions, are provided with emotional outlets that cannot be found in most school assignments. These products become a representation of the self, totally inseparable from the creator. At this point, music deals directly with values, both in terms of the pupil and his creation and in terms of the class and their evaluation of the product. Pupils who find personal fulfillment in their compositions will spend more time and energy in self-improvement than they would through less-creative activities.

One of the most difficult tasks for the teacher is maintaining a supportive atmosphere that accepts and values all pupil products (and hence the pupils themselves) while attempting to assist them in improving the quality of their products (and thus improve themselves in their self-concepts). Instead of allowing free rein in the choice of creative activities, the teacher must structure these experiences by direction or influence. Perhaps most important, the teacher must provide time for experimentation and thinking, or incubation, for the quality of the creative product and the value of the educative experience depend on the presence of these essential elements.

Cognitive Aspects

As the child experiences a variety of auditory events, as she considers their component elements, and particularly as she manipulates sound creatively, she is gaining knowledge. She hears, sings, and creates a melody and knows what a melody is before she understands the term. The principle of placing sense experience before the introduction of terminology or written symbol (which has been part of many music education philosophies for generations) is still valid.

Principles of notation can be taught effectively to preschool children through concrete representation. A rhythmic series of long and short notes may be rep-

---

3. Margery M. Vaughan, "Music as Model and Metaphor in the Culturation and Measurement of Creative Behavior in Children" (Research Report presented to the Music Educators National Conference National Convention, Atlanta, Georgia, March 1972), abstracted in *Journal of Research for Music Education* 20, no. 2 (Summer 1972): 218-19.
4. Krathwohl, Bloom, and Masia, *Taxonomy of Educational Objectives*, p. 133.

resented by large and small building blocks. This representation may be performed by slow and fast clapping, walking, playing on percussion instruments, or singing of a neutral syllable. Likewise, a melodic pattern can be represented by the relative height of the blocks or suggested by graphic notation. A particularly useful pictorial notation has been devised by Mary Helen Richards, who uses animals and familiar environmental objects to represent sounds.[5] Gradually, these informal notational systems may be replaced by standard notation.

The use of notation is introduced to help children interpret sounds objectively and to aid in their remembering of sounds so that communication is facilitated. Through the use of informal notation, a new song, particularly a pupil composition, will be remembered by the child and will permit her future performance of the song.

Pupil observation and analysis of auditory phenomena prepares the child for the use of formal terminology. Whereas the performance of an original composition provides an outlet for the emotions, the learning and use of formal terminology stimulates the intellect. The teacher must sense the appropriate moment to present the terminology, and this moment is dictated by the musical experiences of the children, not by any formal scheme. Generally, children are happy to replace an awkward descriptive phrase with a concise, authentic adult term.

While a child's learning orientation is creative-project-centered, the planning orientation of the teacher should largely be concept-centered. A teacher needs to select the concept to be presented and to define a series of creative projects and classroom strategies that will be most likely to elicit concrete examples and clarification of the concept. Pupils' analyses of the elements of their projects, supplemented by other examples for listening and analysis, prepare them for learning to apply formal terminology and to efficiently state the concept. If careful and extensive analyses have been made, children may realize numerous applications of the concept and may even originate their own projects for future investigation.

Performance Abilities

Music provides a great variety of ways to demonstrate the acquisition of conceptual knowledge by psychomotor performance. Most American school music programs provide, to some degree, experiences in singing, listening, and playing on instruments. With increasing frequency, an attempt also is being made to include creative performance experiences. Each activity in the music education curriculum adds perspective to the pupil's study of music. Listening to music leads to subjective responses, while the analysis of the constituent elements provides rational value. Pupil composition and performance and the input of the teacher further reinforce both of these internal perspectives.

An external approach to the development of appreciation for music (and the other fine arts) is suggested by the systematic methods of aesthetic perspectivism.

---

5.   Mary Helen Richards, *Threshold to Music* (Belmont, Calif.: Fearon Publishers, 1964).

This approach promotes classroom experiences in all the societal roles that collectively define the term *musician*.[6] The child would be a music creator (composer, arranger), performer (singer, dancer, instrumentalist), leader (conductor, teacher), critic (journalist, audience), scholar (musicologist, ethnomusicologist), and technician (electronic manipulator, instrument maker). Through his projects he will develop the performance abilities associated with these roles as he realizes his creativity, increases his auditory sensitivity, and utilizes his cognitive acquisitions. For most children, music performance, even in its broadened definition, should not only be an end in itself but primarily a means to a musical education.

The emphasis on the "average" child is not intended to imply that continued opportunities for high-level performance should not be provided for the musically talented. Excellent bands, choruses, and orchestras are a credit to American schools, and they should be encouraged. Furthermore, these pupils should be able to find many new and challenging outlets in the general music program. Select groups could perform some of the pupil compositions. What should be avoided is the attitude that only the talented should perform; this attitude, fostered by the accessibility of outstanding performances on radio and recordings, has been detrimental to amateur music performance in this country. Performing music is often the key to enjoying it. The modern educator should provide meaningful performance experiences that are geared to the abilities of each individual child.

MUSIC CONCEPTS AND STRATEGIES FOR TEACHING

Modern curriculum planning in music is based on the interrelation of the structure of the subject matter with appropriate stages of development of the child. Lists of required songs for singing and examples for listening are no longer sufficient. There is in music, as in other disciplines, a logical sequence of concepts to be developed in increasing depth and breadth, according to the principles of the spiral curriculum. This process should continue throughout the school years, and hopefully, throughout the pupils' lives.

The concept sequence is patterned on children's maturing sensitivities to aural stimuli, their growing abilities to organize sounds creatively, and their increasing performance abilities. Because of the logical organization of the desired concepts, it is possible to present a framework that becomes a guide for the teacher in the selection of appropriate sense experiences, creative projects, and materials.

Most modern music textbooks are based on a stated or implied hierarchy of musical concepts. This arrangement customarily considers each musical element (for example, rhythm) in turn, according to a system of developmental levels—

---

6. Charles B. Fowler, "Perspectivism: An Approach to Aesthetic Education," *Journal of Aesthetic Education* 2, no. 1 (January 1968); 87-99.

usually one level of each element for each grade. Such a rigid scheme, no matter how freely applied, appears to be contrary to the principles of individualized instruction.

Numerous plans for organizing concepts are available commercially, but there are several reasons for not adopting one of them as a single basis for the curriculum of a music program. Most commercial programs are organized according to the logic of the adult, not the child. There is often a separation of concepts into *component elements* (such as rhythm, melody, harmony, and form) and the *expresssive elements* (including timbre, dynamics, and tempo); whereas children perceive *all* the elements to be expressive.

Frequently, the audiovisual materials required to accompany a concept-oriented music series are available only in a "package deal" (including teachers' manuals, recordings, slides, charts, and photographs), which may be beyond the limits of the school budget. In other cases, the recommended materials may be out-of-print or difficult to obtain. Furthermore, the music represents only the Western art music of the mid-eighteenth through the nineteenth centuries. At best, packaged programs cannot take into consideration the unique needs and past musical experiences of the children in a particular classroom.

Perhaps more importantly, a prepackaged program conveys the impression that curriculum is a product instead of a guide to a developmental process. It is essential that the classroom teacher, with the assistance of a music specialist, consider each individual child in the selection of music concepts, strategies, and materials. The degree of success of one lesson plan should become a feedback mechanism in the construction of the next. In this way, not only the classroom teacher, the music specialist, and the expert sources (including series books) they consult are involved in curriculum construction but also the pupils themselves.

Aesthetic-Response Concepts

Before children are introduced to the concepts through customary music materials, it is necessary that they take active part in basic aesthetic experiences that will heighten their sensitivities. The term *aesthetic experience* connotes "images and trains of thought which, because of their relation to the inner life of the particular individual, may eventually culminate in affect."[7] "Aesthetic sensitivity is man's capacity to respond to the emotional values and cognitive meanings of art."[8] Aesthetic response strategies such as the following develop a conscious awareness of the beauty of objects in space, elements in motion, and sounds in communication.[9]

---

7. Leonard B. Meyer, *Emotion and Meaning in Music* (Chicago: University of Chicago Press, 1956), p. 256.

8. Gerald L. Knieter, "The Nature of Aesthetic Education," in Bennett Reimer, *Toward an Aesthetic Education* (Washington, D.C.: Music Educators National Conference, 1971), p. 3.

9. The strategies presented and much of the environmental approach espoused are the result of several years of experimentation with The Fresh Music Group. These strategies have been used successfully to sensitize a variety of age groups, from preschool to adult, including seminars of teachers. The author is indebted to his associates, Dr. Loran Carrier and Mr. Robert Walters, for their ideas and inspiration.

Strategy: The class and teacher form a circle, thus defining an environment. (The term *environment* is now somewhat familiar even to kindergarten pupils.) The teacher (or a pupil) walks into the environment and considers the space. When he finds a comfortable spot, he may assume any body position that can be maintained for several minutee.

Each pupil (one at a time) may enter the environment when he is ready and contemplate the space as now modified by one or more pupils. He may position himself either touching or detached from those already in place.

After six or eight pupils have entered and formed a "statue," they should look around, while in position, at the structure. The other pupils may look at the formation from all sides. Then the pupils leave the environment (one at a time, not necessarily in the reverse of their original order), dissolving the structure. The exercise is repeated with new volunteers, until all the pupils have had a chance to become part of a structure.

Once the procedure has been learned, the pupils may be divided into groups of six or eight, and structures may be formed simultaneously in various parts of the room. Enough time should be allowed so that pupils can observe and compare results and both internal and verbal responses can occur.

This strategy may be repeated numerous times over a span of years, with a gradual development of the concept that an object by itself and in relation to its environment has beauty. This concept can be further related to the arts of sculpture and architecture.

Strategy: Proceed as in the previous strategy, except that when each child finds her place, she makes a motion that feels right for her position in the environment. The motion may be made with her head, arms, legs, or whole body, but it should be something that can be done repeatedly while the group assembles and dissolves, and it should not interfere with anyone else's movement.

This exercise sometimes results in a human "machine," with many intricately relating parts. Sometimes it is not mechanistic but pictorial or allegorical. In any case, the pupils should observe the creative products and have time to respond to them.

As with the first strategy, this latter one benefits from repetition. The teacher may guide the discussion toward an analysis of similar and contrary forms and motions, separate and interrelated objects and actions, and the affective states each suggests. These procedures develop an appreciation for mobiles and for the dance as an art form.

Strategy: Each group proceeds as before, only a nonverbal vocal sound is used by each pupil to accompany his motion. The sound should "fit" the motion.

After the entire "organism" has formed and is moving and sounding in concert, the pupils may close their eyes and concentrate on feeling and hearing the motion. Finally, they may stop the motions and continue their sounds in rhythm to only imaginary motion.

Time should again be provided for aesthetic responses and discussion. Frequently, the idea emerges that the motions originally accompanying the sounds can still be felt and visualized when the sound is presented alone. It is likely that the child has informally experienced this sensation outside of school by either dancing to imagined music or visualizing and feeling dance movements when only listening to music.

This latter strategy is the culmination of the two previous ones and ultimately all three exercises should take place in a continuous series. In this way, gesture becomes the realization of an object in motion, and sound becomes audible gesture. Sound can be appreciated in terms of its own beauty and its expressive qualities, for it can represent an object in space as well as in motion.

> *Strategy:* A recording is played and the pupils move to the sounds. (Important considerations for the teacher include the selection of music that implies a variety of moods and motions, large and small, fast and slow. Divergent responses should be respected, as long as they do not inhibit the motions of others or distract from the serious search for musical insights.)

If the previous strategies have been experienced, the quality of pupil responses to this familiar classroom procedure is likely to be better than that of pupils without aesthetic-response training. To repeat an observation stated in earlier chapters: From infancy, children reflect their affective states through their posture and body movements. Gradually, they learn to use these techniques consciously to communicate fear, pleasure, and other emotions.

> *Strategy:* With the class organized in a circle, the teacher (or a pupil) may be "it." He considers how he feels and tries to express his feelings in a gesture or movement. He continues the movement as he walks slowly inside the circle. He stops in front of one of his classmates, who is to copy the movement while imagining the way the movement feels to the first pupil, who returns to his place in the circle.
>
> After repeating the motion a few times, the new "it" can modify the movement to fit her mood, but the change should be gradual. When she has settled on her own version, she moves around the circle and selects a new "it."

After all the pupils have participated, time should be provided to reflect and discuss what transpired and how the activity made the observers feel. The pupils may compare the last movement with the one made by the pupil who started the exercise.

Many children's games involve motion and sound; they frequently employ body percussion (clapping hands, stomping feet) or nonverbal sounds (shouts, nonsense syllables). Some of these games are played in the classroom for the development of rhythmic coordination and for their added asset of providing change and variety from sedentary and purely intellectual pursuits.[10] The most helpful of these activities, from the standpoint of music instruction, are those that personify a movement by the sounds that are used.

---

10. See Chapter 14 for suggestions.

Music Elements Concepts

To be useful to the modern elementary curriculum, a conceptual plan for music education should be based on a definition of music that is both acceptable to professional musicians and practical to use in the schools. Although some contemporary composers and theorists would include in the definition of music both silence and visual displays that generate sound only accidentally, the following definition of music seems to be workable for most educational purposes: *"a span of time in which there is a change due to conscious manipulation within the sound gamut audible to man."*[11]

Children are first of all aware of the *presence* of sound, even when the sound is an isolated event. It is not perceived as a neutral stimulus but rather as one that has a specific identity in terms of timbre. The child can also hear and describe in general terms whether a sound is loud or soft in volume and long or short in duration.

The relative highness or lowness of the tone's pitch is perceived by the child, perhaps almost inseparably from the timbre. However, this element of sound is difficult for most children to express. After all, how many times have they been told to turn the television down (low) when it was too high (loud)?Furthermore, young people, who, because of their short stature, make highpitched sounds, while adults, who are taller, make lower ones.

In other words, children come to school with a wealth of perceptual impressions filed in their memories for future application and refinement. But these usually include contradictory items that are likely to block the formation of certain music concepts. Thus, the child generally lacks the fundamental concepts for relating himself in aesthetic interaction with his environment.[12]

The conceptual scheme illustrated in Charts 13.1 and 13.2 (see pages 348-54) adapts and applies some of the principles suggested by one authority whose hierarchy is based on stages of intricacy and organizational complexity.[13] Two sequences consider tone and time concepts independently in increasing depth. At the highest levels, in terms of summary form, style, social function, and synthesis of the arts, the sequences merge to consider concepts that involve tone and time simultaneously.

Refinements of the scheme were made by the application of Guilford's model of the intellect[14] to musical concepts, in ascending complexity: units, classes, relations, systems, transformations, and implications. The general plan of development commences with cognitive restructuring of the pupils' informal sense experiences through analysis and the application of elementary terminology. Subsequent concepts deal with increasingly complex methods of defining tone and time events as well as the relationships within these categories. The merger of the two takes place in terms of applications and implications.

---

11. George G. Biggs, Jr., "A Suggested Taxonomy of Music for Music Education," *Journal of Research in Music Education* 19, no. 2 (Summer 1971): 171-72.
12. Bennett Reimer, "Aesthetic Behaviors in Music," *Toward an Aesthetic Education* (Washington, D.C.: Music Educators National Conference, 1971), p. 77.
13. Biggs, "A Suggested Taxonomy of Music," pp. 168-82.
14. Guilford, *The Nature of Human Intelligence* (New York: McGraw-Hill, 1967).

Chart 13.1. Tone Concepts

Sound and silence

1. A sound is a change in the environment that we perceive with our sense of hearing.

   Strategy: Experiment with the audible possibilities of some of the sound generators in the classroom. Try to perceive the sound while restricting some sense function (touch, taste, sight, smell, and finally, hearing). Discuss results.

2. Sound is caused by vibration.

   Strategy: Compare sound generators when they are emitting a sound and when silent by feeling vibrations. Improvise and compose pieces that involve silence and sound using various sound generators.

3. Silence may be used to separate notes in melodies.

   Strategy: Identify by a physical movement (moving the arm or body) when a sound is present. Stop the motion during silence. Compare the feelings conveyed by continous melodies and those with rests.

4. Silence may be used to separate the sections of musical compositions.

   Strategy: Compare the feelings conveyed by pieces that have a pause between sections and those that are continuous. What happens to the listener during the silent period? What are the practical aspects in regard to the performer (such as time for rest, tuning, or page turning)? Very short-sectioned contemporary works can be compared to long-sectioned pieces from India and the Orient.

5. Silence may be used for special musical effects.

   Strategy: Compare the effect made by pauses in Beethoven (usually for dramatic effect) and Haydn (frequently for humorous effect). Analyze the impacts in other works and compose examples of music with pauses made for different purposes.

Timbre (tone color)

1. Sounds may be tones (definite pitch) or noises (indefinite pitch).

   Strategy: Distinguish the presence of tones from noises by the presence or absence of a specific pitch. Try to match the tones by singing or by using classroom instruments. Classify the sound generators in the room in terms of whether their sound is a tone or a noise.

2. The timbre of sounds is determined by the physical characteristics of the sound generator.

   Strategy: Associate tones and noises with their sound generators. Learn the names of instruments and associate their sounds with their appearances. Develop generalizations about timbre relating to the shape, size, and vibrating material involved.

3. Timbre may be changed by modifying the sound generator.

   Strategy: Listen to the differences between the sounds of instruments with and without mutes. Compare the typical timbre of Western singing and playing with that of other cultures. Perform on a variety of instruments, employing open and muted sounds. Compare in terms of volume, pitch, and tone color. Sing while holding the nose or muffling the voice, or sing through a cardboard tube. Modify the treble and bass controls of a playback machine.

4. Timbre may be changed by modifying the method of vibrating the sound generator.

   Strategy: Pluck and bow string instruments. Play percussion instruments with a variety of beaters (and brushes); hit a cymbal, rub it with a bow, stroke it with a coin.

Find various ways to sound environmental objects. Try different vocalizing techniques. Organize all these techniques into compositions. Compare the timbres.

Compare similar instruments and decide if the differences in timbre are due to the sound generator, the method of sounding it, or both. Include fretted string sounds (Renaissance lute music, the guitar—Spanish, classical, and electonic, and the ukelele), brass instruments (Tibetan and Western), varieties of woodwinds, and vocal sounds (such as those heard in rock opera, Gregorian chants, and gospel music).

5. Instruments representing more than one timbre category may be grouped together in terms of their musical function.

Strategy: Listen to the sound of standard instumental combinations, including those from a single timbre group (string or brass quartet) and those that combine different timbre groups (woodwind quintet or piano trio). List the instruments and the timbre families represented and compare the sounds. Include jazz and rock groups. Compose works for environmental sounds and classroom instuments that illustrate similar and mixed-timbre groupings.

6. By varying the orchestration (instrumentation) of a composition, contrasts in timbre may be produced.

Strategy: Listen to the sounds in a piece that uses different orchestrations of the same melody in adjacent sections. Theme and variation works (such as the Haydn Variations by Brahms) are ideal for this purpose.

7. Changing the orchestration of a composition alters its effect.

Strategy: Compare the feeling of orchestrated versions of piano music with the original version. Contrast the art-song version of such works as "Londonderry Air" with the Ralph Vaughan Williams orchestrated sound and a current rock interpretation. Contrast the original Beatles' tunes with the Boston Pops Orchestra's arrangements. Re-orchestrate original compositions and comment on the change of feeling.

Dynamics (volume, or loudness)

1. All sounds can be measured in terms of loudness.

Strategy: Using a variety of sound generators, describe the different examples as loud or soft. Use large body movements to express loud sounds, small movements for soft sounds. Play and sing, exaggerating dynamics; also perform with the opposite dynamics.

2. Dynamics may change suddenly or gradually.

Strategy: Identify and compare the effect of gradual (for example, Ravel's "Bolero") and sudden (Haydn's "Surprise Symphony") dynamic changes. Use songs and creative projects to demonstrate understanding and performance abilities regarding both types. Gradually replace the terms *loud* and *soft* with *forte* and *piano* and the abbreviations *f* and *p*. Refine dynamic levels by the use of the term *mezzo* for *moderately,* as in *mp* and *mf*. Likewise, introduce < , or *crescendo (cresc.)* for *gradually louder;* and >, or *diminuendo (dim.)* for *gradually softer.* Use these terms in all subsequent creative projects.

3. Dynamic changes may give variety to sections of a composition.

Strategy: Compare compositions that proceed at one dynamic level with those that employ contrasts. Sing and play pieces without dynamics, then repeat them with dynamic variety.

4. Dynamic variation changes the effect of a composition.

Strategy: Comment on the change of feeling that dynamics cause. Perform a piece using dynamics that are opposite to what is indicated; analyze how this changes the mood as well as the sound.

5. Dynamics can be a function of orchestration.

   Strategy: Contrast the dynamic range of a single singer or instrumentalist with that of a small ensemble and a large group. Contrast the dynamic range of some instruments with others. Compose examples using these contrasts.

6. Certain dynamic levels are associated with certain types of music.

   Strategy: Compare marches, lullabies, church music, and dance music in terms of dynamics. Relate the loudness to the nature of the function. Discuss the relationship of highly amplified music to noise pollution and physical injury.

7. Certain dynamic levels are associated with specific historical eras.

   Strategy: Compare the dynamic levels associated with the music of various historical eras of Western music and the dynamics of non-Western cultures. State a rule regarding the type of music or era. Consider dynamics in relationship to the instruments, musical functions, and social emphases of the era.

Pitch

1. All sounds may be measured in terms of pitch.

   Strategy: Categorize sounds in terms of high and low pitch. Group sounds and sound generators that are in similar ranges.

2. The pitch of a sound is determined by the physical characteristics of the sound generator.

   Strategy: Develop generalizations regarding the size of the sound generator and its range of pitches. Experiment with numerous sound generators (including the voice) to discover what their range of pitches are and how their pitches can be modified.

3. Tones (sounds that have specific pitch) may be related to other tones in terms of the same, higher, or lower pitch.

   Strategy: Imitate pitches vocally and instrumentally. Play or sing pitches higher and lower than a given pitch. Analyze a song learned by rote in terms of the pitch or each successive note.

4. Pitches may be organized into systems called "scales."

   Strategy: Listen to, sing, and perform works in a variety of scale systems. Young pupils may start with two-tone chants (such as those used in playground games) and gradually progress to five-tone (pentatonic), seven-tone (major, minor, and modal), and twelve-tone (chromatic and serial) music. Identify the pitches used by employing hand signals, letters, or numbers. Learn a new piece by first identifying the scale system.

5. The sound of composition is affected by the scale system employed.

   Strategy: Compare pieces written in different scale systems. Write examples of different scale systems.

Harmonic interval (involves two or more sounds that combine into a compound, simultaneous sound event)

1. Sound blends are made of two or more sounds.

   Strategy: Identify the component parts of sound blends. Compose and perform sound blends.

2. Tone blends may involve the same or different pitches.

   Strategy: Compare the sound of one person playing or singing alone with a group performing in unison. Contrast this sound with that of a blend of different notes (harmony). Write tone blends.

3. A blend can be made up of equally important sounds or of an important sound and a background sound.

   Strategy: Determine whether blends are made up of equal sounds or whether one sound is more important. Sing songs with rhythmic accompaniment of drums, rhythm sticks, or body percussion. If the parts are equal, both are melodies. Refer to the background parts as the "accompaniment."

4. The choice of tones that form a harmonic interval depends on the scale system employed.

   Strategy: Using melodies with ostinatos, bourdons, descants, rounds, and harmony, analyze the notes in the melody and the accompaniment. Compare them and relate them to a single scale system. Perform the scale system and compose a piece using that system in a melody and accompaniment parts.

5. Chords are blends of specific tones of a scale system. (This concept should follow the study of the seven-tone scale systems.)

   Strategy: Analyze the tones used in chordal accompaniments, starting with songs that use only one chord and then those using the primary chords (I, IV, and V). Learn to accompany melodies on the autoharp, piano, guitar, or bells; first choose the chord by ear and then learn to play chords as indicated by letter and number symbols.

6. Blends may be made up of only the tones of a chord, or they may include other (nonharmonic) tones.

   Strategy: Compare the sound of music that uses nonharmonic tones with music that does not. Test each note of a melody with the chord that accompanies it to isolate nonharmonic tones. Compare the effect of music composed of many nonharmonic tones with a piece using mainly chord tones. Compose examples of each.

Melodic interval

1. A melody is a series of tones.

   Strategy: Repeat the third strategy under "Pitch" in terms of all the melodic motion of a melody. Use short examples at first, preferably known tunes.

2. A melodic pattern is a shape in sound.

   Strategy: Draw (or construct with blocks) the shape of a melody. Try to find similar patterns within a melody. Compose and perform new melodies using graphic or concrete notation.

3. Melodic patterns can be repeated at the same pitch or at higher or lower pitch levels.

   Strategy: Identify, by sound and notation, melodic patterns that are repeated at the same pitch ("Twinkle, Twinkle Little Star": phrases one and five, two and six, and three and four) and at different pitches (phrase three repeats phrase two a step higher). Represent repeated patterns by similar body movements, contrasting patterns by different movements. Use both of these types of patterns in original compositions.

4. Melodic movement is measured in intervals.

   Strategy: Melodic movement can be defined in more refined terms, first differentiating between step and skip movement, then using interval names (a *second* for one letter name to the next, and so forth) and finally determining the exact interval (for example, a major second equals two half-steps; a minor second equals one half-step). Melodies can be defined by the starting note and subsequent melodic movement, performed from this description, and compared with the original notation.

5. Melodic phrases are shapes, or combinations of shapes, that form a musical thought.

   Strategy: Melodic phrases can be expressed by bodily movement. Mark the ends of melodic ideas with appropriate gestures. Rock music and non-Western music are readily adaptable to this procedure.

6. Phrases may be composed of similar and/or different melodic patterns.

   Strategy: Identify similar and contrasting phrases and express them with similar and contrasting physical movements. Compare the feeling of phrases that employ repeated patterns with those that do not. Compose and perform examples of both types of phrases.

7. A melody may have resting places, or cadences.

   Strategy: Contrast the feeling of works that have a continuous flow of melody (such as many sixteenth-century compositions) with others that have distinct phrase divisions (such as many eighteenth-century compositions, particularly in dance forms). Analyze how the melody communicates a feeling of repose, considering the choice of notes and the melodic patterns employed.

Chart 13.2. Time Concepts

Beat and tempo (speed)

1. The basic unit of rhythm is the beat, or pulse.

   Strategy: Listen to music or environmental sounds that have a marked, recurring beat. Indicate the beat by clapping or tapping. Compare it to the heartbeat or the tick of a clock.

2. The beat may be fast or slow.

   Strategy: Compare the beats of different pieces by describing them as fast, slow, or about the same. Try performing a piece at a markedly different speed than usual. Discuss the result.

3. A sound may have the same length (duration) as a beat, or it may be longer or shorter than a beat.

   Strategy: Establish the beat by foot tapping. Then compare the notes and the beat. Describe whether the notes are equal to or shorter or longer than the beat.

4. The speed of the beat may change in different sections of a composition.

   Strategy: Compare pieces that have a continuous tempo with those that alternate sections in slow and fast tempos. Discuss the effect of tempo changes.

5. The tempo of a composition may change within a section of the work.

   Strategy: Establish the beat of a selection by foot tapping or by using a metronome. Discover brief sections of faster or slower tempos in expressive romantic music or music in the gypsy tradition. Also check endings of pieces that are generally regular in tempo. Discuss the expressive result. Perform pieces with changing tempos, using the pupil as a conductor.

Accent

1. Beats may be strong (accented) or weak (unaccented).

   Strategy: Find the beat of the words to a song and indicate it by clapping. Clap harder on the accented syllables. Do this with various kinds of music, including marches, waltzes, dirges, and rock.

2. Accented beats may be stronger in certain kinds of music.

   Strategy: Compare the strength of the accented beats in a variety of music, from plain chant to jazz. Discuss the effect.

3. Accented and unaccented beats may be grouped into rhythmic patterns.

   Strategy: Count the number of beats between accented beats. Counting the accented beat as one, determine the number of beats in each group (measure). (In quadruple meter, contrast the strong beat one with the somewhat-less-strong beat three.) Express the pattern by exaggerated conducting patterns.

4. Meter signatures indicate the accent pattern, the kind of note receiving a beat, and the beat subdivisions.

   Strategy: Transfer the physical representation of sound groupings to the notation of meter. Contrast the indications of subdivisions (for example, the duple accent pattern may have two subdivisions in 2/4 meter and three subdivieions in 6/8). Perform and compose in a variety of meters.

5. Accented beats may be displaced from their expected beat.

   Strategy: Using jazz, folk, and rock music as well as art music, locate examples of displaced accent. If this is a regular pattern, tap to the beat and clap to the syncopation. Discover whether the syncopated feeling is due to a missing accent, an accented note on a weak beat, or an accent between beats.

6. The meter signature may be changed in a composition to indicate shifting accents.

   Strategy: Clap to the accent pattern indicated by a sequence of changing meters (which the pupils can compose). Rewrite in one meter with strong beats indicated by accents (>). Decide whether one meter or changing meters is easier to perform and write an example.

7. Meter signatures may be asymmetrical (not equally divisible by two or three).

   Strategy: Listen to the beat patterns of asymmetrical meters to determine the signature. Include examples from art music and jazz (Dave Brubeck frequently employs asymmetrical meters). See if they are truly asymmetrical or merely recurring compounds of duple and triple patterns.

Duration (length)

1. Sounds may be short or long in duration.

   Strategy: Indicate the duration of sounds by continuous body movements during the sound and no motion when the sound stops. Describe the sounds in terms of whether they are long or short.

2. A sound may be measured in terms of a beat or multiples of or fractions of beats.

   Strategy: Represent the beat with blocks, pictures of objects, or graphic notation. Indicate the length of short notes by short blocks or the like, and longer notes, by longer representations. Count the number of beats in long notes and the number of short notes to a beat. Gradually introduce standard notation (whole notes and so forth).

3. Some long notes may not be even multiples of the beat.

   Strategy: Analyze the length of sounds involving dotted notes. ("America" has examples of the dotted quarter note.) Perform and compose examples of long, short, and dotted notes.

Rhythm

1. A melody can be made up of tones of equal or unequal duration.

   Strategy: Discuss some of the ways that you can move to music (slow and heavy, quick, and light, skipping, hopping, sliding, and so forth). Move to the sounds of a variety of examples. Describe the movements in terms of whether they are of even or uneven duration.

2. The rhythm of a composition suggests a certain type of music.

   Strategy: Move to a variety of types of music. Listen to the sounds without moving. Analyze the different types of feelings each type of music elicits (fast, slow, happy, sad, serious, funny, and so on).

3. Rhythmic patterns may involve elements of repetition and contrast.

   Strategy: Identify and clap to rhythmic patterns in a song. Indicate every time the pattern is repeated. Compose a piece that uses repeated and contrasting rhythmic phrases.

4. Rhythmic phrases may combine similar and contrasting elements.

   Strategy: Locate repeated patterns in phrases that combine a pattern with a contrasting beginning or ending pattern. Also locate similar but varied patterns (such as in theme and variations).

5. A cadence is a rhythmic resting place.

   Strategy: Find the resting place at the ends of phrases. Discuss which resting places indicate relative and complete repose.

6. A rhythmic pattern may be used as a theme (motive) for an entire composition.

   Strategy: Listen for rhythmic motives in songs, instrumental works (including Beethoven eymphonies), dance music of many periods and cultures, and rhythmic games. If the rhythmic motive is used constantly (as in much dance music), clap the motive or play it on a percussion instrument throughout. If it is used periodically, indicate each time it is employed.

Advanced Concepts

The concepts related to tone and time tend to merge at a level of advanced development. Such constructs as melody and cadence involve both time and tone concepts.

All the technical elements of a composition taken as a whole constitute *style*, which may be considered in relation to a type of music, an era, a region or tribe, or an individual composer. The organizational elements of a composition collectively define *summary form*. The utilization of a composition by society is its *social function*. Likewise, music merges conceptually in a *synthesis of the arts* in works that employ music simultaneously with other arts.

All these advanced concepts emerge gradually during the development of the child's aesthetic sensitivity, creative abilities, performance skills, and conceptual growth regarding music elements.

Using the Conceptual Approach

A teacher must translate the general strategy into terms that are appropriate for specific children. If the concept statements and general strategies are reviewed in terms of sense experiences, creative activities, cognitive abilities, and performance skills, a number of specific strategies for use in the classroom should suggest themselves.

One of the first songs that many children learn in school is "Twinkle, Twinkle, Little Star." It may be taught by rote for the sheer enjoyment of singing together and to develop performance ability in singing (including matching pitches and keeping the rhythm). However, the same song can be used to develop numerous music concepts. For example, it may be used to illustrate melodic direction (first two pitches the same, leap up, repeated tone, stepwise up, and so forth), and it becomes a clear illustration of repeated and contrasting phrases (see Chart 13.1 [third strategy under "Melodic Interval"]). Since this particular song is limited to six tones, it is ideal for early experiences in music reading, using either hand signals (such as those devised by Zoltan Kodaly and modified for use in American schools by Mary Helen Richards) or standard notation.

Older pupils may wish to analyze the chords employed (conveniently, only the I, IV, and V^7, or primary chords) and to learn the accompaniment on the autoharp, piano, bells, or guitar. Some children may wish to conduct the song, demonstrating their knowledge of meter concepts. With a lab situation, this project could be parceled out in several individual contracts, leading to a culminating activity involving class singing, with pupil conductors (one indicating the beat and another the pitches with hand signals), one or more pupils providing accompaniment, and still another indicating phrases by defining arcs with arm movements. Intermediate-age pupils may even wish to compare the theme with the original by Mozart.

Creative projects related to "our germinal masterpiece" also suggest themselves. After singing one verse to accompaniment, the children could perform the second verse by expressing the feeling of twinkling stars through movement and then singing the original as a third verse. This procedure of presenting a musical idea, contrasting it, and then repeating it exemplifies ABA form, which is used in many songs. In addition, the subject matter might be used as the basis for a pupil improvisation or composition using nonverbal sounds, environmental or classroom instruments. Possible spin-off activities include art interpretations of the song or a play with a star as the main character.

The concept structure is intended merely to aid a teacher in promoting musical experiences. Most concepts will be returned to numerous times, with progressively complex specific strategies leading the pupils to greater understanding of the concepts. In some cases, a specific strategy can be returned to after intervening experiences with other concepts, and the strategy takes on new significance to the pupils.

Although the hierarchy is related to the likely learning sequence, it is not only acceptable but highly desirable to bypass certain elements and go more deeply into others. These decisions will be based on the dynamics of the classroom experience and the interest of individual pupils.

EVALUATION

Music offers an ideal discipline for the application of behavioral objectives to conceptual goals. Traditionally, teachers have set their goals for music education in terms of appreciation, understanding, and enjoyment—terms in which it is difficult if not impossible to measure behavioral development. The performance behaviors of singing, playing, dancing, analyzing, and writing music are eminently measurable and can be used to exhibit such cognitive abilities as selecting, comparing, constructing, describing, naming, arranging, and stating or applying a rule.

The measurement of affective responses is in its infancy. The anecdotal report is probably the most valuable evaluation instrument of affective development. Learning can be assessed in terms of voluntary participation, readiness to respond, facial expressions, nonverbal sounds, direct comments about the activities and assignments, continuation of musical activities in free time, and other observable affective response behaviors. These may be compared with responses in other curriculum areas to indicate the relative status of attitudes toward music. Observations at the beginning of a year may establish a base line to facilitate the measurement of affective changes during the term.

THE CHALLENGE

The music program in the elementary school has two goals: to make children aurally sensitive to their environments and to make music, the highest form of humanity's organization of sound, a vital part of children's lives. Youngsters should show an awareness of the enriching role of this auditory environment through expanding sensitivity, creative activity, and cognitive development. Finally, they need to be aware of the societal applications of sound through performance activities.

Aural awareness of the environment can affect many diverse life activites. The sound of fall leaves crunching underfoot adds to the appreciation of their patchwork of color and the crisp feel of the frosty air. The ability to be able to sing a melody in tune and discriminate timbre differences may help to develop the authentic pronunciation of a foreign language. Sensitivity to rhythmic variation may provide the first clue that the family car is in need of a tune-up. Although humankind may never again regain the acute aural sensitivity of our preliterate forebearers, children can be helped to develop their aural interaction with the environment, and in this sense, directly improve the quality of their lives.

EXERCISES FOR THOUGHT AND ACTION

1. Interview several elementary school teachers about their music programs. Determine, if possible, whether their programs provide for children to be

individually creative. To what extent do these instructors teach the concepts presented in this chapter?

2. Ask some elementary school children, perhaps third and fourth graders, about the music they like. Note the range from rock to folk to patriotic to television commercials.

3. Find out if in your area there are schools that have music laboratories. Are these labs similar to the one described in this chapter?

4. Interview one or more music specialists about any problems they may feel they have in working with classroom teachers.

5. Examine the teacher edition for a series of music textbooks. To what extent is the instructional plan applicable to individualizing instruction? Are the concepts identified in this chapter included in the instructional plan?

6. Record various sounds around your house or dormitory—clock ticking, refrigerator running, chair scraping on the floor, and so forth. See how well children can identify each of these sounds.

SELECTED READINGS

Bergethon, Bjornar, and Boardman, Eunice. *Musical Growth in the Elementary School.* New York: Holt, Rinehart & Winston, 1963. This volume includes a year-by-year developmental progression involving listening, playing, moving, creating, and reading. Musical examples and teaching suggestions are provided. (Supporting long-playing record available.)

Biggs, George G., Jr. "A Suggested Taxonomy of Music for Music Education." *Journal of Research in Music Education* 19, No. 2 (Summer 1971): 171–72.

Cheyette, Irving, and Cheyette, Herbert. *Teaching Music Creatively.* New York: McGraw-Hill, 1969. The discovery method and creative approach to music is the emphasis in this text, which provides a wealth of practical and stimulating ideas.

Ernst, Karl D., and Gary, Charles L., eds. *Music in General Education.* Washington, D.C.: Music Educators National Conference, 1965. This collection of essays, written by prominent music educators, deals with the totality of music education in terms of philosophy and specific practices.

Gary, Charles L., ed. *Music in the Elementary School–A Conceptual Approach.* Washington, D.C.: Music Educators National Conference, 1967. This is a clear exposition of the conceptual approach in music and a careful detailing of conceptual development in the elements of music. Standard series books and recorded examples are suggested.

Gelineau, P. Phyllis. *Experiences in Music.* New York: McGraw-Hill, 1970. This is a good source of musical information and suggested lessons for the musically inexperienced teacher. A wealth of sources are cited, including books, music, and recordings.

Hermann, Edward J. *Supervising Music in the Elementary School.* Englewood Cliffs, N.J.: Prentice-Hall, 1965.

Meyer, Leonard B. *Emotion and Meaning in Music.* Chicago: University of Chicago Press, 1956.

Reimer, Bennett. "Aesthetic Behaviors in Music." *Toward An Aesthetic Education.* Washington, D.C.: Music Educators National Conference, 1971.

Richards, Mary Helen. *Threshold to Music.* Belmont, Calif.: Fearon Publishers, 1964.

Good health is rather widely considered to be a necessary factor in learning; certainly ill health may prevent or retard learning. As the author of this chapter suggests, both health and physical education programs in the schools have had difficulty in maintaining roles commensurate with the importance of health to learning. The reasons for this situation, as implied in this chapter, are worthy of the reader's attention.

The author treats separately health education and physical education—as many school programs do—but stresses the importance of relating other areas of the curriculum to both. Examples of activities which do just that are included. The author's interest in mental health is evident, along with his concern for the interaction that should be taking place among children. The reader will find helpful the styles of teaching in the physical education section, since problems in teaching physical education frequently arise.

W.T.P.

Children's Health and Physical Education

Jerrold S. Greenberg

Discussing health instruction and physical education in a single chapter necessitates some explanation. Many persons think of the two areas as essentially one, since in the not-too-distant past it was not uncommon for health information to be taught in a somewhat "fringe" manner by the physical education instructor. However, specialists in health education and specialists in physical education have both proclaimed the identity of each area. In addition, a good many elementary school teachers have taught health as one subject area and physical education as another. (In contrast to the minimal treatment of health by physical education instructors, the elementary school teacher has traditionally done little about physical education other than permitting children to play.)

To properly keep the two curriculum areas separated, yet related, it is necessary to recognize that physical education relates to movement and the acquisition of psychomotor skills, whereas health education is involved with all aspects of learning—psychological, sociological, physiological, and intellectual—that relate to health. With the differentiation between health education and physical education in mind, the chapter will delineate the objectives, curriculum content, instructional practices, and evaluation procedures that relate and are specific to each area.

The assumption in this chapter is that classroom teachers will be responsible for the health and physical education of elementary school children. If a teacher is fortunate enough to be in a school with a specialist in either area, then the activities presented may serve to supplement offerings of these specialists. If no specialist is available, the classroom teacher can still conduct meaningful health and physical education instruction. This chapter was designed to help teachers who find themselves in either of these situations. It should also be remembered that physical activity can itself serve to motivate and refresh children for other learning activities and therefore should be engaged in periodically throughout the school day. Employing the physical activities described in this chapter should result in increased motivation for learning in general as well as for achieving the health and physical education objectives described.

HEALTH EDUCATION

As implied previously, health has often been taught when the weather was too inclement for physical activity or when incidental time was available. Thus, health education often consisted of not much more than asking children to stand at an open classroom window and hyperventilate, inspecting fingernails, or determining whether or not a clean handkerchief could be produced.

Although the trend is presently toward health teachers being trained specifically in health education, a recent investigation in the Michigan public schools indicated approximately fifty percent of those teaching health had majored in physical education during their undergraduate schooling, only thirty-five percent had minored in health education at the undergraduate level, and less than fifty percent majored in health in graduate schools.[1] On the other hand, the increasing awareness of such health-related problems as environmental pollution, drug abuse, dental decay, and the increasingly impersonal nature of human existence (a mental health educational concern) has created teaching positions for educators who focus their attention on health. One reaction to this need is the increasing numbers of teacher preparation programs in health education.[2] Also, in school districts not employing health education teachers, the classroom teacher is increasingly expected to offer learning experiences related to health education. Because of this trend, many schools offer in-service instruction to teachers so they can acquire the health knowledge and teaching competency necessary for adequate health instruction.

Health Problems

The United States is in the midst of a not-very-publicized health crisis. Although health-related problems affecting the populace of the world are usually

---

1. *Patterns and Features of School Health Education in Michigan Public Schools.* (Michigan Department of Education, 1969), pp. 7-8.
2. *Institutions Offering Programs of Specialization in Health Education.* (Washington, D.C.: School Health Education Study, 1970), p. 3.

recognized by Americans, the prevalence of problems associated with health in the United States is not common knowledge. A reported twenty-two thousand suicides each year (and many suicides are not reported) are evidence of mental-health problems. While the number of mentally ill patients above age twenty-four is decreasing, the number of such patients under this age is increasing. The contribution of the school to the mental health of its pupils can therefore be called into question.

Related to health problems is the question of safety: 10,900,000 people suffered disabling injuries in the United States in 1970, and only two million of those people were hurt in accidents associated with motor vehicles. Accidents at home, accounting for four million disabling injuries, are of concern. The frequency of such injuries might be decreased by safety education in the schools.

Accidents and mental illnesses are but two health problems.[3] Further evidence of the state of health in the United States are the following:

1. Thirty-two percent of persons over age thirty-five have lost their natural teeth.
2. Fifty percent of all children under age fifteen have never visited a dentist.
3. Three out of four Americans have evidence of gingivitis or periodontal disease.
4. If all forms of cancer were eliminated, the life expectancy in the United States would increase by two or three years; if all obese people in the United States were reduced to ideal weight, the life expectancy would increase by more than seven years.
5. Fifty-five percent of all college students have smoked marijuana.
6. One-third of all marriages end in divorce.
7. Every 15 seconds, an American contracts a venereal disease.[4.]

Objectives of Health Education

A reeducation relative to health seems in order. Consequently, the formalized health education of the populace should commence no later than the early elementary school grades. The attaining of positive attitudes toward health is not an overnight occurrence but rather a continuing process requiring time and thought. The process should be incorporated into the life of all children, if for no other reason than their intrinsic interest in health-related topics. Topics such as drugs, sex, and food are discussed by children in varied settings and should therefore be fair game for the classroom. Rather than chance misinformation and the development of distorted health-related attitudes, the teacher can provide opportunities for the study of truth related to health and for the development of healthy attitudes.

Specific objectives in the several health education areas are cited in this section. But since the philosophy of education espoused in this chapter (and in earlier chapters) advocates pupil involvement at all phases of the educational

---

3. For a further description of the health of Americans, see Boisfeuillet Jones, ed., *The Health of Americans* (Englewood Cliffs, N.J.: Prentice-Hall, 1970).

4. James Muth, Jack Arndt, and Melvin Weinwig, "Community Action in Venereal Disease Education," *The Journal of School Health* 43, no. 6 (June 1973): 393.

process, there will be no extensive detailing of numerous health education objectives. To select objectives *for* pupils rather than *with* them is antithetical to the recommendations presented. It is intended that specific objectives be developed through dialogue between pupils and teacher and that those objectives stated here be viewed as points of departure for such communication.

Particularly related to objectives is the fact that health education is often perceived as a preventive act. This attitude prevails even though, today, all our national resources appear to be largely directed toward therapeutic measures rather than preventive ones. Health education is still viewed as an instrument to help prevent diseases and illnesses from developing. Thus, the current focus of health education is on these three areas:

1. The acquiring of health knowledge
2. The developing of healthy attitudes
3. The establishing of healthy practices

Health Knowledge, Attitudes, and Behavior

The interrelatedness of health knowledge, attitudes, and behavior has been expressed in a government bulletin:

> We have chosen to express in forthright fashion our belief that communication and education are elements of one process by which states of knowledge, attitudes, and behavior are modified, and that any separation of those components will impede the progress sought by all.[5]

In effect this means that the acquisition of health knowledge should result in the development of healthy attitudes that, in turn, should be manifested in healthy behaviors. To illustrate, this should mean that the knowledge that ten times as many cigarette smokers as nonsmokers contract lung cancer will lead to the attitude that smoking cigarettes is harmful to a person's health and to the behavior of stopping or never starting to smoke cigarettes.

It has been suggested that having the correct information and the proper attitude is of little value without the desired behavior. If children have knowledge of the incidence of lung cancer among cigarette smokers and nonsmokers and believe cigarette smoking to be hazardous to their health but continue to smoke cigarettes, the question arises as to the value and success of the health education program. Many health educators purport to evaluate their programs by the number of cigarette smokers and nonsmokers among graduating pupils, by the diets observed, and by the extent of drugs used.

Health behaviors, of course, need not precede knowledge and attitudes. For instance, if a child should be playing with a toothbrush and be taught how to brush his or her teeth before understanding the reasons for brushing, the behavior might serve as motivation for acquiring the necessary knowledge and developing the desired attitude.

---

5. U.S. Dept. of Health, Education and Welfare, Public Health Service. *Surgeon General's Conference on Health Communications*. Public Health Service Publication no. 998, Superintendent of Documents (U.S. Government Printing Office, Washington, D.C., February, 1963).

The Problem of Set Objectives

The democratic process of schooling may be regarded by some persons as suspect if a child is programmed through learning experiences so that he or she behaves in a particular way. "At question is the issue of whether we regard the educational process as a means of teaching one how to learn—to search for the truth—or as a means of controlling behavior (psychologists might call this 'shaping')."[6] Even if there is agreement that behavior should be specified, the question of who should decide which behaviors are desirable remains. For example, at first glance it may seem that a person who weighs 250 pounds and is six feet tall should diet to reduce toward an ideal weight. Assuming this person to be somewhat physically unhealthy, the health educator might determine an objective (decreased caloric intake) to achieve this goal, along with presenting learning experiences to accomplish it. However, physical health is only one aspect of a person's health. Mental and social health need also to be considered. If this person is a member of a gourmet club and his or her social and intellectual health are related to that club, to decrease caloric intake and not eat with the club members might harm his or her social and mental welfare. The person best qualified to determine whether this person should lose weight is probably that individual. However, he or she should have knowledge of the relationship between weight and physical health and should understand his or her own motivations before arriving at a decision.

The point of this example is that a prescription for behavior should involve the person who is expected to incorporate that behavior as part of his or her life-style. Of course, children are not adults, and their life-styles are being established by their experiences—those in school and, more importantly, those related to their home lives.

The Focus of Health Education Objectives

The point of view here is that health education should be concerned with providing information rather than with teaching attitudes and behaviors that may be related to such knowledge. Teachers should not be preoccupied with children's health behaviors; rather they should help them understand their motivations and answer their questions.

The following are examples of worthwhile knowledge to be acquired through health instruction: knowledge of self and self-motivations, knowledge related to content in health curriculum content areas, and knowledge of objectives set by oneself. To illustrate the kind of knowledge that seems appropriate, consider the matter of bicycle safety. The pupil should recognize his or her motivation for crossing in the middle of the street or for riding a bicycle in an unsafe manner. The child should be aware of the possible consequences of this behavior and should know about safe behavior and have the opportunity to experience safe behavior. The objectives of safety education should relate to this

---

6. Gere Fulton, "Drug Abuse Education—Tell It Like It Is," *School Health Review* 3, no. 4 (July-August 1972): 33.

knowledge and experience. Objectives formed in this manner will be much more meaningful than a list of statements that simply direct the child not to cross in the middle of the street or to stop at red lights when on a bicycle.[7]

If a teacher only prescribed behaviors relative to bicycle riding, it is possible that a process has been established that some people may consider undemocratic in nature and potentially dangerous to a free society? What other kinds of behaviors should teachers then be allowed to prescribe? Who else can prescribe behaviors?

There is much health knowledge from which to choose particular elements for instruction. Unfortunately, there are few criteria to apply to the process of choosing just what to teach. It is recommended that children be asked their interests in health topics and that what is taught be closely related to these interests. In this manner, the health instructional experience will be relevant and meaningful to the children. Below are some examples of questions that are related to just one area of health education, sex education, and that were asked by children who were in a study that was reported by the Connecticut State Education Department:

1. Where does a baby come from? When will they grow teeth? Start to walk? Learn to understand? (asked by third graders)
2. What causes birth deformities? (asked by fourth graders)
3. How do we stay alive in our mothers' stomach? (asked by fifth graders)
4. Does smoking have anything to do with babies being formed wrong? (asked by sixth graders)
5. When people are going to get married, why do they have a blood test? (asked by seventh graders)
6. How do kids stay well-liked without being one of the gang; smoking, drinking, etc.? (asked by eighth graders)[8]

A Conceptual Approach to Health Objectives

As with other subject areas, health education programs have recently adopted a behavioral focus to the stating of instructional objectives. This is illustrated in one recent study of school health education, identified as a conceptual curriculum design, which incorporates objectives stated in terms of observable and measurable behaviors exhibited by the learner.[9] The objectives grow out of three key concepts: growing and developing, interactions, and decision making. Each of these concepts includes several others, which in turn consist of numerous

---

7. Of course, to stop at red lights when on a bicycle is a desirable behavior. It is also a behavior that is required by law in most states, even though it is often ignored by law enforcement officers, parents, and others (a fact that teaches the child much more than how to ride a bicycle).

8. Ruth Byler et al., *Teach Us What We Want To Know* (New York: Mental Health Materials Center, Connecticut State Board of Education, 1969). For an example of how children's questions related to health may be incorporated into a meaningful learning experience, see Robert Brooks, "The Use of Student Questions as a Partial Format for Instruction Regarding Smoking and Health," *The Journal of School Health* 40, no. 10 (December 1970): 542–44.

9. School Health Education Study, *Health Education: A Conceptual Approach; Experimental Curriculum Project* (Washington, D.C.: School Health Education Study, 1965).

Figure 14.1. A Conceptual Model for Health Education

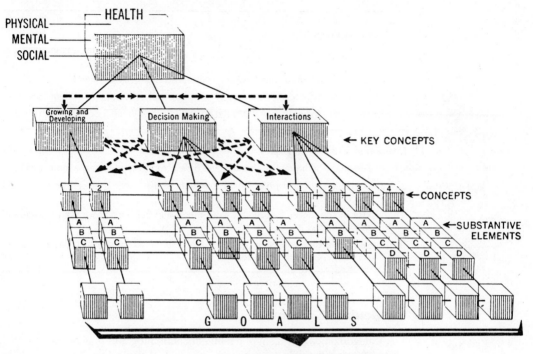

BEHAVIORAL OUTCOMES

Source: School Health Education Study, Health Education: A Conceptual Approach; Experimental Curriculum Project (Washington, D.C.: School Health Education Study, 1965). Reprinted from John T. Fodor and Gus T. Dalis, *Health Instruction: Theory and Application* (Philadelphia: Lea & Febiger, 1966), Figure 3, p. 50. Used with permission of the publisher.

subconcepts or principles. Figure 14.1 diagrammatically depicts this conceptual health education curriculum. The key concepts and those derived from them are shown in Chart 14.1.

Figure 14.1 shows that each concept is comprised of several subconcepts, which are stated in behavioral terms and serve as instructional objectives.[10] An example of this is given in Chart 14.2 on page 367.

Chart 14.1. School Health Education Study Curriculum Concepts

Growing and developing (key concept)

1. Growth and development influences and is influenced by the structure and functioning of the individual.

10. A listing of all concepts, subconcepts, and principles in this study can be obtained from 3M Education Press, Minnesota Mining and Manufacturing Co., St. Paul, Minn.

2. Growing and developing follow a predictable sequence yet are unique for each individual.

Interacting (key concept)

1. Protection and promotion of health is an individual, community, and international responsibility.
2. The potential for hazards and accidents exists in any environment.
3. There are reciprocal relationships involving people, disease, and the environment.
4. The family serves to perpetuate the human race and to fulfill certain health needs.

Decision making (key concept)

1. Personal health practices are affected by a complexity of forces, often conflicting.
2. Utilization of health information, products, and services is guided by values and perceptions.
3. Use of substances that modify both mood and behavior arises from a variety of motivations.
4. Food selection and eating patterns are determined by physical, social, mental, economic, and cultural factors.

Curriculum Content

Categorizing the content of health education programs may not be as useful as it was before the development of the conceptual curriculum design model just described, but it still may provide insights for teachers regarding their concerns about health education. For want of other labels, the teacher may conceive of health content as related to the following three areas: human relationships, personal health, and community health. Human relationships content consists of the study of family living, sex education, emotional and attitudinal development, and the skills necessary for individuals to relate to one another. Personal health areas include knowledge of the care of skin, hair, eyes, ears, teeth, hands, and nails and about such preventive practices as medical examinations, avoidance of the transmission of disease, and protection from the contracting of diseases (inoculation, for example). Community health pertains to the study of communicable diseases, environmental health, safety education, and first aid as well as involves familiarity with community health resources, such as the fire, police, and health departments. An apparent omission in the above listing is drug education. Since drug abuse is said to be related to an inability to relate to others, pertains to one's personal health, and has been described as epidemic, it is apparent that drug education can be included within any of the three major categories.

Instructional Strategies

Since the school is a place in society where it should be possible to discover truth, it is important that teachers provide for open and objective investigations of

Chart 14.2. Example of a Conceptual Health Education Curriculum

Key Concept: Decision Making

Concept: Use of substances that modify mood and behavior arises from a variety of motivations

Level I subconcepts:

1. Identifies substances commonly used by many individuals in society that modify mood and behavior
2. Names ways common mood and behavior modifying substances are used in homes and community
3. Is aware that there are differences between alcoholic beverages and other beverages
4. Realizes there are differences in family practices and feelings about use of tobacco and alcoholic beverages

Level II subconcepts:

1. Describes the range of substances used by man to modify mood and behavior
2. Differentiates among controls on purchase, possession, and use of substances that modify mood and behavior
3. Illustrates how, when, and where certain mood and behavior-modifying substances are used for dietary, ceremonial, social, pain relieving, and other reasons
4. Discusses why certain mood and behavior-modifying substances are used rather commonly and others under special circumstances

Source: Adapted from *Health Education: A Conceptual Approach to Curriculum Design.* Copyright 1967 by School Health Education Study. Used with permission of the publisher, Minnesota Mining & Manufacturing Co.

those health topics that are deemed important by children. Children need to participate in the decisions that determine how the curriculum and teachers should serve them. To be sure, parents and the community should also be involved in decisions that pertain to schooling, as should experts in subject matter areas and textbook writers. However, the rights of children should be protected. If learning is to take place, children's concerns and interests need to receive paramount consideration.

Health Texts

Textbooks are often excellent sources from which to choose topics for suggested study and from which to learn about those topics. The following are some current elementary level, health education books:

Bauer, W.W., et al. *Health for All Series.* Glenview, Ill.: Scott, Foresman & Co., 1965. (Grades 1-8).

Byrd, Oliver E., et al. *Laidlaw Health Series.* River Forest, Ill.: Laidlaw Brothers, 1966. (Grades 1-8).

Cornwell, Oliver K., and Irwin, Leslie W. *My Health Book Series*. Chicago: Lyons & Carnahan, 1963. (Text-workbooks for grades 3-8).

Hallock, Grace T., et al. *Health for Better Living Series*. Boston: Ginn & Co., 1963. (Grades 1-8).

Irwin, Leslie W., et al. *Dimensions in Health Series*. Chicago: Lyons & Carnahan, 1965. (Grades 1-8).

Schneider, Herman, and Schneider, Nina. *Health Science Series*. Boston: D.C. Heath & Co., 1961-65. (Kindergarten through grade 8).

Wilcox, Charlotte E., et al. *The Health Action Series*. Chicago: Benefic Press, 1961-62. (Grades 1-8).

Wilson, Charles C., M.D., and Wilson, Elizabeth A. *Health for Young America Series*. Indianapolis, Ind.: Bobbs-Merrill, 1965. (Grades 1-8).

Process Versus Content

Given the increase in knowledge due to technological and scientific advances, it seems imperative that teachers be willing to continue to be learners and be willing to adjust, to make more accurate statements about knowledge and "facts," and to have inquiring attitudes. It should be realized that the role of the school is to prepare children for a changing and somewhat unpredictable society. Thus, children need to maintain the desire to learn; they need to know how to pursue interests and knowledge rather than simply to learn what is a "fact" today. It is this rationale, the need to be flexible in terms of the future, that necessitates a greater concern for process than content.

As has been suggested in earlier chapters, in order for children to pursue their interests in the classroom in the sense described here, they must acquire the ability to relate to others, possess positive self-concepts, and remain tolerant of other opinions. The necessity of possessing these attributes applies to all learning in groups. The discussion of such health-related topics as a child's role in the family, the use and abuse of drugs, and why and how boys differ from girls requires discussion and group process skills to an extent as great as that required in studying any other school subject.

Learning Activities—Process

The activities suggested below are related to the learning process in elementary school health instruction. Essentially, they are concerned with the development of the skills and attitudes important to all communication processes. The reader will note their relationship to learning activities suggested in earlier chapters, particularly those in Chapters 4 and 5.

1. *Listening Practice*. Children are formed into groups of three members each for the purpose of discussing a question. Questions may range from "How does someone make friends?" to "What's the safest way to ride a bicycle?" During the ensuing discussion, in order for a member of the group to communicate verbally, he or she must paraphrase, to the satisfaction of the previous speaker, what was last said. If a paraphrase is attempted but is incorrect, the person who is being paraphrased repeats

what he or she said and the paraphraser makes another attempt. The purposes of this exercise are as follows:

a. To provide a framework for classmates to talk in small groups and get to know one another

b. To emphasize that people often think about what they want to say next and do not really listen to what others are saying

c. To discuss fully the topic at hand in an interesting and effective manner

d. To underline the idea that communication is often impeded by emotional involvement in the topic, by someone who talks for a long period of time, by someone who presents a lot of ideas all at once, by serious biases, or by poor facility in speaking and listening

(If this exercise is conducted for a twenty-minute period of time and discussed fully, pupils will become aware of their listening skills and will attempt to sharpen them. A periodic repeat of this exercise will provide feedback as to progress in listening-skills development.)

2. *Clarifying Values.* Many classroom activities designed to help pupils clarify values can be found.[11] This is one example:

Children list, in any order, twenty things that they really enjoy doing. (The completion of this phase of the exercise is not always easy to accomplish, thereby providing evidence as to how little thought is directed toward the things we do.) After completing the list, the child is to:

a. Place a letter *p* next to those items the child thinks his or her parents would have listed when they were in the grade he or she is in. (In this manner, a discussion of the presence, or absence, of a generation gap can be introduced.)

b. Place a dollar sign next to those items that cost money to do.

c. Place an *X* next to each item that can be done alone and a *Y* next to each item that requires another person.

d. Place the approximate date when the five "most enjoyed" items on the list were last done.

(A discussion of the above points will help the children to clarify what they value by comparing what they *enjoy* doing with what they *actually* do.

3. *Self-Portrait.* It is important for good mental health that children have accurate, if not positive, self-concepts. To help them learn how they are perceived by others, ask each child to draw a self-portrait, attempting to show as much feeling as possible in the picture. Then, the children pair off and discuss the accuracy of their portraits. (Note: There is some danger that this activity will develop inaccurate, as well as negative, self-concepts; thus, this exercise should be used with caution.)

4. *Role Reversal.* Another technique for helping children see how they are perceived by others is to ask them to act as someone else in the class. The person who is being imitated should have the opportunity to imitate the actor as well. A discussion centering on the acts does much for fostering self-awareness.

---

11. See Louis Raths, Merrill Harmin, and Sidney Simon, *Values and Teaching: Working with Values in the Classroom* (Columbus, Ohio: Charles E. Merrill Publishing Co., 1966).

5. *Acting Out Feelings.* Emotional health and the study of feelings are difficult topics to discuss in a school setting. Children can show much about their feelings in dramatics—as has been suggested—but they may play roles to show feelings. From the list below, children could select a feeling to act out. The role playing may be limited to verbal expression only or physical movements only (as in pantomime), or it may be a combination of both forms. A discussion of the acting and the feeling itself should follow.

pride	happiness	glory
determination	love	sadness
joy	warmth	freedom
fascination	loneliness	confidence

Learning Activities—Content

The activities described below are suggestive of many others that might be used to help teach those aspects of health that are important for elementary school children to know. Many of these are games and other activities similar to those suggested in earlier chapters for teaching content rather than skills.

1. *Cognitive Football.* A content area in health education is selected; for example, drug education. The class is divided into two teams. A football field is drawn on the chalkboard, and the teacher holds three sets of cards, which contain questions pertaining to the content area selected. One set of cards contains relatively easy questions, and each question answered correctly results in a five-yard gain. Another set of cards have somewhat difficult questions, and each correct answer results in a ten-yard gain. The last set of questions is worth fifteen yards for each correct answer. With the ball on the fifty-yard line, the toss of a coin determines which team commences the game. Team members decide from which set of cards the questions should be selected and thereby how much of a gain will be attempted. Before trying to answer the question, the team decides which member will answer the question, and this child is not allowed to receive help from his or her teammates. Teams alternate answering questions, and the team that puts the ball over the opponent's goal line is the winner.

2. *Family Drawings.* Sometimes children have misunderstandings about the roles of family members. An activity designed to bring to the surface a child's feelings about his or her family involves drawing a picture of his or her family in a group activity or some other context. Drawings are then exchanged until each classmate has had the opportunity to review each drawing. Every pupil writes a one-sentence comment, which expresses his or her reaction, on the back of each drawing reviewed. Comments may relate to the family as a whole or to individuals depicted. Drawings are then returned to their owners, and time is provided for reading the comments and for discussing the objectives of this exercise.

3. *Daily Menu.* To help make nutrition education relevant to their lives, pupils may be asked to keep a record of all foods they ingest. They may

conduct an analysis of these foods by nutrient content and nutritional value as well as by cultural differences. Expressions such as "You are what you eat" can then be discussed.

4. *Health Experiments.* There are many experiments that can be conducted in health classes to illustrate cause and effect relationships or to make learning more interesting. Examples of such experiments follow:

a. *Smoking Experiments.* To demonstrate the effect of smoking on the lungs, the teacher accumulates smoke from a cigarette in his or her mouth, and with the handkerchief then placed over the mouth, exhales the smoke. The dark spot that appears on the handkerchief demonstrates the effect of cigarette tar on the lungs. The teacher repeats this process, but this time the smoke is inhaled. The difference between the effects from an inhaled puff and a noninhaled puff is shown by the stains on the handkerchief. This difference suggests that tar remains in the lungs.

   An experiment indicating the effect of nicotine on the heart can also be conducted. The teacher's pulse rate which indicates the heart beat, is measured before and after smoking a cigarette. The higher pulse rate after smoking the cigarette suggests that smoking has a stimulative effect on the heart.

b. *Dental Experiment.* Available from the Colgate-Palmolive Company at a cost of fifty cents per kit is a "Cavity Fighter Kit," which includes "disclosing tablets." When these tablets are chewed, tablet particles cling to places on the teeth that aren't clean, thereby allowing the pupils to test the effectiveness of various methods of brushing the teeth.

c. *Environmental Experiments.* Water collected from polluted creeks, rivers, or lakes is compared with water collected from nonpolluted sources. When both samples are mounted on slides and viewed through a microscope, the organisms present provide evidence of differences between the two water sources.

5. *Correlated Activities.* As has been suggested in earlier chapters, there are many opportunities for combining the health curriculum with one or more other areas, such as:

a. *English.* Discussing environmental and personal health problems. Writing or giving oral reports on health problems and issues. Holding panel discussions and debates on health topics.

b. *Social Studies.* Visiting community health institutions. Mapping areas having health problems or activities. Studying inner-city or rural problems related to health.

c. *Science.* Demonstrating how the lungs work. Injecting a mouse with nicotine. Studying the effects of environmental factors on the body.

d. *Mathematics.* Gathering statistics pertaining to health-related absences from school. Making graphs and charts that show health statistics.

e. *Art.* Studying the effects of color on emotions. Drawing diagrams of the human body.

f. *Physical Education.* Studying the effects of exercise on the human body. Investigating the reasons for school health regulations governing the use of the pool, gymnasium, lunchroom, bathrooms, drinking fountains, and so forth. Studying sport as an emotional outlet.

Evaluation

Evaluation in health instruction assumes several modes. If the teacher perceives the role of health instruction to be one of affecting children's behaviors, then evaluation may largely consist of assessing the attainment of health-related behaviors. Evaluation should be made in terms of these behaviors; that is, determinations may be made of dental habits, patterns of exercise and rest, and so forth. If the concern is more with children's knowledge of health information, then tests may be administered before and after learning experiences. Similarly, if the concern is with attitudinal development, instruments to measure attitudes are available. For instance, teachers professing to be concerned with the self-concepts of their students may assess the effect of the health class on that variable by administering Stanley Coopersmith's *Self-Concept Scale*.[12] Generally, teachers are concerned with children's acquisition of knowledge about health and with attitudes and behaviors concerning it; thus, they employ various measures in the assessment of their instruction.

Teachers should determine what they are attempting to do and then assess whether they have done it. This may seem obvious, but systematic evaluation by teachers, health instructors included, is the exception rather than the rule. Increasingly advanced is the point of view that if teachers are not able to provide evidence in some objective manner that learning has taken place, they are in the awkward position of not being able to justify their existence as teachers.[13] Certainly there is a need for meaningful and valid evaluation of health instruction at all levels. Thus, even though "there is a shortage of valid and useful elementary health education tests, scales, and other appraisal devices,"[14] teachers can assess the health instruction by several means.

Observation

As mentioned earlier, observing children's behavior is a means of determining what they may have learned in the health program. This behavior can be observed in the school and its environs. For example, some things to look for in the school and in children's behavior include:

1. Evidence of a cleaner and more attractive school building
2. Improved behavior during safety and fire drills

---

12. Stanley Coopersmith, *The Antecedent of Self Esteem* (San Francisco: Freeman, 1968).
13. Robert F. Mager, *Preparing Instructional Objectives* (San Francisco: Fearon Publishers, 1962), p. 47.
14. Carl Willgoose, *Health Education in the Elementary School*, 3rd ed. (Philadelphia: W.B. Saunders Co., 1969), p. 389.

3. Increased cooperation in helping to maintain a healthful classroom
4. Evidence of practices to limit the use of sweets and carbonated drinks during class trips and parties
5. Improved practices with regard to working and playing in properly heated and lighted rooms[15]

Published Tests

Though not bountiful, some health tests are available. These include:

Adams, G.S., and J.A. Sexton. *California Tests in Social and Related Sciences, Part 3, Test 5, Health and Safety*. Monterey, Calif.: California Test Bureau, 1963. (Grades 4-8).

AAHPER Cooperative Health Education Test. Washington, D.C.: American Association for Health, Physical Education and Recreation, 1972. (Grades 7-9).

Bicycle Safety Information Test. Chicago, Ill.: National Safety Council. (Elementary level).

Colebank, A.D. *Health Behavior Inventory*. Monterey, Calif.: California Test Bureau, 1963. (Grades 7-9).

Crow, L.D., and L.C. Ryan. *Health and Safety Education Test*. Rev. ed. Edited by C.L. Brownell. Chicago, Ill.: Psychometric Affiliates, 1960. (Grades 3-6).

Getting Along: Grades 7, 8, 9. Temple City, Calif.: T. Lawrence, 6117 No. Rosemead Blvd., 1964.

Kindergarten Health Check for Parents. Los Angeles, Calif.: Los Angeles City Schools, Division of Educational Services, 1958.

Yellen. S. *Health Behavior Inventory*. Monterey, Calif.: California Test Bureau, 1963. (Grades 3-6).

Health Records

Records, usually kept by a school nurse, are frequently available to teachers. These records usually review the pupils' illnesses and injuries and contain related information useful for evaluation of the program.

Surveys

Communications from pupils, parents, other teachers, and school administrators may provide evaluative information about the health program. Questionnaires or requests for comments are both appropriate means for obtaining such information.

---

15. Willgoose, *Health Education*, p. 390.

PHYSICAL EDUCATION

Since physical education activities are largely of a motor and psychomotor nature, the physical education program should largely focus on the development of these skills. Later, when the child is sufficiently skilled, the activities are extended, and the pupil may choose those activities he or she wishes to participate in. The development of these basic skills may be considered analogous to achieving the process objectives of health education programs, with the subsequent choosing of activities being similar to the content objectives.

Physical education has not always been perceived as a vital part of the school curriculum. There are several reasons for this, with perhaps the principal one being an ignorance of the aims and objectives to which physical educators subscribe. Although recently identified environmental problems have resulted in an emphasis on the quality of our lives, physical education teachers have been concerned with the quality of living for many years. The worthwhile use of leisure time, the appreciation of complex movement, and the ability to do one's best and accept defeat or success with grace all pertain to qualitative living. These are only some of the goals of physical education programs. As is shown in the following section, an investigation of the objectives of physical education provides evidence of this quality-of-life theme.

Objectives

The concerns of physical education can be classified under four major headings: basic skill development, sport skill development, physical fitness development, and social development.

Basic Skills

Basic skills pertain to psychomotor activities that are not specific to any sport. Such skills include:

Walking	Bouncing
Skipping	Jumping
Running	Kicking
Throwing	Leaping
Catching	Striking

In addition to these, the development of skills related to perception is important, and possibly this development can be aided through physical activities. Such perceptual-motor skills as directionality, laterality, figure-ground perception, balancing, and body awareness are related to learning skills in other curriculum areas. Directionality is the skill needed to move in a specific direction to reach an object. Laterality is concerned with the concepts of right and left and the ability to control each side of the body separately and simultaneously. Figure-ground perception refers to visual distinctions that enable the child to focus on an object and see that object as separate from and forward of a background. Balancing may be defined as the ability to equalize the distribution of weight and thereby maintain control of the body. Body awareness is the ability to identify the different parts of the body and their relationships to one another. The presence or absence of these perceptual-motor skills can be determined by administering the Purdue Perceptual-Motor Survey.[16]

Sport Skills

Basic skill development should have occurred by the end of the third grade. By this time the motor skills developed can be incorporated into sports activities. Such skills as those used for dribbling a basketball, hitting a baseball, trapping a soccer ball, throwing a football, and dancing then become the basis for developing objectives for the upper elementary grades program. However, the development of these skills should not be sought prior to the satisfactory achievement of basic motor skill development. In considering objectives, it is important to stress that the development of sport skills should not be directed at supplying Olympic or professional teams with talented athletes but rather at helping children become competent in one or more sports so that they may enjoy them and the exercising and socializing they provide. Skill in a sport allows children to use their leisure time in a productive manner as well as helps them to develop healthy attitudes toward competition, cooperation, winning and losing, fair play, and trying their best. Additionally, the sense of an individual's uniqueness and ability to contribute may be perceived and/or realized through sporting events. It is for these many reasons that sport skills should be developed, with the accompanying knowledge and attitudes intended to last a lifetime.

Physical Fitness

The development and maintenance of adequate physical fitness should coincide with the development of basic motor and sport skills. Physical fitness consists of the following eight factors:
1. *Strength:* the ability to perform large-muscle activity
2. *Power:* the process of using strength for effective movement (sometimes referred to as dynamic strength)
3. *Endurance:* the ability to carry out muscular activity over a period of time
4. *Agility:* the ability to change direction swiftly, easily, and with the body under control
5. *Flexibility:* the range of movement at the body's joints
6. *Speed:* the ability to move quickly and effectively
7. *Balance:* the ability to maintain body equilibrium in a variety of positions
8. *Coordination:* the harmonious functioning of muscles to produce complex movements

---

16. Eugene Gayle Roach and Newell Carlyle Kephart, *The Purdue Perceptual-Motor Survey* (Columbus, Ohio: Charles E. Merrill Publishing Co., 1966).

The goals of physical fitness development are directed at quality living. Physical fitness of a minimal degree is required if a child is to be fit to perform daily tasks (including learning in school), to possess the ability to meet emergency situations, and to participate in socializing sports activities. Furthermore, the relationship between being physically unfit and illnesses of a degenerative nature (for example, heart disease) has been well established. This suggests that physical fitness developed at an early age and then maintained can contribute to health in later years.

Social Development

Social development is also a goal of physical education, even though it is one that often is not recognized, particularly in the evaluation of programs. Tests of motor skills, sports skills, and physical fitness levels are available and are often administered to aid in the evaluation of physical education objectives; however, tests of sportsmanship, cooperation, and perseverance are more difficult to develop and therefore more difficult to find and administer. The fact that social development, especially that of sportsmanship, may be observed by the teacher does not mean that the program is achieving social development. Regardless of the instructional problems, physical education programs should attempt to teach:

Cooperation
Sportsmanship
Perseverance
Leadership
Ability to follow
Judgment
Respect for rules
Courtesy

As with the development of physical fitness, social development is concurrent with all learning in physical education. While a sport skill is being taught, for instance, rules associated with how that skill must be performed to be socially acceptable (and possibly legal) may be taught.

Curriculum Content

The content for achieving many of the objectives in physical education may be considered in several patterns. One consists of classifying activities as individual, dual, or team efforts. Illustrative of this type of classification is golf as an individual sport, tennis as a dual sport, and basketball as a team sport. Rhythmic activities, stunts, and other games can also be classified according to this pattern. Another way is to categorize the activities as movement explorations, rhythmic activities, sports activities, stunts, and gymnastics.

Movement Exploration

Movement exploration utilizes problem solving to learn movement skills. As described later, problems that can be solved by choosing any one movement or combination of movements from a group of correct responses are developed. For instance, children may be asked to shake single parts of their bodies. Then they may be requested to shake additional parts of their bodies. It is at this point that the problem becomes more complex, requiring combinations of movements.

There are many advantages to the utilization of movement exploration. This approach lends itself to evaluation by simple observation. Since the solution to a problem is the purpose of a movement, the child or teacher can assess the quality of the movement by determining if the problem has been solved. In addition, the lack of teacher-predetermined standards of performance allows for creative responses by children and for immediate feedback as to the success of these responses. Furthermore, the child learns not only *what* he is doing but *how* to perform various movements. Whereas some physical activities require size, weight, or advanced motor ability for adequate performance, movement exploration activities allow children of different physical abilities and attributes to learn and to achieve success. To illustrate this point, if asked to move a weight from one end of the room to another, one child might lift it, another pull it, and a third topple it end over end but each child would have solved the problem.

Movement exploration activities can be varied by time (slow, fast, even, uneven), space (high, low, large, small), flow (sustained, interrupted), or by equipment (ball, bat, pegs). In all cases, problem solving in relation to movement seeks to provide a wide experience in motor activity, to elicit creative movement responses, and to provide opportunitites for each child to appreciate his or her movement possibilities.

Rhythmic Activities

Rhythmic activities are included in the physical education curriculum to develop a sense of timing, maintain physical fitness levels, enhance specializations, and stimulate interest in movement. Varied movements are necessary in rhythmic activities. These include walking, running, hopping, leaping, skipping, sliding, bending, swaying, striking, lifting, and pulling. The movements may be varied as to tempo, beat, meter, accent, and mood. The relationship between rhythmic experiences in physical education programs and those in music programs are quite similar (see Chapter 13). Such equipment as tom-toms, drums, bells, sticks, records, and cymbals may be employed to achieve the objectives of rhythmic activity.

Rhythms may be related to the movement of objects as well as to movements of the body. For example, ball bouncing, rope jumping, baton twirling, or hoop twisting are rhythmic activities requiring coordinated body movements.

Rhythmic activities may also be employed to develop social knowledge and skills. Singing and dancing are both socializing and rhythmic activities that may be related to history and to understanding and appreciating various international differences.

Sports Activities

Sports activities, usually begun about grade three, utilize movement skills learned through movement exploration and rhythmic activities. Basketball requires ball-bouncing skills; football requires coordinated movements of the body in dodging and in kicking the ball; and volleyball players need to strike the ball in a rhythmic manner. In developing sport skills, however, games requiring less skill and organization precede an involvement in the sport itself. Such games, called games of low organization, can best be described with an example: Third graders might not be able to bat a volleyball over an eight-foot net, pass a volleyball from one player to another, or spike the ball over the net. In preparation for volleyball, the game of Newcomb is played. Newcomb requires a lower net and allows the player to catch and throw rather than strike the ball. Half-court basketball and slap ball (slapping a baseball rather than hitting it with a baseball bat) are other examples of games of low organization.

Participation in these sports activities is directed toward the development of physical fitness, the learning of sport skills for use during leisure time, and the providing of enjoyment. Sports activities should not be conducted to develop interscholastic, intercollegiate, or professional athletes. The exceptional child, though, should have an opportunity to manifest his or her advanced skills. Therefore, limited competitive activities between classrooms or schools has a place in the physical education curriculum, but these activities should not be the focus of the curriculum.

Stunts and Gymnastic Activities

The development of courage and the accompanying feeling of satisfaction on successful completion of the activity as well as the development of coordination, balance, and general body management are major goals of stunts and tumbling. But although these activities have long been an enjoyable aspect of physical education for some children, they have been an unenjoyable part of the curriculum for others. Since stunts and tumbling require a degree of courage, the teacher should allow children to participate electively in these activities. If children are forced into an activity that frightens them, they will not usually enjoy participation and may display tight, uncontrolled movements that tend to precipitate injury.

Those children who do wish to join in tumbling activities may attempt to master the forward roll, the backward roll, and a three-point head stand. Stunts for elementary school children include the tip-up (balancing on the palms while in a squat position with elbows inside the knees), duck walk (walking in a squat position with hands grasping the ankles), and the chinese get-up (two partners seated back to back with elbows interlocked while attempting to stand).

Related to stunts and tumbling are gymnastic activities, which develop courage, physical fitness, and general body management. The natural desire of the young to climb and swing account for the interest elementary school children show for gymnastics. The apparatus used in these activities may include the side horse, parallel bars, rings, horizontal bar, or trampoline. The equipment tends to motivate children who have seen experts on television and perhaps at gymnasiums in their own hometowns. The individual nature of apparatus work affords each child the opportunity to create movements of his or her own, succeed by his or her own ability, and develop self-confidence—all of which hopefully will transfer to other aspects of the child's life.

Instructional Strategies

As with all school subject matter, physical education can be interesting or boring. Rather than describe particular physical education activities that could be employed by the classroom teacher, references to sources that discuss these activities are included at the end of this chapter. The purpose of this section is to describe a progression of teaching styles that will free the child to determine *what* to learn and *how* to learn it.

One of the most influential sources on the teaching styles of physical education teachers is Muska Mosston's *Teaching Physical Education: From Command to Discovery*.[17] The author describes and recommends a progression of teaching styles that range from a highly teacher-dominated one to one that is totally pupil-determined. The analogy between the group process skills described earlier in relation to self-directed health education and Mosston's teaching styles should not be lost. In both physical and health education, such skills are necessary for freeing the learner. A brief description of Mosston's teaching styles is included here, but the reader is referred to the original source.

Styles of Teaching

1. *Command Style.* The teacher predetermines the objectives, content, learning activities, and means of evaluation. Pupils are not involved in the planning. During lessons the teacher directs or gives commands to the pupils. The teacher evaluates performances of pupils and periodically offers suggestions for improvement of such performances.

   The teacher who conducts a calisthenic drill so that all pupils raise their arms and spread their legs simultaneously is using the command style of teaching. This style can be recognized by such teacher directives as:
   a. On the count of 1, raise the right arm.
   b. Place the thumbs on the seam of the ball with your remaining fingers spread as far as possible.
   c. Kick the ball with the instep of your foot as you shift your weight from the back foot to the front. Ready, go!

2. *Task Style.* When some children are told that by the end of the class session they will be required to perform a forward roll and others who have mastered this skill will be required to demonstrate a backward roll, the task style of teaching is being employed. In this style, the planning is also done by the teacher, but there is less predetermination of other aspects of the program; that is, the amount of time devoted to any one activity will be determined during the lesson and dependent on the abilities of the children, and tasks will be assigned according to performance levels of the pupils. Children participate at their own pace but are expected to complete tasks within a specified period of time. Evaluation is made by the teacher, although a degree of self-evaluation by the child occurs in relation to the completion of many activities.

---

17. Muska Mosston, *Teaching Physical Education: From Command to Discovery* (Columbus, Ohio: Charles E. Merrill Publishing Co., 1966).

3. *Reciprocal Teaching.* Reciprocal teaching requires children to form pairs. One partner performs the task while the other partner observes the performance and offers suggestions for improvement. The performer and observer then switch roles. The teacher may stop the activity periodically to either demonstrate a skill, correct mistakes, or introduce the next task. Planning, as in the previously described styles of teaching, is done by the teacher with no pupil input. Evaluation is also made by the teacher, principally by observation as he or she moves about the learning area.

4. *Individualization.* A program for each child is predetermined by the teacher and communicated to the child, with the execution of the program done by the child. The teacher provides instruction but only occasionally offers corrections or hints as to how to complete the tasks. Giving each child his or her own program provides direction for the pupils while at the same time freeing them during the learning process itself. Each child evaluates himself or herself, with assistance from the teacher when requested. The following is one example of a sequence of tasks for this teaching style:

   a. Balance on just your hands that are placed on the floor. Keep your elbows inside your bent knees (tip-up).
   b. Perform a forward roll to a seated position.
   c. Perform a forward roll to a standing position.
   d. From a seated position, perform a backward roll.
   e. Perform a forward roll to a seated position and immediately perform a backward roll.
   f. Perform a backward roll from a seated position landing on feet, with legs bent at the knees, and immediately perform a forward roll to a standing position.

5. *Guided Discovery.* This style of teaching requires the teacher to predetermine the content and the steps involved in the learning of that content. Then questions or clues that will result in responses leading to the other questions are formulated so that the process is continually repeated. In this manner, children learn to perform an activity without the teacher ever telling them how. In effect, guided discovery teaches a *process*—the process of inquiry. The learning of the activity is subordinate to the learning of the process. To aid children in learning this process, the teacher always waits for their responses to his or her questions and reinforces correct responses. Evaluation during guided discovery is built into the style itself. The fact that the process is completed and that the subject matter has been learned is evidence of the effectiveness of the procedures followed.

   The following example is used by Mosston to illustrate a guided discovery lesson:

Subject matter:	Soccer.
Specific purpose:	To discover the use of the toe-kick in long and high-flying kicks.
Question 1:	"What kind of kick is needed when you want to pass the ball to a player who is far from you?"

Anticipated answer:	"A long kick!!" (Response: "Good!")
Question 2:	"Suppose there is a player from the opposing team between you and your teammate?"
Anticipated answer:	"Then the ball must fly high!" ("Right!" says the teacher.)
Question 3:	"Where should the force produced by the foot be applied on the ball in order to raise if off the ground?"
Anticipated answer:	"As low as possible!" ("Yes!" responds the teacher.)
Question 4:	"Which part of the foot can comfortably get to the lowest part of the ball without interference with the direction of the run and its momentum?"
Anticipated answer:	"The toes!" ("Very good!" proclaims the teacher.)
Question 5:	"Would you like to try it?"[18]

6. *Problem Solving.* As with previous teaching styles, problem solving requires the teacher to predetermine the subject matter taught. However, the subject matter is presented in the form of a problem. Once the problem is presented, the child is on his or her own to formulate questions and seek answers that will help solve the problem. Self-inquiry and self-discovery are encouraged and mistakes are expected.

This style of teaching allows the child to test cognitive solutions through physical responses. The following are some problems that may be presented to the children:
   a. How narrow can you be?
   b. How small can you be?
   c. Move as though you were very wide.
   d. Can you twist yourself like a dishrag and then shake yourself out?
   e. Move very slowly like a turtle, elephant, or a person working on skis.
   f. Be a food.
   g. Run as if you are being pursued, catching a bus, or dodging missiles.
   h. Fall as if you are dizzy, exhausted, stumbling.
   i. Throw the ball with one part of your body and catch it with another.
   j. Pretend you are very angry, sad, or happy.
   k. Imitate an animal.
   l. Pretend you are a musical instrument.
   m. Move like you are smoke in the air.

7. *Creativity.* As might be expected, the progression of teaching styles just described will culminate in the ability of children to formulate problems, pose questions relative to those problems, provide answers to them, and to evaluate their own performance. The teacher will then act as a resource available to students. It is therefore possible to have each child participating in different activities and practicing different tasks as long as an ac-

---

18. Mosston, *Teaching Physical Education*, p. 153.

counting of safety precautions has been made. Such possibilities as children running into one another, equipment being misused, and activities being conducted in an unsafe manner (for example, using a trampoline without people along its sides) should be considered.

Conditions for Effective Motor Learning

Regardless of the teaching style chosen, certain conditions are necessary if motor learning is to be achieved. The following is a discussion of several of these conditions:

1. *Communication must be appropriate for the learner.* There are three forms of communication to consider: verbal, visual, and manual guidance. Verbal and visual communications are self-explanatory. Manual guidance consists of moving the learner through a physical activitiy to provide him or her with a kinesthetic sense of the activity. It has been found that visualization and manual guidance are most effective with poorly skilled learners, while verbalization is most effective with skilled learners.

2. *Practice sessions for the learning of motor behavior can be distributed (many short periods of time) or massed (several long periods of time).* Especially at the beginning stages of learning, distributed practice is suggested because beginners need continuous reinforcement of correct physical responses. Massed practice becomes more appropriate as the pupils become more skilled.

3. *Physical skills can be learned by the whole method or the whole-part method.* The whole method involves practice of the total movement, whereas the whole-part method entails learning each part of the movement separately and then combining these parts to perform the total movement. Studies have indicated that when the skill to be learned is composed of continuous movements and when timing and speed are necessary to the pattern and coordination of the movement, the whole-part method is less effective than the whole method. For example, teaching children how to serve a tennis ball is best conducted by the whole method. If, on the other hand, an activity is composed of a number of subskills, the teaching of each subskill separately is appropriate. The whole-part method then is best employed in the teaching of a game like basketball, with a teacher showing pupils how to dribble a basketball and how to shoot a basketball before they play the game.

4. *Mental practice, or thinking of how to perform a skill, by itself results in motor learning.* However, mental practice combined with physical practice is the most effective condition for motor learning.

5. *Feedback relative to physical performance is an important condition for motor learning.*

6. *Skills should be practiced as realistically as possible.* If speed is part of the skill, the skill should be practiced at a speed as close to the appropriate speed as possible so long as the learner is still able to maintain control of the movement. If accuracy is a necessary part of the skill, the skill should be practiced from the beginning with attention to accuracy.

7. *Overlearning (practicing until a skill becomes automatic) is necessary for effective motor performance.* Overlearning results in consistency of performance and in the ability to retain and repeat performance.

Evaluation

To evaluate physical education teaching is both a simple and complex task. It is relatively easy to construct tests of such matters as the rules of games, the strategy of sports activities, and the proper movements to perform a skill. Similarly, whether or not children can perform a particular motor activity or task can be determined by observing their performances. Much of this evaluation can and should be done informally by teachers—and by pupils. However, published tests and testing procedures for evaluating motor skill development and physical fitness as well as knowledge about them should also be employed. On the other hand, it is difficult to evaluate sportsmanship, cooperation, leadership, and the development of attitudes pertaining to awareness of the beneficial nature of physical activity. Observing children allows assessment of these qualities to a limited extent, particularly as they are expressed in various sports activities. The following questions serve as an example of observational assessment of behaviors that indicate affective learning *(appreciation for physical activity* in this case):

1. Is the child prepared for physical education (for example, does he or she have sneakers and shorts)?
2. Does the child participate in after-school physical activities?
3. Is the physical fitness of the child maintained at a satisfactory level?
4. Does the child participate in physical activity during recess or lunch hour?

Of course, affirmative responses to these questions may indicate something other than appreciation of physical activity, but if the behaviors suggested by the questions are present, the teacher may conclude with some confidence that the child does indeed possess an appreciation of physical activity.

EXERCISES FOR THOUGHT AND ACTION

1. What values are associated with involving children in selection of objectives, with choosing learning activities, and with evaluation?
2. What health-related resources are available in your school's community? Respond in terms of people, organizations, facilities, and equipment.
3. What are the major health problems in your school? List these by the following categories: communicable disease problems, safety problems, mental-health problems, and other problems (for example, dental cares, drug experimentation).
4. If accessible, survey the health folders maintained in your elementary school. What information is in the folders? Which pieces of information seem unnecessary? What important information seems to be missing?

5. How much emphasis should be placed on competition in sports activities? Is competition necessary for pupils to excel? Does an attitude of cooperativeness suffer when competitive activities are conducted?
6. What kinds of physical education activities can take place within the classroom?
7. Suggest ways in which physical education activities may be correlated with other subject areas. What are the advantages and disadvantages to the correlations you suggest?

SELECTED READINGS

I. *Health Education*

Felice, Joseph P., and Carolan, Patrick J. *Tune in to Health.* New York: College Entrance Book Co., 1971.

Fodor, John T., and Dalis, Gus T. *Health Instruction: Theory and Application.* Philadelphia: Lea & Febiger, 1966.

Improving Elementary School Safety. 2nd ed. Chicago: National Safety Council, 1970.

Kilander, H. Frederick. *School Health Education.* 2nd ed. New York: Macmillan Co., 1968.

Miles, Matthew B. *Learning To Work in Groups.* New York: Teachers College Press, 1965.

New York State Education Department. *A Multimedia Reference Listing of Materials on Drug Education.* New York: University of the State of New York, 1971.

Oberteuffer, Delbert; Harrelson, Orvis A.; and Pollock, Marion B. *School Health Education.* 5th ed. New York: Harper & Row, 1972.

Sax, Saville, and Hollander, Sandra. *Reality Games.* New York: Macmillan Co., 1972.

Turner, C.E.; Randall, Harriet B.; and Smith, Sara Louise. *School Health and Health Education.* 6th ed. St. Louis, Mo.: C.V. Mosby Co., 1970.

Zuckerman, David W., and Horn, Robert E. *The Guide to Simulation for Education and Training.* Cambridge, Mass.: Information Resources, 1970.

II. *Physical Education*

Bucher, Charles, and Reade, Evelyn. *Physical Education and Health in the Elementary School.* 2nd ed. New York: Macmillan Co., 1971.

Dauer, Victor. *Dynamic Physical Education for Children.* 3rd ed. Minneapolis, Minn.: Burgess Publishing Co., 1968.

Geri, Frank H. *Illustrated Games and Rhythms for Children.* Englewood Cliffs, N.J.: Prentice-Hall, 1955.

Gilliom, Bonnie C. *Basic Movement Education for Children: Rationale and Teaching Units.* Reading, Mass.: Addison-Wesley Publishing Co., 1970.

Kirchner, Glenn. *Physical Education for Elementary School Children.* Dubuque, Iowa: Wm. C. Brown Publishing Co., 1970.

Kirchner, Glenn; Cunningham, Jean; and Warrell, Eileen. *Introduction to Movement Education.* Dubuque, Iowa: Wm. C. Brown Publishing Co., 1970.

Miller, Arthur G., and Whitcomb, Virginia. *Physical Education in the Elementary School Curriculum.* 3rd ed. Englewood Cliffs, N.J.: Prentice-Hall, 1969.

Mosston, Muska. *Teaching Physical Education: From Command to Discovery.* Columbus, Ohio: Charles E. Merrill Publishing Co., 1965.

Nagel, Charles. *Play Activities for Elementary Grades.* St. Louis, Mo.: C.V. Mosby Co., 1964.

Radler, Donald, and Kephart, Newell. *Success Through Play.* New York: Harper & Row, 1960.

Salt, E. Benton; Fox, Grace I.; and Stevens, B.K. *Teaching Physical Education in the Elementary School.* 2nd ed. New York: Ronald Press Co., 1960.

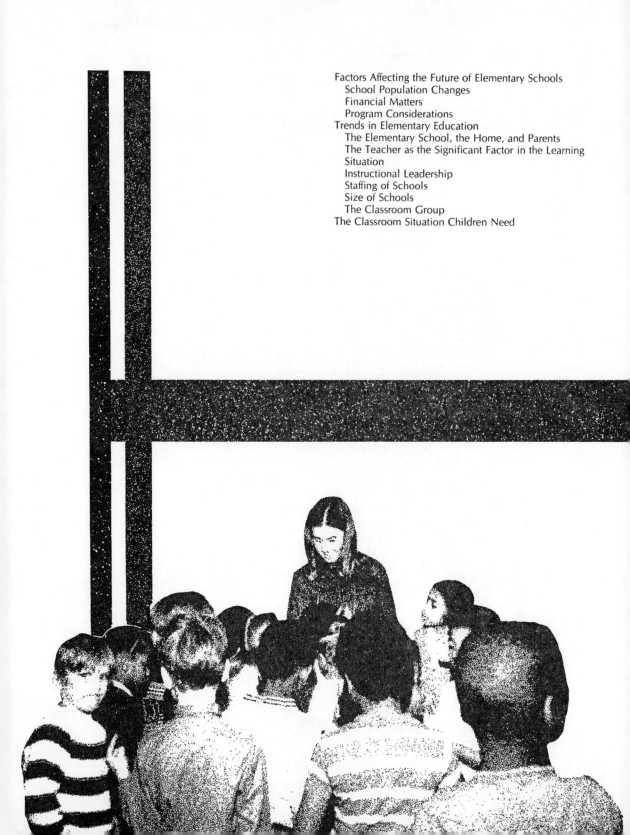

This chapter is not a forecast of the future in the sense that "a look ahead" usually implies. Neither is it a review of trends in the various subject areas, those points having been made in the chapters devoted to each field. Rather, the discussion stresses possible directions that elementary education might conceivably take— depending on how the schools respond to external forces and what sorts of educational decisions are made.

In any attempt to outline the future of American elementary schools, it must be kept in mind that institutions are inherently conservative and resistant to change. Another important consideration is that the educational system can only reflect the values and conflicts of the society it serves. The elementary school of the future may well be significantly different from its predecessor, depending on the nature and the extent of changes that occur in the larger culture. Those in charge of the schools will be confronted with the extremely difficult task of deciding which aspects of societal change and variation to emphasize as the principles on which the education of children can be based.

Certainly all pervasive societal trends eventually affect the schools. The pattern of employment opportunities, family living arrangements, the types of implicit messages conveyed by the mass media, the degree of concern about energy and the environment, and other similar concerns will influence curriculum and administration. The discussion presented in this chapter does not include analysis of these general matters but is, rather, restricted to areas that are immediately and directly controlling what the elementary school can do.

W.T.P.

A Look Ahead
The Elementary School Beyond the 1970s

Richard T. Salzer and Walter T. Petty

FACTORS AFFECTING THE FUTURE OF ELEMENTARY SCHOOLS

Looking ahead requires consideration of the "here and now," and there are data available concerning a number of factors that will affect elementary education. For one important point, the school population is no longer growing in size and is actually decreasing in many districts. (The nation, for the first time in a generation, has a surplus of qualified teachers.) Yet even though the school-age group is not increasing in numbers, school-system budgets grow larger each year, a condition that causes many citizens to wonder about the worth of the educational system. Citizens are beginning to demand reliable information concerning the effectiveness of the schools in meeting society's objectives.

School Population Changes

In the United States the school-age population has been steadily declining since 1970. There were more than one million fewer schoolchildren in 1973 than there were in 1970, with the prospect that by 1982 there will be as many as four million fewer pupils.

This drop in enrollment has many implications. The regular opening of new schools has provided opportunities to try construction and organizational innovations of many kinds. The appointment of a new principal and staff has often been accompanied by decisions to use a particular educational approach throughout a school. Reduced numbers of pupils not only means that few buildings will be opening but also that innovation and program development will now evidently be a matter of efforts to change the practices of the present staff rather than the recruitment of new faculty members. Furthermore, some existing school buildings will be closed. Such closings mean fewer opportunities for variation within a school system, an important stimulus to program innovation.

If all else remains the same, a decrease in the number of schoolchildren must bring a decline in the number of teaching positions. Perhaps decisions will be made to establish smaller classes or add additional specialized personnel, in which case more teaching positions would be made available. But it seems more likely that, in most situations, fewer teachers will be employed. Such a development represents a serious problem for the society at large, for higher education, and for the individuals involved.

Financial Matters

While financial aspects of education have always received substantial attention and occasionally have become central concerns, most Americans have been willing to support their school system without much complaint. There is reason to believe, however, that this situation is changing. Taxes, including those for schools, are rising, and in most localities the education levy remains under the direct control of the electorate. Increasingly, voters have been acting to place limitations on expenditures for education.

Several states now provide school funds substantially or entirely through state agencies, and the federal government has become increasingly involved in the financial affairs of the educational system. While some observers welcome these developments, other groups deplore the resultant effect, which is the removal of much control from the local setting. It appears clear that many citizens want local control of the budget as a means of maintaining substantial influence over the conduct and content of education. The citizens of this nation have usually had authority over their school system, and many of them are not eager to surrender such power.

Professional educators have sought to assure the taxpayers that quality education is possible only when school systems are well financed. While it is not possible to offer absolute proof of such a contention by showing a direct relationship between specific expenditures and particular results, there are some general indications that seem consistent with the statement. Results of nationwide testing programs indicate that areas of the country in which spending for education is greatest do have the lowest rates of illiteracy—although either factor might be cause or effect. Certainly any observer can see substantial differences between well-funded and minimally financed school systems, and these differences have become the subject of court decisions that may have far-reaching implications.

All of this—questions of school governance, degree of local control, willingness to pay for all recommended educational services—reflects concern over whether or not the school system is worthy of support.

Program Considerations

Large numbers of citizens are at least as much concerned with what the schools do as with what they cost. There are, as might be expected, continuing complaints that the curriculum and the library contain offensive material or that individual teachers are doing something objectionable. Strongly expressed concerns about the absence of minimum educational standards are not new either, of course, but recently, independent agencies have attempted to go beyond the customary complaints that performance is not what it used to be and examine what children in the school system can and cannot do.

Whether or not the average child of today knows as much or can read or do mathematics as well as the pupil of twenty or fifty years ago is a question that cannot be resolved. What does seem clear is that large numbers of youngsters cannot do well enough to function satisfactorily in our complex modern world. Various surveys have identified significant portions of the populace who cannot complete simple information forms or perform basic calculations.

Disappointing outcomes from examinations of pupil achievement lead to debates about the nature of the school program. Many people are tempted to take the position that improvement will result only from the careful specification of objectives, the utilization of routinized practice materials and frequent testing, and the holding of school personnel "accountable" for the results. Others, including most of the authors of this book, would argue that improvement will come with the devising of inherently interesting tasks that provide realistic opportunities to learn and apply knowledge and skills. And it may be useful to stress that the school is only one aspect of education in this society and therefore cannot be held entirely responsible for the abilities and performances of the young.

TRENDS IN ELEMENTARY EDUCATION

Examination of the present scene in elementary education reveals the existence of several areas of potentially important change. The trends in these areas derive principally from well-established forces that are closely related to the field of education. In the discussion of each point, an attempt has been made to draw implications and describe future developments should the trend continue in its present direction.

The Elementary School, the Home, and Parents

Social science researchers are now coming to a conclusion long since reached by educators: Once it is known what kind of home and family the pupil comes from, his or her success in school can be rather accurately predicted.

Clearly, the home situation is the most important factor in determining what the child is and is likely to become, in and out of school. While educators usually acknowledge that they cannot do much without the support of parents, the school system does not have a very good record of cooperation with the home.

If, as appears likely, the number of children per family continues to be fewer than was the case in the past, parents will have greater opportunity to concern themselves with the welfare of every boy and girl. They will be more and more insistent that the school pay attention to their children's needs and demonstrate interest in each child.

There are several implications for the elementary school in view of this recognition of the importance of the home situation and of the likelihood of greater parental attention to the teaching/learning conditions:

1. Schools must seek ways to be more significantly involved with parents, extending their services into the homes and encouraging parents to participate in educational planning and program development.
2. The schools will be opening their doors to younger children in a variety of ways. In some situations four-year-olds are now being enrolled as a matter of course. The educational system may well come to be responsible for daily care of infants and toddlers and the after-school hours of older children.
3. Programs of parent education should be offered through the elementary schools. There is substantial evidence that young parents are interested in having assistance in such areas as prenatal development, infant care, and parent-child interaction. The school can be the base for these services, using the opportunity to build a relationship with the home and assisting parents to be effective in their roles.

The Teacher as the Significant Factor in the Learning Situation

There is much support for the generalization that the teacher is the most important element in the school learning environment. This recognition is based on both conventional professional wisdom and the results of research investigations, such as the "First Grade Studies" in reading, and the evaluation of the "Follow Through" program for disadvantaged children. The preponderance of educational research results indicates that learning outcomes are influenced first of all by the backgrounds of the pupils and second by who the teacher is. Several points would seem to follow from such a generalization:

1. Those interested in school programs should cease their searches for the "right" method and "best" organization of materials of instruction. Such activity is not worth the time and money expended. All programs are no better or worse than the people using them.
2. Attention should be given to identifying and studying outstanding teachers. Attempts should be made to find out who these people are, what they do, and whether or not others can be helped to be more like them.
3. It should be possible, as a start, to discover the factors that inhibit teachers from doing their best work and reduce or eliminate these barriers.

4. The effectiveness of teachers is mainly due to their personal qualities. Programs should be devised that give teachers better opportunities for the expression of their personalities. This means support for open-ended instruction rather than overly specified curriculum programs and routinized procedures.

Instructional Leadership

In most school districts there is much confusion over the question of the source of educational leadership. No doubt there remain a few districts in which all matters related to curriculum and instruction continue to be resolved in the central office, with directives to the rest of the staff emanating from there regularly. More common, however, are arrangements that provide for shared responsibility among teachers, building principals, and supervisory personnel. The usual procedure is for various groups with different perspectives to be involved in such areas as choice of textbooks and consideration of organizational approaches. Increasingly, private citizens and even pupils have participated in these decision-making processes.

Opposing this trend to wider involvement is the proposal by some teachers' organizations that the teacher group be given more direct control over school programs. Historically, the American teacher has been viewed as an employee who implements policies adopted by school boards and put into operation by administrators. Some influential people in the education profession now believe that teachers and their representatives should make all major decisions and that administrators at the building level ought to be responsible for putting these into effect. Under such arrangements, principals would function as executive officers of teacher committees and, perhaps, be known as "managers."

The drastic difference between these two directions in which educational leadership might go indicates to some extent the nature of the problem. In many elementary schools, principals have all but abandoned any pretense to instructional expertise. Teachers either do anything they want or follow directives from curriculum coordinators, reading specialists, and other authorities from the central office. Teachers in the same building may be found criticizing the principal for not exercising enough control and for interfering in areas that are properly the domain of others.

When principals assert themselves in terms of programming, they frequently find that they are then in a confrontation with some one of the program directors or supervisors. In most school systems, the general rule that principals are responsible for what goes on in their buildings means that in nearly all cases a dispute between principal and a curriculum or instructional staff member will be resolved in favor of the principal. It is not unknown for particular buildings to be ruled off limits to certain supervisors or central-office administrators. It is not likely that such states of affairs will lead to improvement of the instructional program.

Given such a complex situation, it seems likely that difficulties will continue to arise in the area of educational leadership. However, some basic points, such as the following, seem evident:

1. With respect to the trend toward more democratic participation in decision making, it should be kept in mind that no matter what the advantages

in terms of the promotion of positive attitudes, such practices do not automatically result in the selection of good alternatives, much less guarantee their effective execution. Substantial difficulties have also arisen as to the rights and responsibilities of participants, particularly in the matter of selection of textbooks and other teaching materials.

2. In the matter of choosing between a principal and a teacher committee as the leader, it should be recognized that committees are not well known for their capacity to oversee the day-by-day operations of institutions. In the last analysis some one person must assume responsibility for guiding and executing the work of a faculty. It seems inevitable that the building principal must be a leader.

3. To agree that the principal should lead does not confer the ability to do so. In a large number of cases, principals are appointed for reasons that have little to do with their understanding of children or educational programs. If teachers are to acknowledge principals as instructional experts, school administrators and those who work with them will have to take steps to improve the selection and education of school principals.

Staffing of Schools

In addition to teachers and principals, other adults can be important in determining the quality of children's school experiences. It has been customary to emphasize the need for specialized personnel in the schools—remedial teachers, child-behavior consultants, early-childhood experts, and the like—and certainly if all conceivable services were available many pupils would benefit.

There are, however, practical limitations as to how many professionals ought to be added to the budget and provided space and time in the schools. Furthermore, experience with some programs of employing teachers' aides and seeking voluntary participation on the part of citizens interested in the schools has indicated that such efforts have much to recommend them. Future staffing may be based, in part at least, on the following:

1. If there are numerous adults involved in the school program, for one important example, each child has a greater opportunity to find someone with whom to establish a relationship. A warm, responsive person can make a significant contribution, no matter what his or her professional qualifications.

2. Nonprofessionals as well as additional professional personnel could often be welcome in roles directly supportive of instructional activities. As classroom programs become more individualized and organizationally complex, a higher ratio of adults to pupils would be a real advantage. Also, a staff with diversity in backgrounds and skills will make it possible to introduce children to a wide range of interesting experiences, an important contribution to program attractiveness and quality.

3. Projects in schools serving economically disadvantaged children demonstrate that there is something to be gained by adding to the school staff individuals with close ties to the community and families from which the pupils come. Such programs often result in substantial improvement in

school-community relations. Equally important, many citizens have gone on from such experience to further their formal education and to qualify as teachers, social workers, and clinicians themselves, thus enriching the professions as well as their own lives in a significant way.

Size of Schools

Many service agencies are criticized because they seem too large. While size alone may not determine whether or not an agency performs its functions well, there can be no doubt that many who are served feel alienated from huge bureaucracies and structures. Schools are no exception.

Since the school-age population is declining in some areas, districts confront the question of the advisability of retaining buildings with small enrollments or closing them and transferring the pupils. While the economic pressure to consolidate will likely prove irresistible in most cases, there may be situations in which other considerations will prevail. Certainly many arguments supportive of smaller schools may be advanced:

1. As already mentioned, size has an inhibiting effect on many people. Children, parents, and even teachers often suffer a loss of identity in large buildings. Any new school buildings constructed should be planned for maximum enrollments of three or four hundred pupils.
2. Buildings with large enrollments present many difficulties in organization and administration. Huge numbers require the careful scheduling of everything from lunch periods to the appearance of special teachers to the use of the gymnasium and bus-loading platforms. All of this makes for regimentation and confusion, with a consequent loss of flexibility and adoption of practices that are not consistent with children's needs.
3. In smaller schools children have many opportunities to participate in special events and programs, the activities that will be remembered all their lives. Every youngster, not just the most able pupils, should have the chance to succeed in such areas as dramatic performances and service to the school. Participation in these kinds of activities may be expected to result in improved attitudes toward academic work and school in general.
4. For a variety of reasons children's behavior may be expected to be better in small schools. All of the adults know all of the students, so contact is personal. In particular, the principal can be expected to be well acquainted with every child. In large schools it is not unusual to find that a relatively small number of disruptive children is causing the entire building to be operated in a manner that emphasizes discipline and control rather than teaching and learning. Reducing the number of troubled students to a handful will not only in itself produce a better atmosphere but also will provide a greater opportunity for those individuals to receive the assistance they require.
5. If buildings with low enrollments are kept open there would be extra space that might be used in several ways. Community agencies may wish to establish programs for senior citizens or groups of young parents interested in holding child-study classes. The school district might find it

possible to establish a day-care center or prekindergarten rooms. Resource centers containing learning materials could be developed to serve several teachers or an entire building. Teachers might expand their instructional program into an additional room, thus creating a much more varied learning· situation. These are some of the direct and immediate benefits that could be derived from thinking of unused space as an opportunity rather than a problem. School districts may enjoy the advantages of smaller schools by retaining their large buildings and assigning fewer pupils to them.

The Classroom Group

For so long as the teacher's role has been viewed essentially as one involving the dissemination of knowledge and the demonstration of skills to class assemblages, a major goal of school organizers has been to create groups of highly similar pupils. The achievement of such an objective would mean that instructional presentations should be rendered highly efficient, since most of what was happening would be appropriate to most of the pupils most of the time. But given even the most advantageous sets of circumstances, human variability works against those seeking to establish homogeneous groups. And certainly the school situation has been made increasingly complex by significant changes in such matters as the establishment of continuous promotion policies and the defining of attendance areas that may not take into account the variability in children's experiences. As a result of these trends the classroom group has moved toward greater diversity rather than similarity, and responsible teachers have devoted less time to whole-class instruction and more to small-group work and the devising of individualized learning experiences.

As teachers have become more flexible, they have found it possible to accommodate even more variability among pupils. Thus, diversity requires flexibility, and an open-ended program makes it possible to deal effectively with an even greater range of individual differences. Given certain trends now operating, there are reasons to believe that classroom groups will become even more variable:

1. Legal decisions as well as conscious planning by school systems will result in the placement of children of quite different socioeconomic backgrounds in the same classes.
2. Increasing numbers of children with various types of handicaps are being removed from special classes entirely or for part of the school day and "mainstreamed" into regular classrooms.
3. Some schools will adopt the practice of deliberately placing children of different ages in the same classroom group.

THE CLASSROOM SITUATION CHILDREN NEED

The flexible classroom, whether such a situation is referred to as "activity oriented," "developmental," "open," or the like, can best afford the opportunities to accomplish most of what is called for in these chapters:

Diagnostic teaching of the basic skills
Individualization
Improved quality of life
Natural rather than forced language development
Increased use of real-life experiences
Encouragement of personal cognitive development
Greater attention to career education
More involvement with the community
Realistic setting for the practice of skills
Personal fulfillment
Use of services of many adults as resources for learning
Increased opportunities for self-expression
Integration of human knowledge
Establishment of good relationships with others

Learning environments that make these conditions possible are within the power of teachers to create. The authors have intended that this book would help the reader to recognize this. They also have hoped that this book would give the reader the knowledge of the curriculum content and teaching/learning practices as well as an understanding of the forces operating on them to make attainable the elementary schools desired by everyone interested in the best possible education for young children.

INDEX